# Interpreting Qualitative Data
## SECOND EDITION

# Interpreting Qualitative Data

*Methods for Analysing Talk, Text and Interaction*

## SECOND EDITION

# David Silverman

SAGE Publications
London • Thousand Oaks • New Delhi

© David Silverman 2001

First edition published 1993, reprinted 1994 (three times),
1995, 1997, 1999

New edition first published 2001. Reprinted 2001, 2002

SAGE Publications Ltd
6 Bonhill Street
London EC2A 4PU

SAGE Publications Inc
2455 Teller Road
Thousand Oaks, California 91320

SAGE Publications India Pvt Ltd
32, M-Block Market
Greater Kailash – I
New Delhi 110 048

**British Library Cataloguing in Publication Data**

A catalogue record for this book is available from the British Library

ISBN 0 7619 6864 4
ISBN 0 7619 6865 5 (pbk)

**Library of Congress catalog record available**

Typeset by Keystroke, Jacaranda Lodge, Wolverhampton.
Printed in Great Britain by The Cromwell Press Ltd, Trowbridge, Wiltshire

# Contents

# Preface

Writing a book, like most things we do, is related to our own biography. I say 'related to' because it is both inappropriate and foolish to reduce a piece of writing to the personal experiences of its author. Indeed, nothing makes me cringe more than those endless chat shows where the topic is always someone's 'personality' rather than their work. Here, as elsewhere, then, one should trust the tale and not the teller.

However, the convention is that, in a preface like this, tellers should reveal something about their past and their reasons for writing this work. I will comply with this convention. Of course, whatever gloss I put on these matters, my readers will make their own judgements.

Thirty-five years ago, I began my research career with a study of the beliefs and values of junior 'white collar' workers. Influenced by sociological theories of class and social status, I wanted to see how far the way you perceived yourself was influenced by where you worked and by your future job prospects. I used a structured interview schedule and my methodology was cast in the standard forms of quantitative research: an initial hypothesis, a two by two table and statistical tests (see Silverman, 1968). If I had completed this study, my future career might have taken a completely different path.

However, I started to have nagging doubts about the credibility of my research. Although I could manipulate my data so as to provide a rigorous test of my hypotheses, these data were hardly 'raw' but were mediated by various kinds of interpretive activities. Not the least of these arose in my administration of the interview schedule. As I was interviewing my respondents, I was struck by the need to go beyond my questions in various unforeseen ways so as to obtain the sort of answers I wanted. Perhaps, I thought, I hadn't pre-tested my questions properly. Or, perhaps, how we make sense in conversations necessarily relies on everyday conversational skills that cannot be reduced to reliable techniques (see Antaki and Rapley, 1996).

In any event, I abandoned this study and turned to organization theory in a work that was to be both my PhD and a successful textbook (Silverman, 1970). I spent the following decade exploring the uses of two contemporary social science theories. An ethnography of the personnel department of a public sector organization (Silverman and Jones, 1976) was heavily influenced by Harold Garfinkel's (1967) *ethnomethodology* (see Section 5.3.1). And an analysis of literary texts (Silverman and Torode, 1980) derived from Ferdinand de Saussure's (1974) *semiotics* (see Section 7.2). These studies confirmed my belief in the value of theoretically informed research – a belief affirmed throughout the present text.

However, guiding principles tend to be double-edged. So, while we should assert their benefits, we should also be aware of their possible costs. Looking back on this early work, I now feel that it was a trifle over-theorized. Perhaps I had been so enthused by a newly discovered theory that I hadn't allowed myself to be sufficiently challenged, even surprised, by my data.

Such over-theorization is an ever-present danger given that many social science disciplines still, I believe, live in fear of being discovered, like the fabled Emperor, without any clothes (for a recent valuable exception see Kendall and Wickham's, 1999, fine text on Foucault). It is for this reason that what has been called the *postmodern* period of experimental ethnographic writing (Denzin and Lincoln's, 2000: 17, 'fifth moment') barely figures in this book (see Silverman, 1997a: 239–40).

In my later research, I tried to find a better balance between the theoretical 'armchair' and the empirical 'field'. In both an *ethnography* of hospital clinics (Silverman, 1987) and a *conversation analytic* study of HIV test counselling (Silverman, 1997b), I adopted a more cautious approach to my data, inductively establishing hypotheses, using the comparative method, and identifying deviant cases (see Section 8.3.2). In both studies, unlike my earlier work, I explored ways of making my research relevant to a wider, non-academic audience in a non-patronizing way (see Chapter 9).

However, these later studies also derived from two related methodological assumptions present in my 1976 study. All three studies were based not on interviews but on *naturally occurring data*. And all of them looked at how the participants talked to one another and focused on the skills they used and the local functions of what they did.

As with the first edition of this book, these concerns structure my argument here. What I have to say stems from my discomfit with a fairly large proportion of the 'qualitative' research to be found in the leading contemporary academic journals. This discomfit arises from four related tendencies which, in the context of this introduction, I can only list without giving any evidence (more detail is provided in Silverman, 2000: 283–97):

1  A failure of analytic nerve in that the issues of theory building are, at best, addressed only in the first few lines of an article, while the remainder reads like what C. Wright Mills (1959) called 'abstracted empiricism'. This is often allied to a stress on the 'exploratory' nature of the research undertaken as opposed to the attempt to test hypotheses deriving from the increasing body of empirical knowledge and analytical approaches.
2  The attempt to identify qualitative research with 'open-ended', 'informal' interviews. Unlike quantitative researchers, it sometimes seems, our aim is to 'empathize' with people and to turn ourselves into mirrors of other people's 'experiences'.
3  The use of data extracts which support the researcher's argument, without any proof that contrary evidence has been reviewed. Alternatively, the attempt to downplay such issues of validity and reliability in research (as either inappropriate or politically incorrect) and to replace them with

other criteria like the 'authenticity' with which we have reproduced 'experience'.

4 A belief that a particular partisan moral or political position determines how we analyse data and what constitutes a 'good' piece of research.

As opposed to each of these arguments, I propose the following. First, social theory is not an 'add-on' extra but is the animating basis of social research. Second, while 'open-ended' interviews can be useful, we need to justify departing from the naturally occurring data that surround us and to be cautious about the *romantic* impulse which identifies 'experience' with 'authenticity' (see Section 1.1.2 and Atkinson and Silverman, 1997).

Third, I insist on the relevance of issues of validity and reliability to field research: we cannot be satisfied merely with what I have called elsewhere (Silverman, 1989a) 'telling convincing stories'. Contrary to the assumption of many social scientists, as well as funding bodies, generalizability need not be a problem in qualitative research.

Finally, I follow Max Weber (1946) in recognizing the value positions that can arise in the choice of research topics and in discussion of the relevance of research findings. Nonetheless, I totally reject 'partisanship' as a basis for assessing research findings or even as a standard for determining for others what are the most appropriate topics for investigation. Unfortunately, I am not convinced that 'political correctness' (either of the radical left or of the managerial right) does not enter into the decisions of some funding bodies and editorial boards.

None of this means that the reader should expect to find that this book contains a polemic. My central aim is to show the value of a range of methodologies in social research and to equip the reader with some of the skills necessary to apply these methodologies.

It is the *craft* of social research that this book sets out to convey rather than the passive ability to regurgitate appropriate answers in methodology examinations. Mick Bloor has put this point very clearly:

> It seems something of a commonplace among research sociologists that texts on methodology are only of very limited utility in study design, certainly they contain no templates which can be applied unproblematically for the resolution of particular research problems . . . the methodological writings which most sociological researchers seem to find most useful tend to be those which are grounded in particular research projects rather than general surveys of methodological techniques. (1978: 545)

As before, I still believe that learning has little to do with rote learning about the advantages and disadvantages of various approaches or methods. To this end, my discussion is illustrated by many, detailed examples of qualitative research studies.

To be effective, a textbook should offer an active learning experience. In Ancient Greece, Socrates encouraged understanding by asking his students pointed questions. Much more recently, another philosopher, Ludwig Wittgenstein, filled his book *Philosophical Investigations* with hundreds of provocative questions. Interestingly enough, a period of teaching in an elementary school had shown him how real learning often comes by working through particular examples.

Learning through doing is a wonderful way of appropriating knowledge and turning it into useful skills. The point has not been lost in distance learning programmes (like those at the British Open University). Thus I provide many exercises, linked to the surrounding text. These exercises involve the reader in gathering and/or analysing data. My aim is that the users of this book will learn some basic skills in generating researchable problems and analysing qualitative data. As I have confirmed through using these materials for assessment on an undergraduate course, the exercises also give students an ability to show the skills of their craft in a way that is not usually possible in the confines of a usual examination method.

I believe that the most challenging of these skills arises in defining research problems and in analysing data. So this present book is not a 'cookbook': it does not discuss in detail many of the practical issues involved in the research process (e.g. how to obtain access, how to present oneself to research subjects). Some of these matters can only be settled by practical experience. Others involve concealed analytic issues (e.g. about the character of observation) which are discussed in this book.

All of these arguments were present when *Interpreting Qualitative Data* was first published. What, then, are the reasons for this new edition? A list of major changes in this second edition may be helpful:

- This is an expanded and updated text which takes account of the flood of qualitative work in the 1990s.
- All chapters have been substantially rewritten with the aim of greater clarity.
- A new chapter on visual images (Chapter 7) and a considerably expanded treatment of discourse analysis (Section 6.4) are provided.
- The number of student exercises has been considerably increased and they are now present at the end of every chapter.
- I have attempted to provide an even greater degree of student accessibility. Key points and recommended readings now appear at the end of each chapter, and technical terms are presented in bold and appear in a glossary at the end of the volume.
- I have consciously tried to make this a more interdisciplinary social science text which takes account of the growing interest in qualitative research outside sociology and anthropology, in disciplines ranging from psychology to geography, information systems, health promotion, management and many others.

I envisage this reshaped text as a companion volume to my recent book *Doing Qualitative Research* (Silverman, 2000). That book was a guide to the business of conducting a research project. This book is more introductory and, together with its accompanying volume of key readings (Silverman, 1997a), seeks to offer the background that students need before contemplating their own qualitative research study.

For my sense of this 'background', I will use the words of Wittgenstein who, in closing his *Tractatus Logico-Philosophicus*, tells us:

> My propositions serve as elucidations in the following way: anyone who understands me eventually recognises them as nonsensical, when he has used them – as steps – to climb up beyond them (he must, so to speak, throw away the ladder after he has climbed up it). He must transcend these propositions, and then he will see the world aright. (1971: 6.54)

It is my hope that this book may serve as something like Wittgenstein's ladder, providing an initial footing for students then to go off to do their own research – charting new territories rather than restating comfortable orthodoxies.

A number of friends have contributed to this second edition. Among those who have helped are: Vladimir Andrle, Mick Bloor, Norman Denzin, Mike Emmison, Jay Gubrium, Jim Holstein, Moira Kelly, Anssi Peräkylä, Jonathan Potter, Anne Ryen and Paul ten Have. Grateful thanks are also due to my editor at Sage, Simon Ross. Naturally, I alone am responsible for any errors or omissions contained in this book.

David Silverman
London

# Part One

# THEORY AND METHOD IN QUALITATIVE RESEARCH

# 1

## Beginning Research

Some people become qualitative researchers for rather negative reasons. Perhaps they are not very good at statistics (or think they are not) and so are not tempted by quantitative research. Or perhaps they have not shone at library work and hope that they can stimulate their sluggish imagination by getting out into 'the field'.

Unfortunately, as most scientists and philosophers are agreed, the facts we find in 'the field' never speak for themselves but are impregnated by our assumptions. For instance, the initial reports of bystanders in Dallas at the time of the assassination of President Kennedy in 1963 were not of shots but of hearing a car backfiring (Sacks, 1984: 519). Why did people hear it this way?

We all know that people who think they have heard a shot every time a car backfires may be regarded as unstable or even psychotic. So our descriptions are never simple reports on 'events' but are structured to depict ourselves as particular kinds of people who are usually 'reasonable' and 'cautious'.

But, you may say, surely social scientists are more objective than that? After all, they have scientific methods for making observations more trustworthy.

Well, yes and no. Certainly, social scientists will usually go through a more cautious process of sorting fact from opinion than most of us ever need to do in everyday life (see Chapter 8). However, even scientists only observe 'facts' through the use of lenses made up of concepts and theories. Sacks has a basic example of this:

Suppose you're an anthropologist or sociologist standing somewhere. You see somebody do some action, and you see it to be some activity. How can you go about formulating who is it that did it, for the purposes of your report? Can you use at least what you might take to be the most conservative formulation – his name? Knowing, of course, that any category you choose would have the[se] kinds of systematic problems: how would you go about selecting a given category from the set that would equally well characterise or identify that person at hand? (1992, I: 467–8).

Sacks shows how you cannot resolve such problems simply 'by taking the best possible notes at the time and making your decisions afterwards' (I: 468). Whatever we observe is impregnated by assumptions.

### Attempt Exercise 1.1 about now

In scientific work, these assumptions are usually given the fancy term 'theories'. But what are 'theories'?

Martin O'Brien (1993) has used the example of a kaleidoscope to answer this question. As he explains:

> a kaleidoscope . . . [is] the child's toy consisting of a tube, a number of lenses and fragments of translucent, coloured glass or plastic. When you turn the tube and look down the lens of the kaleidoscope the shapes and colours, visible at the bottom, change. As the tube is turned, different lenses come into play and the combinations of colour and shape shift from one pattern to another. In a similar way, we can see social theory as a sort of kaleidoscope – by shifting theoretical perspective the world under investigation also changes shape. (1993: 10–11)

How theory works as a kaleidoscope can be seen by taking a concrete, if crude, example. Imagine that a group of social scientists from different disciplines are observing people at a party through a two-way mirror. The sociologist might observe the gender composition of various conversational groups, while the linguist might listen to how 'small-talk' is managed between speakers. The psychologist might focus on the characteristics of 'loners' versus people who are the 'life and soul' of the party, and the geographer might observe how the spatial organization of the room influenced how people conversed.

The point is that none of these observations are more real or more true than the others. For instance, people are not essentially defined in terms of either their social characteristics (like gender) or their personalities (extrovert or introvert). It all depends on your research question. And research questions are inevitably theoretically informed. So we *do* need social theories to help us to address even quite basic issues in social research.

However, O'Brien's analogy of a kaleidoscope only takes us so far. For instance, how does a 'theory' differ from a 'hypothesis'? And how do we develop both of them?

Questions like this mean that I can no longer postpone the potentially tiresome business of defining my terms. In this chapter, we shall be discussing models, concepts, theories, hypotheses, methods and methodologies. In Table 1.1 I set out how each term will be used.

As the table implies, what I call 'models' are even more basic to social research than theories. **Models** provide an overall framework for how we look at reality. In short, they tell us what reality is like and the basic elements it contains ('ontology') and what is the nature and status of knowledge ('epistemology'). In this sense, models roughly correspond to what are more grandly referred to as 'paradigms' (see Guba and Lincoln, 1994).

TABLE 1.1 *Basic terms in research*

| Term | Meaning | Relevance |
|------|---------|-----------|
| Model | An overall framework for looking at reality (e.g. behaviouralism, feminism) | Usefulness |
| Concept | An idea deriving from a given model (e.g. 'stimulus–response', 'oppression') | Usefulness |
| Theory | A set of concepts used to define and/or explain some phenomenon | Usefulness |
| Hypothesis | A testable proposition | Validity |
| Methodology | A general approach to studying research topics | Usefulness |
| Method | A specific research technique | Good fit with model, theory, hypothesis and methodology |

In social research, examples of such models are functionalism (which looks at the functions of social institutions), behaviourism (which defines all behaviour in terms of 'stimulus' and 'response'), symbolic interactionism (which focuses on how we attach symbolic meanings to interpersonal relations) and ethnomethodology (which encourages us to look at people's everyday ways of producing orderly social interaction). Drawing on Gubrium and Holstein (1997), I will discuss the importance of models further in Chapter 2.

**Concepts** are clearly specified ideas deriving from a particular model. Examples of concepts are 'social function' (deriving from functionalism), 'stimulus–response' (behaviouralism), 'definition of the situation' (inter-actionism) and 'the documentary method of interpretation' (ethnomethod-ology). Concepts offer ways of looking at the world which are essential in defining a research problem.

**Theories** arrange sets of concepts to define and explain some phenomenon. As Strauss and Corbin put it: 'Theory consists of plausible relationships produced among concepts and sets of concepts' (1994: 278). Without a theory, such phenomena as 'gender', 'personality', 'talk' or 'space' cannot be understood by social science. In this sense, without a theory there is nothing to research.

So theory provides a footing for considering the world, separate from, yet about, that world. In this way, theory provides both:

- a framework for critically understanding phenomena
- a basis for considering how what is unknown might be organized (Gubrium, personal correspondence).

By provoking ideas about what is presently unknown, theories provide the impetus for research. As living entities, they are also developed and modified by good research. However, as used here, models, concepts and theories are self-confirming in the sense that they instruct us to look at phenomena in particular ways. This means that they can never be disproved but can only be found to be more or less useful.

This last feature distinguishes theories from **hypotheses**. Unlike theories, hypotheses are tested in research. Examples of hypotheses, discussed later in this book, are:

- How we receive advice is linked to how advice is given.
- Responses to an illegal drug depend upon what one learns from others.
- Voting in union elections is related to non-work links between union members.

In many qualitative research studies, there is no specific hypothesis at the outset. Instead, hypotheses are produced (or induced) during the early stages of research. In any event, unlike theories, hypotheses can and should be tested. Therefore, we assess a hypothesis by its validity or truth.

A **methodology** refers to the choices we make about cases to study, methods of data gathering, forms of data analysis etc. in planning and execut-ing a research study. So our methodology defines how we will go about studying any phenomenon. In social research, methodologies may be defined very broadly (e.g. qualitative or quantitative) or more narrowly (e.g. grounded theory or conversation analysis). Like theories, methodologies cannot be true or false, only more or less useful.

Finally, **methods** are specific research techniques. These include quanti-tative techniques, like statistical correlations, as well as techniques like observation, interviewing and audio recording. Once again, in themselves, techniques are not true or false. They are more or less useful, depending on their fit with the theories and methodologies being used and the hypothesis being tested and/or the research topic that is selected. So, for instance, behaviouralists may favour quantitative methods and interactionists often prefer to gather their data by observation. But, depending upon the hypo-thesis being tested, behaviouralists may sometimes use qualitative methods – for instance in the exploratory stage of research. Equally, interactionists may sometimes use simple quantitative methods, particularly when they want to find an overall pattern in their data.

Having set out some basic concepts, we can now turn to the more practical issue of using models and theories to generate a research problem.

## 1.1 GENERATING A RESEARCH PROBLEM

After long experience in supervising research, at both undergraduate and graduate levels, I find that beginning researchers tend to make two basic errors. First, they fail to distinguish sufficiently between research problems and problems that are discussed in the world around us. The latter kind of problems, which I shall call 'social problems', are at the heart of political debates and fill the more serious newspapers. However, although social problems, like unemployment, homelessness and racism, are important, by themselves they cannot provide a researchable topic.

The second error to which I have referred is sometimes related to the first. It arises where researchers take on an impossibly large research problem. For instance, it is important to find the causes of a social problem like homelessness, but such a problem is beyond the scope of a single researcher with limited time and resources. Moreover, by defining the problem so widely, one is usually unable to say anything in great depth about it.

As I tell my students, your aim should be to say 'a lot about a little (problem)'. This means avoiding the temptation to say 'a little about a lot'. Indeed, the latter path can be something of a 'copout'. Precisely because the topic is so wide-ranging, one can flit from one aspect to another without being forced to refine and test each piece of analysis (see Silverman, 2000: 61–74).

In this part of the chapter, I shall focus on the first of these errors – the tendency to choose social problems as research topics. However, in recommending solutions to this error, I shall imply how one can narrow down a research topic.

### 1.1.1 *What is a problem?*

One has only to open a newspaper or to watch the TV news to be confronted by a host of social problems. In the mid 1990s, the British news media was full of references to a 'wave' of crimes committed by children – from the theft of cars to the murder of old people and other children. There were also several stories about how doctors infected by HIV have continued to work and, by implication, have endangered their patients.

The stories have this in common: both assume some sort of moral decline in which families or schools fail to discipline children and in which physicians fail to take seriously their professional responsibilities. In turn, the way each story is told implies a solution: tightening up 'discipline' in order to combat the 'moral decline'.

However, before we can consider such a 'cure', we need to consider carefully the 'diagnosis'. Has juvenile crime increased or is the apparent increase a reflection of what counts as a 'good' story? Alternatively, might the increase be an artefact of what crimes get reported? Again, how many health care professionals have actually infected their patients with HIV? I know of only one (disputed) case – a Florida dentist. Conversely, there is considerable evidence of patients infecting the medical staff who treat them. Moreover, why focus on HIV when other conditions like hepatitis B are far more infectious? Could it be that we hear so much about HIV because it is associated with 'stigmatized' groups?

However, apparent 'social' problems are not the only topics that may clamour for the attention of the researcher. Administrators and managers point to 'problems' in their organizations and may turn to social scientists for solutions.

It is tempting to allow such people to define a research problem – particularly as there is usually a fat research grant attached to it! However, we must first look at the terms which are being used to define the problem. For instance, many managers will define problems in their organization as problems of 'communication'. The role of the researcher is then to work out how people can communicate 'better'.

Unfortunately, talking about 'communication problems' raises many difficulties. For instance, it may deflect attention from the communication 'skills' inevitably used in interaction. It may also tend to assume that the solution to any problem is more careful listening, while ignoring power relations present inside and outside patterns of communication. Such relations may also make the characterization of 'organizational efficiency' very problematic. Thus 'administrative' problems give no more secure basis for social research than do 'social' problems.

Of course, this is not to deny that there are any real problems in society. However, even if we agree about what these problems are, it is not clear that they provide a researchable topic.

Let me return to the case of the problems of people infected with HIV. Some of these problems are, quite rightly, brought to the attention of the public by the organized activities of groups of people who carry the infection. What social researchers can contribute are the particular theoretical and method-ological skills of their discipline. So economists can research how limited health care resources can be used most effectively in coping with the epidemic in the West and in the Third World. Among sociologists, survey researchers can investigate patterns of sexual behaviour in order to try to promote effective health education, while qualitative methods may be used to study what is involved in the 'negotiation' of safer sex or in counselling people about HIV and AIDS.

As these examples demonstrate, the initial impetus for a study may arise from the needs of practitioners and clients. However, researchers from different disciplines will usually give an initial research topic their own theoretical and methodological 'twist'. For instance, in my research on HIV counselling (Silverman, 1997b), the use of tape-recordings and detailed transcripts, as well as many technical concepts, derived from my interest in *conversation analysis* (see Chapter 6).

This example shows that it is usually necessary to refuse to allow our research topics to be totally defined in terms of the conceptions of 'social problems' as recognized by either professional or community groups. Ironically, by beginning from a clearly defined social science perspective, we can later address such social problems with, I believe, considerable force and persuasiveness. This issue is discussed in more detail in Chapter 9.

---

**Attempt Exercise 1.2 about now**

---

### 1.1.2 The absolutist trap

At last, by showing what social research *can* do, we seem to be hitting a positive note. However, there is one further trap which lies in our path when we are trying to define a research problem. What I call the 'absolutist' trap arises in the temptation to accept uncritically the conventional wisdoms of our day. Let me list the four such 'wisdoms' I will be considering:

- scientism
- progress
- tourism
- romanticism.

The first two issues mainly relate to quantitative social scientists; the last two are more of a problem for qualitative researchers. We will consider each in turn.

*Scientism*
This involves uncritically accepting that 'science' is both highly distinct from, and superior to, 'common sense'. For instance, the quantitative researcher might study the relationship between the 'efficiency' of an organization and its management 'structure'. The aim might be to get a more reliable and valid picture than that we might get from common sense.

However, efficiency and the management structure cannot be separated from what the participants in the organization do themselves. So, efficiency and structure are not stable realities but are defined and redefined in different organizational contexts (e.g. internal meetings, labour–management negotiations, press releases etc.). Moreover, the researchers themselves will, inevitably, use their common-sense knowledge of how organizations operate in order to define and measure these 'variables' (see Section 2.2).

This is *not* to say that there is no difference between science and common sense. Of course, social science needs to study how common sense works in a way which common sense would not and could not follow for itself. In doing so, however, it will inevitably draw upon common-sense knowledge. Scientism's mistake is to position itself entirely apart from, and superior to, common sense.

*Progress*
In the nineteenth century, scientists believed they could detect a path leading towards 'progress' in history (e.g. popular readings of Charles Darwin on 'the

evolution of the species' and of Karl Marx on the inevitability of the demise of 'regressive' economic systems). This belief was maintained, with some modifications after the experiences of the two world wars, well into the twentieth century.

However, an uncritical belief in progress is an unacceptable basis for scientific research. For instance, it is dangerous to assume that we can identify social progress when doctors listen more to their patients (Silverman, 1987: ch. 8), or when prison inmates are offered parole, or when all of us feel freer to discuss our sexuality (Foucault, 1977; 1979; Silverman, 1997b: ch. 9). In each case, if we assume 'progress', then we may fail to identify the 'double-binds' of any method of communication and/or new forms of power.

Both scientism and a commitment to progress have had most impact on quantitative researchers. I now turn to two traps that have had a more direct influence on qualitative research.

### Tourism

I have in mind the 'upmarket' tourist who travels the world in search of encounters with alien cultures. Disdaining package tours and even the label of 'tourist', such a person has an insatiable thirst for the 'new' and 'different'. The problem is that there are worrying parallels between the qualitative researcher and this kind of tourist. Such researchers often begin without a hypothesis and, like the tourist, gaze rapaciously at social scenes for signs of activities that appear to be new and different. The danger in all this is that 'touristic' researchers may so focus on cultural and subcultural (or group) differences that they fail to recognize similarities between the culture to which they belong and the cultures which they study. Once you switch away from asking 'leading' questions (which assume cultural differences) to observation of what people actually are doing, then one may find certain *common* features between social patterns in the West and East (see Ryen and Silverman, 2000; and my discussion in Section 1.1.3 of Moerman's, 1974, study of a Thai tribe).

### Romanticism

Just as the nineteenth century was the age of 'progress', so it was the time in which people expected that literature, art and music would express the inner world of the artist and engage the emotions of the audience. This movement was called 'romanticism'.

As I argue in Chapter 4, there is more than a hint of this romanticism in some contemporary qualitative research (see also Gubrium and Holstein, 1997; Atkinson and Silverman, 1997). This particularly applies where the researcher sets out to record faithfully the 'experiences' of some, usually disadvantaged, group (e.g. battered women, gay men, the unemployed etc.).

As I later suggest, the romantic approach is appealing but dangerous. It may neglect how experience is shaped by cultural forms of representation. For instance, what we think is most personal to us ('guilt', 'responsibility') may be simply a culturally given way of understanding the world (see my discussion of the mother of a young diabetic person in Section 6.4.2). So it is problematic to justify research in terms of its 'authentic' representation of experience when what is authentic is culturally defined.

This argument has implications for analysing interview data which I touch upon below. For the moment, I will conclude this section on generating a research problem by examining how different kinds of sensitivity can provide a solution to the twin traps of absolutism and sliding into societal versions of social problems.

### 1.1.3 Sensitivity and researchable problems

I have been arguing that it is often unhelpful for researchers to begin their work on a basis of a social problem identified by either practitioners or managers. It is a commonplace that such definitions of problems often may serve vested interests. My point, however, is that if social science research has anything to offer, its theoretical imperatives drive it in a direction which can offer participants new perspectives on their problems. Paradoxically, by refusing to begin from a common conception of what is 'wrong' in a setting, we may be most able to contribute to the identification both of what is going on and, thereby, of how it may be modified in the pursuit of desired ends.

The various perspectives of social science provide a sensitivity to many issues neglected by those who define social or administrative problems. Let me distinguish three types of sensitivity:

- historical
- political
- contextual.

I will explain and discuss each of these in turn.

*Historical sensitivity*
Wherever possible, we should examine the relevant historical evidence when we are setting up a topic to research. For instance, in the 1950s and 1960s it was assumed that the 'nuclear family' (parents and children) had replaced the 'extended family' (many generations living together in the same house-hold) of pre-industrial societies. Researchers simply seemed to have forgotten that lower life expectancy may have made the extended family pattern relatively rare in the past.

Again, historical sensitivity helps us to understand how we are governed. For instance, until the eighteenth century, the majority of the population were treated as a threatening 'mob' to be controlled, where necessary, by the use of force. Today, we are seen as individuals with 'needs' and 'rights' which must be understood and protected by society (see Foucault, 1977). But, although oppressive force may be used only rarely, we may be controlled in more subtle ways. Think of the knowledge about each of us contained in computerized databanks and the pervasive video cameras which record movements in many city streets. Historical sensitivity thus offers us multiple research topics which evade the trap of thinking that present day versions of social problems are unproblematic.

## Political sensitivity

Allowing the current media 'scares' to determine our research topics is just as fallible as designing research in accordance with administrative or managerial interests. In neither case do we use political sensitivity to detect the vested interests behind this way of formulating a problem. The media, after all, need to attract an audience. Administrators need to be seen to be working efficiently.

So political sensitivity seeks to grasp the politics behind defining topics in particular ways. In turn, it helps in suggesting that we research how social problems arise. For instance, Barbara Nelson (1984) looked at how 'child abuse' became defined as a recognizable problem in the late 1960s. She shows how the findings of a doctor about 'the battered baby syndrome' were adopted by the conservative Nixon administration through linking social problems to parental 'maladjustment' rather than to the failures of social programmes. Political sensitivity does not mean that social scientists argue that there are no 'real' problems in society. Instead, it suggests that social science can make an important contribution to society by querying how 'official' definitions of problems arise. To be truthful, however, we should also recognize how social scientists often need to accept tacitly such definitions in order to attract research grants.

## Contextual sensitivity

This is the least self-explanatory and most contentious category in the present list. By 'contextual' sensitivity, I mean the recognition that apparently uniform institutions like 'the family', 'a tribe' or 'science' take on a variety of meanings in different contexts. Contextual sensitivity is reflected most obviously in Moerman's (1974) study of the Lue tribe in Thailand. Moerman began with the anthropologist's conventional appetite to locate a people in a classificatory scheme. To satisfy this appetite, he started to ask tribespeople questions like 'How do you recognize a member of your tribe?'

He reports that his respondents quickly became adept at providing a whole list of traits which constituted their tribe and distinguished them from their neighbours. At the same time, Moerman realized that such a list was, in purely logical terms, endless. Perhaps if you wanted to understand this people, it was not particularly useful to elicit an abstract account of their characteristics.

So Moerman stopped asking 'Who are the Lue?' Clearly, such ethnic identification devices were not used all the time by these people, any more than we use them to refer to ourselves in a Western culture. Instead, Moerman started to examine what went on in everyday situations.

Looked at this way, the issue is no longer who the Lue essentially are but when, among people living in these Thai villages, ethnic identification labels are invoked and what are the consequences of invoking them. Curiously enough, Moerman concluded that, when you looked at the matter this way, the apparent differences between the Lue and ourselves were considerably reduced. Only an ethnocentric Westerner might have assumed otherwise, behaving like a tourist craving for out-of-the-way sights. For further discussion of Moerman's research, see Section 4.1.

But it is not only such large-scale collectivities as tribes that are looked at afresh when we use what I have called contextual sensitivity. Other apparently stable social institutions (like the 'family') and identities (gender, ethnicity etc.) may be insufficiently questioned from a social problem perspective.

For instance, commentators say things like 'the family is under threat'. But where are we to find the unitary form of family assumed in such commentary? And doesn't 'the family' look different in contexts ranging from the household to the law courts or even the supermarket (see Section 3.5)? Rather than take such arguments at face value, the researcher must make use of the three kinds of sensitivity, to discover how things actually operate in a social world where, as Moerman shows us, people's practices are inevitably more complex than they might seem.

One final point. The three kinds of sensitivity we have been considering offer different, sometimes contradictory, ways of generating research topics. I am not suggesting that all should be used at the beginning of any research study. However, if we are not sensitive to any of these issues, then we run the risk of lapsing into a 'social problem' based way of defining our research topics.

**Attempt Exercise 1.3 about now**

## 1.2 THE VARIETY OF QUALITATIVE METHODS

There are four major methods used by qualitative researchers:

- observation
- analysing texts and documents
- interviews
- recording and transcribing.

These methods are often combined. For instance, many case studies combine observation with interviewing. Moreover, each method can be used in either qualitative or quantitative research studies. As Table 1.2 shows, the overall nature of the research methodology shapes how each method is used.

Table 1.2 underlines the point made in Table 1.1: methods are techniques which take on a specific meaning according to the methodology in which they are used.

So, in quantitative research, observation is not generally seen as a very important method of data collection. This is because it is difficult to conduct

TABLE 1.2 *Different uses for four methods*

| Method | Methodology | |
| --- | --- | --- |
| | Quantitative research | Qualitative research |
| Observation | Preliminary work, e.g. prior to framing questionnaire | Fundamental to understanding another culture |
| Textual analysis | Content analysis, i.e. counting in terms of researchers' categories | Understanding participants' categories |
| Interviews | Survey research: mainly fixed-choice questions to random samples | Open-ended questions to small samples |
| Audio and video recording | Used infrequently to check the accuracy of interview records | Used to understand how participants organize their talk and body movements |

observational studies on large samples. Quantitative researchers also argue that observation is not a very 'reliable' data collection method because different observers may record different observations. If used at all, observation is held to be only appropriate at a preliminary or 'exploratory' stage of research.

Conversely, observational studies have been fundamental to much qualitative research. Beginning with the pioneering case studies of non-Western societies by early anthropologists (Malinowski, 1922; Radcliffe-Brown, 1948) and continuing with the work by sociologists in Chicago prior to the Second World War (Thomas and Znaniecki, 1927), the observational method has often been the chosen method to understand another culture (see Section 3.1.1).

These contrasts are also apparent in the treatment of texts and documents. Quantitative researchers try to analyse written material in a way which will produce reliable evidence about a large sample. Their favoured method is 'content analysis' in which the researchers establish a set of categories and then count the number of instances that fall into each category. The crucial requirement is that the categories are sufficiently precise to enable different coders to arrive at the same results when the same body of material (e.g. newspaper headlines) is examined (see Berelson, 1952).

In qualitative research, small numbers of texts and documents may be analysed for a very different purpose. The aim is to understand the participants' categories and to see how these are used in concrete activities like telling stories (Propp, 1968; Sacks, 1974), assembling files (Cicourel, 1968; Gubrium and Buckholdt, 1982) or describing 'family life' (Gubrium, 1992). The reliability of the analysis is less frequently addressed. Instead, qualitative researchers make claims about their ability to reveal the local practices through which given 'end-products' (stories, files, descriptions) are assembled.

Interviews are commonly used in both methodologies. Quantitative researchers administer interviews or questionnaires to random samples of the population; this is referred to as 'survey research'. 'Fixed-choice' questions (e.g. 'yes' or 'no') are usually preferred because the answers they produce lend themselves to simple tabulation, unlike 'open-ended' questions which produce answers which need to be subsequently coded. A central methodological issue for quantitative researchers is the reliability of the interview schedule and the representativeness of the sample.

For instance, after surveys of voting intention did not coincide with the result of the British general election of 1992, survey researchers looked again at their methodology. Assuming that some respondents in the past may have lied to interviewers about their voting intentions, some companies now provide a ballot box into which respondents put mock ballot slips – thereby eliminating the need to reveal one's preferences to the interviewer. Attention was also given to assembling a more representative sample to interview, bearing in mind the expense of a completely random sample of the whole British population. Perhaps as a result of these methodological revisions, pollsters' final figures of voting intentions fitted much more closely the actual result of the 1997 British election.

'Authenticity' rather than reliability is often the issue in qualitative research. The aim is usually to gather an authentic understanding of people's experiences and it is believed that open-ended questions are the most effective route towards this end. So, for instance, in gathering life histories or in interviewing parents of handicapped children (Baruch, 1982) people may simply be asked: 'tell me your story'. Qualitative interview studies are often conducted with small samples and the interviewer–interviewee relationship may be defined in political rather than scientific terms (e.g. Finch, 1984). Finally, transcripts of audio or video recordings are rarely used in quantitative research, probably because of the assumption that they are difficult to quantify. Conversely, as we shall see (Chapters 6 and 7), audio and video recordings are an increasingly important part of qualitative research. Transcripts of such recordings, based on standardized conventions, provide an excellent record of 'naturally occurring' interaction. Compared to field-notes of observational data, recordings and transcripts can offer a highly reliable record to which researchers can return as they develop new hypotheses.

This rather abstract presentation can now be made more concrete by examining a number of qualitative studies using each method. I will take the example of research on social aspects of AIDS because it is a highly discussed, contemporary topic and an area in which I have worked. For each study presented, I will show how different theoretical and methodological imperatives shaped the choice and use of the method concerned.

### 1.2.1 Observation

In 1987, I began sitting in at a weekly clinic held at the genito-urinary department of an English inner-city hospital (Silverman, 1989c). The clinic's purpose was to monitor the progress of HIV-positive patients who were taking the drug AZT (Retrovir). AZT, which seems able to slow down the rate at which the virus reproduces itself, was then at an experimental stage of its development.

Like any observational study, the aim was to gather firsthand information about social processes in a 'naturally occurring' context. No attempt was made to interview the individuals concerned because the focus was upon what they actually did in the clinic rather than upon what they thought about what they did. The researcher was present in the consulting room at a side angle to both doctors and patient.

Patients' consent for the researcher's presence was obtained by the senior doctor. Given the presumed sensitivity of the occasion, tape-recording was not attempted. Instead, detailed handwritten notes were kept, using a separate sheet for each consultation.

The sample was small (15 male patients seen in 37 consultations over seven clinic sessions) and no claims were made about its representativeness. Because observational methods were rare in this area, the study was essentially exploratory. However, as we shall see, an attempt was made to link the findings to other social research about doctor–patient relations. As Sontag (1979) has noted, illness is often taken as a moral or psychological metaphor. The major finding of the study was the moral baggage attached to being HIV-positive. For instance, many patients used a buzzer to remind them to take their medication during the night. As one commented (P = patient):

P: It's a dead giveaway. Everybody knows what you've got.

However, despite the social climate in which HIV infection is viewed, there was considerable variation in how people presented themselves to the medical team. Four styles of 'self-presentation' (Goffman, 1959) were identified. Each style is briefly noted below:

- *Cool* Here even worrying medical statements were treated with an air of politeness and acceptance rather than concern or apparent anxiety. For example, one patient generally answered all questions in monosyllables. His only sustained intervention was when he asked about the name of a doctor he would be seeing at another hospital for his skin infection. He made no comment when a doctor observed that AZT was keeping him alive.
- *Anxiety* At the other extreme, some patients treated even apparent greetings as an opportunity to display 'anxiety'. For instance:

Dr: How are you?
P: Heh. Pretty weak. Something I can't put my finger on. Not right. Don't know.

- *Objective* As has been noted in other studies (see Baruch, 1982, discussed in Section 4.8), health professionals commonly present themselves to doctors as bundles of objective symptoms. One such professional, who was a patient in this clinic, behaved in exactly this way. For instance:

P:   I was wondering whether Acyclovir in connection with the AZT might cause neutropenia . . . [describing his herpes symptoms]. It was interesting. So you'd suggest it four times a day. Because normally they recommend five times a day.

- *Theatrical*  One way of responding to questions about one's physical condition was to downplay them in order to make observations about social situations, acknowledging the listening audience. For instance:

Dr:  How are you feeling physically?
P:   Fine. The other thing was [account of doctor who didn't wave to him in the street]. He's just a bloody quack like you. No offence.
     [to researcher and medical student] I'm a bad case by the way so don't take no notice of me.

Three important points need to be made about this discussion. First, there was no simple correspondence between each patient and a particular 'style' of self-presentation. Rather, each way of presenting oneself was available to each patient within any one consultation, where it might have a particular social function. So the focus was on social processes rather than on psychological states. Second, I have only been to able to offer brief extracts to support my argument. As we shall see in Chapter 8, such use of evidence has led to doubts about the validity or accuracy of qualitative research.

My third point is that these findings reflect only part of the study. We also discovered how the ethos of 'positive thinking' was central to many patients' accounts and how doctors systematically concentrated on the 'bodies' rather than the 'minds' of their patients. We get a sense of this in the extract immediately above where the patient resists an attempt by the doctor to get him to talk more about his physical condition. This led on to some practical questions about the division of labour between doctors and counsellors.

## 1.2.2  Textual analysis

Kitzinger and Miller (1992) have looked at the relation between media reporting of AIDS and the audience's understanding. Their analysis of British television news bulletins provides a good example of how textual analysis may be used in qualitative research on social aspects of AIDS.

It also shows how qualitative researchers try to avoid questions deriving from 'social problem' perspectives, while recognizing that phenomena are always socially defined. Kitzinger and Miller's concern with the social definition of phenomena is shown by the inverted commas they place around concepts like 'AIDS', 'Africa' and what is 'really' the case. As the authors explain:

This chapter focuses on audiences and the role of the media in changing, reinforcing or contributing to ideas about AIDS, Africa and race. It does not argue that HIV either does or not, originate in Africa . . . Here we are not directly addressing questions about where the virus 'really' came from or the actual distribution of infection. Instead we are focusing on how different *answers* to these questions are produced, framed and sustained, what these tell us about the construction of 'AIDS' and 'Africa' and what socio-political consequences they carry with them. (1992: 28, my emphasis)

Over three years of television news reports were examined. In one such report, statistics on HIV infection were given for the whole of Africa and a map of Africa was shown with the word 'AIDS' fixed across the continent. The map was also stamped with the words '3 Million Sufferers'.

In the three-year period, the only country to be distinguished as different from the rest of Africa was South Africa. Indeed, on one occasion, South Africa was described as 'holding the line' against an HIV invasion from black Africa. By contrast, images of black Africans with AIDS were used in all the news reports studied. Moreover, the spread of the epidemic was related to 'traditional sexual values' or, more generally, to 'African culture'.

To see how these media images impacted upon their audience, many discussion groups were established among people with particular occupations (e.g. nurses, police, teachers), with perceived 'high involvement' in the issue (e.g. gay men, prisoners) and with 'low involvement' (e.g. retired people, students).

Although members of all groups were sceptical about media coverage of news issues, they nonetheless accepted the general assumption that AIDS came from Africa and is prevalent there. White people usually began from the assumption that Africa is a hotbed of sexually transmitted diseases. This was based on the belief that sexual intercourse typically begins at an early age and that sexual diseases are spread through polygamy.

However, not all individuals shared these beliefs. Kitzinger and Miller refer to several factors which led people to doubt the media treatment. Among these were the following: personal contact with alternative information from trusted individuals or organizations, personal experience of being 'scapegoated', personal experience of conditions in Africa and being black oneself.

The authors conclude:

Our research shows both the power of the media and the pervasiveness of stock white cultural images of black Africa; it is easy to believe that Africa is a reservoir of HIV infection because 'it fits'. Journalists draw on these cultural assumptions when they produce reports on AIDS and Africa. But, in so doing, they are helping to reproduce and legitimize them. (1992: 49)

Kitzinger and Miller's study has a much bigger database than my study of one medical clinic. However, it shares two features in common. First, in both studies, the researchers began without a hypothesis. Instead, as in much qualitative research, they sought to induce and then test hypotheses during their data analysis. Second, both studies were theoretically driven by the assumption that social phenomena derive their meaning from how they are defined by participants. Both these features are found in the remaining two studies we shall consider.

### 1.2.3 Interviews

Weatherburn et al. (1992) note that many studies assert that there is an association between alcohol and drug 'misuse' and 'risky' sexual behaviour. Conversely, Weatherburn et al. suggest the following:

> [that] the link is asserted but not proven; that the evidence is at best contradictory and that this assertion is informed by a puritanical moral agenda. (1992: 119)

In their own research, we find two postulates which are absent from these earlier, generally quantitative, research studies:

1 No assumption is made about a strong interrelation between alcohol use and engagement in unsafe sex.
2 Psychological traits (like defects of character or weakness of resolve under the influence of alcohol) are held to be an inadequate explanation of enduring unsafe sexual practices (1992: 122–3).

Weatherburn et al.'s research was part of Project SIGMA which is a British longitudinal study of a non-clinic-based cohort of over 1000 gay men. Like other qualitative researchers, they distrusted explanations of behaviour which reduced social life to a response to particular 'stimuli' or 'variables'.

Consequently, they favoured open-ended questions to try to understand the meanings attached to alcohol use by their sample. For instance:

> The first question asked respondents: 'Would you say alcohol plays a significant role in your sex life?' Those respondents who said 'yes', were probed in detail about its exact nature. Respondents were also asked whether alcohol had *ever* influenced them to engage in unsafe sexual behaviours. (1992: 123)

Typically, in an open-ended interview study, respondents were encouraged to offer their own definitions of particular activities, 'unsafe sex' for example.

The findings of the study reflect the complexity of the attempt to explain the 'causes' of social behaviour. The effects of alcohol were found to depend upon 'the context of the sexual encounter and the other party involved in the sexual negotiation' (1992: 129). Only in a minority of reports was alcohol treated as the 'cause' of unsafe behaviour. In the majority of cases, although people might report themselves as 'fairly drunk', they described their sexual activities as the outcome of conscious deliberation.

However, the authors raise a crucial issue about the meaning we should attach to such descriptions, given that people may recall those features that depict their behaviour as socially desirable:

it is recognized that asking people retrospective questions about alcohol use may well be problematic, both because of social desirability phenomena and because alcohol itself impairs recall. (1992: 123)

As we shall see in Chapter 4, this observation goes to the heart of an unresolved debate about the status of interview accounts, namely whether such accounts are:

- true or false representations of such features as attitudes and behaviour; or
- simply 'accounts' whose main interest lies in how they are constructed rather than in their accuracy.

This interview study highlights the advantages of qualitative research in offering an apparently 'deeper' picture than the variable-based correlations of quantitative studies. However, it also implies why it can be difficult to get funding or acceptance for qualitative research. However questionable are the assumptions behind some quantitative research, it tends to deliver apparently reliable and valid correlations between 'variables' that appear to be self-evident. Moreover, these correlations usually lead in clear-cut policy directions.

However, some qualitative research can combine sensitivity to participants' definitions with correlations carrying direct policy implications. We shall see this in our final research study.

### 1.2.4 *Audiotapes*

Silverman's (1997a) study was based on audiotapes of HIV/AIDS counselling from ten different medical centres in Britain, the USA and Trinidad. The focus was on advice (both how advice was given and how it was received). The interest in advice derived from three sources:

1 The research was part funded by the English Health Education Authority: this meant that analysis of advice sequences would be appropriate to its interest in health promotion.
2 Early work on the project had identified two basic 'communication formats' through which such counselling was conducted. The analysis of these 'information delivery' and 'interview' formats provided a crucial resource for the analysis of how advice-giving worked (see Peräkylä and Silverman, 1991).
3 A study by Heritage and Sefi (1992) of health visitors and mothers had provided important findings about the relationship between different forms of advice-giving and their uptake by the client.

As I show in Section 8.3.2, we were able to tabulate the relationship between the form in which advice was given and how it was received in 50 advice sequences. Broadly speaking, personalized advice, offered after clients had been asked to specify their concerns, was associated with a 'marked acknow-ledgement' (e.g. a comment on the advice or a further question from the client). Conversely, counsellors who gave generalized advice, without first getting their clients to specify a particular problem, generally received only 'unmarked acknowledgements' (e.g. 'mm', 'right', 'yes').

However, the availability of detailed transcripts meant that we could go beyond this predictable finding. In particular, we sought to address the functions of counsellors' behaviour – particularly given the fact that, if asked, many of them would have recognized that generalized advice-giving is likely to be ineffective. We hoped, thereby, to make a constructive input into policy debates by examining the *functions* of communication sequences in a particular institutional context.

Let us look at a relevant data extract (Extract 1.1). The transcription symbols are provided in the Appendix (see p. 303).

**Extract 1.1 (SW2 – A)**
(C = Counsellor; P = Patient)

```
 1   C:  .hhhh Now when someo:ne er is tested (.) and they
 2       ha:ve a negative test result .hh it's obviously
 3       ideal uh:m that (.) they then look, after themselves to
 4       prevent [any further risk of=

 5   P:           [Mm hm

 6   C:  =infection. .hhhh I mean obviously this is only
 7       possible up to a point because if .hhh you get into a
 8       sort of serious relationship with someone that's long
 9       ter:m .hh you can't obviously continue to use condoms
10       forever. .hh Uh:m and a point has to come where you
11       make a sort of decision (0.4) uh:m if you are settling
12       down about families and things that you know (0.6)
13       you'd- not to continue safer sex.
14       [ .hhhh Uh:m but obviously: (1.0) you=

15   P:  [Mm:

16   C:  =nee:d to be (.) uh:m (.) take precautions uhm (0.3)
17       and keep to the safer practices .hhh if: obviously you
18       want to prevent infection in the future.

19   P:  [Mm hm

20   C:  [ .hhhh The problem at the moment is we've got it here
21       in {names City} in particular (.) right across
22       the boar:d you know from all walks of life.

23   P:  Mm hm

24   C:  Uh : :m from you know (.) the sort of established high
25       r- risk groups (.) now we're getting heterosexual (.)
26       [transmission as well. .hh Uhm=

27   P:  [Mm hm
```

28   C:   =so obviously everyone really needs to careful. .hhh
29         Now whe- when someone gets a *positive* test result er:
30         then obviously they're going to ke- think very
31         carefully about things. .hhhh *Being* HIV positive
32         doesn't necessarily mean that that person is going to
33         develop AI:DS (.) later on.

34         (.)

35   P:   Mm hm

We can make three observations about this extract. First, C delivers advice without having elicited from P a perceived problem. Reasons of space do not allow us to include what immediately precedes this extract but it involves another topic (the meaning of a positive test result) and no attempt is made to question P about her possible response to this topic, i.e. how she might change her behaviour after a negative test result.

Moreover, within this extract, C introduces fresh topics (what to do in a 'serious' relationship on lines 7–13; the spread of HIV in the city on lines 20–22) without attempting to elicit P's own perspectives. Second, predictably, P only produces variations on 'mm hm' in response to C's advice. While these may indicate that P is listening, they do not show patient uptake and might be taken as a sign of passive resistance to the advice (see Heritage and Sefi, 1992). Third, C does not personalize her advice. Instead of using a personal pronoun or the patient's name, she refers to 'someone' and 'they' (lines 1–3) and 'everyone' (line 28).

Advice sequences like these were very common at three out of the five centres we examined. So we have to ask ourselves why counsellors should use a format which is likely to generate so little patient uptake. Since our preference was not to criticize professionals but to understand the logic of their work, we need to look at the *functions* as well as the dysfunctions of this way of proceeding. A part of the answer seems to lie in the content of the advice given. Note how in Extract 1.1 the counsellor is giving advice about what she tells patients *after* a particular test result. But the patient here does not yet have his result: indeed he has not yet even consented to the test. This leaves it open to the patient to treat what he is being told not as advice but as information delivery (about the advice C would give if P turned out to be seropositive or seronegative). Moreover, throughout C avoids personalizing her advice. Rather than saying what she advises P to do, she uses the non-specific term 'someone'. All the available research suggests that behaviour change rarely occurs on the basis of information alone. Why, therefore, would counsellors want to package their advice in a way which makes patient uptake less likely?

A part of the answer to this question lies in the *dysfunctions* of recipient-designed advice. Throughout our corpus of interviews, counsellors exit quickly from *personalized* advice when patients offer only minimal responses like 'mm hm'. It seems that, if someone is giving you personalized advice, and if you don't show more uptake than 'mm hm', this will be problematic to the advice-giver. Conversely, if you are merely giving somebody general information, then the occasional 'mm hm' is all that is required for the speaker to continue in this format. Moreover, truncated, non-personalized advice sequences are also usually far shorter – an important consideration for hard-pressed counsellors.

Another function of offering advice in this way is that it neatly handles many of the issues of delicacy that can arise in discussing sexual behaviour. First, the counsellor can be heard as making reference to what she tells 'anyone' so that this particular patient need not feel singled out for attention about his private life. Second, because there is no step-by-step method of questioning, patients are not required to expand on their sexual practices with the kinds of hesitations we have found elsewhere in our research (Silverman, 1997b: ch. 4). Third, setting up advice sequences that can be heard as information delivery shields the counsellor from some of the interactional difficulties of appearing to tell strangers what they should be doing in the most intimate aspects of their behaviour. Finally, predictably, information-oriented counselling produces very little conflict. So in Extract 1.1 there is no *active* resistance from P. Indeed, topic follows topic with a remarkable degree of smoothness and at great speed.

So the character of HIV counselling as a focused conversation on mostly delicate topics explains why truncated advice sequences (like that seen in Extract 1.1) predominate in our transcripts.

Clearly, such sequences are functional for *both* local and institutional contexts. This underlines the need to locate 'communication problems' in a broader structural context. Our research had much to say about how coun-sellors can organize their talk in order to maximize patient uptake. However, without organizational change, the impact of such communication techniques alone might be minimal or even harmful.

For instance, encouraging patient uptake will usually involve longer counselling sessions. Experienced counsellors will tell you that, if they take so long with one client that the waiting period for others increases, some clients will simply walk out – and hence may continue their risky behaviour without learning their HIV status.

Undoubtedly, then, there are gains for the counsellor in setting up advice packages which are truncated and non-personalized. Obviously, however, there are concomitant losses in proceeding this way. As we have shown, such advice packages produce far less patient uptake and, therefore, their function in creating an environment in which people might re-examine their own sexual behaviour is distinctly problematic. Two possible solutions suggest themselves from the data analysed by this study. First, necessarily 'delicate' and unstable advice sequences should be avoided; patients should be encour-aged to draw their own conclusions from a particular line of questioning. Second, more time should be provided since both this method and step-by-step advice-giving are very time-consuming. I take up these matters in greater detail in Chapter 9.

Attempt Exercise 1.4 about now

## 1.3 CONCLUSIONS

By focusing on the topics of HIV and AIDS, I have tried to show how four different research methods can be used in qualitative research. Despite the different kinds of data which they generate, they lead to a distinctive form of analysis which is centrally concerned with avoiding a social problem perspective by asking how participants attach meaning to their activities and problems.

Having set out four different qualitative methods, I want to make two general observations. First, as I have emphasized, no research method stands on its own. So far, I have sought to show the link between methods and methodologies in social research. However, there is a broader, societal context in which methods are located and deployed. As a crude example, texts depended upon the invention of the printing press or, in the case of television or audio recordings, upon modern communication technologies.

Moreover, such activities as observation and interviewing are not unique to social researchers. For instance, as Foucault (1977) has noted, the observation of the prisoner has been at the heart of modern prison reform, while the method of questioning used in the interview reproduces many of the features of the Catholic confessional or the psychoanalytic consultation. Its pervasiveness is reflected by the centrality of the interview study in so much contemporary social research. For instance, in the two collections of papers from which the research studies above have been selected, 14 out of 19 empirical studies are based on interview data. One possible reason for this may not derive from methodological considerations. Think, for instance, of how many interviews are a central (and popular) feature of mass media products, from 'talk shows' to 'celebrity interviews'. Perhaps we all live in what might be called an 'interview society' in which interviews seem central to making sense of our lives (Atkinson and Silverman, 1997).

All this means that we need to resist treating research methods as mere *techniques*. This is reflected in the attention paid in this book to the *analysis* of data rather than to methods of data *collection*.

Part Two of this book sets out each research method in greater detail, and Part Three returns to issues of credibility and relevance which are touched upon in this chapter. However, before we deal with these detailed issues, it will be helpful, in the light of the studies discussed here, to review what other writers have said about the distinctive properties of qualitative research. This is the topic of Chapter 2.

# KEY POINTS

- In both science and everyday life, the facts never speak for themselves. This is because all knowledge is theoretically impregnated.
- Theory provides a framework for critically understanding phenomena and a basis for considering how what is unknown might be organized.
- Research problems are distinct from social problems.
- We can generate valuable research problems by employing three types of sensitivity: historical, political and contextual.
- There are four major methods used by qualitative researchers: observation; analysing texts and documents; interviews; and recording and transcribing naturally occurring interaction.
- There is a broader societal context in which research methods are located and deployed.

## Recommended Reading

The most useful introductory texts are Alan Bryman (1988), Nigel Gilbert (1993) and Clive Seale (1998). More advanced qualitative analysis is offered by Miles and Huberman (1984), Hammersley and Atkinson (1983) and Denzin and Lincoln (2000).

## Exercise 1.1

Harvey Sacks (1992) offers a case where you observe a car drawing up near you. A door opens and a teenage woman emerges and runs a few paces. Two other people (one male, one female) get out of the car. They run after the young woman, take her arms and pull her back into the car, which then drives off.
   Now answer these questions:

1 Without using your social science knowledge, prepare at least *two* different interpretations of what you have seen. Focus on whether this is something you should report to the police.
2 Examine at least *two* different interpretations of your behaviour if: (a) you report this matter to the police or (b) you do not report it.
3 Now use any ideas you know from your own discipline to describe and/or explain what you have seen.
4 Consider (a) whether these ideas are likely to give a more 'accurate' picture than your description in 1, and (b) to what extent we need to choose between the descriptions in 1 and 3.

## Exercise 1.2

Discuss how you might study people who take the law into their own hands ('vigilantes'). Is there any difference between your proposed study and a good television documentary on the same subject (i.e. differences in the questions you would ask and how you would test your conclusions)?

Now consider: (a) whether this matters and (b) what special contribution, if any, social science research can bring to such social problems.

## Exercise 1.3

Return to your interpretation of 'vigilantes' in Exercise 1.2. Now examine how you could generate different research problems using each of the three kinds of 'sensitivity' discussed in the chapter, namely:

- historical
- political
- contextual.

## Exercise 1.4

Once more focus on 'vigilantes'. Now suggest what research questions can be addressed by any *two* of the four methods discussed in the chapter, namely:

- observation
- analysing texts and documents
- interviews
- recording and transcribing.

Now consider (a) what are the relative merits of each method in addressing this topic and (b) what, if anything, could be gained by combining the two chosen methods (you might like to refer forward to my discussion of 'triangulation' in Section 8.3.2).

# 2

# What Is Qualitative Research?

To call yourself a 'qualitative' researcher settles surprisingly little. First, as we shall see at the end of this chapter, 'qualitative research' covers a wide range of different, even conflicting, activities. Second, if the description is being used merely as some sort of negative epithet (saying what we are *not*, i.e. non-quantitative), then I am not clear how useful it is. As Peter Grahame puts it:

> the notion that qualitative research is non-quantitative is true but uninformative: we need more than a negative definition. (1999: 4)

In this second sense, 'qualitative research' seems to promise that we will avoid or downplay statistical techniques and the mechanics of the kinds of quantitative methods used in, say, survey research or epidemiology. The danger in the term, however, is that it seems to assume a fixed preference or predefined evaluation of what is 'good' (i.e. qualitative) and 'bad' (i.e. quantitative) research. In fact, the choice between different research methods should depend upon what you are trying to find out.

For instance, if you want to discover how people intend to vote, then a quantitative method, like a social survey, may seem the most appropriate choice. On the other hand, if you are concerned with exploring people's life histories or everyday behaviour, then qualitative methods may be favoured.

However, other, less practical questions arise when you choose between 'qualitative' and 'quantitative' methods. The researcher has to bear in mind that these methods are often evaluated differently. This is shown in Table 2.1, which is drawn from the terms used by speakers at a conference on research methods.

Table 2.1 shows how imprecise, evaluative considerations come into play when researchers describe qualitative and quantitative methods. Depending on your point of view, the table might suggest that quantitative research was superior because, for example, it is value-free. The implication here is that quantitative research simply objectively reports reality, whereas qualitative research is influenced by the researcher's political values. Conversely, other people might argue that such value freedom in social science is either undesirable or impossible.

The same sort of argument can arise about 'flexibility'. For some people, this flexibility encourages qualitative researchers to be innovative. For others,

TABLE 2.1  *Claimed features of qualitative and quantitative methods*

| Qualitative | Quantitative |
| --- | --- |
| Soft | Hard |
| Flexible | Fixed |
| Subjective | Objective |
| Political | Value-free |
| Case study | Survey |
| Speculative | Hypothesis testing |
| Grounded | Abstract |

*Source:* Halfpenny, 1979: 799

flexibility might be criticized as meaning lack of structure. Conversely, being 'fixed' gives such a structure to research but without flexibility.

However, this is by no means a balanced argument. Outside the social science community, there is little doubt that quantitative data rule the roost. Governments favour quantitative research because it mimics the research of its own agencies (Cicourel, 1964: 36). They want quick answers based on 'reliable' variables.

Similarly, many research funding agencies call qualitative researchers 'journalists' or soft scientists' whose work is:

> termed unscientific, or only exploratory, or entirely personal and full of bias. (Denzin and Lincoln, 1994: 4)

For the general public, there is a mixture of respect for and suspicion of quantitative data ('you can say anything you like with figures'; 'lies, damn lies and statistics'). This is reflected by the media. On the one hand, public opinion polls are treated as newsworthy – particularly immediately before elections. On the other hand, unemployment and inflation statistics are often viewed with suspicion – particularly when they appear to contradict your own experience (statistics which show that inflation has fallen may not be credible if you see prices going up for the goods you buy!).

For this reason, by the 1990s, in many Western countries, the assumed reliability of quantitative research was beginning to be under significant threat. In Britain, for instance, the ways in which inflation and unemployment were calculated during the Thatcher era were regularly changed. This suggested to some that such indexes might be being 'fixed' in order to cast a favourable light upon these matters. Similarly, the failure of surveys of voting intention in the British general election of 1992 (almost comparable to the similar failure of US telephone poll studies in the 1948 Truman–Dewey presidential race) made the public a little sceptical about such statistics – even though the companies involved insisted they were providing only statements of current voting intentions and not predictions of the actual result.

But such concerns may constitute only a 'blip' in the ongoing history of the dominance of quantitative research. Qualitative researchers still largely feel themselves to be second-class citizens whose work typically evokes suspicion, where the 'gold standard' is quantitative research.

However, so far we have been dealing with little more than empty terms, apparently related to whether or not researchers use statistics of some kind. If, as I already have argued, the value of a research method should properly be gauged solely in relation to what it is trying to find out, we need now to sketch out the uses and abuses of both quantitative *and* qualitative methods.

## 2.1   THE SENSE OF QUANTITATIVE RESEARCH

Bryman (1988) has discussed the five main methods of quantitative social science research and these are set out in Table 2.2.

TABLE 2.2   *Methods of quantitative research*

| Method | Features | Advantages |
|--------|----------|------------|
| Social survey | Random samples<br>Measured variables | Representative<br>Tests hypotheses |
| Experiment | Experimental stimulus<br>Control group not exposed to stimulus | Precise measurement |
| Official statistics | Analysis of previously collected data | Large datasets |
| Structured observation | Observations recorded on predetermined schedule | Reliability of observations |
| Content analysis | Predetermined categories used to count content of mass media products | Reliability of measures |

*Source*: adapted from Bryman, 1988: 11–12

To flesh out the bare bones of Table 2.2, I will use one example based on the quantitative analysis of official statistics. The example relates to data taken from the General Social Survey (GSS) carried out every year by the US National Opinion Research Center (NORC) and discussed by Procter (1993).

Procter shows how you can use these data to calculate the relationship between two or more variables. Sociologists have long been interested in 'social mobility' – the movement between different statuses in society either within one lifetime or between generations. The GSS data can be used to calculate the latter, as Table 2.3 shows.

In Table 2.3 we are shown the relationship between father's occupation and son's occupation. In this case, the father's occupation is the 'independent' variable because it is treated as the possible cause of the son's occupation (the 'dependent' variable).

Table 2.3 appears to show a strong association (or 'correlation') between father's and son's occupations. For instance, of the group with non-manual

TABLE 2.3   *Respondent's occupation by father's occupation*

| | | Father's occupation | |
|---|---|---|---|
| | | Non-manual | Manual |
| Son's occupation | Non-manual | 63.4% | 27.4% |
| | Manual | 36.6% | 72.6% |

*Source:* adapted from Procter, 1993: 246

fathers, 63.4% were themselves in non-manual jobs. However, among sons with fathers in manual occupations, only 27.4% had obtained non-manual work. Because the sample of over 1000 people was randomly recruited, we can be confident, within specifiable limits, that this correlation is unlikely to be obtained by chance.

However, quantitative researchers are reluctant to move from statements of correlation to causal statements. For instance, both father's and son's occupations may be associated with another variable (say inherited wealth) which lies behind the apparent link between occupations of father and son. Because of such an 'antecedent' variable, we cannot confidently state that father's occupation is a significant *cause* of son's occupation. Indeed, because this antecedent variable causes both of the others to vary together, the association between the occupation of fathers and sons is misleading or 'spurious'.

Along these lines Procter (1993: 248–9) makes the interesting observation that there appears to be a marked correlation between the price of rum in Barbados and the level of Methodist ministers' salaries, i.e. in any given year, both go up or down together. However, we should not jump to the conclusion that this means that rum distillers fund the Methodist Church. As Procter points out, both the price of rum and ministers' salaries may simply be responding to inflationary pressures. Hence the initial correlation is 'spurious'.

### Attempt Exercise 2.1 about now

While looking at Tables 2.2 and 2.3, you may have been struck by the extent to which quantitative social research uses the same language that you may have been taught in say physics, chemistry or biology. As Bryman notes:

> Quantitative research is . . . a genre which uses a special language . . . [similar] to the ways in which scientists talk about how they investigate the natural order – variables, control, measurement, experiment. (1988: 12)

Sometimes, this has led critics to claim that quantitative research ignores the differences between the natural and social world by failing to understand the 'meanings' that are brought to social life. This charge is often associated with critics who label quantitative research as 'positivistic' (e.g. Filmer et al., 1972).

Unfortunately, **positivism** is a very slippery and emotive term. Not only is it difficult to define but there are very few quantitative researchers who would accept it (see Marsh, 1982: ch. 3). Instead, most quantitative researchers would argue that they do not aim to produce a science of laws (like physics) but simply aim to produce a set of cumulative generalizations based on the critical sifting of data, i.e. a 'science' as defined above.

As I argue, at this level, many of the apparent differences between quantitative and qualitative research should disappear – although some qualitative researchers remain insistent that they want nothing to do with even such a limited version of science (see Section 2.6). By contrast, in my view at least, qualitative researchers should celebrate rather than criticize quantitative researchers' aim to assemble and sift their data critically (see Chapter 8).

## 2.2 THE NONSENSE OF QUANTITATIVE RESEARCH

Procter's attempt to control for spurious correlations was possible because of the quantitative style of his research. This has the disadvantage of being dependent upon survey methods with all their attendant difficulties. As Fielding and Fielding argue:

> the most advanced survey procedures themselves only manipulate data that had to be gained at some point by asking people. (1986: 12)

As we will see in Chapter 4, what people say in answer to interview questions does not have a stable relationship with how they behave in naturally occurring situations. Again, Fielding and Fielding make the relevant point:

> researchers who generalize from a sample survey to a larger population ignore the possible disparity between the discourse of actors about some topical issue and the way they respond to questions in a formal context. (1986: 21)

This is why a dependence on purely quantitative methods may neglect the social and cultural construction of the 'variables' which quantitative research seeks to correlate. As Kirk and Miller (1986) argue, 'attitudes', for instance, do not simply attach to the inside of people's heads and researching them depends on making a whole series of analytical assumptions. They conclude:

> The survey researcher who discusses is not wrong to do so. Rather, the researcher is wrong if he or she fails to acknowledge the theoretical basis on which it is meaningful to make measurements of such entities and to do so with survey questions. (1986: 15)

According to its critics, much quantitative research leads to the use of a set of *ad hoc* procedures to define, count and analyse its variables (Blumer, 1956; Cicourel, 1964; Silverman, 1975). The implication is that quantitative researchers unknowingly use the methods of everyday life, even as they claim scientific objectivity (Cicourel, 1964; Garfinkel, 1967). This is why some qualitative researchers have preferred to describe how, in everyday life, we actually go about defining, counting and analysing.

Let me try to concretize this critique by means of a single example. More than 30 years ago, two American sociologists, Peter Blau and Richard Schoenherr, conducted a study of several large organizations. The study is interesting for our present purposes because it is explicitly based on a critique of qualitative methods. In these authors' view, too much research in the 1960s had used qualitative methods to describe 'informal' aspects of organization – like how employees perceive their organization and act according to these perceptions rather than according to the organizational 'rulebook'.

Blau and Schoenherr (1971) suggested that the time was ripe to switch the balance and to concentrate on 'formal' organization, like how jobs are officially defined and how many 'levels' exist in the organizational hierarchy. Such features can then be seen as 'variables' and statistical correlations can be produced which are both reliable and valid.

Look at how such an apparently simple, quantitative logic worked out in practice. Blau and Schoenherr used as their data organizational wallcharts which show hierarchies and job functions. Unfortunately, from their point of view, as a revealing early chapter acknowledges, these wallcharts are often ambiguous and vary in structure from one organization to another. Consequently, it was necessary to discuss their meaning in interviews with 'key informants' in each organization. Using this information, Blau and Schoenherr constructed standardized measures of various aspects of organizational structure such as 'hierarchy' and 'job specificity'. The result of all this was a set of statistical correlations which convincingly show the relationship between the variables that Blau and Schoenherr constructed.

Unfortunately, given the indeterminancy of the data they were working with, the authors engaged in a series of sensible but undoubtedly *ad hoc* decisions in order to standardize the different forms in which people talk about their own organization. For instance, they decided to integrate into one category the two grades of 'clerk' that appear on one organization's wallchart of authority.

This decision was guided by a statistical logic that demanded clearly defined, 'reliable' measures. However, the researchers' decision has an unknown relationship to how participants in the organization concerned actually relate to this wallchart and how or when they invoke it. Indeed, Blau and Schoenherr are prevented from examining such matters by their decision to stay at a purely 'structural' level and to avoid 'informal' behaviour. This means that their own interpretation of the meaning of the statistical correlations so obtained, while no doubt statistically rigorous, is equally *ad hoc*.

What we have here is a nice case of 'the cart leading the horse'. Blau and Schoenherr adopt a purely statistical logic precisely in order to replace common-sense understandings by scientific explanations based on apparently reliable, quantifiable variables. However, despite themselves, they inevitably appeal to common-sense knowledge both in defining their 'variables' and in interpreting their correlations. So the quantitative desire to establish 'operational' definitions at an early stage of social research can be an arbitrary process which deflects attention away from the everyday sense-making procedures of people in specific milieux. As a consequence, the 'hard' data on social structures which quantitative researchers claim to provide can turn out to be a mirage (see also Cicourel, 1964).

This brief (non-random!) example should allow you to understand the kinds of criticism that are often directed at purely quantitative research by more qualitative 'types'. Because space is short, Table 2.4 attempts to summarize these criticisms.

TABLE 2.4   *Some criticisms of quantitative research*

| | |
|---|---|
| 1 | Quantitative research can amount to a 'quick fix', involving little or no contact with people or the 'field'. |
| 2 | Statistical correlations may be based upon 'variables' that, in the context of naturally occurring interaction, are arbitrarily defined. |
| 3 | After the fact speculation about the meaning of correlations can involve the very common-sense processes of reasoning that science tries to avoid (see Cicourel, 1964: 14, 21). |
| 4 | The pursuit of 'measurable' phenomena can mean that unperceived values creep into research by simply taking on board highly problematic and unreliable concepts such as 'delinquency' or 'intelligence'. |
| 5 | While it is important to test hypotheses, a purely statistical logic can make the development of hypotheses a trivial matter and fail to help in generating hypotheses from data (see Glaser and Strauss, 1967, discussed in Section 3.4.1). |

It should be noted that Table 2.4 contains simply some complaints made about *some* quantitative research. Moreover, because quantitative researchers are rarely 'dopes', many treat such matters seriously and try to overcome them. So, for instance, epidemiologists, who study official statistics about disease, and criminologists are only too aware of the problematic character of what gets recorded as, say, 'cause of death' or a 'criminal offence' (see Hindess, 1973). Equally, good quantitative researchers are conscious of the problems involved in interpreting statistical correlations in relation to what the variables involved 'mean' to the participants (see Marsh, 1982: ch. 5).

In the light of this qualification, I conclude this section by observing that an insistence that any research worth its salt should follow a purely quantitative logic would simply rule out the study of many interesting phenomena relating to what people actually do in their day-to-day lives, whether in homes, offices or other public and private places. But, as the next section shows, a balanced view should accept the strengths, as well as the limitations, of quantitative research.

## 2.3 THE SENSE OF QUALITATIVE RESEARCH

Qualitative researchers suggest that we should not assume that techniques used in quantitative research are the *only* way of establishing the validity of findings from qualitative or field research. This means that a number of practices which originate from quantitative studies may be *inappropriate* to qualitative research. These include the assumptions that social science research can only be valid if based on experimental data, official statistics or the random sampling of populations and that quantified data are the only valid or generalizable social facts.

Critics of quantitative research argue that these assumptions have a number of defects (see Cicourel, 1964; Denzin, 1970; Schwartz and Jacobs, 1979; Hammersley and Atkinson, 1983; Gubrium, 1988). These critics note that experiments, official statistics and survey data may simply be inappropriate to some of the tasks of social science. For instance, they exclude the observation of behaviour in everyday situations. Hence, while quantification may *sometimes* be useful, it can both conceal as well as reveal basic social processes.

Consider the problem of counting attitudes in surveys. Do we all have coherent attitudes on any topics which await the researcher's questions? And how do 'attitudes' relate to what we actually do – our practices? Or think of official statistics on cause of death compared to studies of how hospital staff (Sudnow, 1968a), pathologists and statistical clerks (Prior, 1987) attend to deaths (see Section 5.3.2). Note that this is *not* to argue that such statistics may be biased. Instead, it is to suggest that there are areas of social reality which such statistics cannot measure.

The methods used by qualitative researchers exemplify a common belief that they can provide a 'deeper' understanding of social phenomena than would be obtained from purely quantitative data. However, just as quantitative researchers would resist the charge that they are all 'positivists' (Marsh, 1982), there is no agreed doctrine underlying all qualitative social research (see Section 2.6).

## 2.4 THE NONSENSE OF QUALITATIVE RESEARCH

In many quantitatively oriented social science methodology textbooks, qualitative research is often treated as a relatively minor methodology. As such, it is suggested that it should only be contemplated at early or 'exploratory' stages of a study. Viewed from this perspective, qualitative research can be used to familiarize oneself with a setting before the serious sampling and counting begin.

This view is expressed in the following extract from an early text. Note how the authors refer to 'nonquantified data' – implying that quantitative data are the standard form:

> The inspection of *nonquantified* data may be particularly helpful if it is done periodically throughout a study rather than postponed to the end of the statistical

analysis. Frequently, a single incident noted by a perceptive observer contains the clue to an understanding of a phenomenon. If the social scientist becomes aware of this implication at a moment when he can still add to his material or exploit further the data he has already collected, he may considerably enrich the quality of his conclusions. (Selltiz et al., 1964: 435, my emphasis)

Despite these authors' 'friendly' view of the uses of 'nonquantified' data, they assume that 'statistical analysis' is the bedrock of research. A similar focus is to be found, a quarter of a century later, in another mainly quantitative text:

Field research is essentially a matter of immersing oneself in a naturally occurring . . . set of events in order to gain firsthand knowledge of the situation. (Singleton et al., 1988: 11)

Note the emphasis on 'immersion' and its implicit contrast with later, more focused research. This is underlined in the authors' subsequent identification of qualitative or field research with 'exploration' and 'description' (1988: 296) and their approval of the use of field research 'when one knows relatively little about the subject under investigation' (1988: 298–9).

These reservations have some basis given the fact that qualitative research is, by definition, stronger on long descriptive narratives than on statistical tables. The problem that then arises is how such a researcher goes about categorizing the events or activities described.

This is sometimes known as the problem of **reliability**. As Hammersley puts it, reliability:

refers to the degree of consistency with which instances are assigned to the same category by different observers or by the same observer on different occasions. (1992: 67)

The issue of consistency particularly arises because shortage of space means that many qualitative studies provide readers with little more than brief, persuasive, data extracts. As Bryman notes about the typical observational study:

field notes or extended transcripts are rarely available; these would be very helpful in order to allow the reader to formulate his or her own hunches about the perspective of the people who have been studied. (1988: 77)

Moreover, even when people's activities are audio or video recorded and transcribed, the reliability of the interpretation of transcripts may be gravely weakened by a failure to note apparently trivial, but often crucial, pauses, overlaps or body movements. For instance, a recent study of medical consultations was concerned to establish whether cancer patients had understood that their condition was fatal. When researchers first listened to tapes of relevant hospital consultations, they sometimes felt that there was no evidence that the patients had picked up their doctors often guarded statements about their prognosis. However, when the tapes were retranscribed, it was demonstrated that patients used very soft utterances (like 'yes' or, more usually 'mm') to mark that they were taking up this information. Equally, doctors would monitor patients' silences and rephrase their prognosis statements (see Clavarino et al., 1995).

Some qualitative researchers argue that a concern for the reliability of observations arises only within the quantitative research tradition. Because what they call the 'positivist' position sees no difference between the natural and social worlds, reliable measures of social life are only needed by such 'positivists'. Conversely, it is argued, once we treat social reality as always in flux, then it makes no sense to worry about whether our research instruments measure accurately (e.g. Marshall and Rossman, 1989).

Such a position would rule out any systematic research since it implies that we cannot assume any stable properties in the social world. However, if we concede the possible existence of such properties, why shouldn't other work replicate these properties? As Kirk and Miller argue:

> Qualitative researchers can no longer afford to beg the issue of reliability. While the forte of field research will always lie in its capability to sort out the validity of propositions, its results will (reasonably) go ignored minus attention to reliability. For reliability to be calculated, it is incumbent on the scientific investigator to document his or her procedure. (1986: 72)

A second criticism of qualitative research relates to how sound are the explanations it offers. This is sometimes known as the problem of **anecdotalism**, revealed in the way in which research reports sometimes appeal to a few, telling 'examples' of some apparent phenomenon, without any attempt to analyse less clear (or even contradictory) data (Silverman, 1989a). This problem is expressed very clearly by Bryman:

> There is a tendency towards an anecdotal approach to the use of data in relation to conclusions or explanations in qualitative research. Brief conversations, snippets from unstructured interviews . . . are used to provide evidence of a particular contention. There are grounds for disquiet in that the representativeness or generality of these fragments is rarely addressed. (1988: 77)

This complaint of 'anecdotalism' questions the **validity** of much qualitative research. 'Validity' is another word for truth (see Chapter 8). Sometimes one doubts the validity of an explanation because the researcher has clearly made no attempt to deal with contrary cases. Sometimes, the extended immersion in the 'field', so typical of qualitative research, leads to a certain preciousness about the validity of the researcher's own interpretation of 'their' tribe or organization. Or sometimes, the demands of journal editors for shorter and shorter articles simply mean that the researcher is reluctantly led only to use 'telling' examples – something that can happen in much the same way in the natural sciences where, for instance, laboratory assistants have been shown to select 'perfect' slides for their professor's important lecture (see Lynch, 1984).

**Attempt Exercise 2.2 about now**

Despite these common problems, doubts about the reliability and validity of qualitative research have led many quantitative researchers to downplay the value of the former. However, as we have seen, this kind of 'damning by faint praise' has been more than balanced by criticisms of quantitative research offered by many qualitative researchers.

## 2.5 COMBINING QUALITATIVE AND QUANTITATIVE RESEARCH

> By our pragmatic view, qualitative research does imply a commitment to field activities. It does not imply a commitment to innumeracy. (Kirk and Miller, 1986: 10)

Since the 1960s, a story has got about that no good sociologists should dirty their hands with numbers. Sometimes this story has been supported by sound critiques of the rationale underlying some quantitative analyses (Blumer, 1956; Cicourel, 1964). Even here, however, the story has been better on critique than on the development of positive, alternative strategies.

The various forms of ethnography, through which attempts are made to describe social processes, share a single defect. The critical reader is forced to ponder whether the researcher has selected only those fragments of data which support his argument. Where deviant cases are cited and explained (cf. Strong, 1979; Heath, 1981), the reader feels more confident about the analysis. But doubts should still remain about the persuasiveness of claims made on the basis of a few selected examples.

In this part of the chapter I want to make some practical suggestions about how quantitative data can be incorporated into qualitative research. These suggestions flow from my own recent research experience in a number of studies, one of which is briefly discussed shortly.

I do not attempt here to defend quantitative or positivistic research *per se*. I am not concerned with research designs which centre on quantitative methods and/or are indifferent to the interpretivist problem of meaning. Instead, I want to try to demonstrate some uses of quantification in research which is qualitative and interpretive in design.

I shall try to show that simple counting techniques can offer a means to survey the whole corpus of data ordinarily lost in intensive, qualitative research. Instead of taking the researcher's word for it, the reader has a chance to gain a sense of the flavour of the data as a whole. In turn, researchers are able to test and to revise their generalizations, removing nagging doubts about the accuracy of their impressions about the data.

As Cicourel (1964) noted many years ago, in a bureaucratic-technological society, numbers talk. Today, with qualitative social science on trial, we cannot afford to live like hermits, blinded by global, theoretical critiques to the possible analytical and practical uses of quantification. In the new millennium, I believe this case holds just as strongly.

It is, of course, mistaken to count simply for the sake of counting. Without a theoretical rationale behind the tabulated categories, counting only gives a spurious validity to research.

For instance, in his observation of classroom behaviour, Mehan suggests that many kinds of quantification have only limited value:

> the quantitative approach to classroom observation is useful for certain purposes, namely, for providing the frequency of teacher talk by comparison with student talk . . . However, this approach minimizes the contribution of students, neglects the inter-relationship of verbal to non-verbal behavior, obscures the contingent nature of interaction, and ignores the (often multiple) functions of language. (1979: 14)

To some extent, when I counted patients' questions in a study of cancer clinics (Silverman, 1984), I fell foul of Mehan's criticisms. Although my comparison of clinics was theoretically informed (deriving from Strong's, 1979, discussion of 'ceremonial orders'), the tabulation was based upon dubious, common-sensical categories. For instance, it is very problematic to count participants' questions when your only data are fieldnotes. Without being able to reinspect a tape-recording, my category of 'question' has an unknown relation to the participants' orientations. So quantification can neatly tie in with the logic of qualitative research when, instead of conducting surveys or experiments, we count participants' own categories as used in naturally occurring places.

Let me give you an example of this. In the early 1980s (see Silverman, 1987: chs 1–6) I was directing a group of researchers studying a paediatric cardiology (child heart) unit. Many of our data derived from tape-recordings of an outpatient clinic that was held every Wednesday.

We soon became interested in how decisions (or 'disposals') were organized and announced. It seemed likely that the doctor's way of announcing decisions was systematically related not only to clinical factors (like the child's heart condition) but to social factors (such as what parents would be told at various stages of treatment). For instance, at a first outpatients' consultation, doctors would not normally announce to parents the discovery of a major heart abnormality and the necessity for life-threatening surgery. Instead, they would suggest the need for more tests and only hint that major surgery might be needed. They would also collaborate with parents who produced examples of their child's apparent 'wellness'.

This step-by-step method of information-giving was avoided in only two cases. First, if a child was diagnosed as 'healthy' by the cardiologist, the doctor would give all the information in one go and would engage in what we called a 'search and destroy' operation, based on eliciting any remaining worries of the parent(s) and proving that they were mistaken.

Second, in the case of a group of children with Down's syndrome in addition to suspected cardiac disease, the doctor would present all the clinical information at one sitting, avoiding a step-by-step method. Moreover, atypically, the doctor would allow parents to make the choice about further treatment, while encouraging them to dwell on non-clinical matters like their child's 'enjoyment of life' or friendly personality.

This medical focus on the child's *social* characteristics was seen right at the outset of each consultation. I was able to construct a table, based on a comparison of Down's and non-Down's consultations, showing the different forms of the doctor's questions to parents and the parents' answers. This tabulation showed a strong tendency with Down's children for both the doctor and the parents to avoid using the word 'well' about the child, and this absence of reference to 'wellness' proved to be crucial to understanding the subsequent shape of the clinical consultation.

Moreover, the categories in the table were not my own. I simply tabulated the different questions and answers as actually given. For instance, the most common question that the doctor asked parents was:

A well child?

However, parents of Down's syndrome children were rarely asked this question. Instead, the most common question was:

How is he (she)?

This avoidance of the term 'well' proved to be crucial to understanding the direction which the consultations with Down's syndrome families subsequently took.

This example shows that there is no reason why qualitative researchers should not, where appropriate, use quantitative measures. Simple counting techniques, theoretically derived and ideally based on participants' own categories, can offer a means to survey the whole corpus of data ordinarily lost in intensive, qualitative research. Instead of taking the researcher's word for it, the reader has a chance to gain a sense of the flavour of the data as a whole. In turn, researchers are able to test and to revise their generalizations, removing nagging doubts about the accuracy of their impressions about the data.

I conclude this section, therefore, with a statement which shows the absurdity of pushing too far the qualitative/quantitative distinction:

> We are not faced, then, with a stark choice between words and numbers, or even between precise and imprecise data; but rather with a range from more to less precise data. Furthermore, our decisions about what level of precision is appropriate in relation to any particular claim should depend on the nature of what we are trying to describe, on the likely accuracy of our descriptions, on our purposes, and on the resources available to us; not on ideological commitment to one methodological paradigm or another. (Hammersley, 1992a: 163)

**Attempt Exercise 2.3 about now**

## 2.6   VARIETIES OF QUALITATIVE RESEARCH

Writers of textbooks on qualitative method, including myself (Silverman, 1993), usually feel obligated to define their phenomenon and to risk suggesting what qualitative researchers may have in common. Martyn Hammersley (1992) has taken a cautious path by arguing that, at best, we share a set of preferences. These are set out in Table 2.5.

TABLE 2.5   *The preferences of qualitative researchers*

1   A preference for qualitative data – understood simply as the analysis of words and images rather than numbers.
2   A preference for naturally occurring data – observation rather than experiment, unstructured versus structured interviews.
3   A preference for meanings rather than behaviour – attempting 'to document the world from the point of view of the people studied' (Hammersley, 1992: 165).
4   A rejection of natural science as a model.
5   A preference for inductive, hypothesis-generating research rather than hypothesis testing (cf. Glaser and Strauss, 1967).

*Source*: adapted from Hammersley, 1992: 160–72

Unfortunately, as Hammersley himself recognizes, even such a cautious list as that in Table 2.5 is a huge over-generalization. For instance, to take just item 5 in the table, qualitative research would look a little odd, after a history of over 100 years, if it had no hypotheses to test!

Moreover, if we take the list as a reasonable approximation of the main features of qualitative research, we can start to see why it can be criticized. As already noted, in a world where numbers talk and people use the term 'hard' science, a failure to test hypotheses, coupled with a rejection of natural science methods, certainly leave qualitative researchers open to criticism.

So unless we use the negative criterion of being 'non-quantitative', there is no agreed doctrine underlying all qualitative social research. Instead, there are many 'isms' that appear to lie behind qualitative methods. We have already seen how critics of quantitative research accuse it of positivism. And many readers of this book will have already come across other 'isms' such as feminism and postmodernism.

The most useful attempt to depict these different approaches within qualitative research is in Gubrium and Holstein (1997). They use the term 'idiom' to encompass both the analytical preferences indicated by my term *model* (see Table 1.1) and the use of particular vocabularies, investigatory styles and ways of writing. They distinguish (and criticize) four different 'idioms':

- *Naturalism*   A reluctance to impose meaning and a preference to 'get out and observe the field'.
- *Ethnomethodology*   Shares naturalism's attention to detail but locates it in talk-in-interaction.
- *Emotionalism*   Desires 'intimate' contact with research subjects and favours the personal biography.

- *Postmodernism*  Seeks to deconstruct the concepts of the 'subject' and the 'field'.

Some development of these ideas is found in Table 2.6.

TABLE 2.6  *Four qualitative idioms*

| Idiom | Concepts | Preferred data |
|---|---|---|
| Naturalism | Actors<br>Meanings | Observation<br>Interviews |
| Ethnomethodology | Members' methods for assembling phenomena | Audio/video recordings |
| Emotionalism | Subjectivity<br>Emotion | Interviews |
| Postmodernism | Representation<br>Reflexivity | Anything goes |

*Source*: adapted from Gubrium and Holstein, 1997

According to Gubrium and Holstein, qualitative researchers inhabit the 'lived border between reality and representation' (1997: 102). On this border, in their view, each idiom veers too far to one side as follows:

- *Naturalism*  Its pursuit of the content of everyday lives offers deep insights into the 'what?' of reality at the price of the 'how?' of reality's representation (by both participants and researchers).
- *Ethnomethodology*  Its focus on common-sense practices gives rewarding answers to 'how?' questions but underplays the 'what?' of contextual givens.
- *Emotionalism*  Helps us understand people's experiences but at the cost of privileging a common-sense category ('emotion').
- *Postmodernism*  Reveals practices of representation but can lead to a nihilistic denial of content.

As a way out of this purely critical position, Gubrium and Holstein offer three valuable practical ploys for the qualitative researcher. First, seeking a middle ground to 'manage the tensions between reality and representation' (1997: 114), they show how we can give voice to each idiom's silenced other. The figure of the 'insider', so dear to naturalism, can be treated as 'a represented reality' (1997: 103), as can emotionalism's 'feeling' subject. Equally, conversation analysis's account of institutionality (see Chapter 6) and Sacks's membership categorization analysis (see Chapter 5) show how ethnomethodology can put meat on the bare bones of representation. Last, while we must respect what postmodernism tells us about representation, this can be treated as an incentive for empirically based description, not as its epitaph.

**Attempt Exercise 2.4 about now**

If 'qualitative research' involves many different, potentially conflicting, models or idioms, this shows that the whole 'qualitative/quantitative' dichotomy is open to question.

In the context of this book, I view most such dichotomies or polarities in social science as highly dangerous. At best, they are pedagogic devices for students to obtain a first grip on a difficult field: they help us to learn the jargon. At worst, they are excuses for not thinking, which assemble groups of researchers into 'armed camps', unwilling to learn from one another.

The implication I draw is that doing 'qualitative' research should offer no protection from the rigorous, critical standards that should be applied to any enterprise concerned to sort 'fact' from 'fancy'. Ultimately, soundly based knowledge should be the common aim of all social science (see Kirk and Miller, 1986: 10–11). As Hammersley argues:

> the process of inquiry in science is the same whatever method is used, and the retreat into paradigms effectively stultifies debate and hampers progress. (1992: 182)

## KEY POINTS

- When we compare quantitative and qualitative research, we generally find, at best, different emphases between 'schools' who themselves contain many internal differences.
- Qualitative researchers should celebrate rather than criticize quantitative researchers' aim to assemble and sift their data critically.
- Reliability and validity are key ways of evaluating research.
- Certain kinds of quantitative measures may sometimes be appropriate in qualitative research.
- However, a dependence on purely quantitative methods may neglect the social and cultural construction of the 'variables' which quantitative research seeks to correlate.

### Recommended Reading

The most useful introductory texts are Alan Bryman (1988), Nigel Gilbert (1993) and Clive Seale (1998). Sensible statements about the quantitative position are to be found in Marsh (1982) (on survey research) and Hindess (1973) (on official statistics).

In addition to these general texts, readers are urged to familiarize themselves with examples of qualitative and quantitative research. Strong (1979) and Lipset et al. (1962) are good examples of each.

## Exercise 2.1

This exercise gives you an opportunity to test your understanding of Procter's (1993) arguments about statistical correlations. Table 2.7 relates voting in printers' union elections to having friends who are also printers. Examine it carefully and then answer the questions beneath it.

TABLE 2.7   Club membership and voting in union elections
(% participating in elections)

| | Political interest | | |
| | High | Medium | Low |
|---|---|---|---|
| **Printer friends** | | | |
| Yes | 61% | 42% | 26% |
| No | 48% | 22% | 23% |

Source: adapted from Lipset et al., 1962

1  Does Table 2.7 show that there is an association between having a printing friend and participating in union elections? Explain carefully, referring to the table.
2  Can we be confident that by controlling for the degree of political interest of a printer, we prevent any correlation between friendships and participation being spurious.

## Exercise 2.2

Review any research study with which you are familiar. Then answer the following questions:

1  To what extent are its methods of research (qualitative, quantitative or a combination of both) appropriate to the nature of the research question(s) being asked?
2  How far does its use of these methods meet the criticisms of both qualitative and quantitative research discussed in this chapter?
3  In your view, how could this study have been improved methodologically and conceptually?

---

### Exercise 2.3

This exercise requires a group of at least six students, divided into two discussion groups ('buzzgroups').

Imagine that you are submitting a proposal to research drug abuse among school pupils. Each buzzgroup should now form two 'teams' (team I is 'Quantitative', team II is 'Qualitative').

1 Team I should formulate a quantitative study to research this topic.
2 Team II should suggest limits/problems in this study (team I to defend).
3 Team II should formulate a qualitative study to research this topic.
4 Team I should suggest limits/problems in this study (team II to defend).
5 Both teams should now come to some conclusions.

---

### Exercise 2.4

This exercise will also focus upon drug abuse among school pupils. It can be done in buzzgroups or by individuals.

Following Gubrium and Holstein's (1997) account of four 'idioms' of qualitative research (Table 2.6), suggest how each idiom might:

1 define a delimited research problem on this topic
2 suggest a particular methodology

---

# 3

# Ethnography and Observation

Michael Agar (1986) has described a 'received view' of science. Such a view approaches any research project with these kinds of questions:

- What's your hypothesis?
- How do you measure that?
- How large is your sample?
- Did you pretest the instrument?

Agar argues that it does not always make sense to ask such questions about every piece of social science research:

> For some research styles, especially those that emphasize the *scientific testing* role, those questions make sense. But for other styles – when the social researcher assumes a *learning role* – the questions don't work. When you stand on the edge of a village and watch the noise and motion, you wonder, 'Who are the people and what are they doing?' When you read a news story about the discontent of young lawyers with their profession, you wonder, 'What is going on here?' Hypotheses, measurement, samples, and instruments are the wrong guidelines. Instead, you need to learn about a world you understand by encountering it firsthand and making some sense out of it. (1986: 12)

Although I would dispute Agar's apparent dismissal of the relevance of issues of scientific testing to qualitative research (see Chapter 8), his examples give us an initial hold on the questions that can animate observational studies. An illustration of one observational study may bring to life how social science observers try to answer Agar's question 'What is going on here?' through what he calls 'encountering a world firsthand'.

## Attempt Exercise 3.1 about now

More than half a century ago, William Foote Whyte (1949) carried out over a year's participant observation in a number of Chicago restaurants. He points out how, in a service trade like a restaurant, the organization of work differs from other settings. Instead of the industrial pattern, whereby a supervisor gives orders to a worker, restaurant work originates from a customer's order.

Whyte shows that this difference generates a number of problems for restaurant workers:

- Who originates action?
- For whom?
- How often?
- With what consequences?

The social structure of the restaurant functions as an organized response to these problems. This can be seen in the following three patterns:

1 Many of us will have had the experience of a member of staff snatching away a menu which we have innocently picked up on sitting down at a restaurant table. Whyte argues that this occurs because the skilful waitress/waiter attempts to fit customers into *her* pattern of work (e.g. her need to ensure that the table has been cleared before she takes an order). So, by not passively responding to the initiatives of customers, serving staff preserve their own work routines.
2 Back in the 1940s, widespread gender inequalities caused a particular problem for waitresses because they were expected to transmit orders to mainly male cooks. A structure emerged which concealed this initiation of work by waitresses: rather than shout out orders to the cooks, the women wrote out slips which they laid on the counter to be dealt with in the cooks' own time.
3 Barmen also engaged in informal behaviour to distance themselves from the initiation of orders by waitresses. When they had lots of orders, they would not speed up, and so waitresses (and their angry customers) would just have to wait. Moreover, at busy times, they would not mix one cocktail until they had several orders for it which could be mixed together.

Half a century later, Whyte's work remains impressive. His restaurant study shows the importance of *context* and *process* in understanding behaviour (see item 3 of Table 3.1). Thus Whyte shows the skills of staff in reproducing occupational and gender hierarchies by modifying the flow of work and, thereby, redefining apparently simple acts.

Moreover, despite Agar's strictures against 'scientific testing', Whyte does not let a preference for an unstructured research design lead to a study which merely tells anecdotes about a few choice examples. For instance, the restaurant study uses powerful *quantitative* measures of the number of times different types of people initiate actions.

**Attempt Exercise 3.2 about now**

However, can we call Whyte's observational study an ethnography? What, indeed, is **ethnography**? And how does ethnography differ from observation?

'Observation' is almost self-explanatory. Like Whyte, the observer looks, listens and records. But observation, of course, is not just the province of social scientists. Physicists, engineers and police officers all make their 'observations'. More tellingly, in our everyday lives, we depend upon making observations of each other – for instance about whether to categorize a stranger's question as 'genuine' or a 'pick-up line' (see Sacks, 1992,I: 49,103, 130–1).

Of course, the status of social science observations versus what we observe in everyday life is a big issue (see Section 3.4.3). A common terminological solution is to say that social scientists do something extra with their observations: they write ethnographies. *Ethnography* puts together two different words: 'ethno' means 'folk', while 'graph' derives from 'writing'. Ethnography refers, then, to social scientific writing about particular folks.

The origins of ethnography are in the work of nineteenth-century anthropologists who travelled to observe different pre-industrial cultures (see Section 3.1.1). Today, 'ethnography' encompasses a much broader range of work, from studies of groups in one's own culture to experimental writing to political interventions (see Sections 3.1.2 to 3.1.4). Moreover, ethnographers today do not always 'observe', at least directly. They may work with cultural artefacts like written texts or study recordings of interactions they did not observe firsthand. For this reason, in what follows I shall use 'ethnography' to refer to a general approach and reserve 'observation' to talk about specific issues of ethics and technique.

Some contemporary researchers share the early anthropologists' belief that in order to understand the world 'firsthand', you must participate yourself rather than just observe people at a distance. This has given rise to what is described as the method of *participant observation* (see Section 3.3.2). Indeed, in a very general sense, participant observation is more than just a method. It describes a basic resource of all social research:

> in a sense, *all* social research is a form of participant observation, because we cannot study the social world without being part of it. From this point of view, participant observation is not a particular research technique but a mode of being-in-the-world characteristic of researchers. (Atkinson and Hammersley, 1994: 249)

How does this 'mode of being' impact on the specifics of ethnographic research? Bryman (1988) has provided a useful list of the principal characteristics of qualitative research. As adapted in Table 3.1, it stands as a simple guide for the ethnographer.

TABLE 3.1 *Aims of observational research*

1  *Seeing through the eyes of:* 'viewing events, actions, norms, values, etc. from the perspective of the people being studied'.

2  *Description:* 'attending to mundane detail . . . to help us to understand what is going on in a particular context and to provide clues and pointers to other layers of reality'.

3  *Contextualism:* 'the basic message that qualitative researchers convey is that whatever the sphere in which the data are being collected, we can understand events only when they are situated in the wider social and historical context'.

4  *Process:* 'viewing social life as involving interlocking series of events'.

5  *Flexible research designs:* 'qualitative researchers' adherence to viewing social phenomena through the eyes of their subjects has led to a wariness regarding the imposition of prior and possibly inappropriate frames of reference on the people they study'. This leads to a preference for an open and unstructured research design which increases the possibility of coming across unexpected issues.

6  *Avoiding early use of theories and concepts:* rejecting premature attempts to impose theories and concepts which may 'exhibit a poor fit with participants' perspectives'.

*Source:* adapted from Bryman, 1988: 61–6

Bryman's list provides a useful orientation for the novice. Item 2 is particularly important: 'Description: attending to mundane detail'. One way to understand the import of 'mundane detail' is to say that the ethnographer attempts to answer Agar's question, 'What is going on here?' To show what lies behind this apparently simple question, I will use the example of police movies.

If you go to the cinema primarily in order to see 'action' (car chases, holdups etc.), then it will take a big effort for you to become a good ethnographer. On the other hand, if you are intrigued by the *details* of police work and of criminal activity, you are very much on the right lines. This is because social science observation is fundamentally about understanding the routine rather than what appears to be exciting. Indeed, the good observer finds excitement in the most everyday, mundane kinds of activities.

Take some examples from 'crime' movies. Compare the trite storyline of *LA Confidential* (the usual closing shootout, the happy ending) with the surprises of the Coen brothers' *Fargo* (a pregnant woman as sheriff). Think of how *Fargo* slows down its narrative by detailing the mundane lives of both sheriff and criminals in a small town quite unlike the usual big city setting of such movies. Or the positively ethnographic pursuit of the 'boring' features of the world in Bertrand Tavernier's *L327*, a police story almost without arrests or car chases but with a strong focus on the routines of police work as we see Parisian drug cops spending most of the time sitting in their offices, 'cooking' their official reports.

*Fargo* and *L327* require a certain discipline from their audience, just as the good observer finds interest in what is apparently routine. For example, how police do their paperwork and assemble their files may tell us more about their activities than the occasional shootout (see Cicourel, 1968 and Exercise 5.5).

So far, I have found good reason to accept item 2 ('description') in Table 3.1. However, the reader should proceed with caution about uncritically accepting all the items in the table. As I suggested in Chapter 1, any attempt to base observation on an understanding of how people 'see' things (item 1) can speedily degenerate into a commonsensical or psychologistic perspective. To put the argument in its most extreme form, I believe that the ethnographer should pursue what people actually do, leaving what people say they 'think' and 'feel' to the skills of the media interviewer (see Section 1.3).

However, I run ahead of myself. Let us slow down and provide more background. In the rest of this chapter, I will attempt to illuminate four crucial aspects of ethnographic and observational work:

- the 'focus' of the study, including tribes, subcultures, the public realm and organizations)
- ethical issues, including the issue of informed consent
- methodological choices, including access, identity, defining a research problem, looking as well as listening, methods of recording data, developing analysis of ethnographic data and feedback to participants
- theoretical issues, that is the theoretically derived nature of ethnographic analysis and the main contemporary theoretical approaches including grounded theory, naturalism and ethnomethodology.

## 3.1  THE ETHNOGRAPHIC FOCUS

Just as, according to Bryman, the qualitative researcher seeks to see things in context, so the student needs some basic knowledge of the historical tradition from which observational studies arose. This is because:

> Qualitative research is an empirical, socially located phenomenon, defined by its own history, not simply a residual grab-bag comprising all things that are 'not quantitative'. (Kirk and Miller, 1986: 10)

In this section, we will consider four different topics on which ethnographic studies have focused: tribes, subcultures, the public realm and organizations.

### 3.1.1  Studies of tribes

The initial thrust in favour of observational work was anthropological. Anthropologists usually argue that, if one is really to understand a group of people, one must engage in an extended period of observation. Anthropological fieldwork routinely involves immersion in a culture over a period of years, based on learning the language and participating in social events.

An important early study arose out of Malinowski's (1922) research on the everyday social life of the Trobriand Islanders in the Western Pacific. Like Radcliffe-Brown (1948), Malinowski was committed to rigorous scientific description of the beliefs and practices of 'native' peoples (see Atkinson and Hammersley, 1994: 249–50).

However, in the early twentieth century, the idea of 'native' populations with 'primitive' beliefs was already familiar to the colonial rulers of the British Empire. Indeed, these rulers employed administrators with the explicit task of reporting on the ways of colonial subjects. In this sense, it could be argued that these early anthropologists adopted a 'colonial methodology' (Ryen and Silverman, 2000).

Both anthropologist and colonial civil servant seem to have perceived the foreigner as someone who was outside and different from the white middle class. So the foreign becomes something he can discover, research and understand (of course, most of the middle class persons involved in and writing about foreign cultures were men).

This focus on the difference between foreign and Western culture appears in different ways in both novels and academic works. Daniel Defoe's story about Robinson Crusoe shows how the middle class saw travel to 'the foreign', with Crusoe as the representative of the civilization transforming nature into culture. Joseph Conrad's Mr Kurtz's anxiety for the dark and wild Africa is revealed when fever fantasies make his office-holder mask crack.

In general, however, exotic cultures studied by anthropologists like Malinowski and Evans-Pritchard very often turned out to be folk groups of the Third World countries, or former colonial states far away from the Western world and academic institutions.

Though anthropologists have recognized for a long time that cultural positions are relative, their insistence on the anthropologist as a cultivated European based within classic science seemed to be more long-lived. This perception of the researcher was not challenged until the group of anthropologists itself became more diverse in respect of gender, age, experience and methodological background.

However, while we may today have freed ourselves from most of the earlier assumptions of effortless superiority, not everything has changed. Like the early anthropologists, it is tempting to attempt to fix a boundary around 'native' populations. Like them, we may unreflectively distinguish the 'exotic' by what appears to be 'familiar'. So the early anthropologist may have shared with modern 'upmarket' tourists a belief in the irreplaceable intrinsic value of every culture still not affected by Western influence (see Section 1.1.2).

Contemporary anthropologists do not, however, limit themselves to criticizing the 'colonial' or 'touristic' impulses of their forebears. Providing we can rid ourselves of a colonial mentality, it is both practically and analytically important to attempt to understand other cultures in the context of an increasingly 'globalized' world.

One important contemporary example of such an attempt is to be found in **cognitive anthropology**. As its name suggests, cognitive anthropology seeks to understand how people perceive the world by examining how they communicate. This leads to the production of ethnographies, or conceptually derived descriptions, of whole cultures, focused on how people communicate.

For instance, Basso (1972) discusses the situations in which native American Apache people prefer to remain silent, and Frake (1972) shows how the Subanun, a people living in the Philippines, assign social status when talking together during drinking ceremonies.

While cognitive anthropology is usually content with single case studies of particular peoples, **structural anthropology** is only interested in single cases in so far as they relate to general social forms. Structural anthropologists draw upon French social and linguistic theory of the early twentieth century, notably Ferdinand de Saussure and Emile Durkheim. Their main building blocks are Saussure's account of sign systems (see Section 7.2) and Durkheim's insistence that apparently idiosyncratic forms of behaviour can be seen as 'social facts' which are embedded in forms of social organization. In both cases, behaviour is viewed as the expression of a 'society' which works as a 'hidden hand' constraining and forming human action (see Lévi-Strauss, 1967).

A classic case of an anthropologist using a case study to make such broader generalizations is found in Mary Douglas's (1975) work on a central African tribe, the Lele. Douglas noticed that an anteater, that Western zoologists call a 'pangolin', was very important to the Lele's ritual life. For the Lele, the pangolin was both a cult animal and an anomaly.

In part, this was because it was perceived to have both animal and human characteristics: for instance, it tended only to have one offspring at a time, unlike most other animals. It also did not readily fit into the Lele's classification of land and water creatures, spending some of its time on land and some time in the water. Curiously, among animals that were hunted, the pangolin seemed to the Lele to be unique in not trying to escape but almost offering itself up to its hunter.

True to her structuralist perspective, Douglas resisted a 'touristic' response and moved beyond curiosity to systematic analysis. She noted that many groups who perceive anomalous entities in their environment reject them out of hand. To take an anomalous entity seriously might cast doubt on the 'natural' status of your group's system of classification

The classic example of the rejection of anomaly is found in the Old Testament. Douglas points out that the reason why the pig is unclean, according to the Old Testament, is that it is anomalous. It has a cloven hoof which, following the Old Testament, makes it clean – but it does not chew the cud, which makes it dirty. So it turns out that the pig is particularly unclean precisely because it is anomalous. Old Testament teachings on intermarriage work in the same way. Although you are not expected to marry somebody of another tribe, to marry the offspring of a marriage between a member of your tribe and an outsider is even more frowned upon. In both examples, anomaly is shunned.

However, the Lele are an exception: they celebrate the anomalous pangolin. What this suggests to Douglas is that there may be no *universal* propensity to frown upon anomaly. If there is variability from community to community, then this must say something about their social organization.

Sure enough, there is something special about the Lele's social life. Their experience of relations with other tribes has been very successful. They exchange goods with them and have little experience of war.

What is involved in relating well with other tribes? It means successfully crossing a frontier or boundary. But what do anomalous entities do? They too cut across boundaries. Here is the answer to the puzzle about why the Lele are different.

Douglas is suggesting that the Lele's response to anomaly derives from experiences grounded in their social organization. They perceive the pangolin favourably because it cuts across boundaries just as they themselves do. Conversely, the Ancient Israelites regard anomalies unfavourably because their own experience of crossing boundaries was profoundly unfavourable. Indeed, the Old Testament reads as a series of disastrous exchanges between the Israelites and other tribes.

By means of this historical comparison, Douglas has moved from a single-case explanation to a far more general theory of the relation between social exchange and response to anomaly. In their discussion of *grounded theory*, Glaser and Strauss (1967) have described this movement towards greater generality as a move from *substantive* to *formal* theory (see Sections 3.3.6 and 3.4.1). In their own research on hospital wards caring for terminally ill patients, they show how, by using the comparative method, we can develop accounts of people's own awareness of their impending death (i.e. a substantive theory) into accounts of a whole range of 'awareness contexts' (formal theory).

### 3.1.2 Studies of subcultures

A crude (and sometimes inaccurate) way to distinguish sociology from anthropology is to say that, unlike anthropology, sociology's 'tribe' is the people around them.

Sociological ethnography is usually assumed to originate in the 1920s when students at the University of Chicago were instructed to put down their theory textbooks and get out on to the streets of their city and use their eyes and ears. The '**Chicago School**', as it became known in the 1930s, had two strands. One was concerned with the sociology of urban life, represented by the work of Park and Burgess on the social organization of the city into different 'zones' and the movement of population between zones over time. The second strand, associated with Everett Hughes, provided a series of vivid accounts of urban settings, particularly focused on 'underdog' occupations and 'deviant' roles.

The Chicago School tradition continued for two decades after the Second World War. In the 1950s, Becker (1953) conducted a classic observational study of drug use. He was particularly concerned with the relationship between marihuana smokers' own understandings and the interactions in which they were involved. He discovered that people's participation in groups of users taught them how to respond to the drug. Without such learning, novices would not understand how to smoke marihuana or how to respond to its effects. Consequently, they would not get 'high' and so would not continue to use it.

Becker outlines a number of stages through which novices pass on their path to become a regular smoker. These include:

1 *Direct teaching* For example, being taught the difference between how to smoke marihuana and how to smoke tobacco; learning how to interpret its effects and their significance.
2 *Learning how to enjoy the effects* Through interaction with experienced users, the novice learns to find pleasure in sensations which, at first, may be quite frightening.
3 *Resocialization after difficulties* Even experienced users can have an unpleasant or frightening experience through using a larger quantity or a different quality of marihuana. Fellow users can 'cool them out', explaining the reasons for this experience and reassuring them that they may safely continue to use the drug.
4 *Learning connoisseurship* Through developing a greater appreciation of the drug's effects, becoming able to distinguish between different kinds and qualities of the drug.

Becker stresses that it is only in the context of a social network, which provides a means of interpreting the effects of the drug, that people become stable marihuana users. It is unlikely, however, that such a network could have been identified by, say, survey research methods concerned with the attitudes of marihuana users.

Studies of different subcultures are the bread and butter of contemporary ethnography (see my discussion of studies of drug use in adolescent cultures and of female members of youth gangs in Section 4.6). However, as most ethnographers recognize, the ethics of observing such potentially vulnerable groups are complicated (see Section 3.2).

### 3.1.3 Studies of the public realm

Many studies of subcultures take place in public areas like streets, shopping malls and parks. However, ethnographers who observe the public domain sometimes have a wider interest than the subculture of particular groups. Instead, their aim is to observe how people in general behave in certain public contexts; for example, while using public transport (see Adler and Adler, 1994: 384–5; Nash, 1975; 1981).

Three sociologists, Simmel, Goffman and Sacks, gave the impetus to this focus on public space. In the nineteenth century, the German sociologist Georg Simmel (1950) developed propositions about the basic forms of human interaction according to the number in a group – for example what happens in 'dyads' (groups of two) compared to 'triads' (groups of three). From these formal propositions, Simmel derived compelling accounts of the 'stranger' and of urban life.

Judging by the number of references to his work by others, Erving Goffman was probably the most influential sociologist working on face-to-face behaviour in the twentieth century.

Goffman's early work, based on a study of the Shetland Islanders in the 1950s, set out the arts of what Goffman (1959) referred to as 'impression management'. This involved people managing their own appearances by controlling the impressions they gave by, for instance, organizing what guests might see in their home. Goffman further distinguished 'face work', which smoothed interaction by maintaining a ceremonial order, from 'character work', which served to maintain or challenge the moral standing of particular individuals.

Goffman shows us two recurrent kinds of rule used to organize social interaction:

- rules of courtesy, manners and etiquette (who is able to do and say what to whom and in what way)
- depending upon the definition of the situation, rules of what is relevant or irrelevant within any setting.

As Goffman points out, these rules give us a clue to understanding what is going on in definitions of situations in face-to-face encounters:

> instead of beginning by asking what happens when this definition of the situation breaks down, we can begin by asking what perspectives this definition of the situation *excludes* when it is being satisfactorily sustained. (1961b: 19, my emphasis)

Harvey Sacks's lectures to undergraduates at the University of California between 1965 and 1972 showed the influence of Goffman's insights in studies of the public realm. For instance, Sacks offers a Goffmanesque discussion of how 'excuse me' rather than 'hello' works as an effective 'ticket' to talk to strangers (Sacks, 1992, II:195; see also Goffman, 1981: ch. 1).

Equally, Sacks's discussion of how appearances are organized when your private space becomes public is very close to that of Goffman (1959). It is routine, for instance, to arrange your living area in a particular way when guests are about to call:

> the magazines on somebody's coffee table are routinely seen to be intended to suggest that they are intellectuals, or whatever else. (Sacks, 1992, I: 329)

Moreover, Sacks develops this example by trading off Goffman's (1959) discussion of how a visitor can contrast such appearances with the appearances that the host was unable to control but 'gave off'. As Sacks puts it:

> And you can walk out of a house and say that somebody's a phoney by virtue of some lack of fit between what you figured you could infer from various things in their house, and what you've found out about them other than that. (1992, I: 329)

Observations like these can be made in the course of everyday life, thereby resolving the ethnographer's problem of access (see Section 3.3.1). Curiously, however, very few novice researchers think about using the public realm as a data source.

### 3.1.4  Studies of organizations

We study and work in organizations like universities and businesses. Often, we spend our leisure time in organized social groups. It is, therefore, hardly surprising that organizations should prove to be a fertile field for the ethnographer. Indeed, most of my research data have been drawn from organizations including a personnel department in local government (see Section 5.3.1), outpatient consultations in hospitals and private clinics (Silverman, 1987) and public and private organizations offering HIV test counselling (see Section 1.2.4).

Recent useful discussions of ethnographic studies of organizations may be found in Boden (1994) and Czarniawska (1998). To simplify matters, I will take examples once more from the work of Erving Goffman and Harvey Sacks.

Goffman's (1961a) book *Asylums* is probably the only sociological monograph ever to have become widely read by the general public. *Asylums* even entered (usually misunderstood) into the recent debate about the 'community care' of mental patients.

The 'character work' that he observed among the Shetland Islanders was very much to the fore in Goffman's ethnographic study of what he called 'the moral career of the mental patient'. Goffman suggested that mental hospitals, like other 'total institutions', such as barracks, prisons, monasteries and boarding schools, broke down the usual boundaries between work, rest and play through using various strategies to strip people of their non-institutional identities, e.g. dressing inmates in uniforms, calling them by a number or institutional nickname.

Faced with what he called a 'mortifying process', Goffman argued that inmates were by no means passive. In particular, they engaged in various 'secondary adjustments' which served to preserve a non-institutionally defined identity. These adjustments ranged from minor infringements of rules ('make-dos') to actively 'working the system' for their own benefit by making skilful use of 'free places' and establishing private and group 'territories'.

Like Goffman, Sacks had no interest in building data-free grand theories or in research methods, like laboratory studies or even interviews, which abstracted people from everyday contexts. Above all, both men marvelled at the everyday skills through which particular appearances are maintained.

We can catch sight of Sacks's use of Goffman's ideas in his article 'Notes on police assessment of moral character' (Sacks, 1972b) which was originally written as a course paper for Goffman's course at Berkeley in the early 1960s (Sacks, 1972a: 280n). For Sacks, police officers face the same kind of problem as Goffman's Shetland Islanders: how are they to infer moral character from potentially misleading appearances?

To solve this problem, police 'learn to treat their beat as a territory of normal appearances' (1972a: 284). Now they can treat slight variations in normal appearances as 'incongruities' worthy of investigation, working with the assumption of the appearances of 'normal' crimes (cf. Sudnow, 1968b).

So observational data can contribute a great deal to understanding how organizations function. However, as Sacks realized, a problem of such ethnographic work is that its observations may be based upon a taken-for-granted version of the setting in question. For instance, Strong's (1979) powerful analysis of the 'ceremonial order' of doctor–parent consultations undoubtedly depends, in part, upon our readiness to read his data extracts in the context of our shared knowledge of what medical consultations look like.

Consequently, ethnographic work can only take us so far. It is able to show us how people respond to particular settings. It is unable to answer basic questions about how people are constituting that setting through their talk (see my discussion of 'ethnomethodology' in Section 3.4.3).

As Maynard and Clayman argue:

> using terms such as 'doctor's office', 'courtroom', 'police department', 'school room', and the like, to characterise settings . . . can obscure much of what occurs within those settings . . . For this reason, conversation analysts rarely rely on ethnographic data and instead examine if and how interactants themselves reveal an orientation to institutional or other contexts. (1991: 406–7)

By not relying on ethnographic data, Maynard implies that observational fieldnotes must be wedded to more reliable data such as audio or video recordings of actual organizational (or institutional) behaviour (see Section 3.3.4). The precise methods and concerns of what he calls 'conversation analysis' will be discussed in Section 6.3.

## 3.2  ETHICAL ISSUES IN ETHNOGRAPHY

In a lecture delivered in the early years of the twentieth century, the German sociologist Max Weber (1946) pointed out that all research is contaminated to some extent by the values of the researcher. Only through those values do certain problems get identified and studied in particular ways. Even the commitment to scientific (or rigorous) method is itself, as Weber emphasizes, a value. Finally, the conclusions and implications to be drawn from a study are, Weber stresses, largely grounded in the moral and political beliefs of the researcher.

From an ethical point of view, Weber was fortunate in that much of his empirical research was based on documents and texts that were already in the public sphere. In many other kinds of social science research, ethical issues are much more to the fore. For instance, both qualitative and quantitative researchers studying human subjects ponder over the dilemma of wanting to give full information to the people they study but seeking not to 'contaminate' their research by informing subjects too specifically about the research question to be studied. This shows that, when you are studying people's behaviour or asking them questions, not only the values of the researcher but the researcher's responsibilities to those studied have to be faced.

Jennifer Mason (1996: 166–7) discusses two ways in which such ethical issues impinge upon the qualitative researcher:

1 The rich and detailed character of much qualitative research can mean intimate engagement with the public and private lives of individuals.
2 The changing directions of interest and access during a qualitative study mean that new and unexpected ethical dilemmas are likely to arise during the course of your research.

Mason suggests that one way to confront these problems is to try to clarify your intentions while you are formulating your research problem. Table 3.2 contains her advice on ethical matters.

TABLE 3.2   *Ethical questions for the ethnographer*

| |
| --- |
| 1   Decide what is the purpose(s) of your research, e.g. self-advancement, political advocacy etc. |
| 2   Examine which individuals or groups might be interested or affected by your research topic. |
| 3   Consider what are the implications for these parties of framing your research topic in the way you have done. |

*Source:* Mason, 1996: 29–30

Some examples will help to clarify the issues that Mason raises. Ordinarily, one should consult the ethical guidelines of one's professional association. All such guidelines stress the importance of 'informed consent' where possible (see Punch, 1994: 88–94; Silverman, 2000: 201–5).

Covert observation, where the observer does not inform subjects about the study, can lead to severe ethical problems regarding 'informed consent' as well as physical danger to the researcher (see also Section 3.3.1). For example, Fielding (1982) obtained permission to research a far right British political party but still felt it necessary to supplement official access with covert observation. In this new situation, he put himself at some potential risk as well as creating ethical dilemmas relating to how much he revealed to his subjects and to outside authorities.

However, we should not assume that 'covert' access always involves possible offence. For instance, on a course I used to teach, students were asked to engage in a small exercise where they observed people exchanging glances in an everyday setting (see Sacks, 1992, I: 81–94). Providing the students were reasonably sensitive about this and refrained from staring at others, I did not envisage any problems arising.

Mason's worthwhile ethical aims are also highlighted when we observe 'underdog' subcultures. First, despite the physical and ethical dangers that may arise in studying groups which are often on the edge of the law, the researcher must remember that relatively easy access to such groups also suggests their vulnerability.

For instance, the behaviour of 'underdog' groups like these is sometimes open to inspection by closed circuit television (CCTV) and other forms of official surveillance. This is hardly the case with the activities of 'top dogs' (unless, like President Nixon, they are foolish enough to preserve audio recordings of their conversations!). So the ethnographer who studies sub-cultures may unthinkingly be preying upon groups who are unable to protect themselves.

Second, although 'underdog' ethnographers may say that their studies are meant to improve public understanding of their chosen group's situation and perspective, their motives can also be criticized. For instance, Dingwall (1980) has noted how such work 'undoubtedly furnishes an element of romance, radical chic even, to liven the humdrum routine of academic inquiry'. He then goes on to note that a concern to champion the 'underdog' is

> inimical to the serious practice of ethnography, whose claims to be distinguished from polemic or investigative journalism must rest on its ability to comprehend the perspectives of top dogs, bottom dogs and, indeed, lap dogs. (1980: 874)

Dingwall concludes that social research, whatever its methods, must seek to produce valid generalizations rather than 'synthetic moral outrage' (1980: 874). One should have doubts about a study which fails to deal even-handedly with the people it describes or to recognize the interactive character of social life. Dingwall's ethic of 'fair dealing' implies that we should ask of any study:

> Does it convey as much understanding of its villains as its heroes? Are the privileged treated as having something serious to say or simply dismissed as evil, corrupt or greedy without further enquiry? (1992: 172)

Clearly, this is as much a scientific as an ethical issue.

## 3.3  METHODOLOGICAL ISSUES

Atkinson and Hammersley (1994: 248) have suggested that ethnographic research usually involves the following four features:

1  a strong emphasis on exploring the nature of particular social phenomena, rather than setting out to test hypotheses about them
2  a tendency to work primarily with 'unstructured' data, that is, data that have not been coded at the point of data collection in terms of a closed set of analytic categories
3  investigation of a small number of cases, perhaps just one case, in detail
4  analysis of data that involves explicit interpretations of the meanings and functions of human actions, the product of which mainly takes the form of

verbal descriptions and explanations, with quantification and statistical analysis playing a subordinate role at most.

Atkinson and Hammersley's list implies ethical issues regarding access to particular cases (see Section 3.3.1) and theoretical concerns (e.g. point 4's focus on 'the meanings and functions of human actions'). In Section 3.4, I will examine how theory enters into ethnography.

At first sight, however, Atkinson and Hammersley's characterization of ethnography appears to deal primarily with *methodology*, i.e. the choices that confront us in planning and executing a research study. In this section, we will examine the following methodological issues in conducting an ethnography:

- gaining access
- finding an identity
- defining a research problem
- looking as well as listening
- recording observations
- developing analysis of field data.

## 3.3.1 Gaining access

Textbooks (e.g. Hornsby-Smith, 1993: 53; Walsh, 1998: 224–5) usually distinguish two kinds of research setting:

- 'closed' or 'private' settings (organizations, deviant groups) where access is controlled by gatekeepers
- 'open' or 'public' settings (e.g. vulnerable minorities, public records or settings) where access is freely available but not always without difficulty, either practical (e.g. finding a role for the researcher in a public setting) or ethical (e.g. should we be intruding upon vulnerable minorities?).

Depending on the contingencies of the setting (and the research problem chosen), two kinds of research access may be obtained:

- 'covert' access without subjects' knowledge
- 'overt' access based on informing subjects and getting their agreement, often through 'gatekeepers'.

The impression you give may be very important in deciding whether you get overt access:

> Whether or not people have knowledge of social research, they are often more concerned with what kind of *person* the researcher is than with the research itself. They will try to gauge how far he or she can be trusted, what he or she might be able to offer as an acquaintance or a friend, and perhaps also how easily he or she could be manipulated or exploited. (Hammersley and Atkinson, 1983: 78)

This clearly brings us on to how the ethnographer finds an identity in the field.

### 3.3.2 Finding an identity

Denzin (1970) notes that participant observers' focus on the present may blind the observer to important events that occurred before his or her entry on to the scene. Second, as Dalton (1959) points out, confidantes or informants in a social setting may be entirely unrepresentative of the less open participants. Third, observers may change the situation just by their presence, and so the decision about what role to adopt will be fateful. Finally, observers may 'go native', identifying so much with the participants that, like a child learning to talk, they cannot remember how they found something out or articulate the principles underlying what they are doing.

Many of these issues fit into Atkinson and Hammersley's (1994: 249) account of four problematic features of fieldwork identity:

1  whether the researcher is known to be a researcher by all of those being studied or only by some, or by none
2  how much, and what, is known about the research by whom
3  what sorts of activities are and are not engaged in by the researcher in the field, and how this locates her or him in relation to the various conceptions of category and group membership used by participants
4  what the orientation of the researcher is, and how completely he or she consciously adopts the orientation of insider or outsider.

Let me just focus on point 3, which relates the observer's behaviour to how (s)he is defined by research subjects. In a study of a ward for terminally ill patients, Anssi Peräkylä (1989) has shown how staff can use four different ways to define themselves and their patients.

Following Goffman (1974), how people treat what is currently relevant and irrelevant defines the **frame** through which a setting is constituted. Using what Peräkylä calls a psychological frame, staff define themselves as objective surveyors of the emotional reactions of patients; patients are both subjects (who feel and experience) and objects (of the knowing psychological gaze. The psychological frame is a powerful means of resolving the identity disturbances found in other frames: where a patient is resisting practical or medical framing, for instance, this can be explained in terms of his psychological state.

But the psychological frame was also relevant to how staff defined the researcher's own identity. This frame seemed to be a convenient means for the staff to talk about their activities to Peräkylä himself and to define his presence to each other and to patients. So, although Peräkylä was actually a sociologist, staff found it convenient to define him as a psychologist.

In a comparative study of public and private cancer clinics (Silverman, 1984; see Section 3.3.4), I saw how the emphasis on privacy in British 'private' medicine creates a special problem of identity for the researcher. While at the NHS clinics I sheltered happily behind a name-tag, at the private clinic my presence was always explained, if ambiguously ('Dr Silverman is sitting in with me today if that's alright?'). Although identified and accepted by the patient, I remained uncomfortable in my role in this setting. Its air of quiet seclusion made me feel like an intruder.

Like the doctor, I found myself dressing formally and would always stand up and shake hands with the patient. I could no longer merge into the background as at the NHS clinics. I regularly experienced a sense of intruding on some private ceremony.

Finding an identity in the field may not, of course, just be about your professional affiliation. Your gender in relation to the gender of the people you are studying may turn out to be very important in relation to how you are defined and, therefore, what you find out.

Although, as we have seen, in his study of restaurants Whyte (1949) treated gender as a topic, it was not until 20 years later that social scientists began to think systematically about the impact of gender on the fieldwork process as a whole.

In part, this reflected an interest in the interplay between gender and power. For instance, almost all the 'classics' of the Chicago School were written by men, and almost all the researchers who rose up the academic hierarchy to become full professors were also men (see Warren, 1988: 11). Increasingly, the gender of fieldworkers themselves was seen to play a crucial factor in observational research. Informants were shown to say different things to male and female researchers.

For instance, in a study of a nude beach, when approached by someone of a different gender, people emphasized their interest in 'freedom and naturalism'. Conversely, where the researcher was the same gender as the informant, people were far more likely to discuss their sexual interests (Warren and Rasmussen, 1977, reported by Warren, 1988).

In studies which involved extended stays in 'the field', people have also been shown to make assumptions based upon the gender of the researcher. For instance, particularly in rural communities, young, single women may be precluded from participating in many activities or asking many questions. Conversely, female gender may sometimes accord privileged access.

For instance, Oboler (1986) reports that her pregnancy increased her rapport with her Kenyan informants, while Warren (1988: 18) suggests that women fieldworkers can make use of the sexist assumption that only men engage in 'important business' by treating their 'invisibility' as a resource. Equally, male fieldworkers may be excluded or exclude themselves from contact with female respondents in certain kinds of situation (see McKeganey and Bloor, 1991).

One danger in all this, particularly in the past, was that fieldworkers failed to report or reflect upon the influence of gender in their fieldwork. For instance, in a study of a large local government organization, mentioned in Section 5.3.1, we discussed but did not report the different kinds of situations to which the male and female researchers gained easy access (Silverman and Jones, 1976). Moreover, even as the role of doing fieldwork as a woman has become more addressed, hardly any attention has been paid by researchers to questions of male gender (McKeganey and Bloor, 1991: 198).

Nonetheless, as fashions change, it is possible to swing too far and accord gender issues too much importance. As McKeganey and Bloor (1991: 195–6) argue, there are two important issues relevant to the significance of gender in fieldwork. First, the influence of gender may be negotiable with respondents and not simply ascribed. Second, we should resist 'the tendency to employ gender as an explanatory catch-all' (1991: 196).

For instance, McKeganey and Bloor suggest that variables other than gender, like age and social class, may also be important in fieldwork. Equally, I would argue, following Schegloff (1991), that we need to demonstrate that participants are actually attending to gender in what they are doing, rather than just work with our intuitions or even with statistical correlations (see Section 2.1; and see Frith and Kitzinger, 1998).

None of this should imply that it would be correct to swing full circle and, like an earlier generation, ignore gender issues in research. It is incumbent on fieldworkers to reflect upon the basis and status of their observations. Clearly, how the researcher and the community studied respond to their gender can provide crucial insights into field realities. Indeed, we would do well to become conscious that even taken-for-granted assumptions may be culturally and historically specific. For instance, Carol Warren suggests that:

> The focal gender *myth* of field research is the greater communicative skills and less threatening nature of the female fieldworker. (1988: 64, my emphasis)

As Warren notes, the important thing is to resist treating such assumptions as 'revealed truths' and to treat them as 'accounts' which are historically situated.

### 3.3.3 Defining a research problem

In Section 2.2 I argued that the premature definition of 'variables' was dangerous in field research. Early 'operational' definitions offer precision at the cost of deflecting attention away from the social processes through which the participants themselves assemble stable features of their social world. So, for instance, the qualitative social scientist may be reluctant to begin by defining, say, 'depression' or 'efficiency'. Instead, it may be preferable to examine how, in different contexts, 'depression' and 'efficiency' come to be defined.

The assumption that one should avoid the early specification of definitions and hypotheses has been common to field researchers since the 1930s. As Becker and Geer argued many years ago, for the field researcher:

> a major part of . . . research must consist of finding out what problems he [sic] can best study in this organisation, what hypotheses will be fruitful and worth pursuing, what observations will best serve him as an indicator of the presence of such phenomena as, for example, cohesiveness or deviance. (1960: 267)

However, this does not mean that the early stages of field research are totally unguided. The attempt to describe things 'as they are' is doomed to failure. Without *some* perspective or, at the very least, a set of animating questions, there is nothing to report. Contrary to the view of crude empiricists, the facts *never* speak for themselves.

Assuming that ethnography consists of simply going out into the field and inducing observations is utterly mistaken. Indeed, this assumption can be an excuse for sloppy, unfocused research.

So Mason (1996: 6) rejects the suggestion that qualitative research can just 'describe' or 'explore' the social world. As Miles and Huberman point out, such unfocused research can be a recipe for disaster:

> the looser the initial design, the less selective the collection of data; everything looks important at the outset to someone waiting for the key constructs or regularities to emerge from the site, and that wait can be a long one. (1984: 28)

So the ethnographer must get beyond the initial experience of fieldwork when every issue seems so fascinating, each aspect seems interconnected and each piece of reading that you do only adds further ideas (and suggests further readings).

Narrowing down is often the most crucial task when fieldworkers are tempted to throw the kitchen sink at their data. As Harry Wolcott puts it, the answer is to 'do less, more thoroughly' (1990: 62). This means strictly defining your research problem, using concepts drawn from a particular *model*. It also means limiting the amount of data you gather to what you can readily analyse.

You can decide which data to use by asking yourself which data are most appropriate to your research problem. For instance, are you more interested in what people are thinking or feeling or in what they are doing?

So, to make your analysis effective, it is imperative to have a limited body of data with which to work. While it may be useful initially to explore different kinds of data, this should usually only be done to establish the dataset with which you can most effectively work.

Does this mean that your data and their analysis will be partial? Of course it does! But this is not a problem – unless you make the impossible claim to give 'the whole picture'. So celebrate the partiality of your data and delight in the particular phenomena that they allow you to inspect (hopefully in detail).

### 3.3.4 Looking as well as listening

In his study of the social organization of a restaurant, W.F. Whyte (1949) reaped rich rewards by using his eyes to observe the spatial organization of activities. However, ethnographers have not always been as keen to use their eyes as well as their ears. Notable exceptions are Humphrey's (1970) *Tea Room Trade* (a study of the spatial organization of gay pickup sites) and Lindsay

Prior's (1987) work on hospital architecture. Michel Foucault's (1977) *Discipline and Punish* offers a famous example of the analysis of prison architecture, while Edward Hall's (1969) *The Hidden Dimension* coined the term 'proxemics' to refer to people's use of space – for instance, how we organize an appropriate distance between each other.

However, these are exceptions. For instance, Stimson has noted how 'photographs and diagrams are virtually absent from sociological journals, and rare in sociological books' (1986: 641; but see Prior, 1997).

But, when it comes to treating what you *see* as data, all is not doom and gloom (see Chapter 7). In a study of interaction in hospital wards, Anssi Peräkylä (1989) notes how spatial arrangements differentiate groups of people. There are the wards and patient rooms, which staff may enter anytime they need to. Then there are patient lounges and the like, which are a kind of public space. Both areas are quite different from areas like the nurses' room and doctors' offices where patients enter only by invitation. Finally, if there is a staff coffee room, you never see a patient there.

As Peräkylä points out, one way to produce different categories of human beings in a hospital is the allocation of space according to categories. At the same time, this allocation is reproduced in the activities of the participants. For instance, the perceptive observer might note the demeanour of patients as they approach the nurses' room. Even if the door is open, they may stand outside and just put their heads round the door. In doing so, they mark out that they are encroaching on foreign territory.

In the early 1980s, like Peräkylä, I tried to use my eyes as well as my ears in a study of medical practice already mentioned in Section 3.3.2. First, I obtained access to a number of clinics treating cancer patients in a British National Health Service (NHS) hospital. Following Phil Strong's (1979) account of the 'ceremonial order of the clinic', I was interested in how doctors and patients presented themselves to each other (see Section 3.4.2). For instance, Strong had noted that NHS doctors would adhere to the rule 'politeness is all' and rarely criticize patients to their faces.

While at the hospital, I noticed that one of the doctors regularly seemed to 'go missing' after his morning clinics. My curiosity aroused, I made enquiries. I discovered that most afternoons he was conducting his 'private' practice at consulting rooms in a salubrious area of London's West End.

Nothing ventured, nothing gained, I tried asking this doctor if I could 'sit in' on his private practice. To my great surprise, he consented on condition that I did not tape-record. I happily agreed, even though this meant that my data were reduced to (what I saw as) relatively unreliable fieldnotes (see Section 3.3.5).

Both NHS clinics were held in functional rooms, with unadorned white walls, no carpets, and simple furniture (a small desk, one substantial chair for the doctor and a number of stacking chairs for patients, families and students). As in most NHS hospitals, heating pipes and radiators were very obtrusive.

To enter the consulting rooms of the private clinic is to enter a different world. The main room has the air of an elegant study, perhaps not unlike the kind of room in a private house where a wealthy patient might have been visited by an eighteenth-century doctor. The walls are tastefully painted and adorned with prints and paintings. The floor has a fine carpet. The furniture is reproduction antique and includes a large, leather-topped desk, several comfortable armchairs, a sofa, a low table covered with books and magazines, and a bookcase which holds ivory figures as well as medical texts. Plants are placed on several surfaces and the room is lit by an elegant central light and a table lamp. To add an executive touch, there are three phones on the desk, as well as a pen in a holder.

This room establishes an air of privacy as well as luxury. At the NHS clinics, patients are nearly always examined in curtained-off areas. Here, however, the examination couch is in a separate room which can only be entered through the consulting room. Although more functional than the latter, it is nonetheless carpeted and kept at a high temperature to keep patients warm. Even the doctor himself may knock before entering this examination room while the patient is dressing or undressing.

Such observations were a very important resource in understanding the character of 'private' medicine at this British clinic. Unfortunately, we have all become a little reluctant to use our eyes as well as our ears when doing observational work. However, there are exceptions. Stimson (1986) discusses a room set out for hearings of a disciplinary organization responsible for British doctors. The Professional Conduct Committee of the General Medical Council sits in a high-ceilinged, oak-panelled room reached by an imposing staircase. There are stained-glass windows, picturing 16 crests and a woman in a classical Greek pose. As Stimson comments:

> This is a room in which serious matters are discussed: the room has a presence that is forced on our consciousness . . . speech is formal, carefully spoken and a matter for the public record. Visitors in the gallery speak only, if at all, in hushed whispers, for their speech is not part of the proceedings. (1986: 643–4)

In such a room, as Stimson suggests, without anything needing to be said, we know that what goes on must be taken seriously. Stimson aptly contrasts this room with a McDonald's hamburger restaurant:

> Consider the decorations and materials – plastic, paper, vinyl and polystyrene, and the bright primary colours. [Everything] signifies transience. This temporary character is further articulated in the casual dress of customers, the institutionally casualised dress of staff and the seating that is constructed to make lengthy stays uncomfortable. (1986: 649–50)

Stimson and Peräkylä show that ethnographers who fail to use their eyes as well as their ears are neglecting a crucial source of data. This lesson is most readily learnt if you imagine a sighted person being forced to make sense of the world while blindfolded! The importance of such visual data is discussed at length in Chapter 7.

Attempt Exercise 3.3 about now

### 3.3.5  Recording observations

Even if you are using both eyes and ears, you will still have to decide how to record your data. Let us assume that you are not using electronic recordings (audiotapes or videotapes) or that you wish to supplement such recordings with observational data. (Working with transcripts deriving from recordings is discussed in Chapter 6 of this book).

In this case, you must rely on contemporary fieldnotes. How should you write fieldnotes?

The greatest danger is that you will seek to report 'everything' in your notes. Not only does this overlook the theory-driven nature of field research (see Section 3.4), it gives you an impossible burden when you try to develop a more systematic analysis at a later stage. As Harry Wolcott puts it:

> The critical task in qualitative research is not to accumulate all the data you can, but to 'can' (get rid of) most of the data you accumulate. This requires constant winnowing. (1990: 35)

At the outset, however, it is likely that you will use broad descriptive categories 'relating to particular people or types of people, places, activities and topics of concern' (Hammersley and Atkinson, 1983: 167). Moreover, items may be usefully assigned to more than one category in order to maximize the range of hypotheses that can be generated. To do this, it may help to make multiple copies of each segment of data, filed under several categories (1983: 170).

One useful aid in filing and indexing is provided by computer software programs. ETHNOGRAPH allows you to code a text into as many as seven different categories. QUALPRO allows text to be broken into still more flexible units and codes. NUD·IST will store information in tree-structured index systems with an unlimited number of categories and highly complex index structures. You can then search your data by these indexes or look for overlap between data indexed under different categories. The NUD·IST program thus helps in the generation of new categories and the identification of relationships between existing categories (see Richards and Richards, 1987; Tesch, 1991; Seale in Silverman, 2000: ch. 12).

In order to make this discussion of note-taking more concrete, I want to give an example from a piece of research I carried out in the early 1980s (see Silverman, 1987: chs 1–6). The study was of a paediatric cardiology unit. Many of my data derived from tape-recordings of an outpatient clinic that lasted between two and four hours every Wednesday.

Secure in the knowledge that the basic data were being recorded, I was free to use my eyes as well as my ears to record more data to help in the analysis of the audiotapes. Gradually, with the help of my co-worker Robert Hilliard, I developed a coding sheet to record my observations.

As an illustration of how I coded the data, Table 3.3 shows the full coding sheet used in this study. In order to explain how we derived the categories, I have included explanations of some of the categories in square brackets.

I ought to stress that this coding form was only developed after observation of more than ten outpatient clinics and after extensive discussions between the research team. During this time, we narrowed down what we were looking for.

Increasingly, we became interested in how decisions (or 'disposals') were organized and announced. It seemed likely that the doctor's way of announcing decisions was systematically related not only to clinical factors (like the child's heart condition) but to social factors (such as what parents would be told at various stages of treatment).

For instance, at a first outpatients' consultation, doctors would not normally announce to parents the discovery of a major heart abnormality and the necessity for life-threatening surgery. Instead, they would suggest the need for more tests and only hint that major surgery might be needed. They would also collaborate with parents who produced examples of their child's apparent 'wellness'.

This step-by-step method of information-giving was avoided in only two cases. First, if a child was diagnosed as 'healthy' by the cardiologist, the doctor would give all the information in one go and would engage in what we called a 'search and destroy' operation, based on eliciting any remaining worries of the parent(s) and proving that they were mistaken.

Second, in the case of a group of children with Down's syndrome in addition to suspected cardiac disease, the doctor would present all the clinical information at one sitting, avoiding a step-by-step method. Moreover, atypically, the doctor would allow parents to make the choice about further treatment, while encouraging them to focus on non-clinical matters like their child's 'enjoyment of life' or friendly personality (Silverman, 1981).

The coding form shown in Table 3.3 allowed us to identify these patterns. For instance, by relating item 14 on the scope of the consultation to the decision format (item 20), we were able to see differences between consultations involving Down's syndrome children and others. Moreover, it also turned out that there were significant differences between these two groups both in the form of the elicitation question (item 16) and in the diagnosis statement (item 19).

The coding form in Table 3.3 followed a practice which derives from:

> that well-established style of work whereby the data are inspected for categories and instances. It is an approach that disaggregates the text (notes or transcripts) into a series of fragments, which are then regrouped under a series of thematic headings. (Atkinson, 1992: 455)

Obviously, in making fieldnotes, one is not simply recording data but also analysing them. The categories you use will inevitably be theoretically saturated – whether or not you realize it! So the coding form shown as Table

TABLE 3.3   *Outpatient coding form*

1   Name of patient

2   Age

3   Clinic and date

4   Doctor

5   Family present

6   Non-family present

7   Length of co-presence of doctor and family [we wanted to record the time of the encounter not including periods when the doctor was out of the room]

8   Diagnosis

9   Stage of treatment:
    First consultation
    Pre-inpatient
    Post-catheter [test requiring inpatient stay]
    Post-operation

10   Outcome of consultation:
    Discharge or referral elsewhere
    Non-inpatient follow-up
    Possible eventual catheter or surgery
    Catheter
    Surgery
    No decision

11   Consultation stages [this derived from Robert Hilliard's attempt to identify a series of stages from a greeting exchange to elicitation of symptoms, through to examination and diagnosis statement: see Silverman, 1985, especially 265–9]:
    Stage
    Questions asked
    Topics covered
    Notes/markers

12   Does doctor invite questions?
    No
    Yes    (When:                )

13   Use of medical terminology:
    Stage
    Doctor/family

14   Scope of consultation:

|  | Family | Doctor |
|---|---|---|
| Prior treatment history | | |
| Extra-cardiac physical states | | |
| Child development | | |
| Child behaviour | | |
| Family's practicalities of treatment or attendance | | |
| Doctor's practicalities of treatment or attendance | | |
| Anxieties and emotional problems of family | | |
| Social situation of family | | |
| External treatment agencies | | |

TABLE 3.3 *continued*

15  Family's presentation of a referral history

16  Format of doctor's initial elicitation question [e.g. how is she? is she well?]

17  Patency [this referred to whether symptoms or diseases were visible or 'patent' to the family]:
     Family's presentation of problems/symptoms
     Doctor's mention of patent symptoms
     Family's assent to problems/symptoms
     Not patent?

18  Location of examination:
     desk
     couch
     side room

19  Diagnosis statement:
     (a)  Use of 'well' (Dr/family/both)
     (b)  Use of 'normal' (Dr/family/both)
     (c)  Possible diagnoses mentioned (0/1/>1)

20  Decisions:
     (a)  Possible disposals mentioned (0/1/>1)
     (b)  Medical preference stated (yes/no)
     (c)  Medical intention stated (yes/no)
     (d)  Family assent requested (yes/no)
     (e)  Family allowed to make decision (yes/no)
     (f)  Family wishes volunteered (yes/no)
     (g)  Family dissent from doctor's proposed disposal (yes/no)

21  Uncertainty expressed by doctor:
     (a)  over diagnosis
     (b)  over treatment

3.3 reflected my interest in Goffman's (1974) concept of 'framing'. This meant that I tried to note down the activities through which the participants managed their identities. For instance, I noted how long the doctor and patient spent on social 'small-talk' and how subsequent appointments were arranged.

These concerns show how theoretically defined concepts drive good ethnographic research (see Section 3.4). They also demonstrate how one can develop analysis of field data after a research problem has been carefully defined.

However, as Atkinson points out, one of the disadvantages of coding schemes is that, because they are based upon a given set of categories, they furnish 'a powerful conceptual grid' (1992: 459) from which it is difficult to escape. While this 'grid' is very helpful in organizing the data analysis, it also deflects attention away from uncategorized activities. In these circumstances, it is helpful to return occasionally to the original data.

In our research, we had our tapes and transcripts which offered endless opportunities to redefine our categories. By contrast, lacking tapes of his data on medical education, Atkinson returned to his original fieldnotes. He shows how the same, original data can be reread in a quite different way.

Atkinson's earlier method had been to fragment his fieldnotes into relatively small segments, each with its own category. For instance, a surgeon's description of post-operative complications to a surgical team was originally categorized under such headings as 'unpredictability', 'uncertainty', 'patient career' and 'trajectory'. Later, when Atkinson returned to his data, they were recategorized as an overall narrative which sets up an enigma ('unexpected complications') resolved in the form of a 'moral tale' ('beware, unexpected things can always happen'). Viewed in this way, the surgeon's story becomes a text with many resemblances to a fairytale, as we shall see in Section 5.2.

There is a further 'moral tale' implicit in using Atkinson's story. The field researcher is always torn between the need to narrow down analysis through category construction and to allow some possibility of reinterpretation of the same data. So, while the rush to categorize is laudable, it should always occur in the context of a solid body of original data. The ideal form for this is a tape-recording or original document. Where these cannot be used, the field researcher must attempt to transcribe as much as possible of what is said and done – and the settings in which it is said and done.

In such transcription, Dingwall (personal correspondence) notes how important it is to record *descriptions* rather than mere impressions. In practice, this means that we should always try to note concrete instances of what people have said or done, using verbatim quotations and 'flat' (or unadorned) descriptions.

**Attempt Exercise 3.4 about now**

### 3.3.6  Developing analysis of field data

One of the strengths of observational research is its ability to shift focus as interesting new data become available. For instance, as already noted, during a study of two cancer clinics at a British National Health Service hospital, I unexpectedly gained access to a 'private' (fee-paying) clinic run by one of the doctors in his spare time. I was thus able to change my research focus towards a comparison of the 'ceremonial orders' of public and private medicine (Silverman, 1984).

However, a strength can also be a weakness. Some qualitative research can resemble a disorganized stumble through a mass of data, full of 'insightful' observations of a mainly 'anecdotal' nature. For instance, in a survey of qualitative papers in two journals in the area of health and social science, I was struck by the number of articles based on one or two 'convincing' examples (Silverman, 2000: 283–96).

There is absolutely no reason why observational research cannot combine insight with rigour. In other words, it is right to expect that such research should be *both* original *and* valid. This will involve testing hypotheses that we have generated in the field. Increasingly, however, as our knowledge of micro-social processes expands, it will mean that we can enter the field with a hypothesis we already want to test. So, in my comparative study of medical practice, Strong's (1979) work on the 'ceremonial orders' of doctor–patient interaction gave me a clear hypothesis which became testable when I gained access to a private clinic.

But how then do we test hypotheses using qualitative data? Many years ago, Becker and Geer (1960) gave us some useful guidelines. In a study of the changing perspectives of medical students during their training, they found three ways of testing their emerging hypotheses:

1 Comparison of different groups at one time and of one cohort of students with another over the course of training. For instance, it could only be claimed with confidence that beginning medical students tended to be idealists if several cohorts of first-year students all shared this perspective.
2 Ensuring that the responses given in interviews were also replicated by what students said and did in more 'naturally occurring' situations (e.g. speaking to one another in classrooms and over lunch).
3 A careful inspection of negative or deviant cases leading to the abandonment, revision or even reinforcement of the hypothesis. For instance: 'if it can be shown that the person who acts on a different perspective is socially isolated from the group or that his deviant activities are regarded by others as improper, unnecessary, or foolish, then one can argue that these facts indicate use of the perspective by all but deviants, hence, its collective character' (Becker and Geer, 1960: 289).
4 The use of simple tabulations where appropriate: for instance, counting statements and activities by whether they were generated by the observer or were more naturally occurring.

More than 30 years later, Dingwall (1992) underlines this search for validity via the comparative method and the use of deviant cases. He also adds a further way of establishing validity:

5 The provision of sufficient 'raw' data (e.g. in long transcripts) to allow the reader to separate data and analysis. As Dingwall comments: 'Clearly, it is no more possible to reproduce all the data than it is for a film-maker to show every inch of film . . . What I am taking exception to, though, is the kind of report that is purely a redescription of the researcher's impressions or sensations. Empathy has its place in ethnography but it should enter after recording rather than being confused with it' (Dingwall, 1992: 169).

The major reason why ethnography should never simply aim to record the researcher's 'impressions' is the theoretically impregnated nature of 'description'. This has been implicit throughout this chapter so it can now be given a relatively short, explicit treatment.

## 3.4  THE THEORETICAL CHARACTER OF ETHNOGRAPHY

One way to assemble data is to begin with a set of very general questions. A good example of such questions is provided by Wolcott:

> What is going on here? What do people in this setting have to know (individually and collectively) in order to do what they are doing? How are skills and attitudes transmitted and acquired, particularly in the absence of intentional efforts at instruction? (1990: 32)

Already here, we can see that Wolcott's questions are guided by a particular theoretical focus on people's knowledge and skills. This emerges out of a set of assumptions common to many field researchers. These assumptions may be crudely set out as follows:

1  *Common sense* is held to be complex and sophisticated rather than naive and misguided.
2  *Social practices* rather than perceptions are the site where common sense operates: the focus is on what people are doing rather than upon what they are thinking, e.g. talking to one another, having meetings, writing documents etc.
3  *Phenomena* are viewed within inverted commas. This means that we seek to understand how any 'phenomenon' is locally produced through the activities of particular people in particular settings.

Of course, any such list glosses over the range of theoretical directions to be found in field research (see Sections 3.4.2 and 3.4.3). Nonetheless, it demonstrates the general point that no research can ever be 'theory-free'.

We only come to look at things in certain ways because we have adopted, either tacitly or explicitly, certain ways of seeing. This means that, in observational research, data collection, hypothesis construction and theory building are not three separate things but are interwoven with one another.

### 3.4.1  Funnels and grounded theory

This process of interweaving different aspects of research is well described by using an analogy with a funnel:

> Ethnographic research has a characteristic 'funnel' structure, being progressively focused over its course. Progressive focusing has two analytically distinct components. First, over time the research problem is developed or transformed, and eventually its scope is clarified and delimited and its internal structure explored. In this sense, it is frequently only over the course of the research that one discovers what the research is really 'about', and it is not uncommon for it to turn out to be about something quite remote from the initially foreshadowed problems. (Hammersley and Atkinson, 1983: 175).

For instance, my research on the two cancer clinics unexpectedly led into a comparison of fee-for-service and state-provided medicine (Silverman, 1984). Similarly, my observation of a paediatric cardiology unit moved unpredictably in the direction of an analysis of disposal decisions with a small group of Down's syndrome children (Silverman, 1981).

We may note three features which these two cases had in common:

1 The switch of focus – through the 'funnel' – as a more defined topic arose.
2 The use of the comparative method as an invaluable tool of theory building and testing.
3 The generation of topics with a scope outside the substantive area of the research. Thus the 'ceremonial orders' found in the cancer clinics are not confined to medicine, while the 'democratic' decision-making found with the Down's children had unexpected effects of power with a significance far beyond medical encounters.

Working this way parallels Glaser and Strauss's (1967) famous account of *grounded theory*. A simplified model of this involves these stages:

- an initial attempt to develop categories which illuminate the data
- an attempt to 'saturate' these categories with many appropriate cases in order to demonstrate their relevance
- developing these categories into more general analytic frameworks with relevance outside the setting.

As we have seen, Glaser and Strauss use their research on death and dying as an example. They show how they developed the category of 'awareness contexts' to refer to the kinds of situations in which people were informed of their likely fate. They call this a grounded *substantive* theory. The category was then saturated and was finally related to non-medical settings where people learn about how others define them (e.g. schools). This is now called a grounded *formal* theory.

Grounded theory has been criticized for its failure to acknowledge implicit theories which guide work at an early stage. It also is more clear about the generation of theories than about their test. Used unintelligently, it can also degenerate into a fairly empty building of categories (aided by the computer software programs already discussed) or into a mere smokescreen used to legitimize purely empiricist research (see Bryman, 1988: 83–7; Silverman, 2000: 285, 287–8).

At best, grounded theory offers an approximation of the creative activity of theory building found in good observational work, compared to the dire abstracted empiricism present in the most wooden statistical studies.

**Attempt Exercise 3.5 about now**

One way to save grounded theory from being a trite and mistaken technique is to treat it as a way of building theories from a particular *model* of social reality. As Kathy Charmaz (2000) has pointed out, a (social) *constructionist* will use grounded theory in a very different way to ethnographers who believe that their categories simply reproduce nature.

In Section 2.6, we noted Gubrium and Holstein's (1997) discussion of such competing models: naturalism, emotionalism, ethnomethodology and post-modernism. For reasons of space, I will just give a short account of how two of these models (naturalism and ethnomethodology) shape the perspective of the ethnographer.

### 3.4.2 The naturalist model

> [Any] researcher, no matter how unstructured or inductive, comes to fieldwork with some orienting ideas, foci and tools. (Miles and Huberman, 1984: 27)

As Gubrium and Holstein note, the apparently atheoretical position of some ethnographers itself derives from a theory:

> The directive to 'minimize presuppositions' in order to witness subjects' worlds on their own terms is a key to *naturalistic* inquiry. (1997: 34, my emphasis)

So the idea of just 'hanging out' with the aim of faithfully representing subjects' worlds is a convenient myth derived from a theory that Gubrium and Holstein term *naturalism*. Of course, without some conceptual orientation, one would not recognize the 'field' one was studying. So the problem is that many closet naturalists fail to come clean about the theory dependence of their research.

I only have space for one example of the problems of naturalism (see Silverman, 2000: 286–96 for more discussion of this and other examples). Engebretson (1996) reports a participant observation and interview study of three groups of healers who 'heal' through the laying on of hands. She locates her findings in terms of three 'dimensions' (setting, interaction and cognitive process) and finds, unsurprisingly, that such healing differed from biomedicine on each of these dimensions.

Unfortunately, Engebretson mentions no explicit model or theory. So, although her descriptions of how healing was organized and how the sessions were opened and closed has at least the potential to suggest practical relevance, it lacks the coherence that a theoretically defined study might offer.

Such a theory would, for instance, inform how data are recorded. Yet Engebretson makes no mention of the system used for recording fieldnotes and its impact on the reliability of her data (see Sections 3.3.3 and 8.2).

Second, her account of her data is presented just as a simple description. Without a discussion of the analytic basis for the researcher's account, her report once more can only have a journalistic status. As I point out in Chapter 10, this is not to criticize journalism which, at its best, can be highly illuminating. It is simply intended to distinguish between journalism and social science.

Third, although Engebretson groups her interview respondents' accounts into a number of categories (physical sensations, emotional experiences and visual images), there is nothing to suggest that these are anything but *ad hoc* labels without a clear analytical basis.

It is unfair to single out just one study when even respected academic journals are overflowing with research reports that refuse to recognize the theoretically guided character of ethnographic description.

But this is not to say that naturalism (even when unacknowledged) has not been the source of insights. Even one of naturalism's fiercest critics, Harvey Sacks, nonetheless found much to admire in the naturalistically informed Chicago School's attention to detail. As Sacks put it:

> Instead of pushing aside the older ethnographic work in sociology, I would treat it as the only work worth criticizing in sociology; where criticizing is giving some dignity to something. So, for example, the relevance of the works of the Chicago sociologists is that they do contain a lot of information about this and that. And this-and-that is what the world is made up of. (1992, I: 27)

Sacks was convinced that serious work paid attention to detail and that, if something mattered, it should be observable. For instance, in a fascinating passage, Sacks noted the baleful influence on sociology of G.H. Mead's (1934) proposal that we need to study things which are not available to observation, e.g. 'society', 'attitudes'. As Sacks comments:

> But social activities are observable, you can see them all around you, and you can write them down. The tape recorder is important, but a lot of this can be done without a tape recorder. If you think you can see it, that means we can build an observational study. (1992, I: 28)

However, the ethnographer's praiseworthy attention to detail rarely satisfied Sacks's rigorous methodological demands. For Sacks, the ethnographer needs to go beyond naturalism in order to analyse the most basic details of interaction. (S)he cannot rely on glosses of 'what everyone knows'. What this might entail will be illustrated in the following discussion of ethno-methodology.

### 3.4.3 *The ethnomethodological model*

Just because something seems 'pretty routine', we cannot assume that it is not difficult to explain. As Harvey Sacks pointed out in one of his lectures:

> the activities that molecules are able to engage in quickly, routinely, have not been described by enormously brilliant scientists. (1992, I: 115)

To understand humans' routine activities, Sacks followed his teacher Harold Garfinkel (1967) in attempting to make common sense into a 'topic', not just a tacit 'resource'. It follows that how societal members (including social researchers) 'see' particular activities is, for Sacks, the central research question.

In this respect, together with Garfinkel (1967), he offers a unique perspective in social science. This perspective is *ethnomethodology* (or the study of folk – or members' – methods) which 'seeks to describe methods persons use in doing social life' (Sacks, 1984: 21).

For Garfinkel and Sacks, when ethnographers 'describe' and 'question', the problem is that they are tacitly using members' methods. If we are to study such methods, it is, therefore, crucial that we don't take for granted what it is we appear to be 'seeing'. As Sacks says:

> In setting up what it is that seems to have happened, preparatory to solving the [research] problem, do not let your notion of what could conceivably happen decide for you what must have happened. (1992, I: 115)

Here Sacks is telling us that our 'notion of what could conceivably happen' is likely to be drawn from our unexamined members' knowledge. Instead, we need to proceed more cautiously by examining the methods members use to produce activities as observable and reportable.

Sacks suggests that people should be seen not as 'coming to terms with some phenomenon' (1992, I: 437) but as actively *constituting* it. Take the phenomenon of 'speeding'. How does one know one is speeding? One solution is to look at your car's speedometer. However, another well-used method is to compare your movement relative to other traffic. And 'traffic' is a phenomenon that is actively organized by road users. As Sacks suggests:

> persons can be seen to clump their cars into something that is 'a traffic', pretty much wherever, whenever, whoever it is that's driving. That exists as a social fact, a thing which drivers do . . . [so] by 'a traffic' I don't mean that there are some cars, but there is a set of cars that can be used as 'the traffic', however it's going; those cars that are clumped. And it is in terms of 'the traffic' that you see you're driving fast or slow. (1992, I: 437)

Sacks here is suggesting that, rather than being a natural fact, 'the traffic' is a self-organizing system, in which people adjust their speed by reference to 'the traffic'. The traffic thus serves as a metaphor for how social order is constructed by reference to what can be inferred. It also shows how the ability 'to read other people's minds' (in this case, the minds of other drivers) is not a psychotic delusion but a condition for social order.

For Sacks, then, 'traffic' and 'speed' are not natural facts but locally assembled phenomena (see also Pollner, 1987). As he notes, the selfsame features can be seen in medical interviews, where what is 'normal' is attended to by doctors on the basis of their elicitation of what is normal for you (1992, I: 57–8). Moreover, while illnesses may be 'erasable', this doesn't usually apply to speeding fines or suicide attempts – and the latter is seen in people's reluctance to identify themselves when calling an emergency psychiatric service (1992, I: 61).

Put at its simplest, researchers must be very careful how they use categories. For instance, Sacks quotes from two linguists who appear to have no problem in characterizing particular (invented) utterances as 'simple', 'complex', 'casual' or 'ceremonial'. For Sacks, such rapid characterizations of data assume:

> that we can know that without an analysis of what it is [they] are doing. (1992, I: 429)

I have only space for one example of the kind of work that follows from Sacks's recommendations. Writing 20 years after Sacks, Maynard (1989) notes how ethnographers are still trying to picture how people see things rather than focus on what is observable. As he puts it:

> In doing ethnography, researchers attempt to draw a picture of what some phenomenon 'looks like' from an insider's account of the phenomenon and for some audience who wants to know about it. The ethnographer, in general, is in the business of describing culture from the members' point of view. (1989: 130)

Maynard notes how such concerns have shaped research in one part of the sociology of law. 'Plea bargaining' has been identified as a process by which defendants plead guilty to a 'lesser' offence, thereby minimizing their punishment and speeding up the work of the courts (evidence does not need to be heard if the defendant pleads guilty). Ethnographers have assumed that this process works on the basis of shared perceptions held by prosecution and defence lawyers.

However, Maynard suggests that such ethnographic work, based on the identification of people's perceptions, has at least three deficiencies:

1 It depends upon common-sense knowledge: 'ethnographers rely on unnoticed abilities to record and recognize such features, just as participants rely on basically uninvestigated abilities in producing them' (1989: 130).
2 It glosses over what 'plea bargaining' actually is – the diversity of discourse that gets called 'plea bargaining'.
3 It fails to treat the common orientation of the parties concerned as an outcome of their interaction, preferring to make such 'mutuality appear to be a matter of cognitive consensus' (1989: 134).

Instead, following Sacks's emphasis on what is observable, Maynard studies 'how a sense of mutuality is accomplished' (1989: 134). This involves examining how plea bargaining sequences are introduced into the talk. For instance, a bargaining proposal can be solicited or it can be announced, as shown in Table 3.4.

TABLE 3.4  *Two forms of plea bargaining*

| PD = public defender, DA = district attorney | | |
|---|---|---|
| *Solicitation* | | |
| (solicit) | PD: | Is there an offer in this case? |
| (proposal) | DA: | I would say in this case a fine, seventy five dollars. |
| | | |
| *Announcement* | | |
| (announcement) | PD: | I'll propose a deal to you. |
| ('go-ahead' signal) | DA: | Tell me what ya got. |
| (proposal) | PD: | If ya dismiss the 242, I might be able to arrange a plea to 460 for a fine. |

*Source*: Maynard, 1989: 134

Maynard's study draws attention to how the phenomenon of 'plea bargaining' is itself locally constituted in the activities of the participants. As I argue later (see Section 10.5), there is a danger that, if ethnography reduces social life to the definitions of the participants, it becomes a purely 'subjectivist' social science which loses sight of *social* phenomena.

Instead, the point is to narrow the focus to what people are *doing*. As Maynard puts it:

> The question that ethnographers have traditionally asked – 'How do participants see things?' – has meant in practice the presumption that reality lies outside the words spoken in a particular time and place. The . . . (alternative) question – 'How do participants do things?' – suggests that the microsocial order can be appreciated more fully by studying how speech and other face-to-face behaviours constitute reality within actual mundane situations. (1989: 144)

**Attempt Exercise 3.6 about now**

## 3.5  CONCLUSION: THE UNITY OF THE ETHNOGRAPHIC PROJECT

I want to conclude this chapter by trying to locate points of contact between ethnomethodology and other forms of ethnography. Consonant with the argument deployed throughout this book, researchers have more to learn by exploring the interstices between analytic positions than by dwelling on one side of fine-sounding polarities.

Moreover, it would be entirely mistaken to believe that all the certainties in observational work derive from ethnomethodological insights. In fact, as I have argued already, a number of ethnographers have either taken on board many of these insights or reached them independently. For instance, a recognition that social phenomena are locally constituted (through the activities of participants) is not confined to Sacks and Maynard. Using the example of studies of the 'family', I want to show another direction from which one can draw the same conclusion.

In a paper on methodological issues in family studies, Gubrium and Holstein (1987) show how much sociological work assumes that 'family life' is properly depicted in its 'natural' habitat – the home. Conversely, they argue that the 'family' is not a uniform phenomenon, to be found in one setting, but is 'occasioned' and 'contexted'. We can see more clearly what they are saying in Table 3.5, which contrasts the 'conventional understanding' with Gubrium and Holstein's alternative.

TABLE 3.5 *Two ways of describing 'family life'*

*The conventional understanding*

1. Families have 'inner' and 'outer' sides.
2. The 'inner' side is located in the household.
3. Outside households we obtain only a 'version' of this 'prime reality'.
4. Members of the household have a privileged access to family order.
5. Participant observation is required to obtain 'authentic understanding' of family life.

*An alternative*

1. 'Family' is a way of interpreting, representing and ordering social relations.
2. The family is not private but inextricably linked with public life.
3. The household does not locate family life.
4. The household is not 'trivial' because it is often appealed to by laypeople and professionals alike as the determinant of family life.

*Source*: adapted from Gubrium and Holstein, 1987

Gubrium and Holstein's alternative direction for family studies closely fits Sacks' approach, while opening up a number of fascinating areas for family studies, as follows:

1. Once we conceive of the 'family' in terms of a researchable set of descriptive practices, we are freed from the methodological and ethical nightmare of obtaining access to study families 'as they really are', i.e. in their own households.
2. We can now study how the structures of family organization are depicted in different milieux (e.g. employment agencies, schools, clinics etc.).
3. This links to studies of the social distribution of 'knowledge' about the family (e.g. when, where and by whom theories of the nature and consequences of 'broken homes' are employed).
4. It also ties in with the study of how different organizational routines constrain particular depictions of family order.

As already noted, issues of household location and privileged access now become redefined as topics rather than troubles: for example, we might study the claims that professionals make for such access. This underlines Gubrium and Holstein's point that family knowledge is never purely private. Family members themselves appeal to collective representations (like maxims and the depictions of families in soap-operas) to explain their own behaviour. Family members also present the 'reality' of family life in different ways to different audiences and in different ways to the same audience (see Gubrium and Holstein, 1990, for a fuller elaboration of this argument).

### Attempt Exercise 3.7 about now

Gubrium and Holstein offer an exciting prospectus for family studies and an appropriate way to conclude this chapter on observation. For this kind of work (elsewhere termed 'articulative ethnography' by Gubrium, 1988), together with ethnomethodology, offers three crucial insights for observational studies, as follows:

1  It switches attention away from a more psychological orientation around what people are thinking towards what they are doing.
2  It shows the analytic issues that lie behind methodological puzzles.
3  It firmly distinguishes social science observational work from journalism and common sense – thus, in a certain sense, fulfilling Durkheim's project.

As Michael Moerman once commented:

> Folk beliefs have honourable status but they are not the same intellectual object as a scientific analysis. (1974: 55)

## KEY POINTS

There are four crucial aspects of observational research:

* the 'focus' of the study
* ethical issues
* methodological choices
* theoretical choices.

Naturalism and ethnomethodology provide very different ways of defining observational research. Each offers a 'toolbox' providing a set of concepts and methods to select appropriate data and to illuminate data analysis.

### Recommended Reading

Introductions to observational and ethnographic work are given by Tedlock (2000) and Angosino and Mays de Perez (2000).

Gubrium and Holstein (1997) offer an important account of four current models used in observational research. Harvey Sacks's lectures offer marvellous insights on the current relevance of the Chicago School (Sacks, 1992, I: 26–31). Kathy Charmaz (2000) provides a good discussion of grounded theory, and Atkinson and Hammersley (1994: 254–7) offer a balanced treatment of postmodernism (not discussed here).

Silverman (2000: 61–74, 138–53) discusses methodological issues in observation such as narrowing down your research problem and developing data analysis.

## Exercise 3.1

An instructor begins an introductory sociology course with the following statement:

> The problem with everyday talk is that it is so imprecise. For instance, sometimes we say: 'too many cooks spoil the broth'. On other occasions, we say: 'many hands make light work'. On this course, based on scientific research, I will demonstrate which of these proverbs is more accurate.

The instructor now reports on laboratory data from an experiment where students have been assigned tasks and then work either in teams or on their own. This experiment seems to show that, all things being equal, team-work is more efficient. Therefore, the instructor claims, we can have more confidence in the validity of the proverb 'many hands make light work'.

Using Agar's criticisms (1986) of the 'received view' of science given at the beginning of this chapter, answer the following questions:

1 Are you convinced by the instructor's claim (e.g. what assumptions does the experiment make? Can proverbs be equally appropriate in different contexts?)?
2 Outline how you might do *observational* work on people's use of such proverbs (e.g. what settings would you look at? What sort of things would you be looking for?).
3 Examine *either* newspaper advertisements *or* advertisements on radio or television. Make a note when proverbs are used. What *functions* do these proverbs seem to have? Do they make the advertisement more convincing? Why?

## Exercise 3.2

When you are next in a restaurant, make observations about how the staff interact with customers. Using Whyte's (1949) findings as a guide, examine:

1 Who originates action?
2 For whom?
3 How often?
4 With what consequences?

If you had an audio or video recording of what you heard and saw, how might that have improved the quality of your analysis?

---

**Exercise 3.3**

This is a research exercise to improve your observational skills in the public realm. These are your instructions:

1  Select a setting in which you regularly participate: good examples would be a student cafeteria, a bus or train, or a supermarket checkout queue.

2  Make a sketch map of the site. What sort of activities does the physical layout encourage, discourage or seem neutral towards? (Refer to Section 3.3.4 for Stimson's comparison of the room for medical hearings and McDonald's.)

3  How do people use the space you are studying? What do they show they are attending to? How do they communicate with one another or avoid communication? Do they look at one another or avoid it? What distance do they keep between one another?

4  In what ways are people using the space to co-operate with one another to *define* themselves (e.g. as a restaurant crowd but not bus passengers)?

5  Is there any difference between how people organize their activities when they are on their own, in pairs or in a crowd?

6  How do people use the setting as a resource for engaging in activities not specifically intended (but not necessarily inappropriate) in that setting (e.g. displaying particular personal characteristics such as wanting to communicate or not wanting to communicate)?

---

## Exercise 3.4

Return to your fieldnotes in Exercises 3.2 and 3.3 and answer the following questions:

1 How were your notes organized (did you just write down verbatim what you saw or heard or did you use some organizing principle, e.g. 'frames')?
2 If there was an organizing principle, which one was it? Why did you choose it? And how did it help or hinder you?
3 If there was no organizing principle, how did you move from the description of what you observed to its analysis?
4 In what ways were your notes dependent on your common-sense knowledge of what was going on?
5 How can that dependence be treated as a problem but also as a help (see Section 3.4.3)?

## Exercise 3.5

Once again, return to your observations in Exercises 3.2 and 3.3. Following Glaser and Strauss's idea of 'grounded theory', answer these questions:

1 How far were your conclusions fully grounded in your data, e.g. were your categories sufficiently 'saturated' with data?
2 What was your 'substantive' theory about your setting?
3 Can you develop a 'formal' theory applying to other settings?
4 Which other settings would you like to observe in order to test this 'formal' theory?

## Exercise 3.6

Once more, return to your observations in Exercises 3.2 and 3.3.

1 In what ways, if at all, were your observations dependent upon a naturalist model of reality?
2 In what ways, if at all, were your observations dependent upon an ethnomethodological model?
3 Were there other models you used or might have used (refer to Gubrium and Holstein's four models discussed in Section 2.6)?
4 What were the advantages/disadvantages of the way you had defined social reality?

**Exercise 3.7**

This exercise encourages you to use the 'alternative' version of describing family life proposed by Gubrium and Holstein.

Imagine that you wish to do an observational study of the family. Now consider the following questions:

1 What are the advantages and disadvantages of obtaining access to the family household?
2 In what ways may families be studied outside the household setting? What methodology might you use and what questions could you ask?
3 What might observation tell you about the 'family' in each of the following settings:

- law courts
- doctor–patient consultations
- television soap-operas?

*Either* do a study of *one* of these settings *or* write hypothetically about all three.
4 What does it mean to say you are studying the 'family' (i.e. within inverted commas)?

# 4
# Interviews

As I argued in Chapter 1, research topics never arise 'out of the blue'. Whether or not we are aware of it, any research topic will derive from particular *models* of looking at the world and/or from certain 'social problems' currently to the fore in society.

However, let us imagine that you have 'innocently' decided to gather some interview data as part of a research methods course. Making use of the accessibility and good nature of your fellow students, you decide to embark on a study of, say, students' perceptions of their future job prospects.

Because you have read a bit about research design, you decide to 'pre-test' some preliminary questions on a friend to find whether they are easily understood (in the way that you intend). Having sorted out your questions, you find half a dozen students and interview them. Now, you think, all you have to do is to summarize their answers and you will have a legitimate research report on your chosen topic.

Well, maybe. Perhaps, along the way, you failed to ask *yourself* a number of questions. These include:

- Why (and in what way) is your chosen research topic significant?
- How far do your topic and findings relate to other research?
- Why is an interview method appropriate for your topic: why not simply look at existing records of graduates' first jobs?
- Is the size and method of recruitment of your sample appropriate to both your topic and your model?
- Did you audio or video record your interviews? How did you transcribe them (if at all)?
- Did you need to interview your respondents face-to-face? Why not use e-mail?
- Did you think about using a *focus group*, where respondents are offered some topic or stimulus material and then encouraged to discuss it amongst themselves?
- What status will you accord to your data? For instance, are you seeking objective 'facts', subjective 'perceptions' or simply 'narratives'?
- How thoroughly have you analysed your data? For instance, have you just reported a few 'telling' extracts? Or have you worked through all your material, searching out examples which don't fit your original suppositions (*deviant-case analysis*)?

Without answers to these questions, your professor may disappoint you with a surprisingly poor grade for your interview project.

I will shortly set out different ways in which social scientists have addressed some of the questions above, paying particular attention to the varying status of interview data in different models of the research process. For discussion of e-mail interviews, see Mann and Stewart (2000); for focus groups, see Bloor et al. (2001).

For the moment, however, I want to illustrate the import of these issues with one helpful case study.

## 4.1   WHEN IS A 'TRIBE' (MOERMAN)?

As an anthropologist, Michael Moerman was interested in learning how a people categorized their world. Like most anthropologists and Chicago School ethnographers (see Chapter 3), he interviewed native informants. His aim was to elicit from them what 'being a Lue' (the name of the tribe) meant to them. So Moerman started to ask tribespeople questions like, 'How do you recognize a member of your tribe?'

He reports that his respondents quickly became adept at providing a whole list of traits which he called 'ethnic identification devices'. These included beliefs and actions which they regarded as unique to the Lue people (e.g. their approach to trading with their neighbours). The final list of such traits seemed to describe the tribe and to distinguish it from its neighbours.

However, Moerman was troubled about what sense to read into the Lue's own accounts. His questions often related to issues which were either obvious or irrelevant to the respondents. As he puts it:

> To the extent that answering an ethnographer's question is an unusual situation for natives, one cannot reason from a native's answer to his *normal* categories or ascriptions. (Moerman, 1974: 66, my emphasis)

So Moerman started to see that ethnic identifications were not used all the time by these people, any more than we use them to refer to ourselves in a Western culture. This meant that, if you wanted to understand this people, it was not particularly useful to elicit from them what would necessarily be an abstract account of their tribe's characteristics given at the behest of an outsider. So, instead, Moerman started to examine what went on in everyday situations through observation.

However, it was not so straightforward to switch to observational methods. Even when ethnographers are silent and merely observe, their presence indicates to people that matters relevant to 'identity' should be highlighted. Consequently, people may pay particular attention to what both the observer and they themselves take to be relevant categorization schemes – like ethnic or kinship labels. In this way, the ethnographer may have 'altered the local priorities among the native category sets which it is his task to describe' (1974: 67).

What, then, was to be done? A clue is given by the initially opaque subheadings of Moerman's article:

- Who are the Lue?
- Why are the Lue?
- When are the Lue?

Moerman argues that there are three reasons why we should *not* ask: 'Who are the Lue?' First, it would generate an inventory of traits. Like all such inventories it could be endless because we could always be accused of having left something out. Second, lists are retrospective. Once we have decided that the Lue *are* a tribe, then we have no difficulty in 'discovering' a list of traits to support our case. Third, the identification of the Lue as a tribe depends, in part, on their successful presentation of themselves as a tribe. As Moerman puts it:

> The question is not 'Who are the Lue?' but rather when, how and why the identification 'Lue' is preferred. (1974: 62)

Moerman adds that this does *not* mean that the Lue are not really a tribe or that they fooled him into thinking they were one. Rather their ethnic identity arises in the fact that people in the area use ethnic identification labels some of the time when they are talking about each other.

Of course, some of the time is not all the time. Hence the task of the ethnographer should be to observe when and *if* ethnic identification labels are used by the participants being studied. Moerman neatly summarizes his argument as follows:

> Anthropology [has an] apparent inability to distinguish between warm . . . human bodies and one kind of identification device which some of those bodies sometimes use. Ethnic identification devices – with their important potential of making each ethnic set of living persons a joint enterprise with countless generations of unexamined history – seem to be universal. Social scientists should therefore describe and analyse the ways in which they are used, and not merely – as natives do – use them as explanations. (1974: 67–8)

So Moerman had changed his research question away from 'Who are the Lue?' and, therefore, abandoned his research design based on interviews. From now on, the issue was no longer who the Lue essentially were but when, among people living in these Thai villages, ethnic identification labels were invoked and what were the consequences of invoking them.

Curiously enough, Moerman concluded that, when you looked at the matter this way, the apparent differences between the Lue and ourselves were considerably reduced. For instance, turn-taking in conversation works in much the same way among Lue and English speakers. Only an ethnocentric Westerner might have assumed otherwise, behaving like a tourist craving for out-of-the-way sights.

Moerman's study reveals that any attempt to describe things 'as they are' is doomed to failure. Without *some* perspective or, at the very least, a set of animating questions, there is nothing to report. Contrary to the view of crude empiricists, who would deny the relevance of theory to research, the facts *never* speak for themselves.

## 4.2 IMPLICATIONS: THREE VERSIONS OF INTERVIEW DATA

Moerman's research points to the way in which idealized conceptions of phenomena like 'tribes' can, on closer examination, become like a will-o'-the-wisp, dissolving into sets of practices embedded in particular settings. The methodological import of this for interview data has been made clear by Carolyn Baker. As she writes:

> When we talk about the world we live in, we engage in the activity of giving it a particular character. Inevitably, we assign features and phenomena to it and make it out to work in a particular way. When we talk with someone else about the world, we take into account who the other is, what that other person could be presumed to know, 'where' that other is in relation to ourself in the world we talk about. (Baker, 1982: 109)

Here Baker is questioning the attempt to treat interview questions and answers as passive filters towards some truths about people's identities (for instance, as members of a tribe). Instead, she is telling us, interviewer and interviewee actively *construct* some version of the world appropriate to what we take to be self-evident about the person to whom we are speaking and the context of the question.

Baker is raising a number of issues about the status of interview data, including:

1  What is the relation between interviewees' accounts and the world they describe? Are such accounts potentially 'true' or 'false' or is neither concept always appropriate to them?
2  How is the relation between interviewer and interviewee to be understood? Is it governed by standardized techniques of 'good interviewing practice'? Or is it, inevitably, based on conversational practices we all use in everyday life?

These issues are central to this chapter. Shortly, I will return to how Baker addresses them in her own interview study of adolescents. First, however, I want to set out three different ways in which most social scientists would answer Baker's questions.

According to **positivism**, interview data give us access to 'facts' about the world. The primary issue is to generate data which are valid and reliable, independently of the research setting. The main ways to achieve this are the random selection of the interview sample and the administration of standardized questions with multiple-choice answers which can be readily tabulated.

According to **emotionalism**, interviewees are viewed as experiencing subjects who actively construct their social worlds. The primary issue is to generate data which give an authentic insight into people's experiences. The main ways to achieve this are unstructured, open-ended interviews usually based upon prior, in-depth participant observation.

According to **constructionism**, interviewers and interviewees are always actively engaged in constructing meaning. Rather than treat this as standing in the way of accurate depictions of 'facts' or 'experiences', how meaning is mutually constructed becomes the researcher's topic. Because of this, research interviews are not treated as specially privileged, and other interviews (e.g. media or professional–client interviews) are treated as of equal interest, i.e. interviews are treated as topics rather than as a research resource. A particular focus is on how interviewees construct narratives of events and people (see Section 5.2) and the turn-by-turn construction of meaning (see the discussion of conversation analysis in Section 6.3).

These three positions are set out in Table 4.1. Let me now describe these three different approaches in greater detail, looking at the type of knowledge each pursues and the different research tasks they set themselves.

TABLE 4.1   *Three versions of interview data*

|  | Status of data | Methodology |
| --- | --- | --- |
| Positivism | Facts about behaviour and attitudes | Random samples Standard questions Tabulations |
| Emotionalism | Authentic experiences | Unstructured, open-ended interviews |
| Constructionism | Mutually constructed | Any interview treated as a topic |

## 4.3   POSITIVISM

In survey research, which is geared to a statistical logic, interview data give access to 'facts' about the world. Although these facts include both biographical information and statements about beliefs, all are to be treated as accounts whose sense derives from their correspondence to a factual reality. Where that reality is imperfectly represented by an account, checks and remedies are to be encouraged in order to get a truer or more complete picture of how things stand.

### 4.3.1   Type of knowledge

Here are the six kinds of topics to which, according to a standard text on survey research (Selltiz et al., 1964), interview questions are addressed. Notice how these writers envisage problems and recommend remedies in relation to each topic.

1 *Facts* These relate primarily to biographical information about the respondent, to statements from informed sources about the structures, policies and actions of organizations, and to descriptions of an event or a community. In this last case, it is possible to weed out 'inaccurate' descriptions by comparing different people's statements: 'If respondents occupying widely different positions in the community agree on a statement, there is much better ground for accepting it as true than if only one of these respondents makes the statement. On the other hand, contradictions between the reports of apparently reliable informants provide important leads for further investigation' (1964: 245).

2 *Beliefs about facts* In questions about beliefs or attitudes, no interpersonal cross-checking of statements is appropriate. However, Selltiz et al. (1964: 246) point out that it is always important to check first whether the respondent has any beliefs about the topic in question, otherwise the researcher may put words into his mouth.

3 *Feelings and motives* Here, 'because emotional responses are frequently too complex to report in a single phrase' (1964: 248), Selltiz et al. recommend the use of open-ended questions, allowing the respondents to choose their own terms

4 *Standards of action* These relate to what people think should or could be done about certain stated situations. Here it helps to link such standards to people's experiences. Where someone has actually faced a situation of the type described, his/her response is likely to be more reliable.

5 *Present or past behaviour* Again, specific questions related to actual rather than hypothetical situations are recommended.

6 *Conscious reasons* (for 1 to 5) Rather than simply ask 'Why?', Selltiz et al. (1964: 253) recommend that the researcher should examine broad classes of considerations that may have determined this outcome (e.g. 'the history of the actor's feeling', or 'the characteristics in a given entity that provoke a given reaction').

For each of these six topics, the task of the interviewer is to elicit a body of facts 'out there' in the world. For positivists, an observation that interview responses might be an outcome of the interview setting would be heard as a charge against the reliability of the technique. To the extent that this possibility arises, checks and remedies are built into the research design. Similarly, for positivists, the language of the interviewee serves primarily as an instrument for the communication of social or psychological facts.

### 4.3.2  Research task

The aim of interviews for positivists is to generate data which hold independently of both the research setting and the researcher or interviewer.

One way of achieving this is by attempting standardized interviews. Consequently, Selltiz et al. are rather suspicious of unstructured interviews which they see as inherently unreliable research instruments. Although they concede that unstructured or open-ended interviews are more flexible than prescheduled interviews and can allow more intensive study of perceptions and feelings, they have inherent problems for positivists:

> The flexibility frequently results in a lack of comparability of one interview with another. Moreover, their analysis is more difficult and time-consuming than that of standardized interviews. (1964: 264)

Even more important for *reliability* than the type of interview selected, is the need to follow a standardized protocol. So Selltiz et al. offer an appendix entitled 'The Art of Interviewing' which provides a set of rules and taboos. Interviewers should ask each question precisely as it is worded and in the same order that it appears on the schedule. They should not show surprise or disapproval of an answer, offer impromptu explanations of questions, suggest possible replies, or skip certain questions. Similarly, Brenner offers a list of dos and don'ts ('basic rules of research interviewing', 1981: 129–30) which are defended in terms of the necessity of standardization:

> In order to ensure adequacy of measurement in a data collection programme it is of primary importance to secure, as much as is possible, the equivalence of the stimulus conditions in the interviews. If these are not equivalent, measurement may be biased, and it may be unwarranted to group responses together for the purposes of statistical analyses. (1981: 115)

Although Brenner (1981: 156) is more sceptical than Selltiz et al. about the prospects of obtaining 'literal measurement' in the interview situation, the statement quoted indicates that he shares with them the same statistical and behaviouralist (or stimulus–response) logic. Following that logic, he calls for more research on social interaction in interviews as a means of:

> improving the quality of research interviews . . . and increasing the degree of social control over the measurement process. (1981: 156)

**Attempt Exercise 4.1 about now**

### 4.3.3 The limits of positivism

For many years, positivist survey research provided the main source of data for sociology. For instance, Brenner (1981) reports studies which indicate that, during the 1960s, around 90 per cent of all the papers in the two leading American sociology journals were based on data derived from interviews and questionnaires.

From a critical position, Maseide (1990) summarizes the most significant premises of the *positivist* approach to interview data. According to positivists:

1 The aim of social science is to discover unknown but actual social facts or essentials.
2 Reality is supposed to be 'out there'. Thus it is a matter of finding the most effective and unbiased methods that, as precisely and objectively as possible, could bring out information about this reality.
3 The existence of typical respondents is explicitly presupposed. These respondents are implicitly supplied with standardized mental structures that match the analyst's reasoning and use of language.
4 Methodological problems are more technical than theoretical or interpretive (adapted from Maseide, 1990: 4).

As Maseide points out, positivists' 'belief in standardized forms of interviewing relies on an exclusive emphasis on the referential functions of language' (1990: 9). However, interview responses 'are delivered at different descriptive levels. The informant does different things with words and stories' (1990: 11).

We will later see that we can extend Maseide's critique of positivism. As Carolyn Baker's research shows, *both* informant *and* interviewer do many 'different things with words and stories'.

To what extent can we understand these 'things' if we switch away from the standardized interview forms of positivism towards more open-ended interviews or even conversations? To answer this question, we must review the arguments of emotionalists.

## 4.4 EMOTIONALISM

For positivists, interviews are essentially about ascertaining facts or beliefs out there in the world. Emotionalists switch this focus but only slightly. Their concern is not with obtaining objective 'facts' but with eliciting authentic accounts of subjective experience. To do so, emotionalists believe that interviewers should try 'to formulate questions and provide an atmosphere conducive to open and undistorted communication' (Holstein and Gubrium, 1997: 116).

The key here is to obtain rapport with respondents and to avoid manipulating them. So, while positivists regard departure from an interview schedule as a possible source of bias, emotionalists may actively encourage it. For instance, feminist interviewers are sometimes advised to take the opportunity to tell their own stories to respondents (Oakley: 1981).

### 4.4.1 Type of knowledge

Emotionalist interviewers want to access the *subject* behind the person given the role of interview respondent. The particular concern is with *lived experience*. Emotions are treated as central to such experience.

An example of this approach will show what this involves in practice. Schreiber (1996) describes an interview study with a snowball sample of 21 women who identified themselves as having recovered from depression. She sets out to establish an account of the depression experience which, she claims, is 'grounded in the real world of the participant' (1996: 471). This 'real world', we are told, contains six 'phases' of '(re)defining the self', each with between three and five 'properties' or 'dimensions'.

In this way, the author attempts to put her readers (and herself) in touch with what she calls 'the depression experience'. However, as Schreiber points out, this was a retrospective study, based on what her respondents told her on being invited to look back at their past. For instance, as she notes, what she calls the first phase of this experience ('My Self Before') 'is only seen upon reflection' (1996: 474).

For positivists, this would cast doubt on the reliability of Schreiber's data and the validity of her claim to access the 'depression experience'. But instead, true to her emotionalist position, Schreiber is less concerned with 'bias' than with 'authenticity'. From this point of view: 'there is merit in hearing the women's understandings of the people they were at the time' (1996: 474).

## 4.4.2 Research task

Emotionalists aim to access emotions by describing respondents' inner experiences, by encouraging interviewers to become emotionally involved with respondents and to convey their own feelings to both respondents and readers (see Gubrium and Holstein, 1997: 58).

This means that emotionalists reject the positivist assumption that both interviewer and interviewee are properly treated as 'objects'. Instead, they depict both as (emotionally involved) subjects. This is set out in Table 4.2.

TABLE 4.2   *Two versions of the interview relationship*

|  | Positivism | Emotionalism |
| --- | --- | --- |
| Interviewer | Object – following research protocol | Subject – creating interview context |
| Interviewee | Object – revealing items relevant to the research protocol | Subject – complying with or resisting definition of the situation |

If interviewees are to be viewed as subjects who actively construct the features of their cognitive world, then one should try to obtain intersubjective depth between both sides so that a deep mutual understanding can be achieved. As Reason and Rowan argue:

Humanistic approaches favour 'depth interviews' in which interviewee and interviewer become 'peers' or even 'companions'. (1981: 205)

In this 'humanistic' version of the interview, *both* the type of knowledge gained *and* the validity of the analysis are based on 'deep' understanding. This is because 'the humanistic framework' supports 'meaningful understanding of the person . . . and wholeness in human inquiry' (1981: 206).

Similarly, Burgess (1980) in his chapter, significantly entitled 'The unstructured interview as a conversation', the interview is seen to give greater depth than other research techniques. This is because, Burgess claims, it is based on 'a sustained relationship between the informant and the researcher' (1980: 109).

For this reason, most emotionalists tend to reject prescheduled standardized interviews and to prefer open-ended interviews. Norman Denzin (1970: 125) has offered three reasons for this preference:

1  It allows respondents to use their 'unique ways of defining the world'.
2  It assumes that no fixed sequence of questions is suitable to all respondents.
3  It allows respondents to 'raise important issues not contained in the schedule'.

### 4.4.3  The limits of emotionalism

These positions might seem to be a welcome alternative to the purely technical version of interviews espoused by positivists. After all, isn't it both more valid and more ethical to recognize that interviews are encounters between human beings trying to understand one another?

This 'humanistic' position is seductive. It seems to blend a self-evident truth about humanity with political correctness about the need for mutual understanding and dialogue. However, it *neglects* three issues which I want briefly to explore:

- the assumptions made in preferring open-ended interviews
- the difference between a 'humanistic' and a social science position
- the role of common-sense knowledge, rather than 'empathy', in allowing us to conduct and analyse interviews.

I will consider each issue in turn.

*Open-endedness*
As Hammersley and Atkinson (1983: 110–11) point out, it is somewhat naive to assume that open-ended or non-directive interviewing is not in itself a form of social control which shapes what people say. For instance, where the researcher maintains a minimal presence, asking few questions, this can create an interpretive problem for the interviewee about what is relevant. Moreover, the passivity of the interviewer can create an extremely powerful constraint on the interviewee to talk (as seen in 'non-directive' styles of psychotherapy and counselling: see Peräkylä, 1995).

I would also add that this preference for a particular form of interview can be defined in terms of avoiding bias which is entirely appropriate to a positivist approach. Conversely, in certain feminist writings, where value freedom is rejected, structured interviews are criticized on political grounds as maintaining a hierarchical relationship in research (see Stanley and Wise, 1983).

## Humanism

Why are interviews so self-evidently based on an exchange of unique human experiences? Indeed, may not this self-evident 'truth' derive not from social science but from a widespread cultural assumption?

Think of our fascination with interviews with celebrities on television news or 'chat shows'. Or consider the way in which sporting events or even Nobel Prize ceremonies are now incomplete without 'pre-match' and 'post-match' interviews. Do the latter give us insights into 'unique' experiences or do they simply reproduce predictable forms of how it is appropriate to account for sporting or academic success or failure (see Emmison, 1988; Mulkay, 1984)?

Only occasionally do sportsmen and women resist their depiction as heroes or villains. For instance, the British decathlete Daley Thompson was well known for nonplussing the media by producing the 'wrong' account – claiming he was 'over the moon' when he had failed and 'sick as a parrot' when he had won. Again, in this vein, a British boxer was recently termed 'arrogant' by a reporter because he had refused to engage in the usual pre-fight slanging match with his next opponent.

This, of course, is the irony. The media aim to deliver us immediate 'personal' experience. Yet what they (we) want is simple repetition of familiar tales. Perhaps this is part of the postmodern condition. Maybe we feel people are at their most authentic when they are, in effect, reproducing a cultural script.

Those approaches in social science which, to some extent, take on board the media's approach and imply that people's experiences are individually meaningful and authentic raise many questions. For instance, from what do these experiences derive? If you can see uniformity in even the most intimate kinds of account, I think there we would see a job for the social scientist.

The well-meaning 'humanistic' social scientist may thus have uncritically taken on board a common-sense assumption about the immediacy and validity of accounts of human experience. This leads to analytic laziness in considering the status of interview data.

## Common sense

Although positivists and emotionalists seek to document different orders of reality (respectively, 'facts' and 'emotions'), there is a surprising degree of tacit agreement between them about one issue. Both are aware of 'traps' in their path which must be overcome if their preferred order is to be properly documented.

So, in an early text, Denzin (1970: 133–8) lists a number of 'problems' which can 'distort' interviewees' responses:

- respondents possessing different interactional roles from the interviewer
- the problem of 'self-presentation', especially in the early stages of the interview
- the problems of 'volatile', 'fleeting' relationships to which respondents have little commitment and so 'can fabricate tales of self that belie the actual facts' (1970: 135)
- the difficulty of penetrating private worlds of experience
- the relative status of interviewer and interviewee
- the 'context' of the interview (e.g. home, work, hospital).

However, to speak of 'distortions' is to play the positivist's game. For positivists are equally concerned with 'misunderstandings' between interviewer and interviewee (or respondent).

By contrast, interviews can also be seen to possess basic properties of all social interaction. These properties derive from both parties' employment of their everyday, common-sense knowledge of social structures to engage in such business as recognizing a question and providing an answer which will be heard as 'appropriate' for a particular identity (see my discussion in Sections 4.7 and 4.8 of the studies by Baker and Baruch). It follows that such properties should be *investigated* rather than treated as a 'problem' standing in the way of accurate reporting of 'facts' or 'experiences'.

### 4.4.4 Emotionalism: summary

For the emotionalist, the open-ended interview apparently offers the opportunity for an authentic gaze into the soul of another, or even for a politically correct dialogue where researcher and researched offer mutual understanding and support. The rhetoric of interviewing 'in depth' repeatedly hints at such a collection of assumptions. Here we see a stubbornly persistent romantic impulse in contemporary social science: the elevation of the experiential as the authentic – the selfsame gambit that can make the TV chat show or news interview so appealing.

There are also real methodological doubts about the emotionalist project which relate to emotionalists' claims to depict the 'authentic' reality they want to access. These doubts have been forcefully presented by Gubrium and Holstein:

> Do we have any evidence of emotion other than its expression? Can researchers give us access to 'real' emotion simply by re-presenting or reenacting subjects' *expressions* of these emotions? Do emotions exist apart from culturally available modes of expression? (1997: 74, emphasis in original)

**Attempt Exercise 4.2 about now**

## 4.5 CONSTRUCTIONISM

While positivists acknowledge that interviewers interact with their subjects, they demand that such interaction should be strictly defined by the research protocol. Consequently, positivists only become seriously interested in interviewer–interviewee interaction when it can be shown that interviewers have departed from the protocol (Brenner, 1981).

Conversely, for emotionalists, interviews are inescapably encounters between subjects. As Norman Denzin has put it:

> I wish to treat the interview as an observational encounter. An encounter . . . represents the coming together of two or more persons for the purpose of focused interaction. (1970: 133)

What distinguishes constructionists from emotionalists is the former's attempt to treat what happens in what Denzin terms 'focused interaction' as a *topic* in its own right, not as something which can stand in the way of 'authentic' understanding of another's experience. This has a direct impact on the type of knowledge which constructionists want to access.

### 4.5.1 Type of knowledge

> Accounts are not simply representations of the world; they are part of the world they describe. (Hammersley and Atkinson, 1983: 107)

Emotionalists help us to see that interviewee respondents are active sense-making subjects. However, they persist in the positivist rhetoric in which accounts are 'simply representations of the world'. By contrast, constructionists are interested in documenting the way in which accounts 'are part of the world they describe'.

What does this mean in practice? The type of knowledge we are concerned with here is how interview participants actively create meaning. This lies behind Holstein and Gubrium's idea of 'the active interview':

> Construed as active, the subject behind the respondent not only holds facts and details of experience, but, in the very process of offering them up for response, constructively adds to, takes away from, and transforms the facts and details. The respondent can hardly 'spoil' what he or she is, in effect, subjectively creating. (1997: 117)

The implication is that methodology texts which advise on 'good' interview technique should only be taken seriously if we are positivists. If not, we need to recognize that the skills involved in bringing off a successful interview are shared by both interviewer *and* interviewee. Ultimately, whatever these methodology texts say, both are drawing upon shared properties of common-sense knowledge.

The earliest attempt to set out this version of interview data was made by Cicourel (1964). For Cicourel, previous advice about good interview technique offers a revealing insight into our dependence on everyday knowledge of social structures. As he writes:

> The subtleties which methodologists introduce to the novice interviewer can be read as properties to be found in the everyday interaction between members of a society. Thus the principles of 'good and bad interviewing' can be read as basic features of social interaction which the social scientist presumably is seeking to study. (1964: 68)

For Cicourel, the remedies recommended by methodologists derive from the very knowledge of the social world which should be made problematic. Moreover, the 'errors' they detect are not really obstacles to social research but rather exhibit basic properties of social interaction. We must learn, he suggests, to 'conceive of the error as evidence not only of poor reliability but also of "normal" interpersonal relations' (1964: 74).

Cicourel parallels Garfinkel's (1967) ethnomethodology with its awe at the 'amazing, practical accomplishment' of research findings. For Garfinkel and Cicourel, such findings are reflexively linked to everyday procedures for 'looking' and 'finding'. Ironically, this makes Cicourel full of praise for methodology texts like Hyman (1954), which is dubbed 'excellent' on two occasions (Cicourel, 1964: 85, 93). The irony arises because he wants to utilize their desired success in achieving a degree of invariance not as a resource but as a topic:

> In spite of the problem of interviewer error, 'somehow' different interviewers with different approaches produce(d) similar responses from different subjects. The question then becomes one of determining what was invariant or, more precisely, how were invariant meanings communicated despite such variations. (1964: 75)

For Cicourel, there is no distinction between the practical skills of methodologists, researchers and interviewers. All are uniformly concerned with what he calls 'the synchronization of meaning'. All use 'rules of evidence' deriving from a single conceptual scheme based on assumed common relevances, stocks of knowledge, typifications, recipes, rules for managing one's presence before others, and so on. These shared 'commonsense devices for making sense of the environment' (1964: 100) are presupposed in conducting or analysing interviews. We must, therefore, learn to 'conceive of the error as evidence not only of poor reliability but also of "normal" interpersonal relations' (1964: 74).

### 4.5.2  Research task

Cicourel's position derived from ethnomethodology, an approach we have already encountered in earlier chapters of this book (most notably in Chapter 3).

Constructionists share ethnomethodologists' focus on how people assemble sense in situations like interviews. This is seen in Holstein and Gubrium's constructionist account of 'the active interview':

> Respondents' answers and comments are not viewed as reality reports delivered from a fixed repository. Instead, they are considered for the ways that they construct aspects of reality in collaboration with the interviewer. The focus is as much on the assembly process as on what is assembled. (1997: 127)

However, most constructionists also want to preserve a concern with *what* interviewees are saying as well as with *how* they get to say it. So Holstein and Gubrium continue:

> The goal is to show how interview responses are produced in the interaction between interviewer and respondent, without losing sight of the meanings produced or the circumstances that condition the meaning-making process. The analytic objective is not merely to describe the situated production of talk, but to show how what is being said relates to the experiences and lives being studied. (1997: 127)

By reinstating a reference to 'the experiences and lives being studied', some ethnomethodologists might say that Holstein and Gubrium are taking us back to the emotionalist position. The issue of whether interview data can tell us anything beyond the local construction of meaning is very much alive today. It leads to two very different criticisms of how constructionists want to treat interviews.

### 4.5.3 Criticisms of constructionism

*Narrowness*

Although the constructionist critique of both positivism and emotionalism may appear to be convincing, its own position seems to have problems and inconsistencies. Cicourel's ethnomethodological concern with the basic properties of social interaction would seem to deny the value of treating interview data as saying anything about any other reality than the interview itself.

Put simply, many interview researchers would complain that, if we follow Cicourel's ethnomethodologically inspired position, we would simply focus on the conversational skills of the participants rather than on the content of what they are saying and its relation to the world outside the interview.

Two responses have been made to this criticism. Those sympathetic to ethnomethodology argue that such content is only to be found through how it is made available by the participants to an interview. Therefore, by focusing closely on the co-production of interview talk, we can say a great deal about content without *importing* our own sense of what content is important (see Schegloff, 1997).

By contrast, many constructionists accept that there is some justification for the alleged 'narrowness' of ethnomethodology and claim that it is possible to combine a concern with both form (how?) and content (what?). Holstein and Gubrium have been the principal exponents of this position, claiming that it is necessary to treat interview data as reporting on both what they call *how* and *what* questions.

In a project on the quality of care and quality of life of nursing home residents (Gubrium, 1997), interview responses were, in part, analysed to address 'what' questions. Here the researcher attempted to:

> link . . . the topics to biographical particulars in the interview process, and thus produce . . . a subject who responds to, or is affected by, the matters under discussion. (Holstein and Gubrium, 1997: 121)

But such a focus on 'what' did not, it was claimed, mean that 'how' questions were neglected:

> The standpoint from which information is offered is continually developed in relation to ongoing interview interaction. In speaking of the quality of care, for example, nursing home residents, as interview respondents, not only offer substantive thoughts and feelings pertinent to the topic under consideration, but simultaneously and continuously monitor who they are in relation to the person questioning them. For example, prefacing her remarks about the quality of life in her facility with the statement 'speaking as a woman', a nursing home resident informs the interviewer that she is to be heard as a woman, not as someone else – not a mere resident, cancer patient, or abandoned mother. (1997: 122)

So, in what Holstein and Gubrium call 'the active interview':

> data can be analyzed to show the dynamic interrelatedness of the *whats* and the *hows*. (1997: 127, emphasis in original)

### Inconsistency?

Holstein and Gubrium's answer to the charge of 'narrowness' leaves them open to a different criticism. Aren't 'what' questions precisely the concerns of emotionalists and positivists? If so, aren't constructionists who want to use interview data to answer such questions simply taking us back to earlier positions?

This is an important and complex issue with no easy answer. So that my readers can try to make up their own minds, most of the rest of this chapter will be used to give telling examples. Each example takes a different position on the appropriateness of using interview data to answer 'what' questions. The first two studies derive from interviews with adolescents.

## 4.6    ADOLESCENT CULTURES: COMBINING 'WHAT' AND 'HOW'

Jody Miller and Barry Glassner (1997) describe a study involving in-depth, open-ended interviews with young women (aged 13 to 18) who claim affiliation with youth gangs in their communities (Miller, 1996). These interviews follow the completion of a survey interview administered by the same researcher.

Here is how they describe the purposes of each form of data:

> While the survey interview gathers information about a wide range of topics, including the individual, her school, friends, family, neighborhood, delinquent involvement, arrest history, sexual history, and victimization, in addition to information about the gang, the in-depth interview is concerned exclusively with the roles and activities of young women in youth gangs, and the meanings they describe as emerging from their gang affiliation. (Miller and Glassner, 1997: 105)

So far Miller and Glassner are focusing on how we can use interviews to understand the meaning of these young women's identity (what Holstein and Gubrium call 'how' questions ). To see how this works out in practice, let us focus on the data that Miller obtained from her in-depth interviews. This is one example:

> Describing why she joined her gang, one young woman told Miller, 'well, I didn't get any respect at home. I wanted to get some love and respect from somebody somewhere else'. (1997: 107)

Here is another respondent's explanation of why she joined a gang:

> 'I didn't have *no* family . . . I had nothin' else.' (1997: 107)

Another young woman, when asked to speculate on why young people join gangs, suggested:

> 'Some of 'em are like me, don't have, don't really have a basic home or steady home to go to, you know, and they don't have as much love and respect in the home so they want to get it elsewhere. And, and, like we get, have family members in gangs or that were in gangs, stuff like that.' (1997: 107)

Let us assume that you have gathered these data and now want to begin analysis. Put at its starkest, what are you to do with it?

In line with the positivist or emotionalist approach, you may start by coding respondents' answers into the different sets of reasons that they give for participation in gangs (perhaps using qualitative software programs such as ETHNOGRAPH or NUD•IST; see Seale, 2000). From these data, two reasons seem to predominate: 'push' factors (unsupportive families) and 'pull' factors (supportive gangs).

Moreover, given the availability of survey data on the same respondents, you are now in a position to correlate each factor with various background characteristics that they have. This seems to set up your research in good shape. Not only can you search for the 'subjective' meanings of adolescent gangs, you can relate these meanings to 'objective' social structures.

Both positivist and emotionalist approaches thus have a high degree of plausibility to social scientists who theorize the world in terms of the impact of (objective) social structures upon (subjective) dispositions. Moreover, the kind of research outputs that it seeks to deliver are precisely those demanded by 'users' in the community, seeking immediate practical payoffs from social science research.

Calling their approach a 'methodology for listening', Miller and Glassner are centrally concerned with emotionalism's desire to 'see . . . the world from the perspective of our subjects' (Glassner and Loughlin, 1987: 37).

However, Miller and Glassner (1997: 103–4) are not entirely satisfied by the apparent plausibility of emotionalism. They now move in a social constructionist direction. For them, this involves thinking about how their respondents are using culturally available resources in order to construct their stories. As Richardson suggests:

> Participation in a culture includes participation in the narratives of that culture, a general understanding of the stock of meanings and their relationships to each other. (1990: 24)

How, then, can the data above be read in these terms? The idea is to see respondents' answers as *cultural stories*. This means examining the rhetorical force of what interviewees say, as:

> interviewees deploy these narratives to make their actions explainable and understandable to those who otherwise may not understand. (Miller and Glassner, 1997: 107)

In the data already presented, Miller and Glassner note that respondents make their actions understandable in two ways. First, they do not attempt to challenge public views of gangs as bad. But, second, they do challenge the notion that the interviewee herself is bad.

However, Miller and Glassner note that not all their respondents glibly recycle conventional cultural stories. As they put it:

> Some of the young women go farther and describe their gang involvement in ways that directly challenge prevailing stereotypes about gangs as groups that are inherently bad or antisocial and about females roles within gangs. (1997: 108)

Here are some of the respondents' accounts that they have in mind:

> 'It was really, it was just normal life, the only difference was, is, that we had meetings.'

'[We] play cards, smoke bud, play dominoes, play video games. That's basically all we do is play. You would be surprised. This is a bunch of big kids. It's a bunch of big old kids in my set.' (1997: 109)

In accounts like these, Miller and Glassner argue that there is an explicit challenge to what the interviewees know to be popular beliefs about youth gangs. Instead of accepting the conventional definition of their behaviour as 'deviant', the girls attempt to convey the normalcy of their activities.

These narratives directly challenge stereotypical cultural stories of the gang. Following Richardson, Miller and Glassner refer to such accounts as 'collective stories' which:

> resist the cultural narratives about groups of people and tell alternative stories. (Richardson, 1990: 25)

Miller and Glassner's sensitive address of the narrative forms from which perspectives arise suggests that interview analysis can, as Holstein and Gubrium suggest, be used to answer both 'what' questions (concerned with identity) and 'how' questions (concerned with matters such as narrative construction).

## 4.7 MEMBERSHIP WORK IN ADOLESCENT–ADULT TALK

Carolyn Baker's (1982) work shows another way of analysing interviews with adolescents. Baker's research is based on her comparative studies of interviews with teenagers in Canada and Australia. Like Miller and Glassner, her initial concern was to use her interviews to learn about how adolescents see themselves relative to children and adults.

However, she soon saw that the participants themselves were constructing a version of adolescent–adult relations for each other. As she puts it:

> at the same time as these passages contain comment about adolescent–adult talk, they are instances *themselves* of adolescent–adult talk. They are conversations between a researcher who could commonsensically be understood to be an adult, and persons who could similarly be describable as adolescents, given their age. (1982: 111)

For Baker, then, it became increasingly clear that the question 'In what ways do adolescents perceive their identity?' is loaded and unhelpful. Instead, she prefers to address the 'how' question: how do people locally construct particular identities?

To show how Baker proceeds, let us take just one extract from one of her interviews (Extract 4.1). Unlike the data given for the previous study, note how Baker's extracts inform us about both interviewee *and* interviewer's talk.

**Extract 4.1 (Baker, 1984: 316)**

(P = Pam, aged 14; I = interviewer)

```
 1   I:   Are there any ways in which you consider yourself to still be partly a child?
 2   P:   Well, I like to watch TV and, uh,
 3   I:   Well, adults do that
 4   P:   Yeah, I still read the comics ((laugh))
 5   I:   Adults do that
 6   P:   That's about, only thing I can think of
```

Note how I assigns P to a place between childhood and adulthood (line 1) and how P enters into the discussion in these terms. Moreover, as Baker (1984: 317) notes, in lines 3 and 5, I treats as invalid P's nominated instances of 'childish' behaviour. By showing that a valid response would involve depicting something exclusive to children, I proceeds on the basis that, although child–adolescent overlap can properly arise (being 'partly a child'), child–adult overlap constitutes an unacceptable answer. The interview continues as in Extract 4.2.

**Extract 4.2 (Baker, 1984: 317)**

(// = overlap)

```
 7   I:   Do you notice any leftovers of childhood in your personality?
 8   P:   Well, my food tastes have all changed differently, like I used to hate lots
 9        of things, now I like most, almost everything. I used to really hate
10        vegetables, and now I'd rather have vegetables than anything else!
11        And um, when I was a child, I used to really be worried about what I
12        looked like and that an now I don't, I don't really care. If peop//
13   I:   // You really don't care?
14   P:   Pe, I don't care what people think, I just, think well I like this, and if no
15        one else does, that's too bad
16   I:   At what point were you, so terrible self conscious about your appearance?
```

Baker draws our attention to the way in which I picks up and pursues the topic of P's feelings about her appearance, while paying no attention to what P says about vegetables. In this way, she shows P that her tastes in food are not entirely compatible with I's attempt to depict overlaps between childhood and adolescence. As Baker suggests:

> by doing this, [the interviewer] shows Pam how adolescence should be done in the interview. While Pam's 'vegetable eating' is passed by, her 'not caring' about her appearance becomes the basis for an identity rich puzzle and solution whose pursuit by the interviewer binds this activity to her category 'adolescence'. (1984: 317–18)

Anssi Peräkylä (personal correspondence) has also pointed out that I's first question, in both extracts, treats P as a subject who might be puzzled by her identity. This can amount to treating P as a *non-child* (because children are not supposed to have that kind of self-consciousness about their identity) and simultaneously as a *non-adult* (because adults are not supposed to be puzzled about who they are). So, straight off, I constitutes P as neither child nor adult (i.e. as an 'adolescent').

This focus on what the interviewer is doing is very different from other approaches to interview data. Positivists treat the interviewer as a possible source of bias, and emotionalists may make assumptions about the role of 'empathy' or 'political dominance' in interviews. However, social constructionists like Baker, who focus on 'how' questions, must address, without prior conceptions, the actual interplay between the interviewer and the interviewee. Moreover, Baker goes further than Glassner and Miller by treating matters of 'identity' as only available through the ways it is locally constituted by all parties.

Baker's analysis draws upon an approach (Harvey Sacks's membership categorization device analysis) that will be presented in Section 5.4. For the moment, we need only note that **membership categorization devices** (MCDs) are used by participants to group together collections of 'similar' identities or categories. Any category is a potential member of more than one MCD. One MCD that can be heard in these attempts to position people as 'children', 'adolescents' or 'adults' is 'stage of life'.

Stage of life is addressed by Pam and the interviewer in both the extracts above. First, in Extract 4.1, in the exchanges between line 1 and 6, I requests and P attempts to provide a set of activities hearable as bound to the category 'still partly a child'. I's comments at lines 3 and 5 now may be heard as attending to the unclear category bounding of activities such as 'watching TV' or 'reading comics'. Similarly, I's pursuit of P's comment about her looks makes sense in terms of the association between the way in which the activity 'being concerned about one's appearance' is category-bound to the category 'adolescent'.

Second, the hierarchical relationship between each of these stage of life categories is attended to by both speakers. For instance, in Extract 4.2, I uses the term 'leftovers' to describe elements left behind from childhood, while P describes her 'non-childlike' self in terms of greater independence and maturity. By reporting her activities in this way, P can be heard to be acting more like an adult than a child.

Most stage of life categories are mutually exclusive, i.e. you are either an 'adult' or a 'child' but, usually, cannot be both at the same time. Hence to refer to an 'adult's' behaviour as 'childish' is hearable as quite a powerful charge.

People recognizable as 'adolescents' may, therefore, want to set up a mutually exclusive framework between such categories. In Extract 4.2, notice how Pam makes a sharp distinction between the past ('when I was a child') and the present (when she has more 'adult' qualities).

At the same time, as Baker notes:

'adolescence' can be made to overlap with 'childhood' or 'adulthood' by discovering 'childness' or 'adultness' in the 'adolescent'. (1984: 303)

The interviewer's question about 'leftovers' (Extract 4.2, line 7) depends precisely on the availability of this sense of overlap. Indeed, people can use both 'childness' or adultness' as simultaneous descriptions of the 'adolescent'. Indeed, as Baker notes, 'this is a classic "problem of adolescence"' (1984: 304) to be found in everyday life just as much as in this interview.

It is worth noting how Baker's analysis departs from positivist approaches to interview data. According to this approach:

1 Standardized sets of questions are part of 'good interview practice', designed to ensure that the interview is a reliable research instrument, free from interviewer error.
2 Any similarities in interviewees' answers are to be explained in terms of 'face-sheet variables' (e.g. social class, gender, ethnicity) external to the interview context.

Conversely, Baker shows that:

1 Standardized questions (and follow-up questions) derive their sense from commonly available conceptions about people's behaviour. Hence, whatever 'scientific' character they have builds upon common-sense knowledge about how the everyday social world operates.
2 Similar answers relate to the interviewees' skills in deploying shared knowledge about this shared social world.

The contrast is very clear. While many interview studies define their approach by technical criteria and treat 'society' simply as an external social fact, Baker shows how *both* interviewer and interviewee rely upon their conversational skills and common-sense knowledge of social structures in order to produce locally 'adequate' utterances. The former approach can be characterized as interview-as-technique; the latter can be called the interview-as-local-accomplishment. This is shown in Table 4.3.

TABLE 4.3 *Two versions of interview data*

| Version of interview | Questions | Answers |
|---|---|---|
| Interview-as-technique | Technical criteria (e.g. pre-testing of questions) | Reflect respondents' place in the social structure |
| Interview-as-local-accomplishment | Common-sense knowledge of social structures used to produce 'adequate' utterances (e.g. to produce a hearable question at an 'appropriate' location) | (e.g. to produce answers which define morally adequate identities) |

From the point of view of interview-as-local-accomplishment, interview data are not 'one side of the picture' to be balanced by observation of what respondents actually do, or to be compared with what their role partners say. Instead, such data show how participants sensitively reproduce and rearticulate identities within the interview. Although such identities (e.g. young person, mother) undoubtedly exist outside the interview in the many contexts of social interaction, the interview-as-local-accomplishment approach encourages us to study the skills used as the parties construct identities and move between them.

Attempt Exercise 4.3 about now

## 4.8 MORAL TALES OF PARENTHOOD

I will give a final example of how we can treat the interview-as-local-accomplishment. The example is taken from a study of 'parenthood' which adopts a similar approach to Baker's discussion of the 'adult–adolescent' relationship.

One of the striking aspects of Baker's data is the way in which her interviewees' accounts have recurrent features in common. This parallels Baruch's (1982) comments about studies of parents' responses to different congenital illnesses in their children.

When parents of handicapped children are first interviewed, they often offer 'atrocity' stories, usually about the late discovery or inadequate treatment of their child's condition. It is tempting to compare what they say with observations of what has happened and with medical workers' accounts. However, as Baruch (1982) notes, such a comparison is based on the positivist assumption that interview responses are to be valued primarily because of their accuracy as objective statements of sets of events. Conversely, we might address the moral forms that give force to 'atrocity' stories, whatever their accuracy. Right or wrong, biased or unbiased, such accounts display vividly cultural particulars about the moral accountability of parenthood.

Baruch begins by looking at data extracts from Burton's (1975) study of parents of children with cystic fibrosis. In Extract 4.3, one such parent tells about an early experience at a baby clinic.

**Extract 4.3 (quoted by Baruch, 1982: Appendix 2)**
Parent: I went to the baby clinic every week. She would gain one pound one week and lose it the next. They said I was fussing unnecessarily. They said there were skinny and fat babies and I was fussing too much. I went to a doctor and he gave me some stuff and he said 'You're a young mother. Are you sure you won't put it in her ear instead of her mouth?' It made me feel a fool.

Baruch compares this data extract with another from his own study, as in Extract 4.4.

**Extract 4.4 (Baruch, 1982: Appendix 2, 1)**
Parent: When she was born, they told me she was perfectly all right. And I accepted it. I worried about her which most mothers do, you know. Worry about their first child.
Int:    Hm

> Parent:  She wouldn't eat and different things. And so I kept taking her to the clinic. Nothing wrong with her my dear. You're just making yourself . . . worrying unnecessarily, you see.

Despite the different illnesses, there are striking similarities in the content of what each mother is saying. Both mothers report their concern about the baby's eating habits. Both complain that the clinic doctor dismissed their worries as groundless.

Nonetheless, Baruch notes that each account is treated very differently by each researcher. More specifically:

> Burton treats her findings as an accurate report of an external event and argues that parents' early encounters with medical personnel can cause psychological damage to the parents as well as lasting damage to the relationship with doctors. On the other hand, I see parents' talk as a situated account aimed at displaying the status of morally adequate parenthood. In this instance, the display is produced by the telling of an atrocity story. (Baruch, 1982: Appendix 2, 2)

If we return to Table 4.3, we can find the basis for this difference of approach. Burton treats parents' answers as deriving from the social structure of mother–doctor interactions, coupled with a given psychological reality to do with parents' feelings of guilt and responsibility. For Burton, then, the interview is a technique used by social scientists to get closer to such 'facts'.

Conversely, Baruch is arguing that mothers are trading on common-sense knowledge of 'what everyone knows' about the concerns of young mothers. Treating the interview as a local accomplishment, he invites us to see how the construction of an 'atrocity story' is an effective way for mothers to display their moral responsibility.

It might appear that Burton and Baruch are offering *competing* versions of mothers' behaviour. Burton seems to be stressing the mothers' goodwill in difficult circumstances, while Baruch appears to be offering a more cynical account which seems to argue that mothers are mainly concerned with how they will look in the eyes of others. However, it must be stressed that, for Baruch at least, the two accounts are *not* competitive.

This is because Baruch is not treating what his mothers tell him as either true or false accounts of what actually happened to them when they took their babies to the clinics. Consonant with his view of these interviews as 'local accomplishments', he is instead focusing on how, in telling their story to a stranger, mothers skilfully produce demonstrably 'morally adequate' accounts.

Notice how, in both extracts, the mothers' report that their babies had eating problems *prior to the disease diagnosis* specifically implies and contradicts the possible identity 'mother who did not monitor her baby sufficiently'. Coupled with their reports that doctors had, at first, played down their fears, this effectively produces the identity of 'mother who thoroughly monitored her baby but was spurned by the doctor'.

So Baruch is asking about the *functions* of the mothers' accounts rather than casting doubt on their motives. He is not competing with what Burton says about the reality of what happens in mother–doctor encounters because he is refusing to treat interviewees' accounts as simple *reports* on such an external reality.

If anything, however, Baruch's analysis offers a more human account of the capacities of his respondents. While Burton's mothers' responses seem determined by social and psychological structures, Baruch reveals that human subjects actively participate in the construction of social and psychological realities.

So far, however, we have been depending on brief extracts to show how such an analysis works. As I shall argue in Chapter 8, a danger of depending on such extracts is that one can use them to support a preconceived argument rather than to test it.

Baruch (1982) overcomes such dangers by two effective strategies:

- tabulating many cases
- investigating deviant cases.

Let me briefly review each strategy in turn.

Baruch used only the parents' initial responses to the interviewer's opening question: 'So could you just tell me the story?' Following Sacks, Baruch was interested in the membership categorization devices (MCDs) employed by respondents. The MCDs used by Baruch's parents were mainly 'parent', 'child' and 'medical professional'. Baruch then tabulated these responses in terms of pairs of MCDs. His analysis showed that these MCDs were grouped in various pairs at different parts of the account according to who had a duty towards the other (e.g. parent–child, professional–parent).

Table 4.4 indicates the pairs identified. In each case, the category mentioned first is described by the parent as having an implied duty towards the second category.

TABLE 4.4 *Membership categories*

| Categories | Number | % |
| --- | --- | --- |
| Parent–child | 160 | 51 |
| Parent–professional | 86 | 28 |
| Professional–child | 49 | 16 |
| Professional–parent | 16 | 5 |
| Total | 311 | 100 |

*Source*: Baruch, 1982: Appendix 2, 17

Baruch notes that earlier studies (e.g. Voysey, 1975) have stressed the perceived importance of parental responsibilities towards their children. Table 4.4 supports this finding, showing that:

Parent–child norms are central to parents' accounts and, on their own, amount to all the other norms put together. Thus, when parents provide an account of their responses, they are heard to attend to their duties, rights and obligations towards their child, even though they might have been expected to emphasise the medical aspects of their child's career, e.g. professional–child relationships. (Baruch, 1982: Appendix 2, 18)

In Sacks's terms, each of these pairs of MCDs implies common expectations about what sort of activities are appropriate. For instance, the parent–child pairing implies a standard obligation of parental responsibility such that we can describe the collection 'parent–child' as a standardized relational pair (SRP).

Looking just at the SRP 'parent–child', Baruch finds the kinds of activities described in the interviews to be as shown in Table 4.5.

TABLE 4.5  *Parent–child activities*

| Type of activity | Number | % |
|---|---|---|
| Emotional responses to the child's illness and treatment | 101 | 63 |
| Action taken in relation to the child's illness | 38 | 24 |
| Taking responsibility for the child's illness | 11 | 7 |
| Showing knowledge about the child's development and illness | 10 | 6 |
| Total | 160 | 100 |

*Source*: Baruch, 1982: Appendix 2, Table 3

We see from Table 4.5, as Baruch puts it, that:

One of the central features of these stories is the way parents appeal to their emotionality as a normal, moral response of anyone who is in their situation. (1982: Appendix 2, 21)

This emotional response (described in 63 per cent of all such descriptions of parents and children) appears to set the backdrop for the other accounts of action taken (24 per cent) in the context of responsibility (7 per cent) and knowledge (6 per cent). Thus parents describe their relationship to their children as primarily grounded in emotion but leading to actions embodying the more cognitive dimensions of responsibility and knowledge.

Using such tabulations, Baruch demonstrates that the construction of what he calls 'moral tales' (see also Baruch, 1981) is not just an isolated feature of one or two extracts but runs throughout his corpus of data. When grounded on MCD analysis, Baruch's tabulation of data is possible without violating the recognition of the interview as a situated encounter.

Nonetheless, as in all datasets, there are always exceptions. As already mentioned, Baruch stringently seeks to identify such exceptions and, through the method of **deviant-case analysis**, uses them to refine his analysis. The most important deviant case is discussed briefly below.

One set of parents, when asked to tell their story, responded entirely in terms of descriptions of what medical professionals had done for their child. They made no mention of their own emotional responses, or of their own actions as parents. Extract 4.5 gives a brief taste of their response.

**Extract 4.5 (Baruch, 1982: Appendix 2, 28)**

```
1  Parent:  Well the story really started with him going in for a minor op last year
2           and the anaesthetist just er investigations discover a murmur which
3           she wasn't very happy about and referred us to a paediatrician after the
4           op who agreed that it was an unusual sight and um murmurs are
5           commonplace really
6  Int:     um
7  Parent:  But on the sight and nature of it, it sort of wanted further investigation.
```

While Baruch's other interviews contained several descriptions of parent–child SRPs, they are totally absent here where the tale is told simply in terms of professional–child activities. If you compare this extract with the ones given earlier, the absence here of references to parents' worries is quite striking.

Baruch suggests that the key to understanding this deviant case lies in the parent's statement on lines 4–5 that 'murmurs are commonplace really'. As he notes, this involves:

> the use of a technical language . . . which is never heard in other parents' accounts at this stage of the child's career. (1982: Appendix 2, 29)

It turns out that these parents are themselves medical professionals and are treating the interviewer's question as a request for a reasonably 'objective' account of events seen from a medical point of view. This 'deviant case' thus highlights the way in which, for parents without these medical resources, the request for a story is heard as an opportunity to display that one is still an adequate parent.

Two points of clarification perhaps need to be made. First, this extract is being viewed as deviant purely in a statistical sense. As Baruch argues:

> we are not viewing [the parent's] account as deviant in terms of pre-conceived assumptions about what constitutes adequate parenthood. Rather, the claims we are making about its status are based on a comparison of the considerable differences between its normative character and that of the rest of the sample. As Strong (1979) has argued, such limiting cases are extremely valuable in illuminating consistent features of social life. (1982: Appendix 2, 30)

The second point derives from this: it might be suggested that Baruch is arguing that the occupation of these parents is the *cause* of why they give their account in this way. If so, Baruch would be treating the interviewees' account as stemming from their place in the social structure and, thereby, be reverting to a version of the interview-as-technique (see Table 4.3).

However, although Baruch is not explicit on this matter, his method would suggest that this is *not* his argument at all. Following Sacks, we must recognize that any person can describe themselves (or be described) in a multiplicity of ways. These parents could have elected to have heard the interviewer's request for 'the story' to be addressed to them purely as 'parents' rather than as 'health care professionals who happen to be parents'. By choosing the latter format they display other, equally moral, qualities, e.g. as people who are, for the moment, able to put their feelings on one side and seek to offer an admirably 'objective' account.

In neither case do we have to see an external, pre-given social structure as the determinant of the account. Rather, all the interviewees invoke a sense of social structure in order to assemble recognizably 'sensible' accounts which are adequate for the practical purposes at hand.

### Attempt Exercise 4.4 about now

The implications are clear-cut. First, in studying accounts, we are studying displays of identities which arise as part of members' artful practices (e.g. in telling a particular kind of 'moral tale'). Second, there is no necessary contradiction in seeking to study *both* identities and practices. Sacks himself, for instance, seeks to establish the norms at work in children's stories in order to give an account of the artful practices through which they are assembled. It is equally possible, as Baruch has shown, to study the cultural norms at work within a narrative and to understand how their power derives from *both* their cultural base *and* their use in relation to a set of formal rules with an apparently inexorable logic.

As Sacks acknowledges, the *content* of his formal membership categorization devices is cultural through and through, arising, for instance, in how the collection 'family' is put together in a particular society. However, as he points out, once a category from one collection is used there are powerful pressures to draw on the same collection in subsequent descriptions. This can have unintended consequences: slanging matches, for instance, can get locked into a pattern of mutual insult once the first insulting term is used.

Following Sacks, Baruch's research reveals that, for analytic purposes and in real life, form and content depend upon each other. In this way, the debate between different kinds of constructionism (focused on either 'what' or 'how' questions) may be resolvable.

## 4.9 THE THREE MODELS: A SUMMARY

### 4.9.1 *The value of interview data*

Positivists argue that interviews based upon pre-tested, standardized questions are a way of increasing the reliability of research. However, both emotionalism and constructionism bring into question the value of data derived from standardized, survey research style interviews.

Some constructionists, like Glassner and Miller, assume that people's cultural worlds are more complex than most positivists will allow. Consequently, it is insufficient simply to 'pre-test' an interview schedule by asking questions of a few respondents. Instead, for Glassner and Miller, it is more appropriate to engage in systematic observation *before* any interviewing takes place.

Ethnomethodologists take the argument far further, rarely using interview methods as a way of gathering data. Instead, ethnomethodologists tend to concentrate on purely 'naturally occurring' settings which are observed and/or recorded at first hand.

It should at once be noted that the critique of the value of interview data unknowingly shares an assumption with more traditional approaches. As Hammersley and Atkinson (1983) have pointed out, an attachment to 'naturally occurring data' is a kind of 'naturalism'. Naturalism, they argue, unwittingly agrees with positivism that the best kinds of data are somehow 'untouched by human hands' – neutral, unbiased and representative. In some senses, then, naturalists are the inheritors of the positivist programme, using different means to achieve the same unquestioned ends.

So, despite the power of naturally occurring data, it does not follow that it is illegitimate to carry out our own research interviews. Everything depends on the status which we accord to the data gathered in such interviews.

### 4.9.2  The 'truth' of interview data

One important dimension which distinguishes both positivists and emotionalists from constructionists is whether interviews are treated as straightforward reports on another reality or whether they merely report upon, or express, their own structures.

According to the former ('externalist') position, interviews can, in principle, be treated as reports on external realities. The only condition for positivists is that strict protocols are observed. For emotionalists, the condition is that the interviewer should seek to overcome the presumed power imbalance with her interviewee.

According to the latter ('internalist') position, interviews do present interesting data. But these data express interpretive procedures or conversational practices present in what both interviewer and interviewee are *doing* through their talk and non-verbal actions (Baker, 1982; see Section 4.7).

As already noted, there is a tension in constructionism between internalist and externalist versions of interview data. Put in simpler terms, some constructionists, like Miller and Glassner, are not too sure whether interviews are purely local events or express underlying external realities.

The debate is seen in its clearest form in discussions about whether interview data can be biased. Within positivist work, there is an assumption that bias is a problem because of both bad interviewers *and* bad interviewees.

Thus we hear about the inability of 10 per cent of the adult population to fill out 'even simple questionnaires' (Selltiz et al., 1964: 241), and about the untrustworthiness of some respondents and their unfortunate lack of comprehension of social scientific language (Brenner, 1981: 116–17).

These fears of bias are reflected when constructionists worry about how informants may be concealing what the interviewer most wants to know (Denzin, 1970: 130). Both positivists and some constructionists may then find a common concern in the various ways in which interviewees are not fully moral or not intellectually up to scratch.

However, there are exceptions. For instance, in what is largely a positivist argument, Brown and Sime claim that:

> an account is neither naive nor an apology for behaviour, but must be taken as an informed statement by the person whose experiences are under investigation. (1981: 160)

Equally, there is a more helpful tendency in constructionism. This suggests that we need not hear interview responses simply as true or false *reports* on reality. Instead, we can treat such responses as *displays* of perspectives and moral forms.

The need to preserve and understand the reality of the interview account is central to the argument of many constructionists. Indeed, the ethnographic tradition (see Section 3.1) contains a way of looking at respondents' accounts which goes beyond categorizing them as 'true' or 'false'. William F. Whyte has observed:

> In dealing with subjective material, the interviewer is, of course, not trying to discover the *true attitude or sentiment* of the informant. He should recognise that ambivalence is a fairly common condition of man – that men can and do hold conflicting sentiments at any given time. Furthermore, men hold varying sentiments according to the situations in which they find themselves. (1980: 117)

Unlike Burgess and Denzin, but like Miller and Glassner, Holstein and Gubrium and Carolyn Baker, Whyte shows us how it is not always necessary to treat respondents' accounts as if they were scientific statements and subject them to possible refutation. This leads Whyte to ask questions about the causes of respondents' accounts ('the events and interpersonal relations out of which (they) arise'; 1980: 117).

Of course, this pays scant attention to the form and structure of such accounts, as discussed by Baker. However, in a paper first published in 1960, we can forgive Whyte neglecting the study of the interview as a narrative. An alternative approach, following Gilbert and Mulkay (1983), would be to treat interviews as giving us access to the *repertoire* of narratives that we use in producing accounts (see my discussion of discourse analysis in Section 6.4).

The question remains whether any bridging position is possible between these two apparently incompatible perspectives. Must we choose between seeing interviews as *either* potentially 'true' reports *or* situated narratives?

Let me make two observations which I hope are helpful. First, everything depends on our purposes at hand. Sometimes, as in Baker's work, it makes sense consistently to concentrate on the local or situated character of interview talk. At the other extreme, for instance in quantitative studies of voting intentions or patient satisfaction, it becomes appropriate to treat what interviewees say as potentially 'true' reports. And again, sometimes, not without some difficulty, one can try to follow up both issues, using Miller and Glassner's and Holstein and Gubrium's apparently 'twin-track' approach.

My second observation relates to Baruch's and Baker's studies discussed earlier. It might seem that if, like them, we focus on the local character of interview talk, we have privileged form over content. However, this is yet another misleading polarity. By analysing how people talk to one another, one is directly gaining access to a cultural universe and its content of moral assumptions. Such a position is intrinsic to Garfinkel's (1967) argument that accounts are part of the world they describe.

## 4.10 THREE PRACTICAL QUESTIONS – AND ANSWERS

In the light of the discussion above, I suggest here three questions that interview researchers might ask themselves.

### What status do you attach to your data?
Many interview studies are used to elicit respondents' perceptions. How far is it appropriate to think that people attach a single meaning to their experiences? May not multiple meanings of a situation (e.g. living in a community home) or of an activity (e.g. being a male football fan) be represented by what people say to the researcher, to each other, to carers and so on (Gubrium, 1997)?

This raises the important methodological issue about whether interview responses are to be treated as giving direct access to 'experience' or as actively constructed 'narratives' involving activities which themselves demand analysis (Holstein and Gubrium, 1995). Both positions are entirely legitimate but the position taken will need to be justified and explained.

### Is your analytic position appropriate to your practical concerns?
Some ambitious analytic positions (e.g. ethnomethodology, discourse analysis) may actually cloud the issue if your aim is simply to respond to a given social problem like 'students' perceptions of their future job prospects'. If so, it might be simpler to acknowledge that there are more complex ways of addressing your data but to settle on presenting your research as a *descriptive* study based upon a clear social problem.

*Do interview data really help in addressing your research topic?*
If you are interested in, say, what happens in school classrooms, should you be using interviews as your major source of data? Think about exactly why you have settled on an interview study. Certainly it can be relatively quick to gather interview data, but not as quick as, say, texts and documents. How far are you being influenced by the prominence of interviews in the media (see Atkinson and Silverman, 1997)?

In the case of the classroom, couldn't you observe what people do there instead of asking them what they think about it? Or gather documents that routinely arise in schools, e.g. pupils' reports, mission statements, and so on?

Of course, you may still want to do an interview study. But whatever your method you will need to justify it and show you have thought through the practical and analytical issues involved in your choice.

## 4.11  CONCLUSION

Interviews share with any conversation an involvement in moral realities. They offer a rich source of data which provide access to how people account for both their troubles and their good fortune.

Such observations are hardly surprising since the evidence for them is immediately before our eyes in our everyday experience. Only by following misleading correspondence theories of truth could it have ever occurred to researchers to treat interview statements as only potentially accurate or distorted reports of reality.

## KEY POINTS

- There are three different models relevant to interview data: positivism, emotionalism and constructionism.
- Each model provides different answers to questions about whether we should gather interview data and, if so, how to analyse them.
- These different answers were illustrated by three case studies of interview-based research.

### Recommended Reading

The best short introduction to analysing interview data, written from a constructionist perspective, is Holstein and Gubrium (1995). Silverman (1997a) contains important chapters by Miller and Glassner, Holstein and Gubrium and Baker. Fontana and Frey (2000) provide a recent survey of the literature which is sympathetic to many of the issues raised in this chapter.

Interviews have always been used to elicit autobiographical tales. For an introduction to the life history approach, see Miller (2000). The advent of the Internet now means that researchers need no longer be face-to-face with interviewees. Mann and Stewart (2000) provide a collection of papers on this issue, and Ryen and Silverman (2000) give an example of research based on e-mail interviews. The best discussion of the focus group method is provided by Bloor et al. (2001).

---

## Exercise 4.1

This exercise gives you an opportunity to think through the debate about whether it is appropriate to assess whether interview accounts are true or false. The following extract is taken from a study in which scientists were interviewed about the factors that influence changes in scientific theories (quoted by Gilbert and Mulkay, 1983: 10).

(S = scientist)

1  S:  To make changes you have to be highly articulate, persuasive, and
2       devastating. You have to go to the heart of the matter. But in doing this
3       you lay yourself open to attack. I've been called fanatical, paranoid,
4       obsessed . . . but I'm going to win. Time is on my side.

1 How might this extract be used to support the view that scientific research is largely influenced by scientific politics?
2 Why might you *not* be convinced by this view on the basis of this extract?
3 Why might it be important to understand the different *social contexts* in which scientists give an account of their work?
4 Can it be said *definitively* whether or not science is *essentially* a political process? If not, why not?

## Exercise 4.2

Below is an extract from an interview with an adult daughter who is caring for her mother – a victim of senile dementia – at home (Holstein and Gubrium, 1997: 124). The daughter is employed part-time, and shares the household with her employed husband and their two sons. The extract begins when the interviewer (I) asks the adult daughter (R) to describe her feelings about having to juggle so many needs and schedules.

```
 1  I:  We were talking about, you said you were a member of the, what did
 2      you call it?
 3  R:  They say that I'm in the sandwich generation. You know, like we're
 4      sandwiched between having to care for my mother . . . and my grown
 5      kids and my husband. People are living longer now and you've got
 6      different generations at home and, I tell ya, it's a mixed blessing.
 7  I:  How do you feel about it in your situation?
 8  R:  Oh, I don't know. Sometimes I think I'm being a bit selfish because I
 9      gripe about having to keep an eye on Mother all the time. If you let
10      down your guard, she wanders off into the back yard or goes out the
11      door and down the street. That's no fun when your hubby wants your
12      attention too. Norm works the second shift and he's home during the
13      day a lot. I manage to get in a few hours of work, but he doesn't like
14      it. I have pretty mixed feelings about it.
15  I:  What do you mean?
16  R:  Well, I'd say that as a daughter, I feel pretty guilty about how I feel
17      sometimes. It can get pretty bad, like wishing that Mother were just
18      gone, you know what I mean? She's been a wonderful mother and I
19      love her very much, but if you ask me how I feel as a wife and mother,
20      that's another matter. I feel like she's [the mother], well, intruding on our
21      lives and just making hell out of raising a family. Sometimes I put myself
22      in my husband's shoes and I just know how he feels. He doesn't say
23      much, but I know that he misses my company, and I miss his of course.
24      [Pause] So how do you answer that?
```

1 What do we learn here about R's feelings?
2 How do R and I together construct a story? What do you learn from that?
3 What have you learned from your analysis about the uses and limitations of emotionalism?

## Exercise 4.3

The extract below is taken from Carolyn Baker's study of 'adolescents' (1984: 308–9).

(I = interviewer; V = Victor, age 12)

```
 1  I:  Are there any ways in which you consider yourself still to be a child, or
 2      to have child-like interests or habits or attitudes?
 3  V:  Yeah I still like doin' things that I did when I was a kid you know like,
 4      y'know, Lego 'n that just building stuff you know like when I, I was a
 5      kid you know.
 6  I:  Yeah. You still take pleasure in that kind of thing.
 7  V:  Yeah, I get a friend over and we just build a, great big house 'n that,
 8      it's still just like doing it.
 9  I:  Do you feel at the same time that you're too – really too old for it or do
10      you not feel it's too
11  V:  Well when people say 'ah, he's still doin' that stuff' I don't really care. I
12      just do it in the living room 'n that, 'n it's still fun. Pretty soon I'll, I'll stop
13      doin' it but, when I get too old for it.
14  I:  Or when you no longer think it's fun.
15  V:  Yeah.
16  I:  Which one?
17  V:  How do you mean?
18  I:  What would make you stop, feeling you were too old for it or
19  V:  Yeah, like everyone buggin' me too much y'know 'n, it's not really that
20      bad just building a house or something y'know like, just show my mom
21      it'n everything just take it apart y'know, sort of something to do on a
22      rainy day
```

(1)   In what sense does this interview give us reliable information about how Victor sees himself?

(2)   With close attention to the text, show:

   (a)   how Victor accounts for potentially childlike activities
   (b)   how the interviewer identifies childlike activities
   (c)   how both Victor and the Interviewer attend to the implications of what the other is saying.

---

### Exercise 4.4

This exercise gives you an opportunity to work with some of Baruch's data and to compare his approach with others. Here are some extracts from interviews with mothers of children with congenital heart disease:

> Well um . . . the first thing the nurse who delivered him said was: 'Don't worry, it's alright. Everything's alright.' And I didn't even realize there was anything wrong with him to start with.

> When she was born they told me everything was perfectly alright. And I accepted it.

> He was very breathless and I kept saying to midwives and doctors and various bods that came round, um I said to the midwife look, I said, he's breathing so fast.

> He was sitting in his buggy just looking absolutely lifeless. So I thought right up to the doctor's and see what she says.

Now answer the following questions:

1 Is it helpful to check the accuracy of what these mothers are saying (e.g. by comparing them to case notes, medical accounts etc.)? Explain your answer.
2 Attempt a psychological interpretation of what these mothers are saying (refer to the discussion of Burton in Section 4.8).
3 Now attempt to show how these mothers construct their own moral adequacy using Baruch's concept of 'atrocity stories'. Is the same strategy used in every story?

---

# 5

# Texts

Having a separate chapter on 'texts' may look a little artificial. After all, to treat an interview as a narrative can mean looking for the same textual features as researchers working with printed material. Indeed, the mere act of transcription of an interview turns it into a written text.

To make things clearer, in this chapter I use *text* to identify data consisting of words and/or images which have become recorded without the intervention of a researcher (e.g. through an interview). For presentational purposes, the chapter will focus on written texts. The analysis of images will be discussed in Chapter 7.

Written texts and interviews have one more thing in common. Both underline the linguistic character of many qualitative data. Even if our aim is to search for supposedly 'external' realities in our data (e.g. class, gender, power), our raw material is inevitably the words written in documents or spoken by interview respondents.

Yet British and American social scientists have never been entirely confident about analysing written texts. Perhaps, in (what the French call) the Anglo-Saxon cultures, words seem too ephemeral and insubstantial to be the subject of scientific analysis. It might seem better, then, to leave textual analysis to literary critics and to concentrate on definite social phenomena, like actions and the structures in which they are implicated.

This uncertain attitude to language is also reflected in the way in which quantitative researchers sometimes begin with fairly arbitrary but measurable definitions of their 'variables'. The classic model is Durkheim's *Suicide* which offers a 'conclusive' definition of the phenomenon in its first few pages and then rushes off to investigate it in these terms. As Atkinson (1978) has pointed out, this method rules out entirely any analysis of the very social processes through which suicide is socially defined – particularly in the context of coroners' own definitions of the meanings of particular acts (see also my discussion of Blau and Schoenherr in Section 2.2).

Even in qualitative research, texts are sometimes only important as 'background material' for the 'real' analysis. Where texts are analysed, they are often presented as 'official' or 'common-sense' versions of social phenomena, to be undercut by the underlying social phenomena apparently found in the qualitative researcher's analysis of her interviewees' stories. The model is: the documents *claim* X, but we can *show* that Y is the case.

Take one example. In the UK, academic disciplines in higher education are subjected to external scrutiny and inspection of their research. The Research Assessment Exercise (RAE) is a system of peer review of every academic department's national and international reputation for high-quality research. As part of this exercise, every four or five years, each academic department prepares a long and detailed statement of its research achievements.

Of course, what might be called the 'politics' of this process is deeply fascinating to academics. For instance, how do departments present themselves to the world and what influences the judgements of their peers?

Because of my interest in these matters, I recently attended a presentation of some research on this very topic. The research data consisted of interviews with members of several departments as well as the documents these departments had submitted for the RAE. Yet the paper I heard dealt only with what these academics said when interviewed about this topic. When I asked about the written material, I was told this was only being used as 'background' material.

Here we see how qualitative researchers can sometimes privilege the accounts people give of themselves over data drawn from what they actually do when not being pestered by an interviewer's questions. Yet this is not the only way to proceed.

Paul Atkinson and Amanda Coffey (1997) have written about another review of British universities known as Teaching Quality Assessment (TQA). As they describe it:

> As part of the TQA, departments must submit a 'self-assessment'. This enshrines statements about the degree schemes, their philosophy and objectives; how those objectives are attained; how courses are intended to impart specific skills and competences to students; how examinations or other forms of assessment are used to test whether those skills have been acquired. In one sense, therefore, such self-assessments constitute a kind of description of the department or degree scheme in question. (1997: 52)

While TQA assessors will be influenced by their meetings with department members and by observation of their teaching, anybody who has submitted a CV when applying for a job knows that your own written depiction of your achievements (and limitations) will be very important.

In deciding the grading given by the TQA assessors, the department's written self-assessment is very important. For instance, those assembling the department's TQA report know that assessors are likely to pay attention to such matters as clarity of structure, recognition of current debates about academic teaching quality and constructive self-criticism.

This means that the rhetorical format of the TQA document matters a great deal. As Atkinson and Coffey note: 'it is clear that TQA self-assessments call for very particular kinds of "description"'.

Atkinson and Coffey now show us how an actual TQA document can be analysed. This document is reproduced as Table 5.1.

TABLE 5.1   *A TQA self-assessment document*

*Quality in sociology and social policy*

In defining quality in our subject areas we stress:

- provision of a core curriculum that incorporates the fundamental theoretical, methodological and substantive issues of the disciplines
- clear connections between research excellence and the teaching programme
- ability to allow students to pursue their own areas of interest, within a clear disciplinary framework.

In order to help students and staff attain these objectives we:

- combine formal lectures with small group teaching
- offer students opportunities for individual practical work
- provide student help and guidance through the personal tutor system.

*Source*: adapted from Atkinson and Coffey's, 1997: 53, presentation of Cardiff University self-assessment in Sociology and Social Policy in 1995

Here is one part of their comments about this document:

The layout itself is a valuable clue (and, more generally, the physical, material character of a document is an important feature for detailed attention). As can be seen, it betrays its character through various stylistic conventions. Most notably, the twin characteristics of lists and 'bullet-points' betray its character as an official document, with an essentially practical function. Lists can be analysed in more general terms. They can, of course, be occasional and ephemeral products, like shopping lists, but they often incorporate some implicit idea of order and importance. In singling out these particular features of the department, and in listing them as we have, we mark them as special and deserving particular attention. We lift them out of all the many things we might find to say about a department of sociology and social policy. Moreover, while no rank order of importance is implied here, the list of key features is intended to convey a sense of purpose and logic. The authors here are pursuing a familiar set of textual conventions in their attempt to convey a particular sense of order and structure to their self-evaluation. (1997: 53–4)

Of course, as Atkinson and Coffey note, many more features of this document may be teased out. For instance, we can analyse the terms actually used by the department to convey its commitment to 'teaching quality'.

**Attempt Exercise 5.1 about now**

Analysing material like the TQA document shows that qualitative researchers are quite wrong to neglect textual data. As Table 5.2 shows, texts are marvellous data for even novice researchers to analyse.

However, there is one obvious trap in analysing documents. Just as we may be tempted to treat interview responses as true or false depictions of inner 'experience', so we may scan texts in terms of their correspondence to 'reality'. If this tempted you when reading Table 5.1, remember that this is the way that the TQA assessors themselves will have read the Cardiff document. By contrast, the role of textual researchers is not to criticize or to assess particular

TABLE 5.2    *The advantages of textual data*

| |
|---|
| *Richness*    Close analysis of written texts reveals presentational subtleties and skills. |
| *Relevance and effect*    Texts influence how we see the world and the people in it and how we act: think of advertisements and CVs! |
| *Naturally occurring*    Texts document what participants are actually doing in the world – without being dependent on being asked by researchers. |
| *Availability*    Texts are usually readily accessible and not always dependent on access or ethical constraints. Because they may be quickly gathered, they encourage us to begin early data analysis. |

texts in terms of apparently 'objective' standards. It is rather to analyse how they work to achieve particular effects – to identify the elements used and the functions these play.

Once more Atkinson and Coffey make my point. As they caution:

> this document may be 'about' an academic department at Cardiff, but it is not a transparent description. You certainly cannot take the document and read off from it a picture of the department and its academic programme. That is not because the author(s) lied. The issue is not about honesty, or even about accuracy, in any simple sense. It reflects the extent to which documentary realities constitute distinctive levels of representation, with some degree of autonomy from other social constructions. (1997: 55)

We now have to examine how these 'levels of representation' can be identified. In this chapter, I consider *four* ways in which textual researchers have analysed how texts represent reality. Each is set out as follows with a brief definition:

1 **Content analysis**   This involves establishing categories and then counting the number of instances when those categories are used in a particular item of text, for instance a newspaper report. Because it is a quantitative method, it will not be discussed in detail in this text. However, I will later present a study of political articles (Silverman, 1982) which combines qualitative textual analysis with some simple word counts (see Tables 5.4 and 5.5).

2 **Analysis of narrative structures**   Ethnographers were not the first researchers to treat texts as creating their own 'realities'. The Ancient Greeks were aware of the transforming power of language and developed the science of rhetoric. Then, in the early years of the last century, Ferdinand de Saussure noted that language is comparable to other social institutions like systems of writing, symbolic rites and sign systems for the deaf. All these institutions are systems of signs and can be studied systematically. Saussure called such a science of signs 'semiology' (from the Greek *semeion* = sign). This science was later to be called *semiotics* and will be explained in detail in Chapter 7. In this chapter I will discuss how, inspired by Saussure, later writers showed us how to treat written texts as organized narratives.

3 **Ethnography**   As we saw in Chapter 3, ethnographers seek to understand the organization of social action in particular settings. Most ethnographic

data are based on observation of what people are saying and doing (and of the territories in which this talk and action takes place). However, in literate societies, written accounts are an important feature of many settings (Hammersley and Atkinson, 1983: 128). Therefore, ethnographers must not neglect the way in which documents, tables and visual material like advertisements and cartoons (see Chapter 7) exemplify certain features of those settings. Notable attention has been paid to the commonsense practices involved in assembling and interpreting written records. This work has refused to reduce texts to a secondary status and has made an important contribution to our understanding of everyday bureaucratic practices.

4 **Ethnomethodology** Following Garfinkel (1967), ethnomethodology attempts to understand 'folk' (*ethno*) methods (*methodology*) for organizing the world. It locates these methods in the skills ('artful practices') through which people come to develop an understanding of each other and of social situations. Following an important paper by Sacks (1974), a major focus of ethnomethodology has been on the skills we all use in producing and understanding descriptions – from a remark in a conversation to a newspaper headline. I will, therefore, conclude this chapter by an account of Sacks's concept of 'membership categorization'.

I now will return to a closer description of each of these four approaches.

## 5.1 CONTENT ANALYSIS

Content analysis is an accepted method of textual investigation, particularly in the field of mass communications. In content analysis, researchers establish a set of categories and then count the number of instances that fall into each category. The crucial requirement is that the categories are sufficiently precise to enable different coders to arrive at the same results when the same body of material (e.g. newspaper headlines) is examined (see Berelson, 1952). In this way, content analysis pays particular attention to the issue of the *reliability* of its measures – ensuring that different researchers use them in the same way – and to the *validity* of its findings – through precise counts of word use (see Selltiz et al., 1964: 335–42).

However, the theoretical basis of content analysis is unclear and its conclusions can often be trite. As Atkinson points out, one of the disadvantages of the coding schemes used in such enterprises as content analysis is that, because they are based upon a given set of categories, they furnish 'a powerful conceptual grid' (1992: 459) from which it is difficult to escape. While this 'grid' is very helpful in organizing the data analysis, it also deflects attention away from uncategorized activities (see my discussion of fieldnotes in Section 3.3.5).

In part, Atkinson's critique vitiates the claims of many quantitative researchers' attempts to produce reliable evidence about a large sample of texts. The meat of the problem with content analysis (and its relatives) is not simply Atkinson's point about overlooked categories but how analysts usually simply trade off their tacit members' knowledge in coining and applying whatever categories they do use.

For instance, in a lecture given in the 1960s, Harvey Sacks compared the social psychologist Bales's (1950) tendency to produce immediate categories of 'interaction process' with the relatively long time taken by experienced physicians to read the output of electroencephalographs (EEGs). For Sacks, you should not 'categorize . . . as it comes out' (1992, I: 28). Indeed, as we shall see in my later discussion of what Sacks called 'membership categorization', our ability to categorize quickly is properly treated as a research topic rather than a research resource.

By contrast, in some qualitative research, small numbers of texts and documents may be analysed for a very different purpose. The aim is to understand the participants' categories and to see how these are used in concrete activities like telling stories (Propp, 1968; Sacks, 1974), assembling files (Cicourel, 1968; Gubrium and Buckholdt, 1982) or describing 'family life' (Gubrium, 1992).

## 5.2 NARRATIVE STRUCTURES

The organization of systems of narration, within literature and elsewhere, has been of constant interest to writers influenced by Saussure's science of signs (see Section 7.2). I shall briefly discuss V.I. Propp's (1968) study *Morphology of the Folktale*, written in Russia in 1928, and its subsequent development by the French sociologist A.J. Greimas (1966).

Propp argues that the fairytale establishes a narrative form which is central to all story-telling. The fairytale is structured not by the nature of the characters that appear in it, but by the function they play in the plot. Despite its great detail and many characters, Propp suggests that 'the number of functions is extremely small' (1968: 20). This allows him to attend to a favourite distinction of structuralists between appearances (massive detail and complexity) and reality (a simple underlying structure repeated in different ways).

Propp suggests that fairytales in many cultures share similar themes, e.g. 'a dragon kidnaps the king's daughter'. These themes can be broken into four elements, each of which can be replaced without altering the basic structure of the story. This is because each element has a certain *function*. This is shown in Table 5.3.

Following this example, we could rewrite 'a dragon kidnaps the king's daughter' as 'a witch makes the chief's wife vanish', while retaining the same function of each element. Thus a function can be taken by many different roles. This is because the function of a role arises in its significance for the structure of the tale as a whole.

Using a group of 100 tales, Propp isolates 31 'functions' (actions like 'prohibition', 'violation' or, as we have seen above, 'disappearance'). These functions are played out in seven 'spheres of action': the villain, the provider,

TABLE 5.3    *A dragon kidnaps the king's daughter*

| Element | Function | Replacement |
| --- | --- | --- |
| Dragon | Evil force | Witch |
| King | Ruler | Chief |
| Daughter | Loved one | Wife |
| Kidnap | Disappearance | Vanish |

*Source*: adapted from Culler, 1976: 207–8

the helper, the princess and her father, the despatcher, the hero and the false hero.

Functions and 'spheres of action' constitute an ordered set. Their presence or absence in any particular tale allows their plots to be classified. Thus plots take four forms:

1  development through struggle and victory
2  development through the accomplishment of a difficult task
3  development through both 1 and 2
4  development through neither.

Thus, although any one character may be involved in any sphere of action, and several characters may be involved in the same sphere, we are dealing with a finite sequence:

> the important thing is to notice the number of spheres of action occurring in the fairytale is infinite: we are dealing with discernible and repeated structures. (Hawkes, 1977: 69)

Writing in 1966, Greimas agrees with Propp about the need to locate narrative form in a finite number of elements disposed in a finite number of ways. However, he modifies Propp's lists of elements. First, Propp's list of seven spheres of action can be reduced to three sets of structural relations: subject versus object (this assumes 'hero' and 'princess' or 'sought-for person'); sender versus receiver (includes 'father' and 'dispatcher'); and helper versus opponent (includes 'donor', 'helper' and 'villain'). As Hawkes shows, this reveals the simple structure of many love stories, i.e. involving relations between subjects and objects and between receivers and senders.

Second, Propp's 31 functions may be considerably reduced if one examines how they combine together. For instance, although Propp separates 'prohibition' and 'violation', Greimas shows that a 'violation' presumes a 'prohibition'. Hence they may be combined in one function: 'prohibition versus violation'. Hawkes points out that this allows Greimas to isolate several distinctive structures of the folk narrative. These include: contractual structures (relating to establishing and breaking contracts); performative structures (involving trials and struggles); and disjunctive structures (involving movement, leaving, arriving etc.).

**Attempt Exercise 5.2 about now**

This summarized presentation of the work of Propp and Greimas has underlined two useful arguments. First, the structuralist method reminds us that 'meaning never resides in a single term' (Culler, 1976) and consequently that understanding the articulation of elements is our primary task. Second, more specifically, it shows some aspects of how narrative structure works.

When one reflects how many qualitative data (interviews, documents, conversations) take a narrative form, as indeed do research reports themselves, then the analysis of the fairytale ceases to look like an odd literary pursuit.

However, although textual analysis, following Propp and Greimas, seems very attractive, we need to proceed carefully. If we are analysing how a text works, we should not forget how our own text has its own narrative structure, designed to persuade the reader that, confronted with any given textual fragment, 'we can see that' a favoured reading applies.

This issue arose when I examined (Silverman, 1982) a collection of papers discussing the future of the British Labour Party (Jacques and Mulhern, 1981). Many of the contributions provided a good instrument for predicting the election outcome in relation to Labour's shrinking social base. I selected two short papers by little-known trade union leaders which seemed to propose alternative versions of Labour's political past and future. In this discussion, I shall only consider the four-page text by Ken Gill.

Gill argues that the post-1950 period had seen a 'picture of advance' for the Labour Party. This advance is indexed by a move towards left-wing policies and left-wing leaders in both unions and the Labour Party.

One immediate critical rejoinder to this argument is that organizational and ideological advances have to be judged in relation to popular support – which, with one or two exceptions, dropped continuously at general elections after 1950.

However, this is to remain in a sense *outside* Gill's text. Such arguments tend to use isolated extracts and summaries as a means of deploying critiques. Following a method inspired by Propp, my aim was to avoid interpreting Gill's text in terms of alternative versions of reality but, instead, to enter within it.

Such *internal* analysis must seek to establish the realities the text itself brings into play. There was no difficulty in the programme. The problem was to find a method which would allow these realities to be described.

In order to get a sense of Gill's paper as a whole, I went through the text listing the subjects or agents mentioned. The agents named fell into three broad categories. References to trade unions and to groups defined by class were counted as instances of economic agents. These were distinguished from references to theorists and from references to political parties or tendencies. This produced Table 5.4.

Table 5.4 supports the suggestion that Gill's analysis concentrates on economically defined subjects or subjects defined with reference to other formal institutions. This apparent preference for formal structures was underlined when I counted the 'level' of agent to which Gill refers. Although not all the agents were classifiable in these terms, I discovered a clear preference for agents with an official or high-level position, as shown in Table 5.5.

| TABLE 5.4   Gill's agents | |
| --- | --- |
| Agent | Number |
| Economic | 16 |
| Theoretical | 5 |
| Political | 9 |
| None of the above | 1 |
| Total | 31 |

| TABLE 5.5   Agents' level | |
| --- | --- |
| Level of agent | Number |
| Leader or theorist | 14 |
| No rank or lower rank | 3 |
| Unclear | 14 |
| Total | 31 |

Tables 5.4 and 5.5 substantiated the impression that Gill has constructed a narrative which tells its tale from the top down. It is largely a tale of economic subjects, organized by existing institutions and their leaders. Moreover, further analysis revealed that Gill's text concentrates on activities relating to policy-making, or occupying particular political positions, like passing resolutions opposing the government. In only five cases did he refer to an agent's action; all these cases related to economic struggles.

These simple tabulations supported my argument that Gill's practice contradicted his theory. While Gill theorizes about movements towards socialism and democracy, the structure of his text is consistently elitist. Put another way, the elitist form of his tale runs directly contrary to its democratic message.

Some of this could, of course, be demonstrated by the use of brief extracts from Gill's piece followed by critical exegesis. However, this standard procedure of traditional (political, literary) criticism cannot generate such an analysis so forcefully or economically. Critical exegesis is prone to two damaging limitations: it may appeal to extra-textual realities, while de-emphasizing the realities constructed in the text under consideration; and/or it may base its case on isolated fragments of a text supported by a 'persuasive' argument.

## Attempt Exercise 5.3 about now

At this point, the alert reader may ask: doesn't your own method bear a striking resemblance to content analysis? If so, doesn't it risk the charges of triviality and of imposing (extra-textual) realities on the data through its methods of classification? In which case, can't your argument against traditional criticism be turned against yourself?

Now, of course, the tabulations I have just presented do share with content analysis one characteristic: both involve counting instances of terms used in a text. However, unlike naive forms of content analysis, the terms counted are *not* determined by an arbitrary or common-sense version of what may be interesting to count in a text.

Note that I have counted Gill's agents or 'subjects'. In Western cultures, at least, subjects are intrinsic to narratives: by analysing the construction of subjects, we get to the heart of the work of the text.

Moreover, I have sought to show how Gill's subjects are positioned in relation to particular activities and 'spheres of action'. This follows Propp's analysis of fairytales and Saussure's crucial argument, discussed in Chapter 7, that signs are not autonomous.

## 5.3 ETHNOGRAPHY

Like students of narrative, ethnographers are more concerned with the processes through which texts depict 'reality' rather than with whether such texts contain true or false statements. As Atkinson and Coffey put it:

> In paying due attention to such materials, however, one must be quite clear about what they can and cannot be used for. They are 'social facts', in that they are produced, shared and used in socially organized ways. They are not, however, transparent representations of organizational routines, decision-making processes, or professional diagnoses. They construct particular kinds of representations with their own conventions. (1997: 47)

The implications of this are clear:

> We should not use documentary sources as surrogates for other kinds of data. We cannot, for instance, learn through records alone how an organization actually operates day-by-day. Equally, we cannot treat records – however 'official' – as firm evidence of what they report . . . That strong reservation does not mean that we should ignore or downgrade documentary data. On the contrary, our recognition of their existence as social facts alerts us to the necessity to treat them very seriously indeed. We have to approach them for what they are and what they are used to accomplish. (1997: 47)

How do ethnographers approach texts 'for what they are'? Table 5.6 shows the many interesting questions that can be asked about texts. In this section, I will examine some of the answers that ethnographers have given to these questions.

Of course, written texts may include novels, newspapers and magazines, e-mail messages and official documents. In this section, I will focus on documents because they have been a fruitful area for ethnographic research. Subsequently, I will examine how newspapers and e-mail messages have been analysed using other approaches.

TABLE 5.6   *Ethnographic questions about texts*

| | |
|---|---|
| 1 | How are texts written? |
| 2 | How are they read? |
| 3 | Who writes them? |
| 4 | Who reads them? |
| 5 | For what purposes? |
| 6 | On what occasions? |
| 7 | With what outcomes? |
| 8 | What is recorded? |
| 9 | What is omitted? |
| 10 | What is taken for granted? |
| 11 | What does the writer seem to take for granted about the reader(s)? |
| 12 | What do readers need to know in order to make sense of them? |

*Source*: Hammersley and Atkinson, 1983: 142–3

I discuss below different kinds of documents, taken in the following order:

- files
- statistical records
- records of official proceedings
- e-mails.

It should be stressed that this is not a hard and fast or an all-embracing list of every kind of document. It is organized in this way purely for ease of presentation. Nonetheless, the discussion that follows tries consistently to pursue the analytic issues involved in dealing with textual data. Although there are always practical problems which arise in data analysis and techniques that can offer assistance, methodological problems should never be reduced to merely practical issues and 'recipe' solutions.

As I have already emphasized, people who generate and use such documents are concerned with how accurately they *represent* reality. Conversely, ethnographers are concerned with the *social organization* of documents, irrespective of whether they are accurate or inaccurate, true or biased.

### 5.3.1   *Files*

Like all documents, files are produced in particular circumstances for particular audiences. Files never speak for themselves. The ethnographer seeks to understand both the format of the file (for instance, the categories used in blank printed sheets) and the processes associated with its completion.

Selection interviews provide a good example of a setting where an inter-action is organized, at least in part, by reference to the categories to be found on some document that will later constitute a 'file'. For instance, a large British local government organization used the following record of job selection interviews with candidates in their final year at university (Silverman and Jones, 1976):

- name
- appearance
- acceptability
- confidence
- effort
- organization
- motivation
- any other comments

Following Hammersley and Atkinson's set of questions in Table 5.6, the ethnographer can immediately ask about which items are represented on this list and which are omitted. For instance, the fact that 'appearance' and 'acceptability' are cited and located at the top of the list, while 'ability' is omitted, gives us clues about the culture of the organization. So:

> successful candidates will be recognised in their preparedness to defer to 'commonsense' and to the accumulated wisdom of their seniors; to 'sell themselves' without implying that a university degree provides any more than a basis for further training. (1976: 31)

Some of this is seen in the completed file of one (unsuccessful) applicant to whom we gave a fictitious name. This is set out in Table 5.7.

TABLE 5.7  *A completed selection form*

| | |
|---|---|
| Name: | Chadwick |
| Appearance: | tall, slim, spotty-faced, black hair, dirty grey suit |
| Acceptability: | non-existent; rather uncouth |
| Confidence: | awful; not at all sure of himself |
| Effort: | high |
| Organization: | poor |
| Motivation: | none really that counts |
| Any other comments: | reject |

*Source:* Silverman and Jones, 1976: 31–2

It is tempting to treat such completed forms as providing the *causes* of selection decisions. However, two important points must be borne in mind before we rush to such a conclusion. First, such forms provide 'good reasons' for any selection decision. This means that we expect the elements of the form to 'fit' the decision recorded. For instance, we would be surprised if the 'reject' decision had been preceded by highly favourable comments about the candidate.

Thus the language of 'acceptability' provides a rhetoric through which selectors define the 'good sense' of their decision-making. It does not *determine* the outcome of the decision.

**Attempt Exercise 5.4 about now**

A telling example of this was provided when we played back tapes of selection interviews to selectors several months later without meeting the selectors' request to remind them of their decision. Predictably, on hearing the tapes, selectors often made a different decision than they had made at the time. Nevertheless, when told of their earlier decision, they were able to adjust their comments to take account of it. The 'acceptability' criterion (and its converse 'abrasiveness') thus served more as a means to 'rewrite history' (Garfinkel, 1967) than as a determinant of a particular selection decision.

The second point is that the files themselves are not simple 'records' of events but are artfully constructed with a view to how they may be read. For instance, in a study of a promotion panel at the same organization, I showed how the committee organized their discussion in a way which made their eventual decision appear to be sound. In particular, I identified a three-stage process:

1 beginning with premises all can accept (e.g. 'facts' everyone can agree upon)
2 appealing to rules in ways which make sense in the present context
3 reaching conclusions demonstrably grounded in the rules as applied to the facts (Silverman, 1973).

In order to produce 'sound' decisions, committees attend to relevant background circumstances which shape how 'facts' are to be seen. For instance, in the case of one candidate who had not made much progress, the following was said:

Extract 5.1  (extracts adapted from Silverman and Jones, 1976: 157–8)
Chair:  and, um, is no doubt handicapped in, you know, his career development
         by the fact that that department suddenly ha, ha
?:       yes, yes
Chair:  came to an end and he was, had to be pitched forth somewhere

Even when the facts are assembled, they ask themselves further questions about what the facts 'really mean'. For instance:

Extract 5.2
May:  He's been there a long while in this job has he not? Does he do it in exactly
         the same way as when he started?

Or again:

**Extract 5.3**
May: supposing he had people under his control who needed the softer form of encouragement (. . .) assistance rather than pushing and driving; could he handle that sort of situation?
?:   Yes, and not only could he, but he has done
May: He has, ah good

Gubrium and Buckholdt's (1982) study of a US rehabilitation hospital shows that a concern to assemble credible files may be a common feature of organizational activities. The authors show how hospital staff select, exchange and present information about the degree of physical disability and rehabilitation of patients and potential patients. Like reports of selection interviews, such descriptions are never context-free but are assembled or 'worked up' with reference to some audience:

> staff members work up descriptions of activities . . . using their knowledge of audience relevance in organizing what they say and write. (1982: ix)

I will briefly illustrate such 'working up' in the context of what the authors call 'third-party description'. This refers to descriptions assembled for insurers and government agencies rather than for patients or their families.

Rehabilitation at the hospital was paid for through government funds (via Medicare and Medicaid programmes) and insurance companies. An essential constraint, established by the US Congress in 1972, was a review agency called the Professional Standards Review Organization (PSRO). The PSRO looks at decision-making over patient intake and discharge with a view to limiting costs. For instance, the acceptable average stay for a rehabilitation patient had been calculated at 38 days.

A further constraint on the organization of patient care were two rules of insurance companies. First, the hospital's charges would not be paid if a patient could not have rehabilitation because of additional medical problems (e.g. pneumonia). Second, if a patient's stay is very short, the insurance company may decide, retrospectively, that the patient should not have been admitted in the first place. These constraints shape how admissions are organized and how patient 'progress' is described.

Admissions staff have to make an initial decision about whether or not a potential patient is suitable for rehabilitation or needs other services involving chronic or acute care. A rule of thumb when considering whether a patient should be admitted is that the patient should be able to benefit from at least three hours of therapy per day. However, staff recognize that the files they are sent are not conclusive and may 'shade the truth'. For instance, another institution may wish to discharge the patient, or the family may have exerted pressure for a transfer to the rehabilitation hospital. Consequently, admissions staff appeal to 'experience' and 'professional discretion' in working out what a potential patient's notes 'really mean'.

Appealing to these kinds of grounds, staff establish a basis for deciding what is 'really' meant by any file. Thus, in sorting out 'facts' from 'fancy', participants use a body of interpretive and rhetorical resources to define what will constitute 'reality' or 'the bottom line'.

Once a patient is admitted, the 'working up' of descriptions continues. 'Progress notes' are prepared at regular intervals and staff work at making them internally consistent and appropriate to the recommendation (just like selectors). For instance, staff talk about 'the need to make sure that the figures tell the right story' and regularly try out their accounts on colleagues by asking, 'How does that sound?'

The institutional interest is to show some sort of progress which will be sufficient to satisfy the funding agencies. Consequently, there is a pressure to identify simple problems where progress can readily be made and to seek patient statements which accord with the therapist's version of progress.

Gubrium and Buckholdt's work shows that hospital files can be treated as the outcome of a series of staff decisions grounded in the contingencies of their work. Similarly, Silverman and Jones reveal how records of selection interviews satisfy organizational conceptions of what is appropriate.

Both studies confirm that qualitative researchers are not primarily concerned with whether files are factually 'true' or 'false'. Instead, they focus on how such files reveal the practical decision-making of employees in the context of the constraints and contingencies of their work.

**Attempt Exercise 5.5 about now**

### 5.3.2 Statistical records

Until the 1960s, official statistics, like files, were treated as a more or less accurate *representation* of a stable reality. Of course, this did not mean that their reliability or validity were taken for granted. Particular statistics or measures were often found to be of dubious scientific status. However, it tended to be assumed, in these cases, that such data or measures could always be improved.

The 1960s saw a massive shift of focus among sociologists as documented below:

- Cicourel and Kitsuse (1963) showed how school statistics on educational performance depended upon the organized, practical judgements of school staff.
- Garfinkel revealed how coroners writing death certificates formulated accounts 'of how death *really*-for-all-practical-purposes happened' (1967: 12). As Garfinkel noted, 'really' in these cases referred, unavoidably, to common-sense understandings in the context of organizational contingencies.
- Sudnow (1968a) showed how hospital 'death' was recognized, attended to, and disattended to by hospital staff.

- Sudnow (1968b) revealed that US criminal statistics depended, in part, on a socially organized process of 'plea bargaining' through which defendants were encouraged to plead guilty.

Now, of course, many of these processes had already been recognized by sociologists and demographers. The difference was that such processes were no longer viewed as 'problems' which distorted the validity or reliability of official statistics. Instead, they were now treated in their own right, not as distortions of the phenomena they ostensibly measured but as *constitutive* of those phenomena. In other words, inspired by these studies, many sociologists now treated such phenomena ('death', 'guilt, 'ability') as *arising* within the very record-keeping activity which was supposed passively to record them.

This shift of focus did not mean that demography based on official statistics suddenly became worthless. As Hindess (1973) showed, one can pay attention to the social context of statistical production and still make use of statistics for both practical and analytical purposes. So the work that developed out of the insights of the 1960s is properly seen as having taken a divergent but non-competitive path to the continuing studies based on the use of official statistics.

For instance, Prior (1987) follows Garfinkel by looking at how 'deaths' are investigated by coroners. Prior puts it this way:

> men are more likely to have their deaths investigated, and to have their deaths regarded as 'unnatural', than are women. The same is true of the middle class as against the working class, the married as against the unmarried, widowed or single, and the economically active as against the inactive. (1987: 368)

However, in the case of decisions to do a post-mortem (autopsy) after 'violent' deaths, Prior finds that the figures go in the other direction: manual workers and the single, widowed or divorced are more likely to have an autopsy than the middle class or married.

Prior suggests that coroners use their 'common-sense knowledge' to treat sudden and violent death as more suspicious among the former groups. Although autopsy is generally more common after a death defined as 'violent', Prior notes that:

> in its search for the origins of death, forensic pathology tends to reserve the scalpel as an investigatory instrument for distinct and specific segments of the population. (1987: 371)

The implication is that statistical tables about causes of death are themselves the outcome of a decision-making process which needs to be described (see also Prior, 1997).

Consequently, for the qualitative researcher, statistics, like files, raise fundamental questions about the processes through which they are produced.

### 5.3.3 Official proceedings

Public or official records are not limited to statistical tables. A common feature of democracies is a massive documentation of official business covering legal proceedings, certain business meetings and the work of parliaments and parliamentary committees.

Such public records constitute a potential goldmine for sociological investigation. First, they are relevant to important issues – revealing how public and private agencies account for, and legitimate, their activities. Second, they are accessible; the field researcher does not have the problem, so common in observational work, of negotiating access.

Despite the potential of such work, it has been sadly neglected by field researchers. However, an important, relatively new source of studies in this area has been provided by the journal *Discourse and Society*.

I will take just one example: a study of the 1973 Watergate Hearings in the US Congress. Molotch and Boden (1985) show how their work on the text of these hearings arises in the context of a debate about the nature of power. They are not concerned with explicit power battles or with the ability to set agendas. Instead, they are concerned with a 'third face of power':

> the ability to determine the very grounds of the interactions through which agendas are set and outcomes determined . . . the struggle over the linguistic premises upon which the legitimacy of accounts will be judged. (1985: 273)

As they show, a problem resolved in all talk is that, while accounts are context-bound, a determinate account has 'somehow' to be achieved (see Garfinkel, 1967). Molotch and Boden apply this insight to the interrogation of President Nixon's counsel (John Dean) by the pro-Nixon Senator Gurney. Dean had made public charges about the involvement of the White House in the Watergate 'cover-up'. Gurney's strategy is to define Dean as someone who avoids 'facts' and just relies upon 'impressions'. This is seen in Extract 5.4.

**Extract 5.4 (Molotch and Boden, 1985: 280, adapted)**
(G = Senator Gurney; D = John Dean)
(Transcription conventions are given in the Appendix)

G: Did you dis*cuss* any aspects of the *Water*gate at that meeting with the President? For example, did you *tell* him anything about (1.4) what *Halde*man *knew* of or what Ehrlichman knew?

D: Well, given the- given the fact that he *told* me I've done a good job I assumed he had been very pleased with what ha- what had been going on . . .

G: Did you discuss what Magruder knew about Watergate and what involvement *he* had?

D: No, I didn't. I didn't get into any – I did not give him a report at that point in time

G: Did you discuss *cover*-up money *money* that was being raised and paid?

D: No, sir . . .

G: Well now how can you say that the President knew all about these *things* from a *simple* observation by him that Bob tells me you are doing a good job?

As Molotch and Boden show, Gurney's strategy is to insist on literal accounts of 'facts', not 'impressionistic' ones. Throughout Extract 5.4, for instance, Gurney demands that Dean state that he actually discussed the cover-up with Nixon. When Dean is unable to do this, Gurney imposes limits on Dean's ability to appeal to a context (Dean's 'assumptions') which might show that Dean's inferences were correct.

However, as Gurney knows, all accounts can be defeated by demonstrating that *at some point*, since they depend upon knowing the context, they are not 'really objective'. Hence:

> Demands for 'just the facts', the simple answers, the forced-choice response, preclude the 'whole story' that contains another's truth . . . [consequently] Individuals can participate in their own demise through the interactional work they do. (1985: 285)

### Attempt Exercise 5.6 about now

### 5.3.4  E-mails

It is now commonplace to remark that communication is increasingly mediated by information technology. Originally, telephone calls were a great impetus to research. Somehow, without visual cues, people managed to communicate with each other. Researchers investigated how we create an orderly structure here with stable expectations of the rights and obligations of, for instance, 'caller' and 'called' (see Section 6.3).

More recently, the Internet has been a crucial medium of largely text-based communication. Dependent upon ethically appropriate access, this has opened up a whole new field for ethnographic investigation of textual data including homepages, chatrooms and e-mail correspondence.

To give a taste of what such ethnographic research can reveal, I will take an example from a recent study in which I participated (Ryen and Silverman, 2000). Our dataset consisted of face-to-face interviews and e-mail exchanges between a Norwegian researcher (Ryen) and Asian businessmen.

The interviewees reported clear boundaries between Tanzanian African and Asian 'culture'. Broadly speaking, these Asian entrepreneurs travelled widely, used the latest technologies and were risk-takers. According to a conventional interpretation, in terms of an appeal to 'culture', our data show how Asian Tanzanian entrepreneurs constitute themselves as different from Tanzanian Africans and similar to Western Europeans.

By contrast, analysis of e-mails between Anne Ryen (AR) and one Asian businessman (to whom we gave the name Sachin) suggests the limits of an analyst's appeal to such use of 'culture' as an explanation. In particular, this Norwegian researcher's relative ease in communicating with Asian businessmen needs further investigation. Rather than explain it away in terms of cultural similarities, it is worth examining how both parties *achieve* mutual understanding.

For instance, we examined how AR and Sachin work at achieving agreed forms of 'sign-off' greetings at the end of their mutual e-mails. Sachin's first message ends as follows:

**Extract 5.5 (extracts from Ryen and Silverman, 2000)**
tell me more about yourself in your next e-mail . . .
love Sachin. [ending of first message 26.10.98]

AR replies, among other things:

**Extract 5.6**
I am married and have two small children. [30.10.98]

Presumably, even if she were married, AR might not have mentioned it. Note how in categorizing yourself, you categorize the other person (e.g. in this case as a 'friend' or something 'more'). Moreover, AR doesn't use 'love' as a greeting but *hilsen* (Norwegian for 'greetings'). Sachin monitors the category-bound implications here. His next message now ends:

**Extract 5.7**
regards Sachin. [05.11.98]

In his later messages, 'love' is again not used by Sachin but 'Well regards' [17.11.98], 'well cheerio' [10.12.98] and 'cheeeers' [26.12.98].

In her later correspondence [23.11.98], AR modifies her somewhat impersonal *hilsen* to *Beste hilsen* and then '*Kjaere* (=dear) Sachin!' [22.12.98].

Despite her self-identification as 'non-available', AR responds to Sachin's information that he intends to get married soon by writing:

**Extract 5.8**
Lucky woman to marry you – tell me more! [10.11.98]

Such banter is used by AR to maintain a 'friendly' relationship with a respondent who is, after all, giving his time freely to help her. As we see above, flattery ('lucky woman') is another reward that can be offered to research subjects. Later AR will refer to Sachin's 'energy' and 'vigour' (e.g. 23.11.98, data not shown). By the next month, after describing her work activities, AR adds:

**Extract 5.9**
And the most interesting, is an e-mail interview with an Asian businessman!!! [10.12.98]

Such 'friendly', non-instrumental framing can be used for a whole message. So one of AR's e-mails begins:

**Extract 5.10**
Sachin, this time I have no research questions. [30.11.98]

In the same message, she uses a reference to the weather to issue a lighthearted invitation:

> **Extract 5.11**
> So if you send me a mild summer wind and loads of sunshine, I'll invite you for dinner.

In these ways, AR and Sachin negotiate the parameters of their relationship, invoking a range of paired identities: researcher–researched; female–male; married woman–single man; friend–friend.

So AR begins by implying her sexual unavailability and this is recognized by Sachin's modification of his sign-off greetings. However, conscious of the rewards that research subjects rightly may expect, AR later shows her respondent that, just because she is 'unavailable', this does not mean that she cannot treat him as a friend or that, indeed, she is unaware of his attractiveness to other women.

Like other ethnographic work on texts, this research shows how, despite their relative newness, e-mails are yet another site, like files, statistical records and records of official proceedings, where identities are actively produced.

## Attempt Exercise 5.7 about now

The issue of identity takes us full circle back to my earlier critique of other approaches to textual analysis. My problem with content analysis was that its numerical outcomes were achieved through counting in terms of analysts' categories. While such categories can be well defined, they have an unknown relation to how participants themselves categorize (and count).

By contrast, narrative analysis does claim to access the active story-telling formats of participants. However, it usually reverts once again to an analyst's set of categories (e.g. hero/villain; leader/led).

Such forms of textual analysis leave themselves open to exactly the same charge that can be made about some observational research. This is why, as we saw in Chapter 3, Harvey Sacks made the following comment about much sociological research, whether qualitative or quantitative:

> All the sociology we read is unanalytic, in the sense that they simply put some category in. They may make sense to us in doing that, but they're doing it simply as *another member*. (Sacks, 1992, I: 41–2, my emphasis)

Fortunately, the kind of ethnographic work we have just been discussing does attempt to identify the categories used by ordinary participants ('members'). In my view, however, ethnography lacks a well-developed model to describe these categories. To find such a model, we must turn to ethnomethodology and, more particularly, Sacks's account of membership categorization devices.

## 5.4 ETHNOMETHODOLOGY: MEMBERSHIP CATEGORIZATION ANALYSIS

As we saw in Chapter 3, the work of the sociologist Harvey Sacks has raised some vital methodological questions for ethnographers and anyone else attempting to construct the social sciences as a set of 'observational' disciplines. Sacks puts the issue succinctly:

> Suppose you're an anthropologist or sociologist standing somewhere. You see somebody do some action, and you see it to be some activity. How can you go about formulating who is it that did it, for the purposes of your report? Can you use at least what you might take to be the most conservative formulation – his name? Knowing, of course, that any category you choose would have [these] kinds of systematic problems: how would you go about selecting a given category from the set that would equally well characterise or identify that person at hand? (1992, I: 467–8)

The classic statement of this problem is found in Moerman's (1974) self-critical treatment of his attempt to do a standard ethnography upon a Thai tribe (see Section 4.1). But the message has also been taken by intelligent ethnographers who, like Gubrium (1988), are centrally concerned with the descriptive process (see Section 3.1).

Sacks shows how you cannot resolve such problems simply 'by taking the best possible notes at the time and making your decisions afterwards' (1992, I: 468). Instead, our aim should be to try to understand when and how members do descriptions, seeking thereby to describe the apparatus through which members' descriptions are properly produced.

Consider this description in which the identities of the parties are concealed:

> The X cried. The Y picked it up.

Why is it that we are likely to hear the X as, say, a baby but not a teacher? Furthermore, given that we hear X as a baby, why are we tempted to hear Y as an adult (possibly as the baby's mother) (1992, I: 248–9)?

In fact, Sacks looks at the first two sentences of a story written by a child: 'The baby cried. The mommy picked it up.' Why do we hear the 'mommy' as the mother of this 'baby'? (1992, I: 236). Why do we hear the baby's cries as the 'reason' why the mommy picks it up?

Not only are we likely to hear the story this way, but we hear it as 'a possible description' without having observed the circumstances which it characterizes. Sacks asks:

> Is it some kind of magic? One of my tasks is going to be to construct an apparatus for that fact to occur. That is, how we come to hear it in that fashion. (1992, I: 236)

No magic lies behind such observations. Instead:

> What one ought to seek is to build an apparatus which will provide for how it is
> that any activities, which members do in such a way as to be recognisable as such
> to members, are done, and done recognisably. (1992, I: 236)

Returning to the way we read the children's story, Sacks observes that our reading is informed by the way we infer that the categories 'baby' and 'mommy' come from a collection of such categories which we call 'family' (1992, I: 238). While the 'family' connection can include many categories (i.e. not just 'baby' and 'mommy' but also 'daddy', 'daughter', 'grandmother' etc.), some categories are or can be built as two-set collections (e.g. gender, race) (1992, I: 47–8).

Of course, not any set of categories will be heard as a collection. As Sacks says:

> We only talk about a collection when the categories that compose it are categories
> that members do in fact use together or collect together, as 'male' and 'female' go
> together. (1992, I: 238)

Sacks notes that, as here, younger children's stories may have just one collection of categories – the 'family'. Young children apply this collection to virtually everyone, e.g. parents' friends become called 'aunt' and 'uncle' (1992, I: 368).

However, for children, like any population, there are always at least two collections of categories available (1972a: 32). This means that young children can at least choose between, say, 'auntie' and 'woman' as a way of categorizing a female.

Of course, one only has to read accounts of the 'same' event in two different newspapers to realize the large number of categories that can be used to describe it. For instance, as feminists have pointed out, women, but not men, tend to be identified by their marital status, number of children, hair colour and even chest measurement. Such identifications, while intelligible, carry massive implications for the sense we attach to people and their behaviour. Compare, for example, the following two descriptions:

A:  shapely, blonde, mother of 5.
B:  32-year-old teacher.

Both descriptions may 'accurately' describe different aspects of the same person. But each constitutes very definitely how we are to view that person (for instance, in A, largely in terms of certain ways of constructing gender).

Each identity is heard as a category from some collection of categories. For instance, in A, we hear 'mother' as a category from the collection 'family'. By contrast, in B, 'teacher' is heard as located in a collection of 'occupation'. The implication is that to choose one category from a collection excludes someone being identified with some other category from the same collection.

Sacks calls such a collection a **membership categorization device** (or MCD). This device consists of a collection of categories (e.g. baby, mommy, father = family; male, female = gender) and some rules about how to apply these categories. Sacks gives the definition of an MCD as follows:

> *Membership categorization device* Any collection of membership categories, containing at least a category, which may be applied to some population containing at least a member, so as to provide, by the use of some rules of application, for the pairing of at least a population member and a categorization device member. A device is then a collection plus rules of application. (1972a: 332)

What are these 'rules of application' to which Sacks refers? First, returning to the child's story, we can note that the characters are described by *single* categories ('baby', 'mommy'). So we are not told, as we might be, about, say, the baby's age or gender or the mommy's occupation or even hair colour. And this did not cause us a problem when we first saw 'The baby cried. The mommy picked it up'.

The intelligibility of single category descriptions gives us what Sacks calls the *economy rule*, defined as follows:

> *Economy rule* A single category from any membership categorization device can be referentially adequate. (1992, I: 246)

Of course, single category descriptions are not confined to childrens' stories: sometimes categories like 'man', 'nurse' or 'pop star' are entirely referentially adequate. Nonetheless, the economy rule gives us a very interesting way of addressing how children's socialization may occur. First, children seem to learn single names ('mommy', 'daddy'). Then they learn how such single categories fit into collections ('family') and come to understand various combinatorial tasks (e.g. man = daddy or uncle). So, even at this early stage of their lives, say before they are two years old, children have already learned 'what in principle adequate reference consists of' (1972a: 35) and, in that sense, have entered into society or been 'socialized'.

A second rule of application of MCDs suggests that once one category from a given collection has been used to categorize one population member, then other categories from the same collection *may* be used on other members of the population. Sacks refers to this as the *consistency rule*. It is formally defined as follows:

> *Consistency rule* If some population of persons is being categorized, and if some category from a device's collection has been used to categorize a first member of the population, then that category or other categories of the same collection *may* be used to categorize further members of the population. (1972b: 33, my emphasis; see also 1992, I: 225, 238–9, 246).

The import of the consistency rule may be seen in a simple example. If we use an abusive term about someone else, we know that a term from the same collection can be used on us. Hence one of the reasons we may avoid name-calling is to avoid the development of this kind of slanging match.

However, any category can belong in more than one collection. For instance, as Sacks points out, 'baby' can belong to the collection 'stage of life' ('baby', 'child', 'teenager', 'adult') as well as the 'family' collection (1992, I: 239). 'Baby' also used to be a term of endearment heard in Hollywood movies; here it belonged to a different collection ('romance'?).

Sacks suggests a 'hearing rule' (1992, I: 239) or *consistency rule corollary* (1992, I: 248) which provides a way for members to resolve such ambiguities. When a speaker uses two or more categories to describe at least two members of a population and it is possible to hear the categories as belonging to the same collection, we hear them that way. That is why, in the story with which Sacks begins, we hear 'baby' and 'mommy' in relation to the collection 'family'.

> *Consistency rule corollary*  If two or more categories are used to categorize two or more members to some population, and those categories can be heard as categories from the same collection, then hear them that way. (1992, I: 247)

The consistency rule and its corollary have explained why we hear 'mommy' and 'baby' as part of the same 'family' collection, but it remains to be seen 'how "the mommy" is heard as "the mommy of the baby"' (1992, I: 247). The answer stems from the way in which 'the family' is one of a series of collections that be heard as constituting a 'team', i.e. as part of the same 'side'. In this respect, 'mommy' and 'baby' belong together in the same way as, say, 'defender' and 'striker' in a football team. Sacks suggests that one of the central properties of teams is what he calls *duplicative organization*.

> *Duplicative organization*  [We treat any] set of categories as defining a unit, and place members of the population into cases of the unit. If a population is so treated and is then counted, one counts not numbers of daddies, numbers of mommies, and numbers of babies but numbers of families – numbers of 'whole families', numbers of 'families without fathers', etc. (1972a: 334; see also 1992, I: 225, 240, 247–8)

Duplicative organization helps us in seeing that 'mommy' and 'baby' are likely to be heard as part of the same 'unit'. But a further rule suggests that this is not just likely but is required (in the sense that if you saw things differently then your seeing would appear to other members to be 'odd'). This rule is the *hearers' maxim for duplicative organization*, defined as follows:

> *Hearers' maxim for duplicative organization*  If some population has been categorized by use of categories from some device whose collection has the 'duplicative organization' property, and a member is presented with a categorized population which *can be heard* as co-incumbents of a case of that device's unit, then hear it that way. (1992, I: 248)

Given that the MCD 'family' is duplicatively organized, the hearer's maxim shows us how we come to hear 'the mommy' as not anyone's 'mommy' but as 'the mommy of this baby' in the children's story (1992, I: 248).

However, 'mommy' and 'baby' are more than co-incumbents of a team; they are a pair of positions with mutual rights and obligations (e.g. the baby's right to be fed but, perhaps, obligation not to cry all the time). In this respect, mothers and babies are like husband–wife, boyfriend–girlfriend and even neighbour–neighbour. Each party has certain standardized rights and obligations; each party can properly expect help from the other.

Sacks refers to such groupings as *standardized relational pairs* (SRPs). SRPs, in turn are found in *collection R* which is defined as follows:

> *Collection R* [A collection of paired relational categories] that constitutes a locus for a set of rights and obligations concerning the activity of giving help. (1972a: 37)

One aspect of the relevance of such paired relational categories is that they make observable the *absence* of the second part of any such pair. In this way, we come to observe that a player in a sporting team is 'missing' or, more seriously, treat non-incumbency of, say, a spouse as being a criterion of suicidalness (see the discussion of suicide at the beginning of this chapter, and see Sacks, 1972a: 38–40).

Such absences reveal what Sacks calls the *programmatic relevance* of collection R:

> *Programmatic relevance* If R is relevant, then the non-incumbency of any of its pair positions is an observable, i.e. can be proposedly a fact. (1972a: 38)

Just as collection R consists of pairs of categories who are supposed to offer each other help, there are also categories of 'experts' who offer specialized help with particular 'troubles'. When paired with some 'troubled' person (e.g. a client), they constitute what Sacks refers to as *collection K*:

> *Collection K* A collection constructed by reference to special distributions of knowledge existing about how to deal with some trouble. (1972a: 37)

Collection R and its programmatic relevance allow someone to analyse their situation as, say, properly 'suicidal'. Collection K then allows such a person to know who can offer dispassionate 'advice'.

Collection K implies something about the proper activities of particular categories of people like professionals and clients. This helps to resolve one further issue in our reading of the children's story: why do we have no trouble with the description, 'The baby cried. The mommy picked it up'? To put it more pointedly: why might it look odd if the story read, 'The mommy cried. The baby picked it up'?

The answer, of course, lies in the way in which many kinds of activities are commonsensically associated with certain membership categories. So, if we know what someone's identity is, we can work out the kind of activities in which they might engage. Similarly, by identifying a person's activity (say, 'crying'), we provide for what their social identity is likely to be (in this case, a 'baby').

Sacks refers to activities which imply identities as *category-bound activities* (CBAs). His definition is as follows:

> *Category-bound activities*  Many activities are taken by members to be done by some particular or several particular categories of members where the categories are categories from membership categorization devices. (1992, I: 249)

CBAs explain why, if the story had read: 'The X cried. The Y picked it up', we might have guessed that X was a baby and Y was a mommy. Crying, after all, is something that babies do, and picking up (at least in the possibly sexist 1960s) is something that mothers did. Of course, as Sacks points out, no description is ever completely unambiguous. For instance, 'crying' is not confined to 'babies' and an adult can themselves sometimes be called a 'baby' (1992, I: 584).

Members employ their understandings of category-bound activities to recognize and to resolve such ambiguities. Above all, everyday understanding is based on the assumption that, as Sacks puts it, 'they' (i.e. some category of people) do such things (1992, I: 179). As Sacks shows, through this means, you can do 'racism' while avoiding the use of explicitly ethnic or religious categories.

Moreover, what we know about CBAs allows us to construct what he calls 'a search procedure' when some problematic occurrence appears to have occurred. For instance, Sacks shows how, at the end of 1963, the claim that the possible assassin of President Kennedy was a 'communist' clinched the case for many people: after all, assassination of capitalist leaders appears to be category-bound to the category 'communist infiltrator'. In this way, CBAs allow us to 'tie' certain activities to particular categories. As Sacks puts it:

> if somebody knows an activity has been done, and there is a category to which it is bound, they can damn well propose that it's been done by such a one who is a member of that category. (1992, I: 180)

So, even though we know people other than babies do cry, we are unlikely to say 'the baby cried' if we mean 'the baby of the family'. In this way, the selection of a category makes many potential ambiguities 'non-arisable' (1992, I: 585).

However, on the face of it, when we observe an activity, it could be ambiguous to find the right category to which the activity is bound. Take the case of a 'confession'. As Sacks points out, we know that *both* Catholics and criminals often 'confess'. Have we observed a Catholic or a criminal?

We see at once that, in everyday life, there is rarely such an ambiguity. For, of course, we all know that a Catholic confessional 'looks' very different from a criminal confessing (1992, I: 584–5). So, if we read about a 'confession', the surrounding features of the story (e.g. as part of a 'criminal' story) will tell us immediately how we are to understand it. And all this happens without any sense of problem or ambiguity.

For instance, we do not have any problem of seeing a struggle between two adults (a man and a woman) and a younger person as a 'family fight' (1992, I: 90–1). Ambiguity about this interpretation is much more likely to appear when parties subsequently review an incident. For example, in a legal context, what unambiguously appeared to be merely a 'family fight' can be transformed into a 'kidnap'. At the time of the incident, however, witnesses properly treat things as 'normal' partly because they assume it's not your job but the police's to note crimes (1992, I: 92). Thus we invoke our knowledge of category-bound activities and standardized relational pairs as ways of resolving incongruity.

Returning to our children's story, 'baby' is also a member of a class which Sacks calls *positioned categories* (i.e. baby, adolescent, adult) in which the next category is heard as 'higher' than the preceding one. This creates the possibility of praise or complaint by using a higher or lower position to refer to some activity. So an adolescent can be described as acting in a very 'adult' way or as acting just like a 'baby'.

> *Positioned categories*  A collection has positioned categories where one member can be said to be higher or lower than another (e.g. baby . . . adolescent . . . adult). (1992, I: 585)

The fact that activities are category-bound also allows us to praise or complain about 'absent' activities. For instance, a baby that does not cry where it might (say at a christening) can be properly praised, while an older child that does not say 'thank you' when passed some food or given a present is properly blamed (1992, I: 585).

In both these cases, certain activities become remarkable because of the way their presence or absence is tied to a stage of life. Stage of life is important not only, say, around the dinner table but also in the compilation of official statistics. As Sacks points out, statisticians, like the rest of us, know that, for instance, being unmarried or unemployed are not usually descriptors appropriate to school-age children (1992, I: 68).

As we have seen, because of the category-bound character of many activities, we can establish negative moral assessments of people by describing their behaviour in terms of performing or avoiding activities inappropriate to their social identity. For instance, it may be acceptable for a parent to 'punish' a child, but it will be usually unacceptable for a child to 'punish' a parent.

Notice that, in both cases, 'punish' serves as a powerful picture of an activity which could be described in innumerable ways. Social life, unlike foreign films, does not come with subtitles attached. Consequently, how we define an activity is morally constitutive of it. So if, like other sociologists, Sacks is talking here about norms, unlike them (and members) he is not treating norms as descriptions of the *causes* of action. Instead, he is concerned with how 'viewers use norms to provide some of the orderliness, and proper orderliness, of the activities they observe' (1972a: 39).

How viewers use norms take us back to the way we read 'the baby cried'. For instance, babies can be boys or girls. Why then, might not a 'cry' be reported as, say, 'the boy cried'? The answer, says Sacks, lies in a *viewer's maxim* for category-bound activities which is set out as follows:

> *Viewer's maxim*  If a member sees a category-bound activity being done, then, if one sees it being done by a member of a category to which the activity is *bound*, see it that way. (1992, I: 259, my emphasis)

Through the viewer's maxim, we can understand why we would see a 'baby' rather than 'a boy' crying, since a 'baby' is a category that we treat as having 'a special relevance for formulating an identification of its doer' (1992, I: 259).

Finally, why do we treat it as unremarkable that the story reports as the next activity: 'The mommy picked it up'? As we have already seen, part of the answer lies in the way in which we hear 'mommy' and 'baby' as part of a 'team'. In this respect, duplicative organization is relevant.

In addition, however, picking a baby up is likely to be heard as a norm such that where a baby cries, a mother properly picks it up. In this regard, we have, therefore, a *second viewer's maxim*, defined as follows:

> *Second viewer's maxim*  If one sees a pair of actions which can be related by the operation of a norm that provides for the second given the first, where the doers can be seen as members of the categories the norm provides as proper for that pair of actions, then (a) see that the doers are such members, and (b) see the second as done in conformity with the norm. (1992, I: 260)

Through using this second viewer's maxim, viewers provide for the 'proper orderliness of the activities they observe' in at least two ways:

1  by explaining the occurrence of one activity given the occurrence of the other; and
2  by explaining the sequential order of the two activities (first one, then the other) (1992, I: 260).

Until now, you may have got the impression that because membership categorization allows people to make sense of people and events, Sacks is implying that everything always proceeds smoothly in the best of all possible worlds. Far from it. First, we have already seen how categorization can just as easily serve to maintain racism as to preserve harmony. Second, the use of quite innocent knowledge of category-bound activities can unintentionally allow horrible crimes to be committed.

For instance, in the recent case of the young British boys who murdered the child Jamie Bulger, witnesses who had seen Jamie holding the hands of his two assassins reported that they had assumed they were watching a child with his two elder brothers. Similarly, as Sacks notes, people working in organizations, faced with possibly life-threatening events, do not take remedial action themselves but report what they have seen to the next person up the hierarchy (1992, I: 64). This is because, in organizations, categories are organized into hierarchies. So people assume that they need to refer to another category to confirm some act or to take some action.

Most readers, I suspect, will by now be pretty sated with concepts. I therefore want to slow up the pace somewhat and offer three illustrations and applications of these concepts. The first comes from one of Sacks's own lectures.

### 5.4.1 The navy pilot story

Given that many categories can be used to describe the same person or act, Sacks's task was:

> to find out how they [members] go about choosing among the available sets of categories for grasping some event. (1992, I: 41)

Of course, Sacks does not mean to imply that 'society' determines which category one chooses. Instead, he wants to show the active interpretive work involved in rendering any description and the local implications of choosing any particular category.

A particularly telling example of this is to be found in Sacks's analysis of a *New York Times* story about an interview with a navy pilot about his missions in the Vietnam War (1992, I: 205–22, 306–11). Sacks is specially interested in the story's report of the navy pilot's answer to a question in the following extract:

> *The navy pilot story*
>
> How did he feel about knowing that even with all the care he took in aiming only at military targets, someone was probably being killed by his bombs?
>
> 'I certainly don't like the idea that I might be killing anybody,' he replied. 'But I don't lose any sleep over it. You have to be impersonal in this business. Over North Vietnam I condition myself to think that I'm a military man being shot at by another military man like myself.' (1992, I: 205)

Sacks invites us to see how the pilot's immediate reply ('I certainly don't like the idea . . .') shows his commitment to the evaluational scheme offered by the journalist's question. For instance, if the pilot had instead said 'Why do you ask?', he would have shown that he did not necessarily subscribe to the same moral universe as the reporter (and, by implication, the readers of the article) (1992, I: 211).

Having accepted this moral schema, Sacks shows how the pilot now builds an answer which helps us to see him in a favourable light. The category 'military man' works to defend his bombing as a category-bound activity which reminds us that this is, after all, what military pilots do. The effect of this is magnified by the pilot's identification of his co-participant as 'another military man like myself'. In this way, the pilot creates a standardized relational pair (military man–military man) with recognizable mutual obligations (bombing/shooting at the other). In terms of this pair, the other party cannot properly complain or, as Sacks puts it:

> there are no complaints to be offered on their part about the error of his ways, except if he happens to violate the norms that, given the device used, are operative. (1992, I: 206)

Notice also that the pilot suggests 'you have to be impersonal in this business'. Note how the category 'this business' sets up the terrain on which the specific SRP of military men will shortly be used. So this account could be offered by either part of the pair.

However, as Sacks argues, the implication is that 'this business' is one of many where impersonality is required. For:

> if it were the case that, that you had to be impersonal in this business held only for this business, then it might be that doing this business would be wrong in the first instance. (1992, I: 206)

Moreover, the impersonality involved is of a special sort. Sacks points out that we hear the pilot as saying not that it is unfortunate that he cannot kill 'personally' but rather that being involved in this 'business' means that one must not consider that one is killing persons (1992, I: 209).

However, the pilot is only proposing an SRP of military man–military man. In that sense, he is inviting the North Vietnamese to 'play the game' in the same way as a child might say to another, 'I'll be third base.'

However, as Sacks notes, in children's baseball such proposals can be rejected:

> if you say 'I'll be third base', unless someone else says 'and I'll be . . .' another position, and the others say they'll be the other positions, then you're not that thing. You can't play. (1992, I: 307)

Of course, the North Vietnamese indeed did reject the pilot's proposal. Instead, they proposed the identification of the pilot as a 'criminal' and defined themselves as 'doing police action'.

As Sacks notes, these competing definitions had implications which went beyond mere propaganda. For instance, if the navy pilot were shot down then the Geneva Conventions about his subsequent treatment would only properly be applied if he indeed were a 'military man' rather than a 'criminal' (1992, I: 307).

Having used one of Sacks's own examples, I now turn briefly to two of my own.

### 5.4.2 A newspaper headline

Father and Daughter in Snow Ordeal

This headline appeared in the inside pages of the London *Times*. I want to examine how we can understand the sense it makes using MCD analysis. A schematic reading of this headline, using MCD analysis, is set out in Table 5.8.

TABLE 5.8    *Father and Daughter in Snow Ordeal*

| Concept | Explanation | Headline |
|---|---|---|
| Category | Any person can be labelled in many 'correct' ways | Persons later described as 'supermarket manager' and 'student' |
| Membership categorization device (MCD) | Categories are seen as grouped together in collections | MCD = 'family' |
| Economy rule | A single category *may* be sufficient to describe a person | Single categories are used here |
| Consistency rule | If one person is identified from a collection, then a next person *may* be identified from the same collection | 'Daughter' is from same MCD as 'father' |
| Duplicative organization | When categories can be heard as a 'team', hear them that way | 'Daughter' is the daughter of *this* 'father' |
| Category-bound activities | Activities may be heard as 'tied' to certain categories | 'Snow ordeal' is *not* heard as tied to 'father–daughter' categories; this is why the story is newsworthy |
| Standardized relational pairs (SRPs) | Pairs of categories are linked together in standardized, routine ways | 'Father' and 'daughter' assumed to be linked together through 'caring' and 'support'; how could 'snow ordeal' have happened? |

I want to develop Table 5.8 by asking you a series of questions. In answering them, you will see the skill involved in constructing headlines which encourage us to read the story beneath the headline.

First, note that the persons are described as 'father' and 'daughter'. Given that people can be described in many 'correct' ways, what are the implications of choosing these categories? For instance, the story below the headline tells us that the 'father' is also a 'supermarket manager' and the 'daughter' is a 'school student'. How would we have interpreted the story if the headline had read as follows?

> Supermarket Manager and School Student in Snow Ordeal

Moreover, given that headline, would we have felt like reading the rest of the story and, if so, why?

What are the implications of the chosen categories being derived from the MCD 'family'? And what does it tell us about the saliency of this MCD, that single categories will do (remember that the economy rule is not obligatory)?

Why don't we doubt that this is not any daughter but the daughter of this 'father'? And why is 'snow ordeal' newsworthy in the context of the MCD 'family'?

**Attempt Exercise 5.8 about now**

### 5.4.3  A lonely hearts advertisement

> Active attractive cheerful blonde widow graduate no ties many interests. Seeks mutually fulfilling life with fit considerate educated 60 year old. Details please to Box 123. (*The Times*, 30 January 1993)

Like the headline, this advertisement was chosen at random in order to show how MCD analysis can fruitfully analyse *any* material of this kind. Let us begin by focusing upon the category 'widow'. Now I take it that, while successful newspaper headlines make you want to read the story, the success of a lonely hearts advertisement is judged by the number of appropriate responses that it elicits. If we look at 'widow' in this light, it may evoke a series of contrasting category-bound activities as follows:

> *Type 1*  Miserable (dressed in black); given up on life.
> *Type 2*  Freed from monogamy, light-hearted and ready for multiple relationships ('the merry widow').

Note how this advertisement attends to both these types of category-bound activities. Type 1 is rejected primarily by the use of the adjective 'cheerful', although 'blonde' also neatly contrasts with the black of mourning. Moreover, this is not a description of someone who has given up on life. This widow is 'active' and has 'many interests'. On the other hand, we are specifically not encouraged to assume that this is a 'merry widow'. She is, after all, an intelligent person ('graduate') who seeks one person for a 'mutually fulfilling life'.

However, the subtleties of the descriptive apparatus particularly stand out in what the advertisement does *not* say as follows:

- We are not told the age of the 'widow' (although the consistency rule might imply that she is close to 60 like the man she seeks, this is not necessarily so).
- We are not told the gender of the person she is seeking.

How can the reader resolve these puzzles? First, the advertiser uses the term 'active' to describe herself. Now we may assume that someone, say, in their twenties is 'active'. To state that you are active is thus hearable as what Sacks calls a category modifier. Consequently, we can assume that this is at least a middle-aged person. Second, since the advertiser describes herself in the context of a previous heterosexual relationship ('widow'), we may assume that, without contrary evidence and following the consistency rule, she is seeking a man here.

**Attempt Exercise 5.9 about now**

### 5.4.4  Summary

The examples that we have just been considering demonstrate that membership categories are far from being the inert classificatory instruments to be found, say, in the more rigid forms of content analysis or in Bales's categorizations of 'interaction process'.

By contrast, MCDs are local members' devices, actively employed by speakers and hearers to formulate and reformulate the meanings of activities and identities. Unlike more formalistic accounts of action found in content analysis and some versions of narrative analysis, Sacks shows us the nitty-gritty mechanisms through which we construct moral universes 'involving appropriate kinds of action and particular actors with motives, desires, feelings, aspirations and sense of justice' (Gubrium, personal communication).

Like Garfinkel (1967), Sacks wanted to avoid treating people as 'cultural dopes', representing the world in ways that some culture demanded. Instead, Sacks approached 'culture' as an 'inference-making machine': a descriptive apparatus, administered and used in specific contexts.

## 5.5  CONCLUSION

I hope that, by the end of this chapter, the reader is not feeling punch-drunk! We have indeed covered an enormous amount of ground.

The wide scope of the chapter arose for two reasons. First, I am convinced that qualitative sociologists make too little of the potentialities of texts as rich data. Second, I am also convinced that there are several powerful ways of analysing such data.

Three threads have run through my presentation of different ways to analyse such textual data (for a development of this argument, see Silverman, 2000: 41–3).

### The importance of a clear analytic approach

Successful textual studies recognize the value of working with a clearly defined approach. Having chosen your approach (e.g. narrative analysis, ethnography or Sacks's analysis of membership categorizations), treat it as a 'toolbox' providing a set of concepts and methods to select your data and to illuminate your analysis.

### The relevance of theory to textual analysis

The distinctive contribution that qualitative research can make is by utilizing its theoretical resources in the deep analysis of small bodies of publicly shareable data. This means that, unlike much quantitative research, including content analysis, we are not satisfied with a simple coding of data. Instead, we have to work to show how the (theoretically defined) elements we have identified are assembled or mutually laminated.

### The importance of detailed data analysis

Like many other qualitative approaches, textual analysis depends upon very detailed data analysis. To make such analysis effective, it is imperative to have a limited body of data with which to work. So, while it may be useful initially to explore different kinds of data (e.g. newspaper reports, scientific textbooks, magazine advice pages), this should usually only be done to establish the dataset with which you can most effectively work. Having chosen your dataset, you should limit your material further by only taking a few texts or parts of texts (e.g. headlines).

In the course of this chapter, we have rapidly moved between several complex and apparently different theories – all the way from narrative analysis to ethnomethodology. However, if the reader has grasped at least one useful way of thinking about textual analysis, then I will have achieved my purpose.

Let me also add that I will return to some of these concepts in a later chapter. In Chapter 6 we will encounter the other side of Sacks's work – on the sequential organization of conversation.

## KEY POINTS

- Texts provide rich, naturally occurring, accessible data which have real effects in the world.
- The role of textual researchers is not to criticize or to assess particular texts in terms of apparently 'objective' standards. It is rather to analyse how they work to achieve particular effects.
- I considered *four* ways in which textual researchers have analysed how texts represent reality: content analysis, analysis of narrative structures, ethnography and membership categorization device analysis.

## Recommended Reading

The most useful texts on narrative analysis and ethnography are Pertti Alasuutari (1995), Amanda Coffey and Paul Atkinson (1996) and Barbara Czarniawska (1998). More advanced books are Paul Atkinson (1990) and the chapters on analysing texts in my edited collection *Qualitative Research* (1997a).

My book *Harvey Sacks* (1998) is an introduction to the ideas of Harvey Sacks (Chapters 5 and 7 deal with MCD analysis). Volume I of Sacks's *Lectures on Conversation* (1992) is a marvellous resource: see especially his discussions of category-bound activities (I: 179–81, Lecture 8, Fall 1965; I: 301–2, Lecture 4, Spring 1966; I: 333–40, Lecture 8, Spring 1966; I: 568–96, Lectures 11–14, Spring 1967); the consistency rule (I: 326–7, Lecture 7, Spring 1966); the hotrodders example (I: 169–74, Lecture 7, Fall 1965; I: 396–403); the navy pilot example (I: 205–22, Research Notes, Fall 1965; I: 306–7, Lecture 5, Spring 1966; and the child's story (I: 223–31, Appendix A and B, Fall 1965; I: 236–66, Lectures 1–2(R), Spring 1966).

---

### Exercise 5.1

Return to the TQA material contained in Table 5.1. We have just seen how the 'bullet point' structure can be analysed. Now examine its *content*.
   Here is a *clue*:

> This material contains many phrases that will seem awfully familiar to academic readers. For instance: 'core curriculum', 'within a clear disciplinary framework' and, in later parts not shown, 'well resourced learning environment', 'student monitoring'. These, and expressions like them, are not necessarily part of the everyday talk, even of academics, but they, and phrases like them, are now massively familiar to academics who find themselves composing and consuming such documents. (Atkinson and Coffey, 1997: 54)

1  What can you say about the words and phrases used here? What terms are used (and what are avoided)?
2  How does this language create a particular 'impression' of the department concerned?
3  Now imagine that you have access to interviews with the academics who prepared this document and with the TQA assessors. What use would such data be in analysing this text?

## Exercise 5.2

This is part of the life story of a Finnish man attending an alcohol clinic (adapted from Alasuutari, 1990):

1  When I was a child, the discipline was very strict. I still remember when
2  my younger brother broke a sugar cup and I was spanked. When my
3  father died, my mother remarried. The new husband did not accept
4  my youngest brother. When I was in the army, my wife was unfaithful to
5  me. After leaving the army, I didn't come home for two days. I started
6  to drink. And I began to use other women sexually. I drank and I brawled,
7  because I was pissed off and because her treacherousness was in my
8  mind. When I came to the alcohol clinic, it made me think. I abstained for
9  a year. There was some progress but also bad times. I grew up
10  somewhat. When the therapist changed, I was pissed off and gave it
11  all up.

1  Using what you have read about Propp and Greimas, identify the following elements in this story:
   (a)  functions (e.g. 'prohibition' or 'violation')
   (b)  spheres of action (e.g. the villain, the provider, the helper, the princess and her father, the dispatcher, the hero and the false hero)
   (c)  structures, e.g. subject versus object (includes 'hero' and 'princess' or 'sought-for person'); sender versus receiver (includes 'father' and 'dispatcher'); and helper versus opponent (includes 'donor', 'helper' and 'villain').
2  What can be said about the *sequence* of actions reported?
3  Having done this analysis, what features would you look for in other life stories?

## Exercise 5.3

The following is an extract from a speech made by an English Member of Parliament in the late 1960s. The topic was a Race Relations Bill then going through the British Parliament. The MP was Enoch Powell and the speech became (in)famous as the 'Rivers of Blood' speech because Powell concludes his argument against laws on racial discrimination by saying: 'Like the Roman, I see the River Tiber foaming with much blood.' This extract occurs earlier in the speech (Mercer, 1990):

1  Nothing is more misleading than comparison between the Commonwealth
2  immigrant in Britain and the American Negro. The Negro population of

3   the United States, which was already in existence before the United States
4   became a nation, started literally as slaves and were later given the
5   franchise and other rights of citizenship . . . The Commonwealth immigrant
6   came to Britain as a full citizen, to a country which knew no discrimination
7   between one citizen and another, and he entered instantly into the
8   possession of the rights of every citizen, from the vote to free treatment
9   under the National Health Service . . . But while to the immigrant entry to
10  this country was admission to privileges and opportunities eagerly sought,
11  the impact upon the existing population was very different. For reasons
12  which they could not comprehend, and in pursuit of a decision by default,
13  on which they were never consulted, they found themselves made strangers
14  in their own country. They found their wives unable to obtain hospital beds
15  in childbirth, their children unable to obtain school places, their homes and
16  neighbourhoods changed beyond recognition . . . At work they found that
17  employers hesitated to apply to the immigrant worker the standards of
18  discipline and competence required of the native-born worker; they began
19  to hear, as time went by, more and more voices which told them that they
20  were now the unwanted. On top of this, they now learn that a one-way
21  privilege is to be established by Act of Parliament: a law, which cannot, and
22  is not intended to, operate to protect them or to redress their grievances, is
23  to be enacted to give the stranger, the disgruntled and the agent-
24  provocateur the power to pillory them for their private actions.

1  Identify the subjects that the text constructs (e.g. 'immigrants', 'native-born'),
   the activities in which they engage and the relations that are established
   between them.
2  On this basis, why was Powell's speech so powerful? (Here is a clue:
   look at how the term 'stranger', first used on line 13, takes on a different
   meaning in line 23).
3  How could the same textual strategies be used to *oppose* his arguments?

## Exercise 5.4

The following is a completed selector's report using the same form as found
in Table 5.7:

| | |
|---|---|
| Name: | Fortescue |
| Appearance: | tall, thin, straw-coloured hair, neat and tidy |
| Acceptability: | high; pleasant, quite mature, sensible man |
| Confidence: | very good; not conceited but firm, put himself across very well |
| Effort: | excellent academic record |
| Organization: | excellent, at both school and university |

| Motivation: | keen on administration and very well informed on it; has had considerable experience; quite well informed about both the organization and its functions generally |
|---|---|
| Any other comments: | call for interview; first-rate. |

1  What conclusions may be drawn from how the selector has completed this form, e.g. what sort of features does he find praiseworthy or not needing comment?
2  Does the completed form help us in understanding why certain candidates are selected at this organization? If so, how? If not, why not?
3  If you were told that this selector came to a different decision when played a tape-recording of the same interview some months later, what would you make of this fact? What research questions could be asked now?

## Exercise 5.5

In a discussion of how records are assembled on 'juvenile delinquents' in the US justice system, Cicourel (1968) considers the case of Linda, aged 13. Linda first came to the attention of the police when she reported that she had been kidnapped by four boys. She said that she had been coaxed away from a party by them and admitted that she had told them that she would get drunk and then have sexual intercourse with one of them. After stealing some alcohol, the boys took her to a club where they all got drunk and she had sex with the youngest boy. Although the boys sought to depict Linda as a 'slut', the police viewed Linda as an 'attractive' victim with no prior record. However, some weeks later, acting on information from Linda's parents, the police saw Linda in a drunken state and obtained an admission that she had had sex with ten boys. She was now charged as in danger of leading a lewd and immoral life.

Here are extracts from an interview between Linda (L) and a female probation officer (PO) after Linda's arrest:

```
 1  PO:  You're not pregnant?
 2  L:   No
 3  PO:  Have you used anything to prevent a pregnancy?
 4  L:   Once X (one of her boyfriends) used one of those things
 5  PO:  Did you ever feel scared about getting pregnant?
 6  L:   No, I was always trying to get even with my parents
 7  PO:  You sort of wanted to get even with them?
 8  L:   Yes. I always wanted to get even with other people. My mother gets
 9       mad at me. I love my father. I know that's what's wrong with me.
10       I talk about this with my parents. I don't know why.
```

The probation officer's report suggests that Linda needs psychotherapy and suggests that she be institutionalized for three to six months' treatment.

1 How does the PO organize her questioning to support her eventual recommendation?
2 Is there any evidence that Linda is colluding with the PO in a particular interpretation of her past behaviour?

---

## Exercise 5.6

Here is a further extract from the Watergate Hearings (see Section 5.3.3). At this point, Dean is trying to implicate Nixon in the 'cover-up' operation:

```
 1   D:    When I discussed with him [Nixon] the fact that I thought he ought
 2         to be aware of the fact I thought I had been involved in the
 3         obstruction of justice . . . He told me, John, you don't have any
 4         legal problems  to worry about . . .
 5   G:    Did you discuss any specific ob- instances of obstruction of justice?
 6   (1.3)
 7   D:    Well, I'd- Senator, from- based on conversations I'd had with
 8         him- I had worked from-
 9   G:    I am talking about this meeting.
10   D:    Yes, I understand. I'm answering your question. Uh- the- eh-you
11         c- y- I can tell when-when uh I am talking with somebody if they
12         have some conception of what I am talking about- I had the
13         impression that the President had some conception of what I
14         was talking ab[out
15   G:                   [But I am not talking about impressions. That is what
                   I am trying to
16         get away from. (0.8) I am talking about specific instances.
```

1 Using this material, show what strategies Senator Gurney is using to discredit John Dean's evidence.
2 Show how Dean tries to sustain the credibility of what he is saying.
3 Why might Dean's appeal to what 'I can tell when I am talking with somebody' be seen as 'a risky strategy' by Molotch and Boden (1985)?

---

### Exercise 5.7

Select a series of past e-mail messages between yourself and another person. To satisfy ethical issues, ask the permission of your correspondent to use her/his messages for research purposes. To simplify analysis, limit your data to messages which total no more than 20 lines.

   Now identify the identities invoked and the activities described in these messages. Examine how the meanings of these identities and activities are maintained or change over the course of the correspondence.

---

### Exercise 5.8

This exercise allows you to use MCD analysis on a newspaper headline (Eglin and Hester, 1992):

   Engagement Was Broken – Temperamental Young Man Gassed Himself

Using what you have learned from MCD analysis, examine:

1 What categories are used here, and with what effects?
2 Why might the headline make us want to read the rest of the story?

---

### Exercise 5.9

Here is another 'lonely hearts' advertisement, chosen from the same newspaper (see Section 5.4.3):

   Good looking (so I am told!) Englishman, 35, tall, professional, seeks very attractive lady, preferably non-smoker, to wine, dine and make her smile. Age unimportant. Photo appreciated. Please reply to Box 789.

1 What does this advertisement *infer* about the advertiser or the 'lady' sought even though it does not tell us these things directly?
2 Show how we can see this by examining how this advertisement uses the following devices:

- categories
- MCDs
- the economy rule
- the consistency rule

- category-bound activities
- standardized relational pairs
- positioned categories.

# 6

# Naturally Occurring Talk

When social science researchers begin to design a research study, they encounter a series of choices about how narrowly to define their research problem and which method or methods of data collection are appropriate to its study. If we consider the methods so far discussed in this book – observation, interviews and texts – our choice appears to be very clear-cut.

Using research interviews (or focus groups) involves actively creating data which would not exist apart from the researcher's intervention (**researcher-provoked** data). By contrast, observation or the analysis of written texts, audiotapes or visual images deals with activities which seem to exist independently of the researcher. This is why we call such data **naturally occurring**: they derive from situations which exist independently of the researcher's intervention.

However, like most social science concepts, the opposition between naturally occurring and researcher-provoked data should not be taken too far. Indeed, no data are ever untouched by human hands. If we choose to observe, our data do not speak for themselves but have to be recorded (and transformed) into fieldnotes. Equally, audio and video recordings usually end up being transcribed using particular researcher-designed interventions which are never 'perfect' but only more or less useful. Moreover, the character of such data will be crucially affected by where you position your recording equipment and/or point your camera.

All this suggests that here, as elsewhere, we should treat appeals to 'nature' (as in the term 'naturally occurring') with considerable caution. Nonetheless, providing we do not push it too far, it can still be helpful to make use of the distinction between two kinds of data: naturally occurring and researcher-provoked. Indeed, if we can, at least to some extent, study what people are actually doing in 'naturally occurring' situations, why should we ever want to work with 'researcher-provoked' data?

Most quantitative researchers have a straightforward answer to this question. Data gathered from naturally occurring settings often appear horribly messy and unreliable to quantitative types. If you want to measure things reliably, then, they argue, it helps to create carefully controlled settings and to use well-tested research instruments like questionnaires or laboratory experiments.

By contrast, qualitative researchers who work with researcher-provoked data do not always seem to have thought through their choices. Certainly, open-ended interviews and focus groups can give you data much more quickly than observation and/or recording – although more slowly than texts. Moreover, many researchers claim that it is often not possible to obtain access to naturally occurring settings appropriate to a given research topic – even though this sometimes shows a lack of imagination on their part (see my discussion of methods for studying 'the family' in Section 3.4.4).

Such instrumental factors (speed, lack of alternatives), however, conceal the appeal of methods like the interview and the focus group to a particular research model (*emotionalism*) and more generally to a set of mass-media-driven assumptions deriving from what I have called the interview society (Section 1.3).

Asking people what they think and feel appears to have an immediacy, even 'authenticity', which curiously is believed to be absent in naturally occurring data. So, even when you have tapes or observations of behaviour, you are tempted to 'complete the picture' by interviewing the people concerned about what they were thinking or feeling at the time. The arguments for and against researcher-provoked data are summarized in Table 6.1.

TABLE 6.1    Why work with researcher-provoked data?

| For | Against |
|---|---|
| Speed | What about texts? |
| Easy access | Public data usually available |
| Authenticity of interviews | Reflects temptations of the interview society |
| Interviews help you to understand behaviour | Participants do not need access to each other's thoughts |

By contrast, some qualitative researchers prefer to work with 'naturally occurring' data although their reasons may differ. For the ethnographers of the Chicago School, the real form of immediacy was out on city streets and they wanted to 'tell it like it is' by observing life as it happened. However, their *naturalistic* focus meant that they usually sought to combine observation with interviews with key informants.

For a later generation of researchers, influenced by *constructionism* and *ethnomethodology*, audiotapes of naturally occurring conversation provided marvellous data to analyse how people actually went about constructing a social world together.

Although you may be inclined to think of conversation as trivial ('merely' talk), it is worth reflecting that conversation is the primary medium through which social interaction takes place. In households and in more 'public' settings, families and friends relate to one another through talk (and silence!). At work, we converse with one another and the outcome of this talk (as in meetings or job selection interviews) is often placed on dossiers and files. As Heritage argues:

the social world is a pervasively conversational one in which an overwhelming proportion of the world's business is conducted through the medium of spoken interaction. (1984: 239)

Indeed, what Heritage calls 'the world's business' includes such basic features as telling news, deciding if one should commit suicide, and a child learning how to converse with its mother (see Sacks, 1992; Silverman, 1998: ch. 1).

Yet, even if you are unconvinced by the argument that conversation is central to making the social world, there is still a strong methodological argument which suggests that audiotapes of naturally occurring talk are useful data. To understand why, we must return to the work of Harvey Sacks.

## 6.1  WHY WORK WITH TAPES?

The kind of phenomena I deal with are always transcriptions of actual occurrences in their actual sequence. (Sacks, 1984: 25)

Sacks stresses that one should work with 'actual occurrences' of talk. So, even though twentieth-century philosophers like Wittgenstein (1968), Austin (1962) and Searle (1969) have had important things to say about the things we do in conversation, they do not study actual talk but work with invented examples and their own intuitions about what it makes sense to say.

For Sacks, on the contrary:

One cannot invent new sequences of conversation and feel happy with them. You may be able to take 'a question and answer', but if we have to extend it very far, then the issue of whether somebody would really say that, after, say, the fifth utterance, is one which we could not confidently argue. One doesn't have a strong intuition for sequencing in conversation. (1992, I: 5)

Unlike philosophers, ethnographers do not usually invent conversations. Instead, they observe and record their observations through fieldnotes (see Section 3.3.5). Why did Sacks prefer to use an audio recorder?

Sacks's answer is that we cannot rely on our notes or recollections of conversations. Certainly, depending on our memory, we can usually sum-marize what different people said. But it is simply impossible to remember (or even to note at the time) such matters as pauses, overlaps, inbreaths and the like.

Now whether you think these kinds of things are important will depend upon what you can show with or without them. Indeed, you may not even be convinced that conversation itself is a particularly interesting topic. But, at least by studying tapes of conversations, you are able to focus on the 'actual details' of one aspect of social life. As Sacks put it:

My research is about conversation only in this incidental way, that we can get the actual happenings on tape and transcribe them more or less, and therefore have something to begin with. If you can't deal with the actual detail of actual events then you can't have a science of social life. (1992, II: 26)

Tapes and transcripts also offer more than just 'something to begin with'. They have three clear advantages compared with other kinds of qualitative data:

1   Tapes are a public record.
2   Tapes can be replayed and transcripts improved.
3   Tapes preserve sequences of talk.

Let me expand a little on this list. In the first place, tapes are a public record, available to the scientific community, in a way that fieldnotes are not. Second, they can be replayed and transcriptions can be improved and analyses can take off on a different tack unlimited by the original transcript. As Sacks told his students:

> I started to play around with tape recorded conversations, for the single virtue that I could replay them; that I could type them out somewhat, and study them extendedly, who knew how long it might take . . . It wasn't from any large interest in language, or from some theoretical formulation of what should be studied, but simply by virtue of that; I could get my hands on it, and I could study it again and again. And also, consequentially, others could look at what I had studied, and make of it what they could, if they wanted to disagree with me. (1992, I: 622)

A third advantage of detailed transcripts is that, if you want to, you can inspect sequences of utterances without being limited to the extracts chosen by the first researcher. For it is within these sequences, rather than in single turns of talk, that we make sense of conversation. In this way, tapes and transcripts preserve sequences of talk. As Sacks points out:

> having available for any given utterance other utterances around it, is extremely important for determining what was said. If you have available only the snatch of talk that you're now transcribing, you're in tough shape for determining what it is. (1992, I: 729)

There remains the potential charge that data based mainly on audio recordings are incomplete. We see Sacks's response to this issue when a student on his lecture course asked a question about 'leaving out things like facial expressions' from his analysis (1992, II: 26). Sacks at once conceded that 'it would be great to study them [such things]. It's an absence.' Nonetheless, he constructs a two-part defence of his data.

First, the idea of 'completeness' may itself be an illusion. Surely, there cannot be totally 'complete' data any more than there can be a 'perfect' transcript? Second, Sacks recognized some of the undoubted technical problems involved in camera positioning and the like if you were to use videos (1992, II: 26–7). These are the very issues that have been addressed, if not resolved, by more recent work based on video-recorded data (e.g. Heath, 1986; Heath and Luff, 1992; Heath, 1997). I will return to this work in Chapter 7.

However, as always in science, everything will depend on what you are trying to do and where it seems that you may be able to make progress. As Sacks put it:

one gets started where you can maybe get somewhere. (1992, I: 26)

Getting started, in Sacks's sense, means repeated, careful listening to your tapes. As you listen, you build an improving version of a transcript. In Section 6.2, I discuss why you need to transcribe your tapes and what you need to put into your transcripts.

## 6.2 TRANSCRIBING AUDIOTAPES

As already noted, even if some people are able to remember conversations better than others, we are unlikely to be able to recall such potentially crucial details as pauses and overlaps. Indeed, even with a tape-recording, transcribers may 'tidy up' the 'messy' features of natural conversation such as length of pauses or overlapping or aborted utterances.

Features like pauses matter to all of us, not just to analysts of conversations. Indeed, they are one basis on which, as Sacks (1992) has pointed out, reading somebody else's mind, far from being some paranoid delusion, is both routine and necessary in everyday life. Look at Extract 6.1.

> **Extract 6.1 (Levinson, 1983: 320, simplified)**
> 1  C:  So I was wondering would you be in your office on Monday by any chance?
> 2       (2.0)
> 3  C:  Probably not

The numbers in brackets on line 2 indicate a 2 second pause. The presence of this pause gives us a clue to how C can guess that the person he is questioning might indeed not be in his office on Monday (line 3). This is because when there is a pause when it is someone's turn to speak, we can generally assume the pause will foreshadow some difficulty. Hence C is able to read the pause as indicating that the other person is unlikely to be in his office on Monday and say 'Probably not' in line 3.

Now consider Extract 6.2. This is taken from an interview between a health adviser (H) and a patient who has requested an HIV test. H is offering a piece of advice about condom use and her patient is a young woman who has just left school.

> **Extract 6.2 (Silverman: counsel: 6.3)**
> 1  H:  it's *important* that you tell them to (0.3) use a condom (0.8) or to practise safe
> 2       sex that's what using a condom means.
> 3       (1.5)
> 4  H:  okay?

In Extract 6.2, line 4, H asks 'okay?', which may be heard as a request for the patient to indicate that she has understood (or at least heard) H's advice about condom use. As with Extract 6.1, we can see that a pause in a space where a speaker might have taken a turn at talk (here at line 3) has indicated some difficulty to the previous speaker.

Indeed, it is likely that H heard an earlier difficulty. Note that in line 1 there is a pause of 0.8 seconds. It is not unreasonable to assume that since the patient has not used this space to indicate some understanding of what H has just said (for instance, by saying 'mm'), H's explanation of what 'using a condom means' (lines 1–2) is given precisely in (what turns out to be) an unsuccessful attempt to overcome this difficulty.

At this point you may be wondering how these transcripts can give such precise lengths of pauses. In fact, you do not need any advanced technology for this. Although transcribers may use complicated timing devices, many others get into the habit of using any four-syllable word which takes about a second to say. If you then say this word during a pause, you can roughly count each syllable as indicating a one-quarter of a second pause.

However, pauses are not the only features that you may need to record. In the Appendix (see p. 303), I provide a simplified set of transcription symbols.

It should not be assumed that the preparation of transcripts is simply a technical detail prior to the main business of the analysis. As Atkinson and Heritage (1984) point out, the production and use of transcripts are essentially 'research activities'. They involve close, repeated listenings to recordings which often reveal previously unnoted recurring features of the organization of talk. The convenience of transcripts for presentational purposes is no more than an added bonus.

As an example, the reader might examine Extract 6.3, based on the transcribing conventions listed in the Appendix, which report such features as overlapping talk and verbal stress as well as pauses (in parts of a second).

**Extract 6.3 (Her: 0II: 2: 4: ST)**
(S's wife has just slipped a disc)
```
1  H:  And we were wondering if there's anything we can do to help
2  S:  [Well 'at's
3  H:  [I mean can we do any shopping for her or something like tha:t?
4       (0.7)
5  S:  Well that's most ki:nd Heatherton .hhh At the moment
6       no:. because we've still got two bo:ys at home
```

In Extract 6.3, we see S refusing an offer made by H. Heritage shows how S's refusal (lines 5–6) of H's offer displays three interesting features. First, when S does not take an early opportunity to accept H's offer (after 'anything we can do to help', line 1), H proceeds to revise it. Second, S delays his refusal via the pause in the slot for his turn at line 4. Third, he justifies it by invoking a contingency about which H could not be expected to know.

Why should S and H bother with these complexities? The answer lies in the way in which they end up by producing an account which blames nobody. In an early work, Erving Goffman (1959) similarly suggested that a persistent consideration of interactants is to protect one another's public self-esteem, or 'face'. In doing whatever people are doing, they take into consideration the moral standing of themselves and their co-interactants that their doings project. In the ordinary course of events, this consideration entails the *protection* of the positive moral standing of the self and of others.

We can develop Goffman's observation by noting that certain actions – typically actions that occur in response to other actions, such as invitations, offers or assesments – can be marked as *dispreferred*, that is, problematic in one way or another. Thus, rejections of invitations or offers, or disagreements in response to assessments, can be performed in such a way that encodes their problematic status. Conversely, an acceptance of an invitation or offer, or an agreement with an assessment, can be performed in a way that does not exhibit such problematic status.

Subsequent research has identified a number of practices through which the *dispreferred* status of an action can be marked. According to Heritage (1984: 265–80), these practices include:

1　The action is delayed within a turn or across a sequence of turns.
2　The action is commonly prefaced or qualified within the turn in which it occurs.
3　The action is commonly accomplished in mitigated or indirect form.
4　The action is commonly accounted for.

These actions together constitute what has been called *preference organization*. But note that the concept of 'preference', when used in this sense, does not refer to inner experiences of the actors about 'problems' or the lack of them involved in performing certain actions (Levinson, 1983). Furthermore, the distinction between preferred and dispreferred actions does not involve an *a priori* categorization of actions as problematic or non-problematic. Rather, the distinction between 'preferred' and 'dispreferred' action formats involves a resource for the interactants, through the use of which they can portray their actions as problematic or as not problematic in the interaction at hand.

We can see how conversationalists can prevent problems arising if we return to Extract 6.1.

**Exract 6.1 (Levinson, 1983: 320, simplified)**
1　C:　So I was wondering would you be in your office on Monday by any chance?
2　　　　(2.0)
3　C:　Probably not

C's question (at line 1) is one of those kinds of questions that we hear as likely to precede some other kind of activity. For instance, we all know that, if somebody asks if we will be free on Saturday night, an invitation is in the offing. Here we can guess that if C had got a positive reply, he would then have gone on to offer a request or an invitation.

Why should speakers proceed in this indirect way? The answer is to do with what Goffman called 'face' and what we have called 'preference organization'. By asking a question about someone's whereabouts or plans, speakers avoid others having to engage in the 'dispreferred' act of turning down an invitation. If we reply that we are busy, the invitation need never be offered. The prior question thus helps both parties: the recipient is not put in the position of having to turn down an invitation and, if the question elicits negative information or a meaningful pause (as in Extract 6.1), the questioner is saved from losing face by being able to avoid offering an invitation that is doomed to be declined.

The detailed transcription symbols shown in Extract 6.3 and explained in the Appendix derive from the approach called conversation analysis (CA). CA is based on an attempt to describe people's methods for producing orderly social interaction. These methods include what we have called 'preference organization'.

As we have seen, CA's concern with the *sequential* organization of talk means that it needs precise transcriptions of such (commonsensically) trivial matters as overlapping talk and length of pauses. Close, repeated listenings to recordings often reveal previously unnoted recurring features of the organ-ization of talk. Such listenings can most fruitfully be done in group data sessions. As described by Paul ten Have (1998), work in such groups usually begins by listening to an extract from a tape with a draft transcript and agreeing upon improvements to the transcript. Then:

> the participants are invited to proffer some observations on the data, to select an episode which they find 'interesting' for whatever reason, and formulate their understanding or puzzlement, regarding that episode. Then anyone can come in to react to these remarks, offering alternatives, raising doubts, or whatever. (1998: 124)

However, as ten Have makes clear, such group data sessions should be rather more than an anarchic free-for-all:

> participants are, on the one hand, *free* to bring in anything they like, but, on the other hand, *required* to ground their observations in the data at hand, although they may also support them with reference to their own data-based findings or those published in the literature. (1998: 124)

### Attempt Exercise 6.1 about now

However, without a way of defining a research problem, even detailed transcription can be merely an empty technique. Thus we need to ask: what sort of features are we searching for in our transcripts and what approach lies behind this search?

The rest of this chapter will outline the two main social science traditions which inform the analysis of transcripts of tapes: conversation analysis (CA) and discourse analysis (DA). I will begin with CA.

## 6.3  CONVERSATION ANALYSIS

Conversation analysis is based on an attempt to describe people's methods for producing orderly social interaction. In turn, CA emerged out of Garfinkel's (1967) programme for ethnomethodology and its analysis of 'folk' ('ethno') methods. Sacks's MCD analysis, discussed in Section 5.4, also derives from this programme.

### 6.3.1  Three fundamental assumptions

I will begin by summarizing John Heritage's (1984: 241–4) account of three fundamental assumptions of CA:

1 *The structural organization of talk*  Talk exhibits stable, organized patterns, demonstrably oriented to by the participants. These patterns 'stand independently of the psychological or other characteristics of particular speakers' (1984: 241). This has two important implications. First, the structural organization of talk is to be treated as on a par with the structural organization of any social institution, i.e. as a 'social fact', in Durkheim's terms. Second, it follows that it is illegitimate and unnecessary to explain that organization by appealing to the presumed psychological or other characteristics of particular speakers.
2 *Sequential organization*  'A speaker's action is *context-shaped* in that its contribution to an on-going sequence of actions cannot adequately be understood except by reference to its context . . . in which it participates' (1984: 242). However, this context is addressed by CA largely in terms of the preceding sequence of talk: 'in this sense, the context of a next action is repeatedly renewed with every current action' (1984: 242).
3 *The empirical grounding of analysis*  The first two properties need to be identified in precise analyses of detailed transcripts. It is therefore necessary to avoid premature theory construction and the 'idealization' of research material which uses only general, non-detailed characterizations.

Heritage sums up these assumptions as follows:

> Specifically, analysis is strongly 'data-driven' – developed from phenomena which are in various ways evidenced in the data of interaction. Correspondingly, there is a strong bias against *a priori* speculation about the orientations and motives of speakers and in favour of detailed examination of conversationalists' actual actions. Thus the empirical conduct of speakers is treated as the central resource out of which analysis may develop. (1984: 243)

In practice, Heritage adds, this means that it must be demonstrated that the regularities described 'are produced and oriented to by the participants as normatively oriented-to grounds for inference and action' (1984: 244). Further, deviant cases, in which such regularities are absent, must be identified and analysed (see Section 8.3.2.5 for a further discussion of the role of *deviant-case analysis* in relation to the validity of field research).

For reasons of space, I will briefly describe just three features of talk with which CA is concerned. These are:

1  turn-taking and repair
2  conversational openings and 'adjacency pairs'
3  how 'institutional' talk builds upon (and modifies) the structures of ordinary conversation.

All three features relate to what Sacks calls 'sequencing in conversation'.

### 6.3.2  Turn-taking and repair

Turns at talk have three aspects (Sacks et al., 1974). They involve:

1  how a speaker makes a turn relate to a previous turn (e.g. 'yes', 'but', 'uh huh')
2  what the turn interactionally accomplishes (e.g. an invitation, a question, an answer)
3  how the turn relates to a succeeding turn (e.g. by a question, request, summons etc.).

Where turn-taking errors and violations occur, 'repair mechanisms' will be used. For instance, where more than one party is speaking at a time, a speaker may stop speaking before a normally possible completion point of a turn. Again, when turn transfer does not occur at the appropriate place, the current speaker may repair the failure of the sequence by speaking again. Finally, where repairs by other than the current speaker are required (for instance because another party has been misidentified), the next speaker typically waits until the completion of a turn. Thus the turn-taking system's allocation of rights to a turn is respected even when a repair is found necessary.

There are three consequences of this which are worth noting:

1  *Needing to listen*  The turn-taking system provides an 'intrinsic motivation' for listening to all utterances in a conversation. Interest or politeness alone is not sufficient to explain such attention. Rather, every participant must listen to and analyse each utterance in case (s)he is selected as next speaker.
2  *Understanding*  Turn-taking organization controls some of the ways in which utterances are understood. So, for instance, it allows 'How are you?', as a first turn, to be usually understood not as an enquiry but as a greeting.

3  *Displaying understanding*  When someone offers the 'appropriate' form of reply (e.g. an answer to a question, or an apology to a complaint), (s)he displays an understanding of the significance of the first utterance. The turn-taking system is thus the means whereby actors display to one another that they are engaged in *social* action – action defined by Weber as involving taking account of others.

Thus CA is an empirically oriented research activity, grounded in a basic theory of social action and generating significant implications from an analysis of previously unnoticed interactional forms. As the next section shows, one such unnoticed form is the structure of questions and answers.

## 6.3.3  *Conversational openings and adjacency pairs*

In the 1960s, the American sociologist Emmanuel Schegloff studied data drawn from the first 5 seconds of around 500 telephone calls to and from an American police station. Schegloff began by noting that the basic rule for two-party conversation, that one party speaks at a time (i.e. providing for a sequence a–b–a–b–a–b, where a and b are the parties), 'does not provide for the allocation of the roles "a" and "b"' (1968: 1077). Telephone calls offer interesting data in this regard because non-verbal forms of communication – apart from the telephone bell – are absent. Somehow, despite the absence of visual cues, speakers manage an orderly sequence in which both parties know when to speak. How?

Schegloff suggests:

> A first rule of telephone conversations which might be called 'a distribution rule for first utterances' is: *the answerer speaks first*. (1968: 1078, original emphasis)

In order to see the force of the 'distribution rule', consider the confusion that occurs when a call is made and the phone is picked up, but nothing is said by the receiver of the call. Schegloff cites an anecdote by a woman who adopted this strategy of silence after she began receiving obscene telephone calls. Her friends were constantly irritated by this practice, thus indicating the force of the rule 'the answerer speaks first'. Moreover, her tactic was successful:

> However obscene her caller might be, he would not talk until she had said 'hello', thereby obeying the requirements of the distribution rule. (1974: 355)

Although answerers are expected to speak first, it is callers who are expected to provide the first topic. Answerers, after all, do not normally know who is making the call, whereas callers can usually identify answerers, and answerers will assume that callers have initiated a call in order to raise a topic – hence the embarrassment we feel when somebody we have neglected to call, calls us instead. Here we may convert ourselves from answerers to hypothetical callers by using some formula like: 'Oh, I'd been trying to reach you.' Having reallocated our roles, we are now free to introduce the first topic.

On examining his material further, Schegloff discovered only one case (out of 500) which did not fit the rule 'answerer speaks first'. He concluded that the person who responds to a telephone bell is not really answering a *question*, but responding to a *summons*. A summons is any attention-getting device (a telephone bell, a term of address such as 'John?', or a gesture like a tap on the shoulder or raising your hand). A summons tends to produce answers. Schegloff suggests that summons–answer (SA) sequences have the following features which they share with a number of other linked turns (e.g. question–answer, greetings) classed as *adjacency pairs*:

1 *Non-terminality* They are preambles to some further activity; they cannot properly stand as final exchanges. Consequently, the summoner is obliged to talk again when the summoned completes the SA sequence.
2 *Conditional relevance* Further interaction is conditional upon the successful completion of the SA sequence.
3 *Obligation to answer* Answers to a summons have the character of questions (e.g. 'What?', 'Yes?', 'Hello?'). This means that, as in question–answer (QA) sequences, the summoner must produce the answer to the question (s)he has elicited. Furthermore, the person who has asked the question is obliged to listen to the answer (s)he has obligated the other to produce. Each subsequent nod or 'uh huh' recommits the speaker to attend to the utterances that follow. Through this 'chaining' of questions and answers, 'provision is made by an SA sequence not only for the coordinated entry in a conversation but also for its continued orderliness' (1974: 378–9).

Schegloff was now able to explain his deviant case as follows: summons (phone rings); no answer; further summons (caller says 'Hello'). The normal form of a telephone call is: summons (phone rings); answer (recipient says 'Hello'). In the deviant case, the absence of an answer is treated as the absence of a reply to a summons. So the caller's use of 'Hello' replaces the summons of the telephone bell. The failure of the summoned person to speak first is heard as an uncompleted SA sequence. Consequently, the caller's speaking first makes sense within the 'conditional relevance' of SA sequences.

The power of these observations is suggested by two examples. The first is mentioned by Cuff and Payne:

> The recipient of a summons feels impelled to answer. (We note that in Northern Ireland, persons still open the door and get shot – despite their knowledge that such things happen.) (1979: 151)

The second example arises in Schegloff's discussion of a child's utterance: 'You know what, Mommy?' (first discussed by Sacks, 1974). The child's question establishes an SA sequence, where a proper answer to the summons (Mommy) is 'What?' This allows the child to say what it wanted to at the start, but as an obligation (because questions must produce answers). Consequently, this utterance is a powerful way in which children enter into conversations despite their usually restricted rights to speak.

**Attempt Exercise 6.2 about now**

As Heritage points out, this should not lead us to an over-mechanical view of conversation:

> conversation is not an endless series of interlocking adjacency pairs in which sharply constrained options confront the next speaker. (1984: 261)

Instead, the phenomenon of adjacency works according to two non-mechanistic assumptions:

1  An utterance which is placed immediately after another one is to be understood as produced in response to or in relation to the preceding utterance.
2  This means that, if a speaker wishes some contribution to be heard as *unrelated* to an immediately prior utterance, he or she must do something special to lift assumption 1 – for instance by the use of a prefix (like 'by the way') designed to show that what follows is unrelated to the immediately prior turn at talk.

### 6.3.4  Institutional talk

Contrary to some critics (e.g. Goffman, 1981: 16–17), who accuse conversation analysts of depicting a mechanical system, CA takes very seriously the contexts of interaction. For instance, in the classic statement of CA, it is noted very early on that:

> conversation is always 'situated' – it always comes out of, and is part of, some real sets of circumstances of its participants. (Sacks et al., 1974: 699)

However, although such matters as place, time and the identities of the participants are undoubtedly relevant to speakers, we are reminded that we must be cautious about how we invoke them:

> it is undesirable to have to know or characterize such situations for particular conversations in order to investigate them. (1974: 699)

Two decades later, this position was clearly laid out by Maynard and Clayman:

> Conversation analysts . . . [are] concerned that using terms such as 'doctor's office', 'courtroom', 'police department', 'school room', and the like, to characterize settings . . . can obscure much of what occurs within those settings . . . For this reason, conversation analysts rarely rely on ethnographic data and instead examine if and how interactants themselves reveal an orientation to institutional or other contexts. (1991: 406–7)

As already noted, talk is a feature of both 'formal' and 'informal' interactions, ranging from a courtroom to a casual 'chat'. In a courtroom, for instance, who can speak when is usually clearly defined and, unlike casual chatter, one can be ruled to be speaking 'out of order' and even held to be 'in contempt of court'.

However, it is dangerous to assume that just because talk is occurring in some 'formal' setting, it necessarily has a different structure to ordinary conversation. As we all know, people still chatter in the course of doing their jobs and some formal move may be needed for the talk to take on a formal (or institutional) character, for instance by the chair of a meeting calling the meeting to order.

In any event, as Sacks et al. (1974) suggest, ordinary conversation always provides a baseline from which any such departures are organized and recognized. This means that, in the study of institutional talk, we need carefully to examine how the structures of ordinary conversation 'become specialised, simplified, reduced, or otherwise structurally adapted for institutional purposes' (Maynard and Clayman, 1991: 407).

I will use research on the organization of TV news interviews as an example before attempting a brief summary of what is known so far about institutional talk.

## TV news interviews

Clayman (1992) characterizes TV news interviewing as a site for much caution, given that news interviewers are supposed to be neutral or objective. How is this achieved?

When interviewers (IVs) come on to relatively controversial opinion statements, they distance themselves, creating what Clayman calls a different 'footing'. This is seen in Extract 6.4.

**Extract 6.4 (Clayman 5: Meet the Press 12/8/85)**
```
1  IV:   Senator, (0.5) uh: President Reagan's elected thirteen months ago: an
2        enormous landslide.
3        (0.8)
4  IV:   It is s::aid that his programs are in trouble
```

In lines 1–2, a footing is constructed whereby IV is the author of a factual statement. However, at line 4, the footing shifts to what 'it is said': hence, here IV is no longer the author and the item is marked as possibly 'controversial'.

Footing shifts are also *renewed* during specific 'controversial' words and IVs avoid affiliating with or disaffiliating from the statements they report. They also may comment on the authoritativeness of the source of an assertion or comment on the range of persons associated with it.

However, the achievement of 'neutrality' is a locally accomplished and co-operative matter. Thus interviewees (IEs) 'ordinarily refrain from treating the focal assertion as expressing the IV's personal opinion' (1992: 180). For instance, they do this by attributing the assertion to the same third party.

As Clayman remarks, this is unlike ordinary conversation, where it seems unlikely that speakers are expected to be neutral. As he says, minimal responses to such things as invitations or advice are *not* usually taken as evidence of the recipient's neutrality but are hearable as constituting actual or possible rejection (as we saw in Extract 6.1).

Like Clayman, Greatbatch (1992) notes the specific ways in which participants produce their talk as 'news interview' talk. He shows how the maintenance of IVs' neutrality ties in with the mutual production of the talk as aimed at an overhearing *audience*. Both parties maintain a situation in which it is not problematic that IEs properly limit themselves to responses to IR questions, while IVs:

- confine themselves to asking questions
- avoid a range of responsive activities which would make them a report recipient rather than just a report elicitor (e.g. acknowledgement tokens like 'mmm hm', 'uh huh', 'yes' and news-receipt objects like 'oh, really, did you') (1992: 269–70).

In this context, 'neutrality' is not the only feature which contrasts with talk in other settings. Greatbatch shows that 'disagreements' have features specific to news interview talk. In ordinary conversation, 'whereas agreements are normally performed directly and with a minimum of delay, disagreements are commonly accomplished in mitigated forms and delayed from early positioning within turns and/or sequences' (1992: 273). This suggests, as we saw earlier, that agreements, like acceptance of invitations or advice, are marked as preferred objects.

Greatbatch shows how disagreements arise in the following two ways in multi-party news interviews. First, following a question repeated to the second IE, (s)he can disagree immediately with the opinion of the first IE. As Greatbatch notes, however, this disagreement is *mitigated* since it is *mediated* by the IV's question. As Greatbatch suggests:

> The structure of turn taking in news interviews . . . means that disagreements between IEs are ordinarily elicited by and addressed to a third party, the IV, with whom neither party disagrees. Disagreements which are produced in this manner are not systematically mitigated or forestalled by the use of the preference features that are associated with disagreement in conversation. (1992: 279–80)

Second, however, IEs may disagree in other turn positions, for instance following a co-interviewee's turn or during such a turn. This is seen in Extract 6.5.

**Extract 6.5 (Greatbatch 12)**
1  IE1:  the government advertising campaign is h *high*ly irresponsible. h It's being
2        given [under huge
3  IE2:       [Utter rubbish

This extract departs from the conversational rules of 'preference organization' (which, as we have seen, mark disagreements as dispreferred and hence delayed objects). It also seems to clash with the normal production of a news interview format (because they are not produced as an answer to an IV's question). However, Greatbatch argues, such disagreements display an underlying adherence to the news interview format, namely:

- IE2 can still be heard as responding to the question that produced IE1's answer.
- IE2 directs his answer to the IV, *not* to IE1, and this is quite different from ordinary conversation where the person being disagreed with is also the addressee of the disagreement. Such disagreements are routinely followed (data not shown here) by IV intervening to manage an exit from the disagreement without requiring them to depart from their institutional roles as IEs but not, for instance, combatants, mutual insulters etc.

Greatbatch summarizes his findings as follows:

1 In news interviews, many of the features of preference organization are rendered redundant, replaced by the interview turn-taking system.
2 Within news interviews, 'the structure of turn taking and its associated expectancies provide simultaneously for the *escalation* and *limitation* of overt disagreement' (1992: 299, my emphasis). As Greatbatch suggests, this may explain why panel interviews are so common and are assumed to produce 'lively' broadcasting.

## Basic features of institutional talk

Drew and Heritage (1992: 22–5) distinguish some dimensions according to which we can analyse institutional talk including TV news interviews:

- It is usually goal-oriented in institutionally relevant ways; thus people design their conduct to meet various institutional tasks or functions, e.g. emergency calls to the police need to be rapidly but accurately accomplished (Zimmerman, 1992). Alternatively the goals of interactions can be ill-defined, creating a need for the participants to fashion a sense of what the interaction will be about (Heritage and Sefi, 1992; Peräkylä and Silverman, 1991).
- It is usually shaped by certain constraints, e.g. what can be done in a court of law or news interview; however, in other situations, like counselling or doctor–patient interaction, participants may negotiate or ignore such constraints.
- It is associated with particular ways of reasoning or inference-making, e.g. meaning of not giving response tokens in news interviews; hearing a charge in health visitor–mother (Heritage and Sefi) or doctor–mother (Silverman, 1987: ch. 10) interactions.

Attempt Exercise 6.3 about now

*The issue of context*

As Drew and Heritage have pointed out, while one can do 'institutional work' on a home telephone, not everything said at work is specifically 'institutional':

> Thus the institutionality of an interaction is not determined by its setting. Rather, interaction is institutional in so far as participants' institutional or professional identities are somehow made relevant to the work activities in which they are engaged. (1992: 3–4)

The question that then arises is how we demonstrate what is 'relevant'. Schegloff (1992) has suggested that this is a basic methodological issue. It causes two problems which he calls 'relevance' and 'procedural consequentiality'. These two problems are set out as follows:

1 *Relevance* This is the problem of 'showing from the details of the talk or other conduct in the materials that we are analyzing that those aspects of the scene are what the parties are oriented to' (1992: 110). The problem arises because, as we saw in Chapter 5, Sacks reveals how people can describe themselves and others in multiple ways. This problem, Schegloff insists, is simply disregarded in social scientific accounts which rely on statistical correlations to 'demonstrate' the relevance of some such description. Instead, we need to demonstrate that participants are currently oriented to such descriptions.

2 *Procedural consequentiality* A demonstration that our descriptions of persons and settings are currently relevant for participants is not enough. We must also consider: 'How does the fact that the talk is being conducted in some setting (e.g. "the hospital") issue in any consequence for the shape, form, trajectory, content, or character of the interaction that the parties conduct? And what is the mechanism by which the context-so-understood has determinate consequences for the talk?' (1992: 111).

Schegloff gives two examples relevant to 'procedural consequentiality'. First, he looks at how a particular laboratory study sought to demonstrate something about how people 'repair' mistakes in talk. He shows that, in this study, only the subject was allowed to talk. Hence many features which arise in whether such repairs should be done by self or other (given that there is a preference for self-repair) were unavailable. Thus it will not do to characterize the context as a 'laboratory setting' because other features (only one person talking) can be shown to have more procedural consequentiality.

Schegloff's second example is taken from an interview between George Bush and Dan Rather in the 1988 US election campaign. The interview became famous because of the apparent 'row' or confrontation between the two men. Schegloff shows that such features were noticeable because Bush refused to co-operate in producing a central feature of 'interviews', i.e. that they consist of question–answer sequences where one party asks the questions and the other holds off speaking until a recognizable question has been posed (Silverman, 1973).

The implication is that we cannot describe what went on as occurring in the context of an 'interview'. Instead, interactions only become (and cease to be) 'interviews' through the co-operative activity of the participants. As Schegloff shows, this may make some of the claims relating gender to interruption (Zimmerman and West, 1975) somewhat premature.

These examples show that the issue of determining context is not a once-and-for-all affair because parties have to continue to work at co-producing any context. Equally, we cannot explain people's behaviour as a simple 'response' to some context when that context is actively constructed (and reconstructed).

This means that we should not assume that what we find in talk is necessarily a feature of the institutional setting or other social structural element that our intuitions tell us is relevant. Since 'not everything said in some context . . . is relevantly oriented to that context' (Schegloff, 1991: 62), we must not risk characterizing a conversational structure possibly found across a range of contexts as institutionally specific.

This point is made elegantly in the editor's introduction to a recent collection of studies of 'institutional talk':

> CA researchers cannot take 'context' for granted nor may they treat it as determined in advance and independent of the participants' own activities. Instead, 'context' and identity have to be treated as inherently locally produced, incrementally developed and, by extension, as transformable at any moment. Given these constraints, analysts who wish to depict the distinctively 'institutional' character of some stretch of talk cannot be satisfied with showing that institutional talk exhibits aggregates and/or distributions of actions that are distinctive from ordinary conversation. They must rather demonstrate that the participants constructed their conduct over its course – turn by responsive turn – so as progressively to constitute . . . the occasion of their talk, together with their own social roles in it, as having some distinctively institutional character. (Drew and Heritage, 1992: 21)

However, this does *not* mean that such work treats institutional talk as a closed system cut off from the wider society. By contrast, without making any prior assumptions about 'context', these studies are able to examine how members themselves invoke a particular context for their talk. As we have seen, Clayman and Greatbatch show how TV news interviewers produce their talk as 'neutral' or 'objective', thereby displaying their attention to an overhearing audience's presumed expectations.

Elsewhere, I have argued (Silverman, 1997b: 34–5) for the value of respecting CA's assertion that one's initial move should be to give close attention to how participants locally produce contexts for their interaction. By beginning with this question of 'how', we can then fruitfully move on to 'why' questions about the institutional and cultural constraints to which the parties demonstrably defer. Such constraints reveal the functions of apparently irrational practices and help us to understand the possibilities and limits of attempts at social reform.

### 6.3.5  Doing CA

Despite the battery of concepts found in this chapter, doing CA is not an impossibly difficult activity. As the founder of CA, Harvey Sacks, once pointed out, in doing CA we are only reminding ourselves about things we already know. As Sacks remarks:

> I take it that lots of the results I offer, people can see for themselves. And they needn't be afraid to. And they needn't figure that the results are wrong because they can see them . . . As if we found a new plant. It may have been a plant in your garden, but now you see it's different than something else. And you can look at it to see how it's different, and whether it's different in the way that somebody has said. (1992, I: 488)

However, the way in which CA obtains its results is rather different from how we might intuitively try to analyse talk. It may be helpful, therefore, if I conclude this section by offering a crude set of prescriptions about how to do CA. These are set out in Tables 6.2 and 6.3.

TABLE 6.2   How to do CA

| |
|---|
| 1  Always try to identify sequences of related talk. |
| 2  Try to examine how speakers take on certain roles or identities through their talk (e.g. questioner–answerer or client–professional). |
| 3  Look for particular outcomes in the talk (e.g. a request for clarification, a repair, laughter) and work backwards to trace the trajectory through which a particular outcome was produced. |

TABLE 6.3   Common errors to avoid when doing CA

| |
|---|
| 1  Explaining a turn at talk by reference to the speaker's intentions. |
| 2  Explaining a turn at talk by reference to a speaker's role or status (e.g. as a doctor or as a man or woman). |
| 3  Trying to make sense of a single line of transcript or utterance in isolation from the surrounding talk. |

If we follow these rules, as Sacks suggests, the analysis of conversations does not require exceptional skills. As he puts it, all we need to do is to 'begin with some observations, then find the problem for which these observations could serve as . . . the solution' (1992, II: xlviii).

## 6.4  DISCOURSE ANALYSIS

Discourse analysis (DA) describes a heterogeneous range of social science research based on the analysis of interviews and texts as well as recorded talk. It shares with CA a common intellectual ancestor in the Oxford philosopher J.L. Austin.

In *How To Do Things with Words* (1962), Austin showed that many utterances do not simply describe a state of affairs but perform an action. For instance:

Help.

I thee wed.

In both cases, the speakers are not heard to describe the state of their mind or to picture reality but are heard to perform some action ('asking for help', 'getting married'). Uttering such 'performatives', as Austin calls them, commits speakers to their consequences. For instance, when people come to give you help and find nothing amiss, it is no defence to say that you were not calling for assistance but simply singing a song. Alternatively, Austin points out, you will not escape a charge of bigamy by saying that you had all kinds of mental reservations when you uttered 'I thee wed' for the second time.

Like nearly all linguistic philosophers, Austin worked with *invented* examples, relying on his native intuition. Social scientists prefer to understand the complexities of naturally occurring talk. What they take from Austin is his concern with the activities performed in talk.

### 6.4.1 *What is discourse analysis?*

At first sight, compared to CA, DA looks like conventional social science. This arises for two reasons:

1  DA is concerned with a range of topics which are often much closer to conventional social science concerns (e.g. gender relations, social control etc.) than is the case in CA. 'Take gender inequalities for example. [DA] Studies have considered both the way in which such inequalities are constructed, made factual, and justified in talk, and they have also considered the resources (**interpretive repertoires**, identities, category systems) that are used to manufacture coherent and persuasive justifications that work to sustain those inequalities' (Potter, 1997: 148).
2  Unlike CA, DA can be quite catholic about what kind of data is acceptable. So, although some DA studies use transcripts of talk from everyday or institutional settings, others are based on transcripts of open-ended interviews, or on documents of some kind. Sometimes these different materials are even combined together in the same study (1997: 147). However, not all DA researchers are entirely happy with using non-naturally occurring data such as interviews (see Potter, 1996a: 134–5).

These two features mean that DA is quite heterogeneous and it is, therefore, difficult to arrive at a clear definition of it. The following is one authoritative version:

> DA has an analytic commitment to studying discourse as *texts and talk in social practices* . . . the focus is . . . on language as . . . the medium for interaction; analysis of discourse becomes, then, analysis of what people do. One theme that is particularly emphasized here is the rhetorical or argumentative organization of talk and texts; claims and versions are constructed to undermine alternatives. (Potter, 1997: 146, emphasis in original)

Potter suggests that this Austinian concern with the rhetorical organization of talk and texts has given DA three unifying assumptions:

1 *Anti-realism*  DA is resolutely against the assumption that we can treat accounts as true or false descriptions of 'reality'. As Potter puts it: 'DA emphasizes the way versions of the world, of society, events, and inner psychological worlds are produced in discourse.'
2 *Constructionism*  DA is concerned with 'participants' constructions and how they are accomplished and undermined'.
3 *Reflexivity*  DA considers 'the way a text such as this is a version, selectively working up coherence and incoherence, telling historical stories, presenting and, indeed, constituting and objective, out-there reality' (1997: 146).

To put some meat on these bare bones, I present below three concepts used in DA research:

- interpretive repertoires (or interpretive repertoires)
- stake
- scripts.

This is not meant to be an exhaustive list. In particular it leaves out DA work concerned with rhetoric and ideology (e.g. Wetherell and Potter, 1992; Billig 1992; 1995) and with issues relating to the construction of scientific texts (e.g. Ashmore, 1989; Potter, 1996b).

### 6.4.2  *Interpretive repertoires*

Early DA studies attempted to identify broad 'discourses' which participants use to define their identities and moral status. As Potter puts it:

> **Interpretive repertoires** are systematically related sets of terms that are often used with stylistic and grammatical coherence and often organized around one or more central metaphors. (1996a: 131)

Two examples will indicate how this concept has been used.

*Science as a repertoire*
Nigel Gilbert and Mike Mulkay (1983) were concerned with scientists' accounts of scientific practice. As they point out, one way of hearing what

scientists say is as hard data which bear on debates in the philosophy of science about the character of scientific practice. It is then tempting to treat such accounts as 'inside' evidence ('from the horse's mouth', as it were) about whether scientists are actually influenced by 'paradigms' and community affiliations more than by sober attempts to refute possible explanations, as in Popper's *critical rationalism* (see Section 8.1.4).

Confusingly, Gilbert and Mulkay's scientists used both quasi-Kuhnian and quasi-Popperian explanations of scientific practice. Understandably, however, they were much keener to invoke the Popperian ('sober refutation') account of how *they* worked and the Kuhnian ('community context') account of how certain *other* scientists worked.

Were these accounts to be treated as a direct insight into how scientists do their work or how they experience things in the laboratory? Not at all, given the anti-realist posture of DA. Instead, these interview data gave Gilbert and Mulkay access to the *vocabularies* that scientists use. These vocabularies were located in two very different interpretive repertoire:

- a *contingent* repertoire, in which scientists used a political vocabulary of 'influence' and 'interest' to talk about each other's institutional affiliations and ability or inability to get big research contracts etc.
- an *empiricist* repertoire, in which scientific activity was described as a response to data 'out there' in 'nature'.

Neither repertoire conveyed the 'true' sense of science. For DA, there is no more an essential form of scientific practice than there is a single reality standing behind 'atrocity stories' told by mothers of handicapped children (see Section 4.8). Everything is situated in particular contexts. So scientists, Gilbert and Mulkay note, are much more likely to use a 'contingent' repertoire in a discussion at a bar than in a scientific paper.

In this way, the research question ceases to be 'What is science?' and becomes 'How is a particular scientific discourse invoked? When is it invoked? How does it stand in relation to other discourses?'

Gilbert and Mulkay's focus on interpretive repertoires leads us to see that 'science', like other social institutions, is a *hyphenated phenomenon* which takes on different meanings in different contexts (see Section 10.7).

### Motherhood as a repertoire

As just noted, it is not only sober institutions like 'science' which dissolve into a set of repertoires. The same process can be seen when we look at how women invoke the identity of 'motherhood'. My example of this will be drawn from a clinic for young diabetics (Silverman, 1987: ch. 10).

Extract 6.6 is the start of a consultation between a mother of a diabetic child aged 16 and her paediatrician. It takes place when her daughter is in another room having her blood taken and the mother has asked specially if she can see the doctor. This extract comes a little way into the consultation.

**Extract 6.6**
(D = doctor; M = mother of June, aged 16)

1  M:  She's going through a very languid stage ( ) she won't do anything unless
2      you push her
3  D:  so you're finding you're having to push her quite a lot?
4  M:  mm no well I don't (.) I just leave her now

At line 4, there is evidence to suggest that M hears the doctor's question as a charge against her parenting. Notice how she withdraws from her initial depiction about 'pushing' her daughter when the doctor, through repeating it, makes it accountable. One way to look at what is happening here, then, is as a *charge–rebuttal* sequence.

Now why would she want to withdraw from her depiction of her daughter and herself in lines 1–2 of this extract? It seems that M hears D's question as depicting her as potentially a 'nagging' mother (it is interesting that only women can nag!). So, when the doctor topicalizes 'pushing', the mother withdraws into an account which suggests that she respects her daughter's autonomy.

Shortly after, June's mother produces another worry about how her daughter is coping with her diabetes. This time her concern is her daughter's diet (Extract 6.7).

**Extract 6.7**
1  M:  I don't think she's really sticking to her diet (.) I don't know the effects
2      this will have on her (.) it's bound to alter her sugar if she's not got the
3      right insulin isn't it? I mean I know what she eats at home but
       [outside
4  D:  [so there's no real consistency to her diet? It's sort
5      [of
6  M:  [no well I keep it as consistent as I can at home

Now look at what the doctor says this time. Unlike in Extract 6.6, he does not topicalize M's 'pushing' her child. Instead, he produces what M hears as a charge against her responsibility towards June ('there's no real consistency to her diet'). In response, the mother now uses the very thing she denied earlier in order to rebut what she hears as the charge of 'irresponsibility' in what the doctor is saying.

This brings us to the issue of interpretive repertoires: in this case a repertoire of 'parental responsibility' and one of 'young adults' autonomy'. M is skilfully operating with two repertoires that apparently are quite contradictory. In purely logical terms, you can't on the one hand say 'I watch everything my child does' and at the same time 'I leave my child to do anything she wants to do'. However, by using each repertoire when situationally appropriate, the mother is able to detect and rebut possible traps in the way the doctor is responding to what she is saying.

Consonant with DA's anti-realist and constructionist position, this naturally occurring material reveals that this mother is not *intrinsically* 'nagging' or 'irresponsible'. Instead, both depictions are *locally* available and *locally* resisted. Conversely, if we had interviewed mothers, the temptation would have been to search for idealized conceptions of their role.

### Attempt Exercise 6.4 about now

The reader will note that the gain of this analysis is that, like many DA studies, it addresses a conventional social science topic (conceptions of gender and motherhood). Moreover, it seems to have an immediate practical application. For instance, doctors were interested to learn about the double-binds present in their attention to the autonomy of their young patients. Likewise, parents' groups (largely mothers) of diabetic children found it very helpful to go through material of this kind. It brought out the way in which things they may feel personally guilty about in their relationships with their teenage children are not something that relates to their individual failings. Instead, such problems arise in our culture in the double-binds built into the parent–adolescent relationship.

### Uses and limitations of interpretive repertoires

Both studies identify the cultural resources that participants bring to institutional settings. At the same time, as we have seen, these resources are not treated as simple determinants of their behaviour but are used locally and skilfully. As Potter puts it:

> these resources have a . . . 'bespoke' flexibility, which allows them to be selectively drawn upon and reworked, according to the setting. (1996a: 131)

However, as Potter himself recognizes, the concept of interpretive repertoires does present certain difficulties. Let me mention two of these difficulties:

1  Although the concept may help in understanding communication in well-defined settings like medicine or science, it is: 'difficult to make clear and consistent judgements concerning the *boundaries* of particular repertoires outside constrained institutional settings' (1996a: 131).
2  Appealing to interpretive repertoires may fail to bring out more basic conversational rules to which participants are attending. Consequently, it lays itself open to the charge of basing its analysis upon taken-for-granted knowledge about the basic structures of talk (e.g. how charges or accusations are hearable by conversationalists). As Potter writes: '[a] problem is that the generality of the notion of a repertoire may obscure local interactional "business" that is being achieved by particular forms of discourse' (1996a: 131).

Because of these difficulties, Potter (1996a) argues that the concept of 'repertoire' is being replaced in DA by rather less broad brush concepts. One such concept is 'stake'.

### 6.4.3 Stake

> How is a particular type of blaming achieved? How is a particular version of the world made to seem solid and unproblematic? How are social categories constructed and managed in practice? (Potter, 1996a: 131–2)

These kinds of questions can only be answered by different concepts which allow a more fine-grained attention to conversational detail. The concept of 'stake' attempts to satisfy this need. 'Stake' is explained by Potter in this way:

> People treat each other as entities with desires, motives, institutional allegiances and so on, as having a stake in their actions. Referencing stake is one principal way of discounting the significance of an action or reworking its nature. (Potter, 1997: 153)

Potter illustrates the concept of stake with a number of data extracts. The first is taken from the interview of Princess Diana by the British TV reporter Martin Bashir. Extract 6.8 is part of the extract that Potter considers.

**Extract 6.8 (adapted from Potter, 1997: 151)**

```
 1  Bashir:    Did you (.) allow your friends, >your close friends,<
 2             to speak to Andrew Morton?
 3  Princess:  Yes I did. Y [es, I did
 4  Bashir:                 [Why?
 5  Princess:  I was (.) at the end of my tether (.)
 6             I was (.) desperate (.)
 7             >I think I was so fed up with being< (.)
 8             seen as someone who was a ba:sket case (.)
 9             because I am a very strong person (.)
10             and I know (.) that causes complications, (.)
11             in the system (.) that I live in.
12             (1.0) (smiles and purses lips)
13  Bashir:    How would a book change that.
14  Princess:  I dunno. ((raises eyebrows, looks away))
15             Maybe people have a better understanding (.)
16             maybe there's a lot of women out there
17             who suffer (.) on the same level
18             but in a different environment (.)
19             who are unable to: (.) stand up for themselves (.)
20             because (.) their self-esteem is (.) cut into two.
21             I dunno ((shakes head))
```

Potter focuses on Princess Diana's two 'I dunno' utterances (lines 14 and 21). Utterances like this, he says, work as 'uncertainty tokens' (words or expressions that people use to report states of uncertainty). So, by using 'I dunno', Princess Diana invites us to minimize her *stake* and *interest* in what she is saying. In this way, she discounts the significance of her actions or reworks their nature (1997: 153).

Potter compares this extract to an interview with Salman Rushdie. In Extract 6.9, David Frost is asking about the fatwah – the religious death sentence on Rushdie.

**Extract 6.9 (Potter, 1997: 153; Public Broadcasting Service, 26 November 1993)**

```
1  Frost:    And how could they cancel it now? Can they cancel it–
2            they say they can't.
3  Rushdie:  Yeah, but you know, they would, wouldn't they, as somebody once
4            said. The thing is, without going into the kind of arcana of theology,
5            there is no technical problem. The problem is not technical. The
6            problem is that they don't want to.
```

Potter draws our attention to Rushdie's comment: 'they would, wouldn't they' (line 3). This treats Frost's suggestion that the fatwah cannot be cancelled as a claim which is motivated by special interests:

> The familiar phrase 'they would, wouldn't they' treats the Iranians' claim as something to be expected: it is the sort of thing that people with that background, those interests, that set of attitudes *would* say; and it formulates that predictability as shared knowledge. This extract illustrates the potential for invoking stake to discount claims. (1997: 153)

The concept of 'script', like that of 'stake', helps us to understand the ways in which participants attend to the normative character of their actions.

### 6.4.4 Scripts

As used in DA, 'script' refers to the ways in which participants construct events 'as **scripted**, as instances of some general pattern, or as anomalies and exceptions' (Edwards, 1997: 144). As Derek Edwards points out, the DA use of this concept is quite different from that found in cognitive psychology in which 'script' refers to a more or less fixed mental schema which people learn to associate with certain activities or settings (e.g. a 'restaurant script' involving a series of roles and props: see Edwards, 1997: 143).

By contrast, in DA, a *script* is a way of invoking the *routine* character of described events in order to imply that they are features of some (approved or disapproved) general pattern. Through this device, participants assemble descriptions that attend to matters of appropriateness, responsibility and blame, and:

> build a picture of what kind of person the actor is – that is, his or her personality, disposition or mental state. (1997: 144)

Extract 6.10 shows how 'script' is used as a participant's device. It is an extract from a counselling session in which Mary and Jeff are talking to a counsellor about their marital problems.

**Extract 6.10 (Edwards, 1997: 142, simplified transcription)**

1  Mary:  I went out Friday night (.) and Jeff was working (.) on call (.) and (.)
2  um (2.2) the place that I went to (.) like (.) *clo*sed at half past twe*l*ve
3  and I got home about one o'clock

Edwards draws attention to Mary's mention of what time the 'place' she went to closed. Her description attends to her earlier account of an argument with Jeff about the time that she had arrived home and the fact that she had met her ex-lover while out (data not shown).

Edwards argues that Mary's simple narrative (the 'place . . . *clo*sed at half past twe*l*ve and I got home about one o'clock') presents what happened as merely a routine set of events (a 'script') in which nothing extraordinary or morally reprehensible took place. As Edwards puts it, through scripting what happened, Mary diverts attention from other kinds of interpretations, for instance that:

> she was enjoying herself and did not *want* to come home, let alone that she was enjoying the attentions of men, or even of the man with whom she had had the affair. Mary's getting home at one o'clock (a.m.) is provided as part of a narrative sequence of going somewhere that happened to close at 12.30. (1997: 142–3)

Mary also says: 'I went out Friday night (.) and Jeff was working'. Note how this part of Mary's description allows us to add to Edwards's account. In this passage, Mary chooses to account for the fact that she went out without Jeff. We are now to hear her evening out not as some wilful action of a woman ignoring her partner but as something that was unavoidable ('scripted') and, therefore, morally acceptable.

In my own data, taken from a counselling session about a possible HIV-test, a male client who had not accompanied his girlfriend on holiday also attended to the matter of his (and her) accountability. I will use Edwards's concept of script to analyse one extract from these data (a fuller discussion, addressed in terms of other related concepts, is to be found in Silverman (1997b: 78–84).

Extract 6.11 is at the very beginning of a pre-test counselling interview held at the sexually transmitted disease department of a hospital in a provincial British city. When asked by the counsellor (C) about why he wants an HIV test, this male patient (P) tells a story about what happened on his girlfriend's holiday.

**Extract 6.11 (Silverman, 1997b: 78–9)**

1  C:  righty ho (0.2) could you tell us (.) why you've come for an HIV test
2  today=
3  P:  =well basically (.) because I'm: *wor*ried that I might have AIDS (0.2) er:
4  (0.2) when my girlfriend (.) like she was on holiday in: (.) [X] (0.2) in
5  April with her friend
6  C:  mm hm
7  P:  I didn't go because I was busy (1.0) er:: (0.6) she came *ba*ck but she was

8    away for three weeks she came back (0.6) er: April ( ) May (.) April (.) May
9    June July August September October Nov*em*ber (0.8) and it's now November
10   she's just told me (.) that she had *sex* with (.) a [Xian] when she was out there
11   well not actually had sex with but this she said that this guy (0.2) this is what
12   she told me this guy had (.) forced herself (.) hisself upon her you know
13   (0.6) er::

As with Edwards's extract, the matter of who goes away from home with whom is made accountable here. 'With her friend' (line 5) tells us that his 'girlfriend' had not gone away on her own, where going away on your own *may* be heard as implying a problem with a relationship. 'Her friend' does not tell us the gender of the 'friend'. However we know that, if that gender had been male, it would have massive implications for the story that is being told and, therefore, P would have been obliged to tell us. Given that he doesn't, we must assume that 'her friend' is 'female'. Moreover, we can also assume, for the same reason, that it is not a sexual relationship.

But P also leaves a question hanging about why he had not accompanied his girlfriend, given that 'going on holiday together' can be heard as a script appropriate to the relationship girlfriend–boyfriend.

'I didn't go because I was busy' (line 7) attends to this question, Here P shows that he analyses these inferences in exactly this way. First, he underlines what we had inferred in his original description: 'I didn't go'. Second, he shows that this 'not going' is accountable and provides its warrant: 'because I was busy'. Just as Mary accounts for her husband's absence because 'Jeff was working', so P makes accountable that he did not accompany his girlfriend on her holiday. In both cases, we have accounts which invoke the *routine* character of described events and, thereby, function to constitute the accounts as *scripts* which describe some morally acceptable 'business as usual'.

Further scriptlike elements in P's account can be seen in the way he begins his answer to C's question. Note how being 'worried' about 'AIDS' (line 3) is appropriate to the implied category 'patient' who, in C's words, has 'come for an HIV test today'. When produced as scripts, descriptions construct a profoundly *moral* universe of 'reasonable' activities conducted and perceived by 'reasonable' people. So, for instance, coming today for an HIV test is not only an 'appropriate' activity if you are 'worried', it is also sensible and reasonable, serving to protect yourself (against further 'worry') and the community (because it shows you are aware of the dangers of receiving and transmitting the HIV virus).

However, P's account also provides a description of an event that may be heard in terms of another *script*. 'She was on holiday' (4) conjures up the category 'holidaymaker' which can be heard to imply innocent enjoyment but may also be associated with other activities, e.g. holiday 'romances', holiday 'flings'. Because we know that holidays may be a time when moral inhibitions may be temporarily lifted, the upcoming description of potentially 'promiscuous' behaviour is potentially downgraded or at least made comprehensible.

'She's just told me (.) that she had *sex* with (.) a [Xian] when she was out there' (line 10) consists of a series of highly implicative descriptions of activities. Having 'sex' with a third party implies 'being unfaithful'. Although the earlier description 'on holiday' (confirmed by the place locater 'when she was out there') may make this description understandable, it may not make it excusable. As we shall see, P engages in considerable interpretive work to preserve the moral status of P's girlfriend in a way that does not threaten his own status as a 'reasonable' person.

'Well not actually had sex with' (11): here the damaging description 'having sex' (with a third party) is immediately repaired by B. Thus we have to suspend the implied category 'unfaithful girlfriend'.

But this repaired description is ambiguous. For instance, are we to hear 'not actually had sex' as a physical or social description of the activity?

'She said that this guy (0.2) this is what she told me this guy had (.) forced herself (.) hisself upon her you know' (line 12). It is clear from his next utterance that P is attending to this ambiguity as something in need of further explication. If 'he forced . . . hisself upon her', then we are given a description which implies the categories rapist–victim, where 'victim' implies the activity of not giving consent.

So P reworks his original category 'having sex', with its damaging implications, by positing the absence of consent and thus a withdrawal of the warrant of the charge 'unfaithful girlfriend' and a return to a description of the events as scripted.

However, there is a further nice feature embedded in P's description. It arises in its preface: 'she said that this guy (0.2) this is what she told me'. P's story of these events is thus doubly embedded (both in 'she said' and in 'this is what she told me'). How does 'this is what she told me' serve to repair 'she said'?

We can unpick the nature of this repair by recognizing that when somebody offers an account the upshot of which puts them in an unfavourable light, we may suspect that they have organized their description in order to put themselves in a more favourable light. So, if P had simply reported what his 'girlfriend' had said about this incident, then, although he would be implying that he was a 'trusting partner', he could be seen as 'too trusting', i.e. as a dope.

Now we see that 'this is what she told me' makes him into an astute witness by drawing attention to the potential credibility problem about his girlfriend's account – just, as in Extract 6.9, Salman Rushdie's observation 'they would, wouldn't they' functions to minimize the credibility of a reported statement. However, note that, unlike this comment, P is *not* directly stating that his girlfriend is to be disbelieved. Rather her story is offered just as that – as her *story* – without implying that P knows it to be true or false.

The beauty of P's repair into 'this is what she told me' is that it puts him in a favourable light (as an astute observer), while not making a direct charge against his girlfriend's veracity (an activity which would allow us to see him as a 'disloyal partner'). This allows a hearer of his story to believe or disbelieve his girlfriend's account and allows him to go along with either conclusion.

P's elegantly crafted story leaves it up to the hearer to decide which script best describes these 'events'. Is this the story of an unfaithful girlfriend or of someone who has been shamefully assaulted? However we decide, P fits into the script of a 'loyal partner' and so is in the clear.

## 6.5 CA AND DA COMPARED

The difference between DA and CA is a matter for debate. Some DA researchers find CA's refusal to engage directly with cultural and political context disconcerting (see Wetherell, 1998). Equally, CA specialists question the validity of some DA researchers' appeals to their own sense of context (see Schegloff, 1997).

CA gains by mobilizing information about the structures of ordinary conversation in the context of very detailed transcripts. Following CA, Derek Edwards has called for a DA which draws from Sacks the assumption that there is

> No hearable level of detail that may not be significant, or treated as significant by conversational participants'. (1995: 580)

At first glance, as Edwards implies, this seems to represent an accurate reading of Sacks's programme. However, as Schegloff points out, in practice DA has not always been responsive to the relevance of all aspects of talk to the local production of sense. For instance, some DA researchers may treat particles like 'mm' and 'uh huh' as:

> conversational 'detritus' apparently lacking semantic content, and not contributing to the substance of what the discourse ends up having said. (Schegloff, 1982: 74)

For Schegloff, then, DA can ignore a basic aspect of CA by treating talk

> as the product of a single speaker and a single mind; the conversation-analytic angle of inquiry does not let go of the fact that speech-exchange systems are involved, in which more and more than one co-participant is present and relevant to the talk, even when only one does the talking. (1982: 72)

However, DA-based research studies do provide important insights into institutional talk based on pressing sociological and practical concerns (like doctor–patient and teacher–pupil communication). Equally, like CA, DA can be attentive to the sequential embeddedness of talk – as, for instance, in Extracts 6.6 and 6.7, when the mother's changes of tack are interpreted in terms of the doctor's glosses on what she has just said.

It is for the reader to judge whether any DA study is susceptible to Schegloff's criticisms. Certainly, there is some evidence in recent work (e.g. Potter, 1997) that at least some DA researchers pay considerable attention to the turn-by-turn organization of talk. Moreover, we cannot assume that transcripts which do not record such details as length of pause are necessarily imperfect. There cannot be a *perfect* transcript of a tape-recording. Everything depends upon what you are trying to do in the analysis, as well as upon practical considerations involving time and resources.

Of course, if this is so, we may end up in a pointless debate about whether such work is DA or CA! Indeed, in some cases, this distinction has more to do with whether the author pays his or her disciplinary dues to, respectively, psychology or sociology.

## 6.6 CONCLUSION

The last thing I want to do is to impose conversation analysis or discourse analysis as the only acceptable ways of doing qualitative research. As noted elsewhere in this volume, everything will depend upon the research problem being tackled. Moreover, thoughtful researchers will often want to use a combination of methods.

However, my benevolent neutrality towards the varying logics of qualitative research coexists with an appeal to two very strong principles. First, researchers always need to address the analytic issues that may lie concealed behind apparently straightforward issues of method. Second, qualitative research's concern for an 'in-depth' focus on people's activities (or representations of those activities) is no warrant for sloppy thinking or anecdotal use of 'telling' examples. We owe it to ourselves and our audiences to generate reliable data and valid observations.

If there is a 'gold standard' for qualitative research, it should only be the standard for any good research, qualitative or quantitative, social or natural science – and that requires affirmative answers to two questions. Have the researchers demonstrated successfully why we should believe them? And does the research problem tackled have theoretical and/or practical significance?

## KEY POINTS

- If we can study what people are actually doing in naturally occurring situations, why should we ever want to work with researcher-provoked data?
- Tapes and transcripts have three clear advantages compared with other kinds of qualitative data: tapes are a public record; they can be replayed and transcripts improved; and they preserve sequences of talk.
- CA attempts to describe people's methods for producing orderly social interaction; it identifies these methods in the sequential organization of talk-in-interaction.
- DA studies discourse as texts and talk in social practices; it is particularly concerned with rhetorical or argumentative organization.

## Recommended Reading

For an introduction to CA, see ten Have (1998); for DA, see Potter and Wetherell (1987) and Potter (1996a; 1997). Sacks's work on conversation analysis is found in his collected lectures (Sacks, 1992, vols I and II). These lectures are introduced in my book *Harvey Sacks: Social Science and Conversation Analysis* (1998). The diabetic clinic data discussed here are taken from my book *Communication and Medical Practice* (1987: chs 9, 10).

## Exercise 6.1

This is a task designed to help you familiarize yourself with the transcription conventions used in conversation analysis. As a consequence, you should start to understand the logic of transcribing this way and be able to ask questions about how the speakers are organizing their talk.

You are asked to tape-record no more than five minutes of talk in the public domain. One possibility is a radio call-in programme. Avoid using scripted drama productions as these may not contain recurrent features of natural interaction (such as overlap or repair). Do not try to record a television extract as the visual material will complicate both transcription and analysis. Now go through the following steps:

1 Attempt to transcribe your tape using the conventions in the Appendix. Try to allocate turns to identified speakers where possible but don't worry if you can't identify a particular speaker (put ? at the start of a line in such cases).
2 Encourage a friend to attempt the same task independently of you. Now compare transcripts and relisten to the tape-recording to improve your transcript.
3 Using this chapter as a guide, attempt to identify in your transcript any features in the organization of the talk (e.g. adjacency pairs, preference organization, institutional talk etc.).

## Exercise 6.2

Examine Extracts 6.12 and 6.13 (drawn from Atkinson and Drew, 1979: 52, and discussed in Heritage, 1984: 248–9).

**Extract 6.12**

```
1  A:  Is there something bothering you or not?
2      (1.0)
3  A:  Yes or no
4      (1.5)
5  A:  Eh?
6  B:  No.
```

**Extract 6.13**

```
1  Ch:  Have to cut the:se Mummy.
2       (1.3)
3  Ch:  Won't we Mummy
4       (1.5)
5  Ch:  Won't we
6  M:   Yes
```

1   Why does Heritage argue that these extracts demonstrate that 'questioners attend to the fact that their questions are framed within normative expectations which have sequential implications' (1984: 249)? Use the concept of 'adjacency pairs' in your answer.

2   What are the consequences of Ch. (in Extract 6.13) naming the person to whom his utterance is addressed? Why might children often engage in such naming? Use the concept of 'summons–answer'.

## Exercise 6.3

Below is an extract from an HIV test counselling interview. Read it through carefully in terms of the transcriptions set out in the Appendix.

**(SS/2/16: DG)**

```
1   C:  Okay. (0.7) It may sou:nd (0.5) perhaps a dumb question but if you
2       did have HIV how: might you have got it.
3       (1.0)
4   P:  I'm sorry?
5   C:  If you did have HIV how might you have gotten it.
6   P:  How might I have er gotten it.
7   C:  Mm=
8   P:  = er: Through gay se:x.
9   C:  Okay:.
10      (0.5)
11  C:  [Uh:m:
12  P:  [How exactly how I don't know:, (0.5) uh::: (3.0) I am (.) really not
13      sure. (.)
```

```
14   C:   Okay. .hhh When you say through gay sex I mean how long have
15        you bee:n (0.4) having relationships with other guys for.
16   P:   Okay: er:::: (1.0) s-well (0.3) since I was a little kid.=As long as I
17        c(h)an reme(h)mbe(h)r. .hhhh er::: (1.5) Bu:t (0.4) before I got my
18        jo:b I: (0.3) started seeing someone, (0.4) a:nd it was the only
19        relationship for two and half years.
20   C:   Mm hm
21   P:   And might add a stormy relationship so: (0.2) I was not (.) the faithful
22        lover. (.) The entire two and a half year:s.
23   C:   Both of you [were unfaithful or you weren't.
24   P:              [er::
25   P:   I: (0.6) I was no:t. I'm sure he wa:s (0.5) er::: (0.2) I mean we had
26        several periods of falling ou:t. (0.6) er:: (0.6)
27   C:   Mm hm
28        (1.0)
```

1  List the devices from ordinary conversation that C and P use to monitor each other's talk.
2  In what ways do C and P produce their talk as 'institutional'?

## Exercise 6.4

Below is a later extract drawn from the consultation presented in Extracts 6.6 and 6.7.

(D = doctor: M = mother)

```
1   D:   It sounds as if generally you're having a difficult time
2   M:   Her temper is vile
3   D:   She with you and you with her
4   M:   Yes. And her control of the diabetes is gone, her temper then takes control
5        of her
```

Using the analysis already given of Extracts 6.6 and 6.7, consider the following:

1  What interpretive repertoires do M and D use to organize their talk?
2  How is D's interpretation on line 3 of M's utterance on line 2 hearable as a charge?
3  How does M's utterance on line 4 respond to D's interpretation? Is it hearable as a rebuttal?
4  Can we learn anything from this extract about:

(a)  M's attitude to her daughter
(b)  cultural assumptions about motherhood?

# 7

# Visual Images

In Chapter 6, we considered how we can transcribe and analyse conversations. As I noted, however, audio recordings will not tell us about such potentially relevant matters as who is looking at whom and their body posture. Similarly, in Chapter 5, we concentrated on written texts to the exclusion of the visual images which coexist with words (as in most advertisements and highway signs) and sometimes replace them (as in traffic lights).

Up to this point, my avoidance (or downplaying) of the visual image follows a tendency in much qualitative research. As I noted in Chapter 3, even ethnographers who gather observational data have sometimes been curiously reluctant to use their eyes as well as their ears.

In defence of this position, it is sometimes argued that concern with the image alone can deflect attention from the social processes involved in image production and image reception. For instance, Slater (1989) argues that a focus on the images used in advertisements has neglected the way in which such images are shaped by the economic logic and social organization of the relationship between advertising agencies and their clients. A similar argument lies behind the switch of film analysis in the 1980s away from the analysis of film images and towards understanding the logic of movie production in terms of the studio system.

Whatever the strength of these arguments, perhaps our focus on the verbal may, in part, reflect something altogether more mundane. Unlike artists, architects, engineers or craftspeople, academic researchers learn to prioritize verbal products ('publish or perish' as the slogan goes). So what we *see* is taken for granted and our first thought tends to associate social research with what we can *read* (texts, statistics) or hear (interviews, conversations).

However, our reluctance to consider using our eyes as a research tool points, I think, to something far deeper than academic politics. In societies where television and cinema are central to leisure, there are grounds to believe that, somewhat ironically, we have become lazy with our eyes. Perhaps our learned appetite for 'action' blinds us to the possibility of a slower, more reflective viewing (see my discussion of an ethnographic appreciation of movies after Table 3.1).

In any event, as I have found to my own cost, sit a bunch of students in front of a movie and they will tend to switch off their brains and just let the experience wash over them. So the likely output will not be close-grained analysis but mental popcorn.

However, it is not just a matter of recognizing the importance of visual phenomena. The analysis of images raises complex methodological and theoretical issues. We can appreciate this point by using a concrete example taken from Eric Livingston (1987).

Livingston asks us to imagine that we have been told to carry out some social research on city streets. Where should we begin? Some alternatives are set out in Table 7.1.

TABLE 7.1   *Viewing a street: data possibilities*

| | |
|---|---|
| 1 | Official statistics (traffic flow, accidents) |
| 2 | Interviews (how people cope with rush hours) |
| 3 | Observation from a tower (viewing geometric shapes) |
| 4 | Observation/video at street level (how people queue/organize their movements). |

*Source:* adapted from Livingston, 1987: 21–7

As Livingston points out, each of these different ways of looking at the street involves basic theoretical as well as methodological decisions. Very crudely, if we are attached to social theories which see the world in terms of correlations between social facts (think of demography or macroeconomics), we are most likely to consider gathering official statistics (option 1 in Table 7.1). By contrast, if we think that social meanings or perceptions are important (as in certain varieties of sociology and psychology), we may be tempted by the interview study (option 2). Or if we are anthropologists or those kinds of sociologists who want to observe and/or record what people actually do *in situ*, we might elect options 3 or 4. But note the very different views of people's behaviour we get by observing from on high (3), where people look like ants forming geometrical shapes like wedges, and from street level (4), where behaviour seems much more complex.

The point is that none of these data are more real or more true than the others. For instance, people are not really more like ants or complex actors. It all depends on our research question. And research questions are inevitably theoretically informed.

### Attempt Exercise 7.1 about now

All this means that visual data are not intrinsically better or worse than any other kind of data. We need social theories to help us to identify what is important in the world around us and then, by analysis, to make something of it.

I will shortly introduce some of the theories that we can use to analyse visual images. First, however, I want to give some more examples of the range of visual images that have been studied in qualitative social research.

## 7.1 EXAMPLES OF VISUAL DATA

Rod Watson has made a list of just some of the visual images that could count as qualitative data:

> Tattoos, 'bus tickets, payslips, street signs, time indications on watch faces, chalked information on blackboards, computer VDU displays, car dashboards, company logos, contracts, railway timetables, television programme titles, teletexts, T-shirt epigrams, 'On'/'Off' switches, £10 notes and other bank notes, passports and identity cards, cheques and payslips, the Bible, receipts, newspapers and magazines, road markings, computer keyboards, medical prescriptions, birthday cards, billboard advertisements, maps, *Hansard*, graffiti on walls, music scores, church liturgies, drivers' licences, birth, marriage and death certificates, voting slips, degree certificates, bookkeepers' accounts, stock inventories, cricket scoreboards, credit cards. (1997: 80)

As Watson notes, his list reveals 'the extraordinary diversity in the work done' by images. Among this work, Watson mentions 'contractual commitment, ratifying work, facilitating work, record-keeping, persuasive work [and] identity-establishing work'. Each item, he tells us, 'help(s) us to orientate ourselves to that activity, occasion or setting and to make sense of it' (1997: 80).

To illustrate further the diverse work that images do, I will use three examples: a bus stop, a set of cartoons and a star atlas.

### 7.1.1 *A bus stop*

Here is how Rod Watson has described some research he carried out with John Lee on video recordings of people at bus stops and shelters in an inner suburb of Paris:

> People formed a cluster in and around the shelter. A 'bus came with the sign '16' on its side. On the front was another '16' plus the name of the destination. Some people in the cluster self-selected for the 'bus and formed a queue in order to board it. Others 'disqualified' themselves for this 'bus, often pulling back to let past those visibly wishing to board. The 'bus route (and destination) sign served to 'partial out' or partition those passengers wishing to board that particular 'bus and those wanting a 'bus for another destination. In addition, there were some young people hanging around the outside of the shelter for a considerable time with no apparent intention of boarding any 'bus, and it is arguable that the sign on the 'bus helped to 'partial out' 'waiting passengers' as opposed to 'non-passengers' too. (1997: 92)

Watson suggests that you can identify 'a variety of courses of action' that follow from how these people responded to the bus sign. These actions include:

1. people who included themselves as part of a queue waiting for the number 16 bus

2 people who showed that they were waiting for other buses on different routes but who still manifested 'waiting behaviour'

3 people whose activities were those of a non-travelling spectatorship, including the researchers (1997: 92).

What distinguishes groups 1 and 2 from group 3 is that the former group actively displayed that they were monitoring the sign on the side of the approaching bus. But even more interpretive work was required by the former group before they could board a bus. Waiting passengers were observed to put questions to the driver and to other passengers getting onto the bus, and to consult other images and texts such as the bus timetable. As Watson notes:

> These courses of action resulted in the re-formatting of the configuration of persons in and around the 'bus shelter in somewhat the same way as a kaleidoscope re-formats patterns. (1997: 92)

Following what we have learned from Livingston (Table 7.1), Watson's approach leads him to interpret pedestrians as forming shapes or patterns. However, the kinds of patterns that Watson identifies are derived from a highly specific ethnomethodological model in which the analyst aims to describe the methods that persons use in doing social life (see Section 7.3). Using this model, Watson treats the social organization of waiting at a bus stop as:

> a textually-mediated, self-administered sorting system. That is, the re-configuration of the people at the shelter, e.g. the formation of some of them into a queue upon the arrival of the 'bus, where before there had simply been a cluster of waiting persons, was their own collaborative, textually-mediated accomplishment. (1997: 93)

Watson's research was based on the video recording of naturally occurring interactions. My next two examples derive from published texts.

### 7.1.2 Cartoons

Emmison and McHoul (1987) gathered a set of cartoons about economic issues that appeared in English-language newspapers and periodicals between roughly 1920 and 1980 (see also Emmison and Smith, 2000: 86–90). According to their analysis, it turns out that there are at least three phases in how 'the economy' is represented:

- Before the 1930s, 'economy' refers only to the classical notion of 'economizing' through cutting back unnecessary expenditure.
- In the 1930s, Keynesian ideas about a national economic structure, able to be modified by government intervention, start to be represented. Thus a contemporary cartoon shows 'Slump' as a half-ghost, half-scarecrow figure, while a jaunty Father Christmas dismisses Slump with a wave of his hand.

For the first time, then, the 'economy' becomes embodied (as a sick person) and collective solutions to economic problems are implied (Father Christmas dispensing gifts via government spending).

• By the 1940s, the economy is understood as a fully collective, embodied being. Often cartoons of that period use animals to represent both the economy and economic policy. One cartoon depicts the economy as a sea-monster. Another shows the Budget as a box of snakes charmed by a finance minister.

Emmison and McHoul give us a way to think about the interplay between words and images in cartoons. As they would recognize, we can apply their approach to how the world is represented in a wide range of media products (see my discussion of newspaper headlines and lonely hearts columns in Section 5.4).

### 7.1.3 A star atlas

Lindsay Prior (1997) refers to a very different artefact. Unlike cartoons, star atlases are intended to be serious and long-lasting. But such atlases share with cartoons the use of particular forms of representation which instruct us how we should view them. As Prior notes:

> The Atlas represents the shape of the universe as we currently understand it, and it describes that universe mainly by reference to the constellations (Pisces, Orion, Cygnus and so on). These constellations are very clearly human constructions in the sense that they exist only in the annals of human culture. (Thus, no one, I think, would argue that the stars in Andromeda belong together in anything other than a star atlas made by earthpersons.) More importantly of course, the Atlas informs us how we should 'observe' the night sky. It tells us what to 'see', it structures our observation and our understanding. Moreover, as its maps and projections of the universe change from one edition to another so do our perceptions of that same universe. (1997: 67)

Watson, Emmison and McHoul, and Prior show us how we come to know the world through the ways it is represented. As Watson tells us, the aim of researching 'visual images' is to examine the 'work' that they do and to understand how they do that work.

However, such examination can never be neutral or purely inductive. Inevitably, therefore, the student of images will need to work with a *model*. In the rest of this chapter, I consider two such models: *semiotics* (Section 7.2) and *ethnomethodology* and *conversation analysis* (CA) (Section 7.3).

This excludes some vital traditions used in visual analysis, notably work drawing upon the French philosopher Michel Foucault (see Kendall and Wickham, 1999) and the somewhat amorphous collection of studies that classifies itself as *postmodernism* and/or cultural studies.

However, what we shall lose in narrowness is, I believe, balanced by the fact that the two models dealt with here will not be entirely foreign to readers of the earlier chapters of this book. We have already come across CA in Section 6.3, and semiotics was briefly discussed early in Chapter 5.

The organization of systems of narration, within literature and elsewhere, has been of constant interest to writers influenced by Saussure's science of signs, to which I turn first.

## 7.2  SEMIOTICS

As already noted, one of the difficulties in working with images is the range of complex theoretical traditions available. One tradition that has been used to considerable effect in this area is concerned with the analysis of sign systems. Following Saussure, it has now been called **semiotics**.

Semiotics is the science of 'signs'. It shows how signs relate to one another in order to create and exclude particular meanings. Semiotics arose in the early years of the last century out of the lectures of the Swiss linguist Ferdinand de Saussure (see Culler, 1976; Hawkes, 1977).

To understand what Saussure was saying (like Harvey Sacks, most of Saussure's work is only available in transcripts of his lectures), we must know a little about the concerns of linguistics.

Before the twentieth century, linguistics viewed language as an aggregate of units (words), each of which had a separate meaning attached to it (Stubbs, 1981). Linguistic research was mainly *etymological*, i.e. it concentrated on historical changes in the meanings of words.

In the early 1900s, Saussure revolutionized this approach. Hawkes (1977) has identified the two crucial aspects of Saussure's reform of linguistic research:

1  His rejection of a substantive view of language – concerned with the correspondence between individual words and their meanings – in favour of a **relational** view, stressing the system of relations between words as the source of meaning.
2  His shift away from historical or **diachronic** analysis towards an analysis of a language's present functioning (a **synchronic** analysis). No matter what recent change a language has undergone, it remains, at any given point in time, a complete system. As Hawkes puts it: 'Each language has a wholly valid existence apart from its history as a system of sounds issuing from the lips of those who speak it now' (1977: 20).

Saussure now makes a distinction between *language* (langue) and *speech* (parole). We need to distinguish the system of language (langue) from the actual speech acts (parole) that any speaker actually utters. The latter are not determined by language, which only provides the system of elements in terms of which speech occurs.

Saussure uses the analogy of a chess game to explain this. The rules and conventions of chess constitute a language (langue) within which actual moves (parole) take place. For Saussure, the linguist's primary concern is not to describe parole but to establish the elements and their rules of combination which together constitute the linguistic system (*la langue*).

Having identified *la langue* as the concern of linguistics, Saussure now notes that language is comparable to other social institutions like systems of writing, symbolic rites and sign systems for the deaf. All these institutions are systems of signs and can be studied systematically. Saussure calls such a science of signs *semiology* (from the Greek *semeion* = 'sign'). Later writers use the same root to describe this method as *semiotics*.

Signs have the four characteristics set out in Table 7.2.

TABLE 7.2   *Four characteristics of signs*

1   Signs bring together an image or word (the 'signifier') and a concept (the 'signified'). For example, in a road sign, a picture of a deer is the signifier and 'take care, animals about' is signified.

2   Signs are not autonomous entities: they derive their meaning only from their place within a sign system. What constitutes a sign is only its difference from other signs (so the colour red is only something which is not green, blue, orange etc.).

3   The linguistic sign is *arbitrary* or unmotivated. This, Saussure says, means that the sign 'has no natural connection with the signified' (1974: 69). Different languages simply use different terms for concepts. Indeed they can generate their own concepts: think, for instance, how difficult it is to translate a game into another culture where, because the game is not played there, they lack the relevant terms.

4   Signs can be put together through two main paths. First, there are combinatory possibilities (e.g. the order of a religious service or the prefixes and suffixes that can be attached to a noun: for example, 'friend' can become 'boyfriend', 'friendship', 'friendly' etc.). Saussure calls these patterns of combinations *syntagmatic relations*. Second, there are contrastive properties (e.g. choosing one hymn rather than another in a church service; saying 'yes' or 'no'). Here the choice of one term necessarily excludes the other. Saussure calls these mutually exclusive relations *paradigmatic oppositions*.

An example may help to pull these various features of signs together. Think of traffic lights:

- They bring together concepts ('stop', 'start') with images ('red', 'green').
- These images are not autonomous: red is identifiable by the fact that it is not green, and vice versa.
- Traffic lights have no natural connection with what they signify: red has simply come to mean 'stop' and green to mean 'start'.
- Traffic lights express *syntagmatic* relations (the order in which the traffic lights can change, from red to green and back again, but much more complicated in countries where there is also an amber light).
- Traffic lights are also interpreted by means of *paradigmatic* oppositions: imagine the chaos created if red and green light up simultaneously!

This means that signs derive their meaning only from their relations with and differences from other signs. This further implies that the meaning of signs cannot be finally fixed. It is always possible to extend the signifying chain.

**Attempt Exercise 7.2 about now**

Semiotics continues to provide a vital apparatus for the analysis of texts – both verbal and visual. For instance, Vladimir Propp's influential analysis of the narrative organization of fairy stories (see Section 5.2) clearly draws upon Saussure's concept of the synchronic organization of a system of signs.

Thirty years after Propp, the French writer Roland Barthes also followed Saussure by arguing that semiotics was a science of *differences*, focused, like economics, on the *value* of different elements in relation to one another. To illustrate this point, Barthes (1967) uses a visual example drawn from one of Saussure's lectures.

Think of a sheet of paper. Imagine that we cut this paper into a number of shapes. Each shape has a 'value' in relation to the others (for instance, it is bigger or smaller than they are); it also has a back and a front.

If we imagine that the sheet of paper corresponds to a system of signs (language), the task of semiotics is to discover how the different shapes (signs) into which it is cut establish a particular set of meanings. This means that we must observe any given system of signs 'from the inside', using a finite corpus of shapes. As Barthes argues:

> [we must not] add anything to it [the corpus] during the course of the research, [we must] exhaust it completely by analysis, every fact included in the corpus having to be found in the system. (1967: 96–7)

However, like many later researchers, Barthes is critical about Saussure's insistence (taken up in *structural anthropology*) that we should focus only on sign systems (what Saussure called langue), not on how signs are actually used (parole).

How signs are actually used (parole) is not, for Barthes, the kind of trivial, psychological domain that Saussure indicated. For Barthes and most later semioticians, the work of signs is not reducible to the mechanics of a given sign system. Indeed, how signs are actually used sets into play and potentially challenges (as well as sustains) the codes of language.

Some examples may help to explain this. Following Saussure, colours are relational – constituted by their differences. Hence red is not orange (or any other colour). Now think of the way in which some great artists use palettes which make us rethink the way particular colours stand in relation to others. Although the spectrum of colours is fixed, the *relation* between particular colours can be endlessly rearticulated. This process is, however, not limited to aesthetics.

Think of the symbolic potential of a cut-price airline's advertising slogans in the 1980s: 'People's Airline'. Here the signifier 'People' is being used to signify that flying is everybody's right. We only have to compare the slogan 'People's Airline' with the term 'People's Republic' (still used to describe the Chinese state) to see that how signs are articulated with each other is not a trivial matter. And, of course, these examples reflect only some of the myriad connections that have been made between these elements.

## Attempt Exercise 7.3 about now

The use of 'nationalism' and 'patriotism' underlines the political implications of how signs are articulated with each other and puts some further meat on Saussure's somewhat bare and abstract bones. What Saussure called a relational view of language shows how nationalism only gets a meaning in relation to other terms: hence the Nazi success in identifying a relation between nationalism or patriotism and fascism (e.g. National Socialism). Conversely, as Laclau (1981) has shown, during World War II communist Italian politicians successfully appealed to the apparently indissoluble links between being a patriotic Italian and supporting a party opposed to the Germans.

Since terms have no fixed meaning derived from their past use, populist politicians will try to incorporate popular signs (such as 'patriotism') into their vocabulary. Think, for instance, of the power of the name of Senator McCarthy's red-baiting hearings in the early 1950s: the *Un-American* Activities Committee.

Following Saussure, these examples show that the meaning of a sign is never totally fixed. However, Saussure's insistence on the 'arbitrary' character of any sign need not mean that we should follow him in downplaying the creative way in which signs can be used to establish a favoured set of meanings.

Let me provide a famous *visual* example of how signs are used in this way. Roland Barthes (1973) discusses a photograph in a French magazine taken at the time that France still possessed an African empire. The photo shows a black man who is wearing the uniform of the French army. This man is depicted saluting the French national flag.

To understand the layers of meaning we can read into this image, Barthes (1967: 89ff) introduces the concept of *denotation*. Denotation, according to Barthes, is the surface meaning of signs. In these terms, we note the sign of the salute, formed between the movement of the soldier's arm and the flag upon which his gaze is fixed, and the sign of colour ('black' being selected from the paradigmatic opposition of primary colours).

However, Barthes tells us, there is a deeper level of meaning to be found in this image. The sign as a whole connotes the free participation of 'subject' peoples in the French Empire. At this level, the surface meaning is used to signify a system of *connotation*. This system unconsciously informs the viewer about what the surface meaning of this image implies – the naturalness and hence unquestionability of French imperialism.

Barthes claims to have identified how this image works to sustain what he terms a 'myth' (indeed his book of essays on different images is called *Mythologies*). Conceived as a 'narrative' (see Section 5.2), the myth recreated in this image is, for Barthes, 'true' because it expresses an ideology actually used to sustain French imperialism. But it is also 'false' because it conceals a particular system of connotation.

Barthes's identification of the semiotic analyst as a 'reader of myths' has an impressive intellectual pedigree. In the nineteenth century, Karl Marx had suggested that we treat textbooks of political economy not as sober academic treatises but as 'adventure stories'. And, as we have seen, in the twentieth century, Saussure, followed by structural anthropology, exhibited the structuralist urge to locate 'deep structures' behind particular signs.

However, as Barthes himself was shortly to recognize, such ploys have at least two limitations:

1　By looking behind and underneath signs, they fail to analyse properly the complex internal workings of relations between signs.
2　Accounts of underlying structures or 'myths' create the illusion of an all-knowing analyst who somehow remains outside sign systems.

Barthes's later work was an attempt to recant much of his position in *Mythologies*. In his collection of essays called *Image, Music, Text* (1977), the concept of 'myth' disappears. It is replaced by an insistence on what Barthes terms a 'play of signifiers'. If there is anything 'ideological' about signs, Barthes now finds it not in ironic contrasts between 'appearance' and 'reality' but wherever this potentially 'indefinite' play of signifiers is terminated or closed off. Barthes's later position was important in the emergence of *postmodernism* and its treatment of signification as a pastiche of insecure and changing elements.

The rest of this chapter is taken up with an account of research on images taken from a very different tradition: ethnomethodology and conversation analysis.

## 7.3  ETHNOMETHODOLOGY AND CONVERSATION ANALYSIS

As I noted in Chapter 5, following Garfinkel (1967), *ethnomethodology* attempts to understand 'folk' (*ethno*) methods (*methodology*) for organizing the world. It locates these methods in the skills ('artful practices') through which people come to develop an understanding of each other and of social situations. I will illustrate the uses of ethnomethodology as a method for the analysis of visual data by looking at how it helps to understand what has been called 'common-sense geography' by studying how our location in space is defined in different contexts.

### 7.3.1  Common-sense geography

Schegloff (1972: 80) suggests that Sacks's work on how we select identifications of *persons* (see Section 5.4) can be extended to how we select formulations for locations. For instance, how do we describe where we are now – as in a particular room, house, street, town etc.? Note the children's game of writing on exercise books not just their name but their 'address' including such items as 'Earth', 'the solar system', 'the universe' etc.!

As Schegloff puts it, the analyst's interest in locational formulations is that:

> For any location to which reference is made, there is a set of terms each of which, by a correspondence test, is a correct way to refer to it. On any actual occasion of use, however, not any member of the set is 'right'. How is it that on particular occasions of use some term from the set is selected and other terms are rejected? (1972: 81)

One rule seems to be: do not refer to locations at which all parties are *co-present*. For instance, in a collection of calls to a police department, none referred to the name of the city in which the call was made and the police department was situated (1972: 83).

A second rule is that people who live or work in a place 'may be expected to recognize place names in or near it' (1972: 92). For instance, Schegloff refers to someone asking him 'Are you going to Columbia?' prior to asking directions to the university (1972: 89). In this way, asking for and providing locations are activities rich in membership category implications because we can inspect them 'to see what sort of person [the speaker] must be to have produced [them]' (1972: 94).

Third, Schegloff distinguishes location formulations such as street address, which he calls geographical (G), from location formulations which relate to members (Rm), such as 'John's place' and 'Al's house' or even 'the supermarket' where this is the place to which we both go (1972: 97). He then suggests that, providing the recipient is not a stranger:

> the preference rule appears to be: use an Rm formulation if you can. (1972: 100)

All this implies, for Schegloff, that members use 'a common-sense geography' to report relevant locations. For instance, in conversations between Americans about foreign travel:

> it appears one goes 'to South America' not 'Peru', just as one goes 'to Europe' not 'France'. If one says one went to France, one is asked 'where else?', rather than 'where in France, did you visit?' Persons who went 'just to France' may have to account for it. (1972: 86)

However, such spoken location formulations cannot be separated from the sequence of talk in which they occur. As Schegloff himself implies, how do we translate 'downstairs', 'in front' and 'across the street' into meaningful objects (1972: 88)? As he puts it:

> on each occasion in conversation on which a formulation of location is used, attention is exhibited to the particulars of the occasion. In selecting a 'right' formulation, attention is exhibited to 'where-we-know-we-are', to 'who-we-know-we-are', to 'what-we-are-doing-at-this-point-in-the-conversation'. (1972: 115)

It is worth pointing out that recognizing the context-boundedness (or *indexicality*) of location formulations is very different from saying that such formulations are *dependent* upon social context. As Schegloff suggests:

> To say that interaction is context-sensitive is to say that interactants are context-sensitive. (1972: 115)

It follows that, rather than try to engage in conventional social science tasks (e.g. relating location formulations to 'contexts'), we must investigate:

> how participants analyze context and use the product of their analysis in producing their interaction. (1972: 115)

The upshot of this seems to be twofold. First, 'location formulations' are undoubtedly an important, investigatable matter. However, second, investigation should be directed to how members, in the contingencies of their interaction, actually 'do' location rather than to the attempt to formulate analysts' rules.

Alec McHoul and Rod Watson (1984) have pursued the topic of location by an analysis of a brief extract from a geography lesson at an Australian high school. They ask:

> how is commonsense geographical knowledge transformed into subject knowledge and how do such methodical features of the co-participants' talk provide for this? (1984: 283)

They trace this movement from 'common-sense' to 'subject' knowledge through the ways participants select and come to agree about 'place references' (1984: 283). Part of the extract which they analyse is reproduced as Extract 7.1. In it T refers to a teacher and CBD to the central business district and Lois is a student.

Using *membership categorization device* (MCD) analysis, McHoul and Watson argue that, in lines 1–2, the teacher establishes a location device with 'court house' as a category drawn from the MCD 'public buildings'. Given court house's positioning with this MCD, the teacher suggests being 'central' as category-bound to it (i.e. a category-bound activity or CBA).

**Extract 7.1 (McHoul and Watson, 1984: 287, simplified)**
```
 1  Lois:  Perhaps a court house is likely to be centred very close-t'the CBD then
 2          again there're other types of public buildings
 3          (0.7)
 4  T:      ee gee (0.3) e:r fire station-which possibly should be- located in the
 5          suburbs-so you'd be wrong if y'had all y'public buildings in the
 6          CBD-y'd probably be wrong if y'had e::::::r a great dispersal of
 7          y'public buildings
 8  Lois:  The university also would be away from the s::: city centre (a bit) too
 9  T:      Why's that Lois?
```

10  Lois:  Oh th's just more space out there I s'pose
11          (1.0)
12  Lois:  Ahm
13  (3.4)
14  Lois:  Ah wouldn't be too far away but it would be right in among all the
15          court houses 'n (0.2) churches 'n things like that

However, McHoul and Watson remind us that Sacks suggested that not all CBAs cover all categories in any MCD. In particular, in 'positioned category devices' (see Section 5.4), each category may be *ranked* in relation to the appropriate CBA. In this regard, they argue, 'fire station' (line 4) is used by the teacher to suggest that the MCD 'public buildings' can include CBAs ranked in the following range: 'probably central' (court houses) to 'possibly suburban' (fire stations).

Lois shows her understanding of this structure by offering a further category ('university', line 8) from the same MCD ('public buildings') ranked in the same way as 'fire station'. Moreover, in line 15, she provides another category ('churches') which she ranks with court house.

Following Schegloff's (1972) insistence that there is no 'right' formulation of location, McHoul and Watson remind us that categories such as 'court house' are not automatically tied to 'central' but depend, on every occasion, upon members' interpretive work. Their analysis, then, distances itself from any claims about the cultural meaning of location terms. Instead, it sets out to be an analysis of what they call 'commonsense geography (or urban ecology)' (1984: 291). As Garfinkel (1967) shows, such a common-sense geography inevitably depends upon the employment of such members' resources as 'ad hocing' and 'the documentary method of interpretation'.

In the classroom, these resources are used by teacher and pupil to produce a recognizable 'geography lesson'. As Paul Drew (1978: 3–4) points out, through the descriptions that members provide, 'interactional tasks' (like a lesson) are accomplished. Sometimes, however, these tasks may be more obviously politicized and so the issue of location descriptions becomes more politically 'loaded' than in either the classroom example or Schegloff's discussion of street directions.

For instance, in British public hearings into 'Violence and Civil Disorder in Northern Ireland' in 1969, Drew shows how witnesses' descriptions of locations appealed to 'the normally organized religious geography of Belfast' (1978: 4). So, for instance, when witnesses refer to the Shankill Road, they will be heard to use a category drawn from the MCD 'Protestant areas' and associated with various category-bound activities (e.g. Orange Orders, marching, wearing bowler hats etc.).

Moreover, this is not an analyst's surmise. As Drew shows, a lawyer at the hearings used such location devices (among other items) as 'indicative of an invasion of Catholic areas by Protestants' (1978: 11). In turn, this formulation is not a passive, culturally determined reading. Rather, it actively constructs a category-bound set of activities with clear political implications – in this case what Drew calls an 'accusation'. We can see the force of Drew's point if we compare, for instance, the word 'invasion' used here with the possible alternative description 'peaceful march'.

Similarly, Georgia Lepper's (1995) study of a 'duty rota logbook' compiled at a British further education college shows how the entries are organized as accusations which encourage further disciplinary action. In one case, for instance, a student's activities are defined as follows: 'spends her time in the refectory and not in the library'. When this location category is combined with the description 'she is rude and aggressive', the reader is provided with a set of CBAs which imply the MCD 'trouble-maker'. Such a membership category powerfully encourages some disciplinary outcome while prospectively exonerating college staff from any possible counter-charge, for example 'harassment' (1995: 197–9).

**Attempt Exercise 7.4 about now**

So far, the ethnomethodological studies we have been considering are concerned with how people establish together a particular location in space and place. However, this only gives us an indirect understanding of visual images as made available in conversations and verbal texts.

For a more direct understanding of the place of the visual in everyday life, we must turn to studies which, through analysis of videotapes, show how participants actually attend to visual elements in their environment. Part of the environment of that talk is the bodily presence and gaze of others and/or the technologies through which people communicate. This area has been a major concern of conversation analysis (CA). In Section 7.3.2 I present three CA-informed studies of how people use such resources.

### 7.3.2  Using visual and mechanical resources

*Conversation analysis* (CA) emerged from the work of Harvey Sacks (1992) who studied with Garfinkel. As we saw in Section 6.3, CA is based on the attempt to describe people's methods for producing orderly talk-in-interaction.

As I remarked in Chapter 6, Sacks was certainly aware of the importance of such non-verbal communication. For instance, his students were given an exercise where they had to observe people exchanging glances. Sacks then showed them how you can analyse the descriptive apparatus involved in the glance (1992, I: 88).

However, Sacks was concerned about the technical problems of working with video recordings. For instance, he responded to a question about gaze and body movements with the assertion that, while 'it would be great to study them', there are, at present, too many technical problems (like where you place the camera) (1992, II: 26).

Since Sacks's time, many of the technical problems of recording and transcribing non-verbal communication have been resolved and some important studies have revealed the fascinating interpenetration of talk, gaze and body movements (e.g. Heath, 1986; Goodwin and Goodwin, 1986; Peräkylä and Silverman, 1991). For instance, Goodwin (1981) has discussed how speakers can assess recipiency for their talk by inspecting the gaze of others. As he shows, speakers who find their addressee looking away restart their speech. This usually solicits the orientation of a recipient to a newly initiated complete turn.

However, people attend to other objects in their environment than just co-conversationalists. For instance, as I noted above, place and location can be an important topic for members. Equally, as I show below, mechanical objects such as computer screens and photocopiers are routinely made the focus of joint attention.

In this part of the chapter, I will not attempt to provide a summary of such research (for a valuable discussion, see Heath, 1997). Instead, I will review three studies: Don Zimmerman's (1992) work on emergency calls, Christian Heath's (1997) discussion of the interrelation of body movements and gaze in medical consultations, and Lucy Suchman's (1987) study of how photocopiers are used. All three studies show how video data can be used in CA. They also bear on a theme discussed in Section 6.3.4: how 'institutionality' is locally produced.

### Calls to emergency services

Zimmerman (1992) is concerned with the interactional organization of the talk occurring in calls to US 911 emergency telephone numbers operated by the emergency services. His research was based on data from three centres (one in the Midwest, two on the West Coast).

The study focuses on calls to two of the centres which have a computer-assisted dispatch system (CAD). This follows the following pattern:

1  Requests for police, fire and medical assistance are taken by call-takers (CTs).
2  CTs enter information received from callers (Cs) into a computer terminal.
3  This information is transmitted to dispatchers (Ds) who further process it and forward it to appropriate field units.

Zimmerman argues that this pattern means that we need to look at each call in terms of the *functions* it fulfils in relation to organizational and callers' concerns. This often involves complicated management in order to align callers to the needs of call-takers.

The work of call-takers responds to a number of organizational constraints, including:

1  obtaining *accurate* locations, e.g. the Midwest centre's CAD will reject intersections it does not recognize
2  establishing the nature of the problem
3  in the case of criminal activity, obtaining 'full' descriptions of suspects

4  obtaining the name and location of the caller
5  fitting all of the above speedily into a 'dispatch package' entered into the available CAD codes which, among other things, characterize the 'problem' (e.g. 'pergun' means person with a gun, and 'p1' means priority 1).

Zimmerman shows that these constraints shape the character of C–CT talk in the following ways. First, CTs have to cut off long-winded or 'hysterical' Cs. They attempt to do this by issuing directives ('stop shouting', 'answer my questions') or offering reassurance ('help is on the way').

Second, by contrast, CTs simultaneously have to ensure that Cs don't hang up before the relevant information has been given. However, 'help is on the way' may be heard as a closing invitation. So, typically, it is combined with a 'stay on the line' request as in Extract 7.2.

> **Extract 7.2 (Zimmerman, 1992: 8)**
> CT:  We have units on the way, okay just stay on the phone with me
> C:    Okay

Finally, at all times, CTs have to attend to Cs' talk in terms of what is reportable via the CAD codes. This means that response tokens from the CT are often replaced by the sound of the computer keyboard as in Extract 7.3.

> **Extract 7.3 (Zimmerman, 1992: 4)**
> (kb = sound of keyboard being used)
>
> 1   C:  hhh Uh there's uh (0.2) oh I think it's uh (.) *white jeep*
> 2        (.) hh jeepster tha[t pulled up here uh in front.
> 3                            [kb - - - - - - - - - - - - - - - - - - -
> 4   C:  =An there's about (0.1)] five Nihgro guys tha' got out, I -
> 5        - - - - - - - - - - - - - - - ]
> 6        heard=um tal[kin about (0.1) hh going (.) to thee] next
> 7                    [- - - - - - - - - - - - - - - - - - - - - - - -]
> 8        apartment building uh fur uh *fight* (0.2) [hh a ]n I jus'
> 9                                                    [- - - -]
> 10       am going down tuh check it out

As Zimmerman notes about this extract:

> At the possible conclusion of C's account of the trouble . . . [on line 8] CT says nothing while she continues her keyboard activity. After a pause of 0.2 second, C initiates [an] elaboration . . . which, in the absence of a receipt of acknowledgment from CT, may be oriented to the possibility of some problem with his narrative. (1992: 427)

This absence of response tokens, one expected feature of hearers' activities when not taking a turn at any given possible turn transition point in ordinary conversation, thus has observable consequences in these calls. As Zimmerman suggests, the absence of such a response token may be heard by C as indicating a trouble in the report. Thus it can lead to hedges and downgrades (e.g. less than ten lines from the end of Extract 7.3, C hedges, stating that 'it might not be anything').

CTs must also orient both to what Cs are saying and to what they are *about* to say. Hence they may defer initiating inquiries if their monitoring of the Cs' talk suggests the upcoming delivery of a piece of pertinent information. Some of these kinds of organizational 'solutions' are oriented to by Cs.

So, here, unlike other telephone calls, the opening sequence does not routinely contain a greeting or a 'how are you' sequence. Both parties typically seek to reach the 'reason for the call' sequence as soon as possible.

However, some callers may be particularly responsive to what CTs require. For instance, organizations routinely in contact with the emergency services offer ordered tellings of problems, oriented to the organizational needs of CTs. This is seen in Extract 7.4 where C is a caller from the staff of a hospital ('General').

**Extract 7.4 (Zimmerman, 1992: 56)**

CT: Emergency
C: Hi hh General, there's been an overdose. (.) Twenty three twenty three hh
   I[daho: hh
CT: [(keyboard) O:kay
C: Upstairs apartment num:ber two: hh
CT: Thank you=
C: =Umhm bye

In Extract 7.4, C's two turns convey all the information that CT needs. Hence her 'thank you' is closing implicative and heard as such by C.

However, in the case of non-institutional callers, there is often an intractable problem in aligning Cs' and CTs' perspectives. For CTs, calls have to be made as routine as possible: hence 'emergencies' have to be transformed into ordinary, predictable events. Conversely, for Cs 'emergencies' are, by definition, non-routine and must be displayed as such.

Zimmerman's study shows the unintended consequences of the use of PCs in emergency call centres. As Heath (1997) shows, the growing use of PCs by general practitioners has also had an unexpected impact on their communication with patients. To understand this further, we need to examine how doctors and patients organize their gaze. Even the simple act of writing a prescription turns out to have important interactional consequences.

## Communicating with patients: the body in action

Heath (1997) discusses a medical consultation with a female patient complaining of pain in her knee. Towards the end of the consultation, the doctor begins to prepare a prescription. As he starts to write, the patient, who is still standing following the physical examination, begins to tell a story.

Extract 7.5 shows how she tells her story. Her words are transcribed using the CA conventions explained in the Appendix. In addition, however, Extract

7.5 shows both body movements and the direction of the participants' gaze (marked as 'up' or 'down').

> **Extract 7.5 (Heath, 1997: 194, Fragment 1, Transcript 3, adapted)**
>
> ```
>      walks
>      up      down          up    down up down    up  down
> P:   I was coming up the steps li:ke this all the way up I felt
>
> Dr:  writes          turns to    turns to          nods and
>      prescription    P's face    P's legs          smiles
> ```

Here is how Heath describes this extract:

> As the patient begins to describe the difficulties she had walking up the stairs at Debenhams, she starts to walk up and down on the spot, illustrating the problems she experienced. More particularly she places her hand on the doctor's desk and balancing her weight, shows the way in which she distorted her hip and leg movement to actually climb the stairs. The movements give sense to the talk they accompany. They lucidly reveal the problems she experienced and provide a vivid picture of the suffering that she incurred. The utterance itself points to the difficulties and provides a framework in which the movements embody, literally, the patient's difficulties and suffering. (1997: 192)

As Heath points out, however, we should not treat these movements as simply to do with the patient herself. For P has a problem: how to encourage the doctor to look as well as listen to her story. For, as this extract begins, Dr is looking down, while writing a prescription. By its end, however, Dr is looking at his patient.

As Heath comments:

> The patient's success in encouraging the doctor to watch the performance and thereby achieving the sequential relevance of the story derives from the ways in which she designs her bodily conduct.
>
> As she begins to step up for the second time, she swings her hips towards the doctor and in particular the area between the document and his face. As the hips move towards the doctor he looks up, turning to the face of the patient. It is as if the patient's movement elicits the reorientation by the doctor, encouraging him to temporarily abandon writing the prescription and transform the ways in which he is participating in the delivery of the story (cf. Heath, 1986).
>
> On turning to the patient's face, he finds her looking at her own legs as she utters 'like this'. He immediately turns and watches the performance as she steps up and down. And, as she brings the performance to completion with 'terribly' and the doctor utters 'yeh', 'yes' and nods she has successfully established a recipient who has not only heard the tale, but witnessed the difficulties experienced by the patient as she walked up the steps. (1997: 194)

By including the video data in his analysis, Heath has elegantly revealed the interplay between words, gaze and bodily movements. As he puts it, P's bodily conduct is both 'part of her story' and functional in gaining Dr's gaze, and thereby 'an audience for the performance and . . . the sequential relevance of the story' (1997: 195). Now that doctors' activities include not only prescription writing but, like Zimmerman's emergency service telephone operators, looking at the screens of their PCs, Heath's address of the visual elements of conduct could not be more practically relevant.

### Communicating with a photocopier

Like Zimmerman, Lucy Suchman (1987) is concerned with the interaction between people and machines. However, in this case, the communication is not mediated through a caller or client. Instead, she takes the example of a computer-based system attached to a photocopier and intended to instruct the user in the photocopier's operation.

Suchman focuses on how rules function in human–computer interaction. She draws upon Gladwin's (1964) account of the navigation methods of a South East Asian tribe, the Trukese. They have no 'rational' Western theory of navigation: instead, they navigate via various *ad hoc* methods (e.g. responding to the wind, the waves, the stars, the clouds etc.). Suchman asks how real is the contrast between Western and Trukese methods of navigation. Theories and plans do not *determine* the actions of either Western or Trukese navigators. Rather Western navigators *invoke* a plan when asked to account for their navigation which, inevitably, depends on *ad hoc* methods (e.g. accounting for disasters like the Exxon Valdez oil spill off Alaska).

This creates a problem in artificial intelligence systems which are:

> built on a *planning model* of human action. The model treats a plan as something located in the actor's head, which directs his or her behaviour. (Suchman, 1987: 3)

As Suchman notes, plans neither determine action nor fully reconstruct it. Thus she argues that 'artifacts built on the planning model confuse *plans* with *situated actions*' and proposes 'a view of plans as formulations of antecedent conditions and consequences that account for actions in a plausible way' (1987: 3). Conversely, she suggests, the successful navigation of the Trukese shows that:

> the coherence of situated action is tied in essential ways not to . . . conventional rules but to local interactions contingent on the actor's particular circumstances. (1987: 27–8)

This implies that, in designing computers that can interact with humans, the system of communication:

> must incorporate both a sensitivity to local circumstances and resources for the remedy of troubles in understanding that inevitably arise. (1987: 28)

This will mean that:

> Instead of looking for a structure that is invariant across situations, we look for the processes whereby particular, uniquely constituted circumstances are systematically interpreted so as to render meaning shared and action accountably rational. (1987: 67)

There is a methodological basis behind Suchman's focus on processes of systematic interpretation that is worth noting. Although we have not reproduced her data here, like Zimmerman and Heath, her analysis is concerned with the sequential organization of verbal and non-verbal interaction.

Suchman's data derive from videos of four sessions, each of more than an hour, involving first-time users of this 'expert system'. In each session, two novices worked together in pairs. She is particularly concerned with how interactional 'troubles' arise and are resolved.

In Suchman's study the computer used in the photocopier:

> project(s) the course of the user's actions as the enactment of a *plan* for doing the job, and then use(s) the presumed plan as the relevant context for the action's interpretation. (1987: 99, my emphasis)

However, the problem is that 'plans' have a different status for computers and users:

> While the [design] plan directly *determines* the system's behaviour, the user is required to *find* the plan, as the prescriptive and descriptive significance of a series of procedural instructions. (1987: 101, my emphasis)

This is shown in Suchman's model of how the computer is supposed to 'instruct' a user, set out in Table 7.3.

TABLE 7.3   *The basic interactional sequence*

| |
|---|
| 1   *Machine presents instruction* |
| User reads instruction, interprets referents and action descriptions. |
| 2   *User takes action* |
| Design assumes that the action means that the user has understood the instruction. |
| 3   *Machine presents next instruction* |

*Source*: based on Suchman, 1987: 107

Despite this rational model, much of the user's behaviour is unavailable to the system, for instance: 'the actual work of locating referents and interpreting action descriptions' (1987: 107). This means that if an instruction is *misunderstood* by the user, the error will go unnoticed.

Predictably, Suchman's study reveals many conflicts between the design assumptions (DA) built into the machine and the user assumptions (UA). Some examples of this are set out in Table 7.4.

TABLE 7.4   *Design assumptions (DAs) and user assumptions (UAs)*

| | |
|---|---|
| DA | Treat the question 'what next?' as a request for the next step – attended to by presentation of the next instruction. |
| UA | Can ask 'what next?' sometimes in order to know how to abort or repair an activity (e.g. where only one photocopy obtained instead of the five desired). |
| | |
| DA | Repeat instructions either (a) where task needs to be repeated or (b) where user's action in response to the instruction is in error, such as to return the system to a state prior to the instruction being given (a loop). |
| UA | In the case of repeated instructions, (b) does *not* occur in human interaction. Instead, the repetition of an instruction indicates that 'the action taken in response to the instruction in some way fails to satisfy the intent of the instruction, and needs to be remedied' (1987: 148). |
| | |
| DA | Users will follow instructions; where they do not, this will be detected by the machine. |
| UA | Can sometimes ignore instructions because of preconceptions about what is appropriate, based on prior experience. |

*Source*: based on Suchman, 1987: 148–67

As the table shows, a faulted action can go unnoticed at the point where it occurs. This is because:

> what is available to the system is only the action's effect and that effect satisfies the requirements for the next instruction. (1987: 167)

As a consequence, while from the point of view of the design the users have achieved precisely what they want, this is not how users actually perceive their situation. Because of these kinds of conflict between the assumptions of designers and users, Suchman concludes that users often fail to get what they want from the photocopier:

> Due to the constraints on the machine's access to the situation of the user's inquiry, breaches in understanding that for face-to-face interaction would be trivial in terms of detection and repair become 'fatal' for human–machine communication. (1987: 170)

Like many studies concerned with the mechanics of our interaction with the objects around us, Suchman's findings are both analytically and practically rich. Among the practical implications of her study, we may note that:

1  It reveals the character of practical decision-making in a way relevant to the design of expert systems.
2  It suggests the constructive role of users' troubles in system design, i.e. troubles arise not by departing from a plan but in the situated contingencies of action. She notes how such systems may seek not to eliminate user errors but 'to make them accessible to the student, and therefore instructive' (1987: 184).

Suchman's work is important because it uses video recordings to focus on the precise mechanics of institutional interaction. In particular, Suchman begins by using everyday interaction as a baseline and then seeing how far human–computer interaction departs from it. This means that she avoids beginning with the common-sense assumption that there is a stable organizational or institutional order separate from everyday interaction.

**Attempt Exercise 7.5 about now**

## 7.4 CONCLUSION

The observant reader may remark that this is rather an unbalanced account of how qualitative researchers have used visual data. For instance, I have barely discussed certain kinds of data, such as photographs or movies and I have under-played the dominant role of postmodernism in the analysis of the image.

I plead 'guilty' to this charge of imbalance. However, I would enter a plea in mitigation.

With the burgeoning of cultural studies within social science, the study of visual images has become a highly fashionable topic. Although this rediscovery of the visual is welcome, it has occurred at some cost.

First, as Emmison and Smith (2000: viii–ix, 22) suggest, cultural studies' usual focus on commercially produced images (like advertisements and TV news bulletins) has led to a relative neglect of research on how everyday participants use the visual and mechanical resources in their environment. Second, I have reservations about the quality of analysis that passes as adequate in many areas of cultural studies. Rather than cautious, rigorous research on visual images, we tend to find either the kind of politically driven 'demythologizing' seen in the early work of Roland Barthes (see Section 7.2) or a postmodernist pastiche where 'anything goes'.

Of course, these are big generalizations. And even I would exclude from my charge sheet certain kinds of research which accept the postmodernist banner (see, for example, Kendall and Wickham's, 1999, argument that we treat Foucault's work as a toolbox for empirical research rather than as an impetus to woolly theorizing).

Nonetheless, this helps to explain why I have given so much attention to how everyday participants use the visual and mechanical resources in their environment. Emmison and Smith elegantly make this point:

> In giving up the idea that visual research is only the study of photographs, advertisements, etc. . . . a far broader range of data becomes available for investigation. From our vantage point, visual inquiry is no longer just the study of the image, but rather the study of the seen and the observable. (2000: ix)

As Emmison and Smith argue, this change of focus to 'the seen and the observable' also serves to reconnect visual research to lively *models* of social research forgotten in the postmodernist fashion parade. These include the approaches discussed in this chapter, as well as the models considered in Chapter 3: the naturalism of the Chicago School and Erving Goffman's analysis of framing.

## KEY POINTS

- The aim of researching 'visual images' is to examine the 'work' that they do and to understand how they do that work.
- Semiotics is the science of 'signs'. It shows how signs relate to one another in order to create and exclude particular meanings.
- Ethnomethodology identifies a 'common-sense geography' by studying how people establish together a particular location in space and place.
- Conversation analysis studies videotapes to show how participants actually attend to visual elements in their environment, e.g. the bodily presence and gaze of others and/or the technologies through which people communicate.

### Recommended Reading

For the most recent, systematic and accessible discussion of how to analyse visual images see Emmison and Smith (2000). For a short treatment of the methodological issues involved when students use video data, see Silverman (2000: 45–8).

Famous examples of semiotic readings of images are to be found in Barthes (1973). For Barthes' semiotic analysis of photographs see Barthes 1977 and 1981.

A difficult but rewarding semiotic treatment of cinema is found in Stephen Heath (1981). For an attempt to apply some of Heath's concepts to a movie, see my paper 'Unfixing the subject: viewing *Bad Timing*' (1991).

Two of Harvey Sacks's lectures give stunning examples of analysing visual data from an ethnomethodological model: glances (1992, I: 81–94) and traffic (1992, I: 435–40).

---

**Exercise 7.1**

This exercise asks you to use some ideas from Table 7.1 about viewing a street. You will need to spend some time observing a local street in order to define a researchable topic.

1 What is your topic? What *models* and *concepts* can you use to understand it?
2 What data will you use? For instance, which position will you choose to observe from? Why? Would you like to use a video camera? If so, where would you position it? Why?
3 What conclusions (about which topics do you) think you will be able to derive from your analysis?

---

**Exercise 7.2**

This is an exercise to help you to use Saussure's abstract concepts. Imagine you are given a menu at a restaurant. The menu reads as follows (for convenience we will leave out the prices):

> Tomato soup
> Mixed salad
>
> Roast beef
> Fried chicken
> Grilled plaice
>
> Ice cream (several flavours)
> Apple pie

Your task is to work out how you can treat the words on the menu as a set of related signs. Try to use all Saussure's concepts, e.g. langue, parole, syntagmatic relations and paradigmatic oppositions.
   Here are some clues:

1 What can you learn from the *order* in which the courses are set out?
2 What can you learn from the *choices* which are offered for each course?

---

**Exercise 7.3**

This exercise is designed to help you to think about how sign systems work in visual images.

1  Select two newspaper or billboard adverts for different makes of the same product.
2  List the signifiers present in each advert.
3  Now consider how these signifying elements are related (or articulated) to each other and the meaning (or 'message') that is, thereby, signified in each advert.
4  Do the two adverts use the same or different strategies to convey their message?

---

**Exercise 7.4**

This exercise invites you to take up some of the issues involved in assembling common-sense location categories. It draws upon an exercise designed by Emmison and Smith (2000: 103).

1  Invite a few friends to draw a map of how to drive by car from where they live to some location in the city centre.
2  Now compare each map. For example, look at what location indicators are used at the 'start' of each map and what are used to indicate the city centre.
3  Consider what you have learned from this exercise about 'common-sense geographies'.
4  Compare your findings with the discussion of map-making in Emmison and Smith (2000: 95–105) or Psathas (1979).

---

### Exercise 7.5

This exercise invites you to build upon Lucy Suchman's work. Before you attempt it, you must get permission for filming from all the photocopier users and from the university authorities responsible for the photocopying room (for a sample consent form, see Table 9.4).

1  Take a video camera into a photocopying room in your university.
2  Film the instructions that each user gives to the photocopier, the message that then follows, and the user's response to each message, and audio record any comments that each user makes during these activities.
3  Carefully transcribe your data, using the method used by Heath in Extract 7.5.
4  What are the similarities and differences evident between user assumptions (UAs) and design assumptions (DAs)?
5  What does your research suggest about (a) how the photocopier could be better designed; and (b) how photocopier users could be better trained?

---

# Part Three
# IMPLICATIONS

# 8

# Credible Qualitative Research

So far in this book we have been describing the different ways in which qualitative researchers gather and analyse their data. But what about the credibility of your research *findings*?

If you think about it, any form of writing involves some sort of attempt to keep your audience with you. Qualitative researchers need to decide, however, if they are satisfied simply with keeping their audience sufficiently interested that they will want to turn the page. Is qualitative research any different from good journalism or novel writing? Should we want to achieve anything more?

Based on these doubts, in this chapter I will examine two questions:

1  Does it matter whether qualitative research findings are credible?
2  If so, how might that credibility be sustained and recognized?

I will begin with the 'does it matter?' question. For, if our answer is no, then this can be a very short chapter!

## 8.1  DOES CREDIBILITY MATTER?

The array of suggestive theories and contrasting methodologies, reviewed in the previous part of this book, may tempt us to believe that credibility does not matter and that the maxim 'anything goes' applies to qualitative research. In this vein, I will first refer to the position of the ethnographer Michael Agar and then touch upon some feminist critiques of how scientists normally claim credibility.

### 8.1.1 Critics of scientific credibility

Agar (1986: 11) has criticized what he calls 'the received view' of science, based on the systematic test of explicit hypotheses. This view, he argues, is inappropriate to research problems concerned with 'What is going on here?' (1986: 12) which involve learning about the world firsthand.

So far, this is not contentious. As you will have gathered from Chapter 3 of this book, it does not always make sense for people doing observational work, like Agar, to begin with prior hypotheses. However, Agar draws a contestable implication from this truism. The implication, according to Agar, is a rejection of the standard issues of credibility in favour of:

> an intensive personal involvement, an abandonment of traditional scientific control, an improvisational style to meet situations not of the researcher's making, and an ability to learn from a long series of mistakes. (1986: 12)

Since it is very difficult for any reader to check the extent of what Agar calls the researcher's 'intensive personal involvement', he is, in effect, asking us to take on trust any research findings based on such claims.

Yet, as Hammersley and Atkinson point out, it is paradoxical to assert that the qualitative research community cannot or should not *check* findings:

> This is a paradoxical conclusion. While culture members freely and legitimately engage in checking claims against facts . . . the social scientist [claims to be] . . . disbarred from this on the grounds that it would 'distort reality'. (1983: 13)

Moreover, negative practical consequences for social science would, I believe, follow from the kind of anarchy that Agar implies. First, by minimizing the credibility of qualitative research findings (at least in conventional terms), it would play into the hands of our quantitative critics. Second, by downplaying the cumulative weight of evidence from social science research, it lowers our standing in the community.

While Agar writes about the 'personal involvement' of the *researcher*, many qualitative researchers also want to emphasize the involvement and experiences of their research *subjects*. This can encourage some to go even further than Agar in rejecting conventional versions of scientific credibility. For instance, Stanley and Wise describe 'objectivity' as:

> an excuse for a power relationship every bit as obscene as the power relationship that leads women to be sexually assaulted, murdered and otherwise treated as mere objects. The assault on our minds, the removal from existence of our experiences as valid and true, is every bit as questionable. (1983: 169)

Like many feminist sociologists, Stanley and Wise argue that the validity of 'experiences' should replace supposedly male-dominated versions of 'objectivity'. Thus, although qualitative methods are held to be most appropriate for understanding women's experience, such experiences are seen as valid or 'true' in themselves. In any event, it is argued, the goal of research is not to accumulate knowledge but to serve in the emancipation of women.

For purposes of exposition, I have chosen an extreme position: readers wanting a less dogmatic feminist approach might turn to Cain (1986). However, Stanley and Wise's argument has the merit that it reveals a methodological assumption which many feminists share.

Nonetheless, from my point of view, all these writers too readily abandon any reference to the credibility of qualitative research findings. First, it simply will not do to accept any account just on the basis of the researcher's political credentials (see my discussion of the researcher as partisan in Section 9.1). Second, we should not be all that impressed if a researcher makes very much of their 'intensive personal involvement' with their subjects. Immediacy and authenticity may be a good basis for certain kinds of journalism but qualitative researchers must make different claims if we are to take their work seriously.

Not only are the effects of these positions potentially dangerous, but the position itself is based on what I take to be somewhat misleading assumptions which I criticize below (for another relevant critique, see Hammersley, 1992):

1 The assumption that 'experience' is paramount is not at all new. Indeed, it was a primary feature of nineteenth-century romantic thought (see Silverman, 1989b). As I have argued in this book (especially in Chapter 4 but also in Section 1.1.2), to focus on 'experience' alone undermines what we know about the cultural and linguistic forms which structure what we count as 'experience'.
2 Rather than being a male standard, the attempt to generate credible knowledge lies at the basis of *any* dialogue. Without the ability to choose between the truth claims of any statement, we would be reduced to name-calling along the lines of 'You would say that, wouldn't you?' Against certain current fashions, we ought to recognize how, when eighteenth-century Enlightenment thinkers emphasized the power of reason, they were seeking just such a way out from prejudice and unreason.
3 To assume that emancipation is the goal of research conflates yet again 'fact' and 'value'. How research is used is a value-laden, political question (see Chapter 9). To my mind, the first goal of scientific research is valid knowledge. To claim otherwise is to make an alliance with an awful dynasty that includes 'Aryan science' under the Nazis, and 'socialist science' under Stalin.

If qualitative research is to be judged by whether it produces valid knowledge, then we should properly ask highly critical questions about any piece of research. And these questions should be no less probing and critical than we ask about any quantitative research study.

## 8.1.2  Key questions for evaluating research

Any systematic attempt at description and explanation, whether quantitative or qualitative, needs to answer many critical questions. A brief summary of these questions is set out in Table 8.1.

TABLE 8.1  *Criteria for the evaluation of research*

| 1 | Are the methods of research appropriate to the nature of the question being asked? |
| 2 | Is the connection to an existing body of knowledge or theory clear? |
| 3 | Are there clear accounts of the criteria used for the selection of cases for study, and of the data collection and analysis? |
| 4 | Does the sensitivity of the methods match the needs of the research question? |
| 5 | Was the data collection and record-keeping systematic? |
| 6 | Is reference made to accepted procedures for analysis? |
| 7 | How systematic is the analysis? |
| 8 | Is there adequate discussion of how themes, concepts and categories were derived from the data? |
| 9 | Is there adequate discussion of the evidence for and against the researcher's arguments? |
| 10 | Is a clear distinction made between the data and its interpretation? |

*Source*: adapted from criteria agreed and adopted by the British Sociological Association Medical Sociology Group, September 1996

Although Table 8.1 was prepared as a set of criteria for the evaluation of *qualitative* research papers, I believe that the criteria I have selected are equally appropriate for quantitative studies. This shows that, in principle, there is no reason to prefer any form of data.

Table 8.1 offers a guide to the criteria that research findings must satisfy if they are to be regarded as credible. The questions in Table 8.1 help us to identify those research reports which appear to tell entertaining stories or anecdotes but fail to convince the reader of their scientific credibility. This is what I mean by *anecdotalism*. I explain this further below.

**Attempt Exercise 8.1 about now**

## 8.1.3  The problem of anecdotalism

As Hugh Mehan (1979) has noted, the very strength of ethnographic field studies – their ability to give rich descriptions of social settings – can also be their weakness. Mehan identifies three such weaknesses:

1 'Conventional field studies tend to have an anecdotal quality. Research reports include a few *exemplary* instances of the behavior that the researcher has culled from field notes.'

2 'Researchers seldom provide the criteria or grounds for including certain instances and not others. As a result, it is difficult to determine the typicality or *representativeness* of instances and findings generated from them.'

3 'Research reports presented in tabular form do not preserve the materials upon which the analysis was conducted. As the researcher abstracts data from raw materials to produce summarized findings, the original form of the materials is *lost*. Therefore, it is impossible to entertain alternative interpretations of the same materials' (1979: 15, my emphasis).

In the light of Mehan's arguments, even a brief perusal of published articles using qualitative methods can be profoundly disturbing (Silverman, 2000: 283–96). Much too frequently, the authors had fallen foul of two problems identified by Fielding and Fielding (1986: 32):

- a tendency to select their data to fit an ideal conception (preconception) of the phenomenon
- a tendency to select field data which are conspicuous because they are exotic, at the expense of less dramatic (but possibly indicative) data.

These problems have been succinctly diagnosed by Bryman:

> There is a tendency towards an anecdotal approach to the use of data in relation to conclusions or explanations in qualitative research. Brief conversations, snippets from unstructured interviews . . . are used to provide evidence of a particular contention. There are grounds for disquiet in that the representativeness or generality of these fragments is rarely addressed. (1988: 77)

This complaint of 'anecdotalism' implies that qualitative researchers cannot exempt themselves from the standard demands that must be met by any research that claims to be 'scientific'. Since what 'social science' is and is not is widely misunderstood and is crucial for what we take to be 'credible' research, some remarks about 'science' are in order.

### 8.1.4 What is social science?

Agar and Stanley and Wise share a common assumption with some social scientists with whom they might otherwise disagree. Many qualitative researchers assume that there is a huge gulf not only between natural science and social science but between qualitative and quantitative social research.

However, we must not make too much of the differences between qualitative research and other research styles (see also Sections 2.5 and 8.3.2.7). For instance, as Hammersley (1990) points out, although replication of an ethnographic study in the same setting may be difficult, we need to understand that replication is not always a straightforward process even in the natural sciences. Hence where research findings are not replicated this is often put down to variation in laboratory conditions and procedures (this relates to the reliability of the research instruments used: see Section 8.2). Moreover, only hard-core laboratory scientists would assume that the controlled experiment offers an appropriate or indeed useful model for social science.

It is an increasingly accepted view that work becomes scientific by adopting methods of study *appropriate* to its subject matter. Social science is thus scientific to the extent that it uses appropriate methods and is rigorous, critical and objective in its handling of data. As Kirk and Miller argue:

> The assumptions underlying the search for objectivity are simple. There is a world of empirical reality out there. The way we perceive and understand that world is largely up to us, but the world does not tolerate all understandings of it equally. (1986: 11)

Following Kirk and Miller, we need to recognize that 'the world does not tolerate all understandings of it equally'. This means that we must overcome the temptation to jump to easy conclusions just because there is some evidence that seems to lead in an interesting direction. Instead, we must subject this evidence to every possible test. This implies that qualitative research can be made credible (and hence resistant to the charge of anecdotalism) if we make every effort to falsify our initial assumptions about our data.

The critical method implied here is close to what Popper (1959) calls **critical rationalism**. This demands that we must seek to falsify our initial hunches about the relations between phenomena in our data. Then, only if we cannot falsify (or refute) the existence of a certain relationship, are we in a position to speak about 'objective' knowledge. Even then, however, our knowledge is always provisional, subject to a subsequent study which may come up with disconfirming evidence.

Popper puts it this way:

> What characterises the empirical method is its manner of exposing to falsification, in every conceivable way, the system to be tested. Its aim is not to save the lives of untenable systems but, on the contrary, to select the one which is by comparison the fittest, by exposing them all to the fiercest struggle for survival. (1959: 42)

Of course, qualitative researchers are not alone in taking Popper's critical method seriously. One way in which *quantitative* researchers attempt to satisfy Popper's demand for attempts at 'falsification' is by carefully excluding 'spurious' correlations (see Section 2.1).

To do this, the survey researcher may seek to introduce new variables to produce a form of 'multivariate analysis' which can offer significant, non-spurious correlations (see Mehan, 1979: 21). Through such an attempt to avoid spurious correlations, quantitative social scientists can offer a practical demonstration of their orientation to the spirit of critical inquiry that Popper advocates. Later in this chapter, in Section 8.3, we will examine the methods, both numerical and non-numerical, that qualitative researchers can use to satisfy Popper's criterion of 'falsifiability'.

One of the most contentious issues in Popper's account of science is his claim that we can appeal to 'facts' to test our findings despite recognizing that we only see such facts through particular theoretical lenses. This relates to my discussion of *models* and *theories* (see Table 1.1).

Hammersley (1990; 1992a) has suggested that qualitative researchers *can* manage the kind of circularity implied by Popper through adopting what he calls a 'subtle form of realism'. This has the following three elements:

1 Validity is identified with confidence in our knowledge but not certainty of its truth.
2 Reality is assumed to be independent of the claims that researchers make about it.
3 Reality is always viewed through particular perspectives. Hence our accounts *represent* reality; they do *not* reproduce it (1992: 50–1).

This is very close to Popper's account of falsification rather than verification as the distinguishing criterion of a scientific statement. Like Popper, Hammersley also argues that claims to validity, based on attempts at refutation, are ultimately sustained by a scientific community prepared 'to resolve disagreements by seeking common grounds of agreement' (1990: 63).

The two central concepts in any discussion of the credibility of scientific research are 'validity' and 'reliability'. In the rest of this chapter, I will discuss each in turn, examining what each concept means in practice in both quantitative and qualitative research.

## 8.2   RELIABILITY

> [Reliability] refers to the degree of consistency with which instances are assigned to the same category by different observers or by the same observer on different occasions. (Hammersley, 1992a: 67)

What reliability involves and its relation to validity can be understood simply by following Kirk and Miller's example of using a thermometer:

> A thermometer that shows the same reading of 82 degrees each time it is plunged into boiling water gives a reliable measurement. A second thermometer might give readings over a series of measurements that vary from around 100 degrees. The second thermometer would be unreliable but relatively valid, whereas the first would be invalid but perfectly reliable. (1986: 19)

Kirk and Miller usefully distinguish three kinds of reliability, as follows:

1 *Quixotic reliability* 'The circumstances in which a single method of observation continually yields an unvarying measurement'; but this kind of reliability can be 'trivial and misleading'. For instance, just because an interview question always elicits a predictable response does not mean that it is analytically interesting or that the response necessarily relates to what people say and do in different contexts.
2 *Diachronic reliability* 'The stability of an observation through time.' For instance, showing that ways of defining advice sequences work equally well with data drawn from different periods.

3 *Synchronic reliability* 'The similarity of observations within the same time-period' (1986: 41–2). A standard way through which this is assessed is the triangulation of methods (e.g. the use of interviews as well as observation). As Kirk and Miller argue, paradoxically the value of such triangulation is that it 'forces the ethnographer to imagine how multiple, but somehow different, qualitative measures might simultaneously be true' (1986: 42).

However, writers who contest the applicability of scientific standards of credibility to qualitative research, predictably also deny the relevance of reliability. Let us examine their arguments before going on to consider how reliability criteria can be applied to different kinds of qualitative data.

### 8.2.1  Reliability not a problem?

Some social researchers argue that a concern for the reliability of observations arises only within the quantitative research tradition. Because such *positivist* work sees no difference between the natural and social worlds, it wants to produce reliable measures of social life. Conversely, it is argued, once we treat social reality as always in flux, then it makes no sense to worry about whether our research instruments measure accurately.

This is an example of such a critical argument:

> Positivist notions of reliability assume an underlying universe where inquiry could, quite logically, be replicated. This assumption of an unchanging social world is in direct contrast to the qualitative/interpretative assumption that the social world is always changing and the concept of replication is itself problematic. (Marshall and Rossman, 1989: 147)

But is this so? It is one thing to argue that the world is processual; it is much more problematic to imply, as Marshall and Rossman seem to do, that the world is in infinite flux (appropriate to the pre-Socratic Greek philosopher Heraclitus, perhaps, but not a comfortable position for social scientists).

Such a position would rule out any systematic research since it implies that we cannot assume any stable properties in the social world. However, if we concede the possible existence of such properties, why shouldn't other work replicate these properties? As Kirk and Miller argue:

> Qualitative researchers can no longer afford to beg the issue of reliability. While the forte of field research will always lie in its capability to sort out the validity of propositions, its results will (reasonably) go ignored minus attention to reliability. For reliability to be calculated, it is incumbent on the scientific investigator to document his or her procedure. (1986: 72)

Following Kirk and Miller, I consider below how reliability can be addressed in qualitative studies. Central to my argument is the assumption that high reliability in qualitative research is associated with what Clive Seale (1999: 148) calls **low-inference descriptors**. As Seale puts it, this involves:

recording observations in terms that are as concrete as possible, including verbatim accounts of what people say, for example, rather than researchers' reconstructions of the general sense of what a person said, which would allow researchers' personal perspectives to influence the reporting. (1999: 148)

I will now look at the methodologies discussed in Part Two of this book: observation, textual analysis, the interview and the transcription of naturally occurring talk and visual data. Using such data, how can we achieve low-inference descriptions and thereby satisfy the criterion of reliability?

### 8.2.2 Reliability and observation

Observational studies rarely provide readers with anything other than brief, persuasive, data extracts. As Alan Bryman notes about the typical ethnography:

field notes or extended transcripts are rarely available; these would be very helpful in order to allow the reader to formulate his or her own hunches about the perspective of the people who have been studied. (1988: 77)

Although, as Bryman suggests, extended extracts from fieldnotes would be helpful, the reader also should require information on how fieldnotes were recorded and in what contexts. As Kirk and Miller argue:

The contemporary search for reliability in qualitative observation revolves around detailing the relevant context of observation. (1986: 52)

Spradley (1979) suggests that observers keep four separate sets of notes:

1  short notes made at the time
2  expanded notes made as soon as possible after each field session
3  a fieldwork journal to record problems and ideas that arise during each stage of fieldwork
4  a provisional running record of analysis and interpretation (discussed by Kirk and Miller, 1986: 53).

Spradley's suggestions help to systematize fieldnotes and thus improve their reliability. Implicit in them is the need to distinguish between **etic** analysis (based on the researcher's concepts) and **emic** analysis (deriving from the conceptual framework of those being studied). Such a distinction is employed in the set of fieldnote conventions set out in Table 8.2.

A concrete example may put some meat on the bare bones of this discussion of reliable observation. In their ethnographic study of adolescent drug users, first discussed in Section 4.6, Barry Glassner and Julia Loughlin (1987) carefully tape-recorded all their interviews. These tapes were then transcribed and coded by:

identifying topics, ways of talking, themes, events, actors and so forth ... Those lists became a catalogue of codes, consisting of 45 topics, each with up to 99 descriptors. (1987: 25)

TABLE 8.2   *Some fieldnote conventions*

| Sign | Convention | Use |
|------|-----------|-----|
| " " | Double quotation marks | Verbatim quotes |
| ' ' | Single quotation marks | Paraphrases |
| ( ) | Parentheses | Contextual data or fieldworker's interpretations |
| < > | Angled brackets | Emic concepts |
| / | Slash | Etic concepts |
| ____ | Solid line | Partitions time |

*Source:* adapted from Kirk and Miller, 1986: 57

On the surface, such tabulation appears to involve the counting for the sake of counting found in some quantitative research. However, the authors make clear that their approach to data analysis is different from positivistic, survey research studies:

> In more positivistic research designs, coder reliability is assessed in terms of agreement among coders. In qualitative research one is unconcerned with standardizing interpretation of data. Rather, our goal in developing this complex cataloguing and retrieval system has been *to retain good access to the words of the subjects,* without relying upon the memory of interviewers or data analysts. (1987: 27, my emphasis)

By retaining this access to subjects' own categories, Glassner and Loughlin satisfy the theoretical orientation of much qualitative research while simultaneously allowing readers to retain some sort of direct access to raw data. In this way, they satisfy Seale's criterion of using low-inference descriptors.

Moreover, Glassner and Loughlin suggest that their analysis fits two criteria of reliability more commonly found in quantitative studies, namely:

1 The coding and data analysis was done 'blind': both the coding staff and the analysts of the data 'conducted their research without knowledge of [the] expectations or hypotheses of the project directors' (1987: 30).
2 The computer-assisted recording and analysis of the data meant that one could be more confident that the patterns reported actually existed throughout the data rather than in favourable examples. This follows Maynard and Clayman's (1991) argument that observational fieldnotes must be wedded to more reliable data such as audio or video recordings of actual behaviour (see Section 8.2.5).

Attempt Exercise 8.2 about now

### 8.2.3 Reliability and texts

When you are dealing with a text, the data are already available, unfiltered through the researcher's fieldnotes. For this reason, textual data are, in principle, more reliable than observations. Of course, I say 'in principle' because it is possible that any text can be forged: think of the example of the so-called 'Hitler diaries'.

Providing there is no evidence of forgery, issues of reliability now arise only through the *categories* you use to analyse each text. It is important that these categories should be used in a *standardized* way, so that any researcher would categorize in the same way.

A standard method of doing this is known as 'inter-rater reliability'. It involves giving the same data to a number of analysts (or raters) and asking them to analyse it according to an agreed set of categories. Their reports are then examined and any differences discussed and ironed out.

In order to see how this method works, you should find a colleague who worked on the same exercise in Chapter 5 as you did. Compare your analysis of the same data and see if you can iron out any differences.

### 8.2.4 Reliability and interviews

The reliability of interview schedules is a central question in quantitative methods textbooks. According to these books, it is very important that each respondent understands the questions in the same way and that answers can be coded without the possibility of uncertainty. This is achieved through a number of means, including:

- thorough pre-testing of interview schedules
- thorough training of interviewers
- as much use as possible of fixed-choice answers
- inter-rater reliability checks on the coding of answers to open-ended questions.

In Chapter 4, I argued that a concentration on such matters tended to deflect attention away from the theoretical assumptions underlying the meaning that we attach to interviewees' answers. Nonetheless, this does not mean that we can altogether ignore conventional issues of reliability, even if we deliberately avoid treating interview accounts as simple 'reports' on reality. So even when our analytic concern is with narrative structure or membership categorization, it is still helpful to pre-test an interview schedule and to compare how at least two researchers' analyse the same data.

Interview studies must also satisfy the criterion of using low-inference descriptors. When we do e-mail interviews, we can readily satisfy this criterion because the participants have already done their own transcribing. When reporting other interviews, we can satisfy the need for low-inference descriptors by:

- tape-recording all face-to-face interviews
- carefully transcribing these tapes according to the needs of reliable analysis (not handing the problem over to an audio-typist!)
- presenting long extracts of data in your research report – including the question that provoked any answer.

**Attempt Exercise 8.3 about now**

### 8.2.5   Reliability and transcripts of audio and video data

Kirk and Miller's argument for the conventionalization of methods for recording fieldnotes can be applied to transcripts. For we need only depend upon fieldnotes in the absence of audio or video recordings. The availability of transcripts of such recordings, using standard conventions (see the Appendix, satisfies Kirk and Miller's proper demand for the documentation of procedures.

In the case of video recordings, standard CA transcription conventions are gradually emerging (see Section 7.3.2). In addition, readers of printed papers can be given prints of still pictures, so-called 'frame grabs' (see ten Have, 1998: 93). With the advent of Internet technologies, we may see a quantum leap where readers and viewers have access to audio- and videotapes while reading the researcher's transcripts.

Although this would go a long way to satisfying the need for low-inference descriptors, we should not make the assumption that it totally overcomes reliability issues. For instance, video researchers still have to make potentially fallible decisions about where to place their camera(s) and when to stop filming.

At a more basic level, when people's activities are tape-recorded and transcribed, the reliability of the interpretation of transcripts may be gravely weakened by a failure to transcribe apparently trivial, but often crucial, pauses and overlaps. For instance, a recent study of medical consultations was concerned to establish whether cancer patients had understood that their condition was fatal.

In this study (Clavarino et al., 1995), we attempted to examine the basis upon which interpretive judgements were made about the content of a series of audiotaped doctor–patient interviews between three oncologists and their newly referred cancer patients. It was during this interview that the patients were supposedly informed that their cancer was incurable. Two independent transcriptions were performed. In the first, an attempt was made to transcribe the talk 'verbatim', i.e. without grammatical or other 'tidying up'.

Using the first transcription, three independent coders, who had been trained to be consistent, coded the same material. Inter-coder reliability was then estimated. Inconsistencies amongst the coders may have reflected some ambiguity in the data, some overlap between coding categories, or simple coding errors.

The second transcription was informed by the analytic ideas and transcription symbols of conversation analysis (CA). This provided additional information on how the parties organized their talk and, we believe, represents a more objective, more comprehensive and therefore more reliable recording of the data because of the level of detail given by this method.

By drawing upon the transcription symbols and concepts of CA, we sought to reveal subtle features in the talk, showing how both doctor and patients produced and received hearable ambiguities in the patient's prognosis. This involved a shift of focus from coders' readings to how participants demonstrably monitor each other's talk. Once we pay attention to such detail, judgements can be made that are more convincingly valid. Inevitably, this leads to a resolution of the problem of inter-coder reliability.

For instance, when researchers first listened to tapes of relevant hospital consultations, they sometimes felt that there was no evidence that the patients had picked up their doctors' often guarded statements about their prognosis. However, when the tapes were retranscribed, it was demonstrated that patients used very soft utterances (like 'yes' or more usually 'mm') to mark that they were taking up this information. Equally, doctors would monitor patients' silences and rephrase their prognosis statements.

In CA, as discussed in Chapter 6, a method similar to inter-rater comparison is used to strengthen reliability. Wherever possible, group data analysis sessions are held to listen to (or watch) audio or video recordings. It is important here that we do not delude ourselves into seeking a 'perfect' transcript. Transcripts can always be improved and the search for perfection is illusory and time-consuming. Rather the aim is to arrive at an agreed transcript, adequate for the task at hand. A further benefit arising from such group sessions is that they usually lead to suggestions about promising lines of analysis.

As already noted, the credibility of qualitative research studies rests not just on the reliability of their data and methods but also on the validity of their findings. I now turn, therefore, to the nature of validity in qualitative research and the means through which we can approach it.

### 8.2.6 Reliability: a summary

I have suggested that both reliability and validity are important issues in field research. I went on to suggest that reliability can be addressed by using standardized methods to write fieldnotes and prepare transcripts. In the case of interview and textual studies, I also argued that reliability can be improved by comparing the analysis of the same data by several researchers.

Let us now turn to validity.

## 8.3   VALIDITY

> By validity, I mean truth: interpreted as the extent to which an account accurately represents the social phenomena to which it refers. (Hammersley, 1990: 57)

Proposing a purportedly 'true' statement involves the possibility of two kinds of *error* which have been clearly defined by Kirk and Miller (1986: 29–30):

- *Type 1 error* is believing a statement to be true when it is not (in statistical terms, this means rejecting the 'null hypothesis', i.e. the hypothesis that there is no relation between the variables).
- *Type 2 error* is rejecting a statement which, in fact, is true (i.e. incorrectly supporting the 'null hypothesis').

Because the idea of *validity* originated in quantitative research, I will begin by considering what it means in that context and how applicable it is to more qualitatively oriented studies.

### 8.3.1   *Validity in quantitative research*

In quantitative research, a common form of type 1 error arises if we accept a 'spurious' correlation. For instance, just because $X$ seems always to be followed by $Y$, does not mean that $X$ necessarily *causes* $Y$. There might be a third factor $Z$, which produces both $X$ and $Y$. Alternatively, $Z$ might be an 'intervening variable' which is caused by $X$ and then influences $Y$ (see Selltiz et al., 1964: 424–31; and my discussion of Procter's, 1993, data in Section 2.1).

   As we saw in Section 2.1, the quantitative researcher can use sophisticated means to guard against the possibility of spurious correlations. However, the survey methods discussed there are not without problems. As Fielding and Fielding argue:

> the most advanced survey procedures themselves only manipulate data that had to be gained at some point by asking people. (1986: 12)

As I suggested in Chapter 4, what people say in answer to interview questions does not have a stable relationship to how they behave in naturally occurring situations. Second, as we saw in Chapter 2, for instance in the work of Blau and Schoenherr (1971), researchers' claims may sometimes be credible merely because they rely on common-sense knowledge which stands in need of explication rather than passive acceptance.

   Again, Fielding and Fielding make the relevant point:

> researchers who generalize from a sample survey to a larger population ignore the possible disparity between the discourse of actors about some topical issue and the way they respond to questions in a formal context. (1986: 21)

So quantitative methods offer no simple solution to the question of validity:

> ultimately all methods of data collection are analysed 'qualitatively', in so far as the act of analysis is an interpretation, and therefore of necessity a selective rendering. Whether the data collected are quantifiable or qualitative, the issue of the *warrant* for their inferences must be confronted. (1986: 12, my emphasis)

We will now examine how qualitative researchers may claim, in Fielding and Fielding's terms, that they have a 'warrant for their inferences' and that their work is valid.

### 8.3.2 Claims to validity in qualitative research

As I have argued, the issue of validity is appropriate whatever one's theoretical orientation or use of quantitative or qualitative data. Few contemporary social scientists are satisfied by naturalism's assumption that credibility is guaranteed provided one 'hangs out' with one's tribe or subcultural group and returns with an 'authentic' account of the field.

However, I shall not discuss here many standard criteria of assessing validity, either because they are available in other methodology texts or because they are commonsensical and/or inappropriate to the theoretical logic of qualitative research as discussed in Section 2.3. These criteria include:

- the impact of the researcher on the setting (the so-called 'halo' or 'Hawthorne' effect) (see Hammersley, 1990: 80–2; Landsberger, 1958)
- the values of the researcher (see Weber, 1949; and this volume, Chapter 9)
- the truth status of a respondent's account (see Section 4.2).

Two other forms of validation have been suggested as particularly appropriate to the logic of qualitative research:

1 Comparing different kinds of data (e.g. quantitative and qualitative) and different methods (e.g. observation and interviews) to see whether they corroborate one another. This form of comparison, called **triangulation**, derives from navigation, where different bearings give the correct position of an object.
2 Taking one's findings back to the subjects being studied. Where these people verify one's findings, it is argued, one can be more confident of their validity. This method is known as **respondent validation**.

Each of these methods is discussed below. In my discussion, I show why I believe these methods are usually *inappropriate* to qualitative research.

### Triangulating data and methods

A major early advocate of the method of triangulation is Norman Denzin (1970). The topic arises in the context of Denzin's discussion of the advantages and limitations of observational work. Unlike survey research, Denzin points out:

> the participant observer is not bound in his field work by pre-judgements about the nature of his problem, by rigid data-gathering devices, or by hypotheses. (1970: 216)

However, Denzin also notes that participant observation is not without its own difficulties. First, its focus on the present may blind the observer to important events that occurred before his entry on the scene. Second, as Dalton (1959) points out, confidantes or informants in a social setting may be entirely unrepresentative of the less open participants. Third, observers may change the situation just by their presence and so the decision about what role to adopt will be fateful. Finally, the observer may 'go native', identifying so much with participants that, like a child learning to talk, (s)he cannot remember how (s)he found out or cannot articulate the principles underlying what (s)he is doing – a perennial threat in naturalism.

Given these difficulties, Denzin offers two related solutions. The first is non-contentious. It involves using multiple sources of data collection, as part of the methodology. Thus Denzin defines participant observation:

> as a field strategy that simultaneously combines document analysis, respondent and informant interviewing, direct participation and observation and introspection. (1970: 186)

Now, as an assembly of reminders about the partiality of any one context of data collection, such a 'field strategy' makes a great deal of sense. However, it seems that Denzin wants to go beyond a recognition of the partiality of data, for his second solution to the difficulties of participant observation is to suggest that a more general practice of 'method triangulation' can serve to overcome partial views and present something like a complete picture.

As Denzin elsewhere notes, actions and accounts are 'situated'. This implies, contrary to what Denzin argues about triangulation, that methods, often drawn from different theories, cannot give us an 'objective' truth (Fielding and Fielding, 1986: 33). So:

> multiple theories and multiple methods are . . . worth pursuing, but not for the reasons Denzin cites . . . The accuracy of a method comes from its systematic application, but rarely does the inaccuracy of one approach to the data complement the accuracies of another. (Fielding and Fielding, 1986: 35)

To counter what Fielding and Fielding rightly call Denzin's 'eclecticism' (1986: 34), they suggest that the use of triangulation should operate according to ground rules. Basically, these seem to operate as follows:

- Begin from a theoretical perspective or model (e.g. naturalism, emotion-alism or social constructionism).

- Choose methods and data which will give you an account of structure and meaning from within that perspective (e.g. emotionalists will want to generate data which give an authentic insight into people's experiences, while social constructionists will prefer to reveal how particular social phenomena are put together through particular interactions).

However, even when we use a single analytical model, it can be tricky to aggregate data in order to arrive at an overall 'truth'. As Hammersley and Atkinson point out:

> one should not adopt a naively 'optimistic' view that the aggregation of data from different sources will unproblematically add up to produce a more complete picture. (1983: 199)

Of course, this does not imply that the qualitative researcher should avoid generating data in multiple ways. Even for social constructionists, data triangulation can serve as an assembly of reminders about the situated character of action. For instance, Dingwall (personal correspondence) has suggested that triangulation has some value where it reveals the existence of public and private accounts of an agency's work. Here 'interview and field data can be combined . . . to make better sense of the other'.

The 'mistake' only arises in using data to adjudicate between accounts. For this reduces the role of the researcher to what Garfinkel (1967) calls an 'ironist', using one account to undercut another, while remaining blind to the sense of each account in the context in which it arises.

To conclude: the major problem with triangulation as a test of validity is that, by counterposing different contexts, it ignores the context-bound and skilful character of social interaction and assumes that members are 'cultural dopes', who need a social scientist to dispel their illusions (see Garfinkel, 1967; Bloor, 1978).

**Attempt Exercise 8.4 about now**

*Respondent validation*
If you privilege 'experience' as 'authentic', as is emotionalism's preference, you will probably want to try to validate your research findings by taking them back to the people you have studied to see whether they conform to their own 'experience'. Along these lines, Reason and Rowan (1981) criticize researchers who are fearful of 'contaminating their data with the experience of the subject'. On the contrary, they argue, good research goes back to the subjects with tentative results, and refines them in the light of the subjects' reactions.

Bloor (1978) incorporates Reason and Rowan's preferred approach (item 3 in the following list) in his discussion of three procedures which attempt respondent validation:

1 The researcher seeks to predict members' classifications in actual situations of their use (see Frake, 1964).
2 The researcher prepares hypothetical cases and predicts respondents' responses to them (see also Frake, 1964).
3 The researcher provides respondents with a research report and records their reactions to it.

Bloor used the third procedure (1978; 1983) in his study of doctors' decision-making in adenotonsillectomy cases, hoping that doctors would validate his descriptions of their practice – what he calls 'a sort of self-recognition effect' (1978: 549). Although Bloor reports that he was able to make some useful modifications as a result of the surgeons' comments, he reports many reservations. These centre around whether respondents are able to follow a report written for a sociological audience and, even if it is presented intelligibly, whether they will (or should) have any interest in it (1978: 550). A further problem, noted by Abrams, is that 'overt respondent validation is only possible if the results of the analysis are compatible with the self-image of the respondents' (1984: 8).

However, Bloor concludes, this need not mean that attempts at respondents' validation have *no* value. They do generate further data which, while not validating the research report, often suggests interesting paths for further analysis (Bloor, 1983: 172).

Bloor's point has been very effectively taken up by Fielding and Fielding (1986) (respondent validation is also criticized by Bryman, 1988: 78–9). The Fieldings concede that subjects being studied may have additional knowledge, especially about the context of their actions. However:

> there is no reason to assume that members have privileged status as commentators on their actions . . . such feedback cannot be taken as direct validation or refutation of the observer's inferences. Rather such processes of so-called 'validation' should be treated as yet another source of data and insight. (1986: 43)

Of course, this leaves on one side the ethics, politics and practicalities of the researcher's relation with subjects in the field (see Chapter 9). Nonetheless, these latter issues should not be *confused* with the validation of research findings.

If we are not fully convinced by either triangulation or members' validation, how, then, are we to overcome the anecdotal quality of much qualitative research in order to claim validity? To answer this question, I will review what I believe to be more appropriate methods for validating studies based largely or entirely upon qualitative data. These include:

- analytic induction
- the constant comparative method
- deviant-case analysis
- comprehensive data treatment
- using appropriate tabulations.

*Analytic induction (AI)*

As I remarked in Section 2.3, qualitative researchers need not accept the assumption that their work can only be exploratory or descriptive. As Glaser and Strauss (1967) argue, grounded theory demands that we often avoid prior hypotheses; this does not mean that we cannot (or should not) generate and test hypotheses 'grounded' in our data.

Having identified some 'phenomenon' and generated some hypothesis, we can then go on to take a small body of data (a 'case') and examine it as follows:

> one case is . . . studied to see whether the hypothesis relates to it. If not, the hypothesis is reformulated (or the phenomenon redefined to exclude the case). While a small number of cases support practical certainty, negative cases disprove the explanation, which is then reformulated. Examination of cases, redefinition of the phenomenon and reformulation of hypotheses is repeated until a universal relationship is shown. (Fielding, 1988: 7–8)

AI is equivalent to the statistical testing of quantitative associations to see if they are greater than might be expected at random (random error). However:

> in qualitative analysis . . . there is no random error variance. All exceptions are eliminated by revising hypotheses until all the data fit. The result of this procedure is that statistical tests are actually *unnecessary* once the negative cases are removed. (Fielding and Fielding, 1986: 89)

An example of AI being used in a field research study will be helpful. In Bloor's study of surgeons, already discussed, he tried:

> to inductively reconstruct each specialist's own standard 'decision rules' which he normally used to decide on a disposal. (1978: 545)

These rules were then compared to each doctor's procedures for searching through relevant information.

Bloor draws upon the distinction between 'necessary' and 'sufficient' conditions for an outcome. 'Necessary' conditions are conditions without which a particular outcome is impossible. 'Sufficient' conditions are conditions which totally explain the outcome in question. For instance, a necessary condition for me to give a lecture is that I should be present at a particular time and place. Sufficient conditions may include me knowing about the subject, having my notes with me, finding an audience awaiting me, and so on. This is how Bloor reports his inductive method:

1 For each specialist, cases were provisionally classified according to the disposal category into which they fell.
2 The data on all a specialist's cases in a particular disposal category were scrutinized in order to attempt a provisional list of those case features common to the cases in that category.

3 The 'deviant cases' (i.e. those cases where features common to many of the cases in the disposal category were lacking) were scrutinized in order to ascertain whether (a) the provisional list of case features common to a particular category could be modified as to allow the inclusion of the deviant cases; or (b) the classificatory system could be so modified as to allow the inclusion of the deviant cases within a modified category.

4 Having thus produced a list of case features common to all cases in a particular category, cases in alternative categories were scrutinized to discover which case features were shared with cases outside the first category considered. Such shared case features were thus judged *necessary* rather than *sufficient* for the achievement of a particular disposal.

5 From the necessary and sufficient case features associated with a particular category of cases sharing a common disposal, the specialist's relevant decision rules were derived (1978: 546, my emphasis).

This is a shortened version of Bloor's list. He adds two further stages where cases are rescrutinized for each decision rule and then the whole process is re-enacted in order to account for the disposals obtained by all the specialists in the study.

Bloor recognizes that his procedure was not *wholly* inductive. Before beginning the analysis, he already had general impressions, gained from contact in the field (1978: 547). We might also add that no hypothesis testing can or should be theory-free. Necessarily, then, analytic induction depends upon both a *model* of how social life works and a set of *concepts* specific to that model.

AI may appear to be rather complicated. However, it boils down to two simple techniques which I shall now consider:

- the use of the constant comparative method
- the search for deviant cases.

### The constant comparative method

The comparative method means that the qualitative researcher should always attempt to find another case through which to test out a provisional hypothesis. In an early study of the changing perspectives of medical students during their training, Becker and Geer (1960) found that they could test their emerging hypothesis about the influence of career stages upon perceptions by comparing different groups at one time and also comparing one cohort of students with another over the course of training. For instance, it could only be claimed with confidence that beginning medical students tended to be idealists if several cohorts of first-year students all shared this perspective.

Similarly, when I was studying what happened to Down's syndrome children in a heart hospital, I tested out my findings with tape-recordings of consultations from the same clinic involving children without the congenital abnormality (Silverman, 1981). And, of course, my attempt to analyse the ceremonial order of private medical practice (Silverman, 1984) was highly dependent on comparative data on public clinics.

However, beginning researchers are unlikely to have the resources to study different cases. Yet this does not mean that comparison is impossible. The constant comparative method involves simply inspecting and comparing all the data fragments that arise in a single case (Glaser and Strauss, 1967).

While such a method may seem attractive, beginning researchers may worry about two practical difficulties involved in implementing it. First, they may lack the resources to assemble all their data in an analysable form. For instance, transcribing a whole dataset may be impossibly time-consuming – as well as diverting you from data analysis! Second, how are you to compare data when you may have not yet generated a provisional hypothesis or even an initial set of categories?

Fortunately, these objections can be readily overcome. In practice, it usually makes sense to begin analysis on a relatively small part of your data. Then, having generated a set of categories, you can test out emerging hypotheses by steadily expanding your data corpus.

This point has been clearly made by Anssi Peräkylä using the example of studies based on tape-recorded data:

> There is a limit to how much data a single researcher or a research team can transcribe and analyse. But on the other hand, a large database has definite advantages . . . a large portion of the data can be kept as a resource that is used only when the analysis has progressed so far that the phenomena under study have been specified. At that later stage, short sections from the data in reserve can be transcribed, and thereby, the full variation of the phenomenon can be observed. (1997: 206)

I employed this constant comparative method, moving from small to larger datasets, in my recent study of AIDS counselling (Silverman, 1997b). For instance, having isolated an instance of how a client resisted a counsellor's advice, I trawled through my data to obtain a larger sample of cases where advice resistance was present. This example is discussed in greater detail later in this section.

### Deviant-case analysis

The comparative method implies actively seeking out and addressing deviant cases. Hugh Mehan makes the point:

> The method begins with a small batch of data. A provisional analytic scheme is generated. The scheme is then compared to other data, and modifications made in the scheme as necessary. The provisional analytic scheme is constantly confronted by 'negative' or 'discrepant' cases until the researcher has derived a small set of recursive rules that incorporate all the data in the analysis. (1979: 21)

Mehan notes that this is very different from the sense of 'deviant-case analysis' in quantitative, survey research. Here you turn to deviant cases in two circumstances:

- when the existing variables will not produce sufficiently high statistical correlations

- when good correlations are found but you suspect these might be 'spurious'.

By contrast, the qualitative researcher should not be satisfied by explanations which appear to explain nearly all the variance in their data. Instead, as I have already argued, in qualitative research, every piece of data has to be used until it can be accounted for.

It is important to stress that 'deviant cases' are properly identified on the basis of *concepts* deriving from a particular *model*. Thus pieces of data are never intrinsically 'deviant' but rather become so in relation to the approach used (see my use of CA to this end in the discussion of tabulations later in this section). This theoretically defined approach to analysis should also properly apply to the compilation and inspection of data in tabulated form.

However, deviant-case analysis in the context of the constant comparative method, because it involves a repeated to and fro between different parts of your data, implies something much bigger. All parts of your data must, at some point, be inspected and analysed. This is part of what is meant by 'comprehensive data treatment'.

### Comprehensive data treatment
Paul ten Have notes the complaint that in CA, like other kinds of qualitative research:

> findings . . . are based on a subjectively selected, and probably biased, 'sample' of cases that happen to fit the analytic argument. (1998: ch. 7, p. 8)

This complaint, which amounts to a charge of anecdotalism, can be addressed by what ten Have, following Mehan (1979), calls 'comprehensive data treatment'. This comprehensiveness arises because, in qualitative research, 'all cases of data . . . [are] incorporated in the analysis' (1979: 21).

Such comprehensiveness goes beyond what is normally demanded in many quantitative methods. For instance, in survey research one is usually satisfied by achieving significant, non-spurious, correlations. So, if nearly all your data support your hypothesis, your job is largely done.

By contrast, in qualitative research, working with smaller datasets open to repeated inspection, you should not be satisfied until your generalization is able to apply to every single gobbet of relevant data you have collected.

The outcome is a generalization which can be every bit as valid as a statistical correlation. As Mehan puts it:

> The result is an integrated, precise model that comprehensively describes a specific phenomena [*sic*], instead of a simple correlational statement about antecedent and consequent conditions. (1979: 21)

Such comprehensive data treatment can be aided by the use of *appropriate* tabulations, where the categories counted are derived from theoretically defined concepts.

*Using appropriate tabulations*

> By our pragmatic view, qualitative research does imply a commitment to field activities. It does not imply a commitment to innumeracy. (Kirk and Miller, 1986: 10)

In this section I want to make some practical suggestions about how quantitative data can be incorporated into qualitative research. These suggestions flow from my own recent research experience in a number of studies, two of which are briefly discussed shortly.

Since the 1960s, a story has got about that no good qualitative researcher should dirty their hands with numbers. Sometimes this story has been supported by sound critiques of the rationale underlying some quantitative analyses (Blumer, 1956; Cicourel, 1964). Even here, however, the story has been better on critique than on the development of positive, alternative strategies.

The various forms of ethnography, through which attempts are made to describe social processes, share a single defect. The critical reader is forced to ponder whether the researcher has selected only those fragments of data which support his argument. Where deviant cases are cited and explained (cf. Strong, 1979; Heath, 1981), the reader feels more confident about the analysis. But doubts should still remain about the persuasiveness of claims made on the basis of a few selected examples.

I do not attempt here to defend quantitative or positivistic research *per se*. I am not concerned with research designs which centre on quantitative methods and/or are indifferent to the interpretivist problem of meaning. Instead, I want to try to demonstrate some uses of quantification in research which is qualitative and interpretive in design.

I shall try to show that simple counting techniques can offer a means to survey the whole corpus of data ordinarily lost in intensive, qualitative research. Instead of taking the researcher's word for it, the reader has a chance to gain a sense of the flavour of the data as a whole. In turn, researchers are able to engage in comprehensive data treatment by testing and revising their generalizations. In this way, the proper use of simple tabulations can remove the researcher's (and reader's) nagging doubts about the accuracy of their impressions about the data.

To illustrate the uses (and pitfalls) of tabulating qualitative data, I discuss below two of my own research studies. The first study, of cancer outpatient clinics, we have already encountered in Sections 3.3.2 and 3.3.4.

## EXAMPLE 8.1 THE CANCER CLINIC

In my observational study of British cancer clinics (Silverman, 1984), I formed an impression of some differences between doctor–patient relations when the treatment was 'private' (i.e. fee-for-service) and those when it was 'public' (i.e. provided through the British National Health Service).

A major aim of this study was to compare what, following Strong (1979), I called the 'ceremonial order' observed in the two NHS clinics with that in a clinic in the private sector. My method of analysis was largely qualitative and, like strong, I used extracts of what patients and doctors had said as well as offering a brief ethnography of the setting and of certain behavioural data. In addition, however, I constructed a coding form which enabled me to collate a number of crude measures of doctor and patient interactions.

This coding form allowed me to generate some simple quantitative measures. The aim was to demonstrate that the qualitative analysis was reasonably representative of the data as a whole. Occasionally, however, the figures revealed that the reality was not in line with my overall impressions. Consequently, the analysis was tightened and the characterizations of clinic behaviour were specified more carefully.

My impression was that the private clinic encouraged a more 'personalized' service and allowed patients to orchestrate their care, control the agenda, and obtain some 'territorial' control of the setting. In my discussion of the data, like Strong, I cite extracts from consultations to support these points, while referring to deviant cases and to the continuum of forms found in the NHS clinics.

The crude quantitative data I had recorded did not allow any real test of the major thrust of this argument. Nonetheless, it did offer a summary measure of the characteristics of the total sample which allowed closer specification of features of private and NHS clinics. In order to illustrate this, I shall briefly look at the data on consultation length, patient participation and widening of the scope of the consultation.

My overall impression was that private consultations lasted considerably longer than those held in the NHS clinics. When examined, the data indeed did show that the former were almost twice as long as the latter (20 minutes as against 11 minutes) and that the difference was statistically highly significant. However, I recalled that for special reasons, one of the NHS clinics had abnormally short consultations. I felt a fairer comparison of consultations in the two sectors should exclude this clinic and should only compare consultations taken by a single doctor in both sectors.

This subsample of cases revealed that the difference in length between NHS and private consultations was now reduced to an average of under 3 minutes. This was still statistically significant, although the significance was reduced. Finally, however, if I compared only *new* patients seen by the same doctor, NHS patients got 4 minutes more on average – 34 minutes as against 30 minutes in the private clinic. This last finding was not suspected and had interesting implications for the overall assessment of the individual's costs and benefits from 'going private'. It is possible, for instance, that the tighter scheduling of appointments at the private clinic may limit the amount of time that can be given to new patients.

As a further aid to comparative analysis, I measured patient participation in the form of questions and unelicited statements. Once again, a highly significant difference was found: on this measure, private patients participated much more in the consultation.

However, once more taking only patients seen by the same doctor, the difference between the clinics became very small and was *not* significant. Finally, no significant difference was found in the degree to which non-medical matters (e.g. patient's work or home circumstances) were discussed in the clinics.

These quantitative data were a useful check on over-enthusiastic claims about the degree of difference between the NHS and private clinics. However, it must be remembered that my major concern was with the 'ceremonial order' of the three clinics. I had amassed a considerable number of exchanges in which doctors and patients appeared to behave in the private clinic in a manner deviant from what we know about NHS hospital consultations. The question was: would the quantitative data offer any support to my observations?

The answer was, to some extent, positive. Two quantitative measures were helpful in relation to the ceremonial order. One dealt with the extent to which the doctor fixed treatment or attendance at the patient's convenience. The second measured whether patients or doctor engaged in polite small-talk with one another about their personal or professional lives. (I called this 'social elicitation'.) As Table 8.3 shows, both these measures revealed significant differences, in the expected direction, according to the mode of payment.

TABLE 8.3  *Private and NHS clinics: ceremonial orders*

|  | Private clinic (n = 42) | NHS clinics (n = 104) |
| --- | --- | --- |
| Treatment or attendance fixed at patients' convenience | 15  (36%) | 10  (10%) |
| Social elicitation | 25  (60%) | 31  (30%) |

Now, of course, the data shown in Table 8.3 could not offer proof of my claims about the different interactional forms. However, coupled with the qualitative data, they provided strong evidence of the direction of difference, as well as giving me a simple measure of the sample as a whole which contexted the few extracts of talk I was able to use.

However, I was very conscious of the fact that my tabulations were dependent on observational fieldnotes. Without access to tape-recordings of these doctor–patient encounters, my database was dependent upon the inferences I had made at the time. Therefore, it lacked some reliability because it could not claim to use low-inference descriptors.

This study also lacked some theoretical credibility. I was using a social constructionist model concerned with describing the actors' own methods of ordering the world. Yet the categories I had counted (e.g. 'social elicitation') were my own and had an unknown relation to the categories actually used at the time by the people I was studying.

My second example, given below, is therefore, I believe, a better one. In this second study, my tabulations were more reliable because they were based on detailed transcripts of tape-recordings of actual interaction. Additionally, my researcher-devised categories could claim to be based on how the participants had demonstrably oriented to the phenomena in question.

## EXAMPLE 8.2 HIV TESTING CLINICS

In their study of first visits by British health visitors (social workers/nurses) to first-time mothers, Heritage and Sefi (1992) found that most advice was initiated by the professional, often prior to any clear indication that it was desired by the client.

Health visitor (HV)-initiated advice took four different forms. At one extreme, advice was given only after a client had mentioned a problem and been questioned about it by the HV (form 1). At the other, HVs gave advice without having generated a perceived 'problem' from the client (form 4). The majority of advice initiations analysed by Heritage and Sefi were of form 4.

The reception of advice by mothers took three forms:

1  A *marked acknowledgement* (MA) (e.g. 'oh right' or repeats of key components of the advice); Heritage and Sefi say such utterances acknowledge the informativeness and appropriateness of the advice.
2  *An unmarked acknowledgement* (UA) (e.g. 'mm', 'yeah', 'right' without an 'oh'). These are minimal response tokens which have a primarily continuative function: (a) they do *not* acknowledge the advice-giving as newsworthy to the recipient; (b) they do not constitute an undertaking to follow the advice; and (c) they can be heard as a form of resistance in themselves because, implicitly, such responses are refusing to treat the talk as advice.
3  Assertions of knowledge or competence by the mother. These indicate that the advice is redundant: hence they also may be taken as resistance.

Mothers' responses were systematically related to the format in which the advice had been given by the HV. This underlines Heritage and Sefi's argument about the advantages of stepwise entry into advice-giving (form 1). In this form of advice-giving, they find less resistance and more uptake displayed by mothers' use of marked acknowledgements. Here the HV's request for her client to specify a problem means that the advice can be recipient-designed and non-adversarial and does not attribute blame.

Like Heritage and Sefi, in a study of AIDS counselling (Silverman, 1997b) I focused on the link between the form in which advice is delivered and its reception. Nearly all advice sequences were counsellor-initiated and many were truncated. As in Heritage and Sefi's study, step-by-step sequences were more likely to produce MAs, and truncated sequences usually produced UAs. The data on uptake are shown in Table 8.4.

Table 8.4 shows a very clear correlation between the way in which an advice sequence is set up and the response that it elicits from the patient. In the total of 32 cases where the counsellor delivers advice without attempting to

TABLE 8.4  *Form of advice and degree of uptake (based on 45 advice sequences)*

| Advice format | Number | Type of acknowledgement[a] | |
|---|---|---|---|
| | | Unmarked | Marked |
| Patient-initiated | 2 | 0 | 2 |
| Counsellor-initiated: | | | |
| Step-by-step, full sequence (type 1) | 11 | 1 | 10 |
| Truncated, no patient problem elicited (type 4) | 32 | 29 | 3 |

[a] 'Unmarked' means *only* unmarked acknowledgements were given in the advice sequence; 'marked' means that at least *one* marked acknowledgement was given.

generate a perceived problem from the patient (type 4), there are only three cases where the patient shows any sign of uptake. Conversely, in the other 13 cases, where the advice emerges either at the request of the patient or in a step-by-step sequence (type 1), there is only one case where the patient does not show uptake.

Table 8.4 thus shows how simple tabulations can offer a valuable means of validating impressions obtained from qualitative data analysis.

Following the discussion above of deviant-case analysis and comprehensive data treatment, I now will show how the analysis of these gross findings was developed by the examination of two deviant cases. In one case a truncated sequence of generalized advice was, unusually, associated with marked acknowledgements (MAs). This is shown as Extract 8.1.

**Extract 8.1 (SW1-8A)**
(C = counsellor, P = patient)

```
 1  C:  But we can't tell you know whether uh one individual is
 2      going to or whether they're [no:t.
 3  P:                              [(It's just on
 4      proportions).=
 4  C:  =That's ri:[ght.
 5  P:            [(      )
 6  C:  .hhhh A:nd obviously if someone looks after themselves they
 7      stand a better chance you know keeping fit and healthy.
 8  P:  Ye:s.
 9  C:  .hhhh The advice we give is commonsense really if you think
10      about it.=To keep fit and healthy, (.) eat a
11      [well) a balanced di:et,
12  P:  [For your natural resistance.=
13  C:  =That's [right.
14  P:          [Ye:s.
15  C:  .hh Plenty of exerci:[se:
16  P:                      [Right.
17  C:  [Uh::m or enough exercise.
```

18  P:  [(I already get that) hheh .hhh [hhh .hhhh Too=
19  C:                                        [Yeah.
20  P:  =much of it. hhuh=
21  C:  =Enough slee:p.
22  P:  Y[es.
23  C:     [You know. All the things we should normally
24      do[: to keep healthy,
25  P:       [Right. Rather than let yourself get run down.=
26  C:  =That's ri:ght.

Extract 8.1 is remarkable for the two marked acknowledgements given by the client (lines 12 and 25). How can we account for this unusual reception of truncated advice?

A part of the answer seems to lie in the content of the advice given. Extract 8.1 is largely concerned with what the counsellor tells people who have a positive test result. This leaves it open to the patient to treat what he is being told not as advice but as information delivery (about the advice C would give if P turned out to be seropositive).

It follows that such uptake obviously need have no direct implication for what the patient does (as opposed to what he thinks) – unlike the uptake of advice. Hence, as in Extract 8.1, P may choose to offer marked acknowledgements to what C says. But, in so doing, he may be simply showing uptake of a sequence that is hearable as information rather than personalized advice.

So when Cs formulate their talk as 'advice' but offer a generalized message (e.g. 'what we tell people who test positive'), they depart from many of the constraints of personalized advice-giving. This is because information delivery is compatible with a wide range of response (from simple continuers to newsworthiness tokens). Whatever the patient says will normally be heard as a receipt of information rather than, as in personalized advice sequences, bearing on the uptake of advice. Consequently, when MAs are found in such truncated advice sequences they function as strong information receipts rather than as positive uptakes of advice.

Through Example 8.2, then, we have seen how a simple tabulation has helped to identify a deviant case. Through the analysis of that case our understanding of the relationship between advice-giving and its reception has been improved.

### Attempt Exercise 8.5 about now

I have concluded this section on validity by focusing upon the uses of simple methods of counting in largely qualitative studies. The 'advice' study uses purely descriptive statistics; the study of private practice consultations introduces some straightforward correlations. This concentration on description is not coincidental.

The kind of research which I have been discussing is doubly interested in description. First, like all scientific work, it is concerned with the problem of how to generate adequate descriptions of what it observes. Second, however, unlike other kinds of qualitative research, it is especially interested in how ordinary people observe and describe their world. Many of the procedures I have discussed here aim to offer adequate (researcher's) descriptions of (lay) descriptions. Once this is recognized as the central problematic of much qualitative research (at least that informed by a constructionist model), then these procedures can be extended to what people say and write in a far broader range of contexts than the medical settings on which I have concentrated in this chapter.

I have tried to show how these kinds of theoretically informed tabulations, combined with the constant comparative method and deviant-case analysis, allow us to generate and to test hypotheses.

### 8.3.3 Validity: a summary

Let me summarize what I have been saying about validity. First, the criterion of *falsifiability* is an excellent way to test the validity of any research finding. Second, *quantitative* researchers have a sophisticated armoury of weapons to assess the validity of the correlations which they generate. Third, we should not assume that techniques used in quantitative research are the *only* way of establishing the validity of findings from qualitative or field research.

This third point means that a number of practices which originate from quantitative studies may be *inappropriate* to field research. The following three assumptions are highly *dubious* in qualitative research:

1  All social science research can only be valid if based on experimental data, official statistics or the random sampling of populations.
2  Quantified data are the only valid or generalizable social facts.
3  A cumulative view of data drawn from different contexts enables us, as in trigonometry, to triangulate the 'true' state of affairs by examining where the different data intersect.

All three assumptions have a number of defects, many of which are discussed (and some displayed) in a number of texts concerned with qualitative research methodology, from Cicourel (1964) through Denzin (1970) to Schwartz and Jacobs (1979), Hammersley and Atkinson (1983) and Gubrium (1988).

Following the same order as in the list above, I note that:

1  Experiments, official statistics and survey data may simply be inappropriate to some of the tasks of social science. For instance, they exclude the observation of 'naturally occurring' data by ethnographic case studies (see Chapter 3) or by conversation and discourse analysis (see Chapter 6).
2  While quantification may *sometimes* be useful, it can conceal as well as reveal basic social processes. Consider the problem of counting attitudes in surveys. Do we all have coherent attitudes on any topics which await the researcher's questions? And how do 'attitudes' relate to what we actually

do – our practices? Or think of official statistics on cause of death compared to studies of the officially organized 'death work' of nurses and orderlies (Sudnow, 1968) and of pathologists (Prior, 1987). Note that this is *not* to argue that such statistics may be biased. Instead, it is to suggest that there are areas of social reality which such statistics cannot measure.

3 Triangulation of data seeks to overcome the context-boundedness of our materials at the cost of analysing their sense in context. For purposes of social research, it may simply not be useful to conceive of an overarching reality to which data, gathered in different contexts, approximate.

So my support for credible qualitative research which takes seriously issues of validity is not based on an uncritical acceptance of the standard recipes of conventional methodology texts or the standard practices of purely quantitative research. I further suggested that data triangulation and member validation are usually inappropriate to validate field research. Instead, I suggested five ways of validating such research:

- analytic induction
- the constant comparative method
- deviant-case analysis
- comprehensive data treatment
- using appropriate tabulations.

However, case study research can rarely make any claims about the representativeness of its samples. How far does this mean that we are unable to make generalizations from case studies?

Since findings can be valid (or 'true') but not generalizable to other cases, I now turn to the issue of generalizability.

## 8.4 GENERALIZABILITY

A regular refrain I hear from student researchers: 'I have so little data, only one case,' they say, 'how can I possibly generalize about it?'

Generalizability is a standard aim in quantitative research and is normally achieved by statistical sampling procedures. Such sampling has two functions. First, it allows you to feel confident about the representativeness of your sample: 'if the population characteristics are known, the degree of representativeness of a sample can be checked' (Arber, 1993: 70). Second, such representativeness allows you to make broader inferences:

> The purpose of sampling is usually to study a representative subsection of a precisely defined population in order to make inferences about the whole population. (1993: 38)

Such sampling procedures are, however, usually unavailable in qualitative research. In such studies, our data are often derived from one or more cases and it is unlikely that these cases will have been selected on a random basis. Very often a case will be chosen simply because it allows access. Moreover, even if you were able to construct a representative sample of cases, the sample size would be likely to be so large as to preclude the kind of intensive analysis usually preferred in qualitative research (Mason, 1996: 91).

This gives rise to a problem familiar to users of quantitative methods:

> How do we know . . . how representative case study findings are of all members of the population from which the case was selected? (Bryman, 1988: 88)

For a few writers who see qualitative research as purely descriptive, generalizability is not an issue. For example, Stake refers to the *intrinsic case study* where 'this case is of interest . . . in all its particularity and ordinariness' (1994: 236). In the intrinsic case study, according to Stake, no attempt is made to generalize beyond the single case or even to build theories.

This is resisted by many qualitative researchers. As Jennifer Mason puts it:

> I do not think qualitative researchers should be satisfied with producing explanations which are idiosyncratic or particular to the limited empirical parameters of their study . . . Qualitative research should [therefore] produce explanations which are generalizable in some way, or which have a wider resonance. (1996: 6)

So, unlike Stake, the problem of 'representativeness' is a perennial worry of many qualitative or case study researchers. How do they attempt to address it? Can we generalize from cases to populations without following a purely statistical logic?

In the rest of this chapter, I will discuss three different but positive answers to this question of how we can obtain generalizability:

- combining qualitative research with quantitative measures of populations
- purposive sampling guided by time and resources
- theoretical sampling.

### 8.4.1  Combining qualitative research with quantitative measures of populations

Quantitative measures may sometimes be used to infer from one case to a larger population. Hammersley (1992) suggests three methods through which we can attempt to generalize from the analysis of a single case:

- obtaining information about relevant aspects of the population of cases and comparing our case to them
- using survey research on a random sample of cases
- co-ordinating several ethnographic studies.

Hammersley argues that such comparisons with a larger sample may allow us to establish some sense of the representativeness of our single case.

However, two of Hammersley's methods are very ambitious for the student researcher. For instance, you are unlikely to have the funds for even a small piece of survey research, while the co-ordination of several ethnographic studies requires substantial resources of time and personnel as well as good contacts with other researchers. Such contacts allowed Miller and Silverman (1995) to apply the comparative approach in describing talk about troubles in two counselling settings: a British haemophilia centre counselling patients who are HIV-positive and a family therapy centre in the US. In this study, we focused on similarities in three types of discursive practices in these settings: those concerned with trouble definitions, trouble remedies, and the social contexts of the clients' troubles (see also Gubrium, 1992).

Lacking such contacts and resources, the student researcher is often left with Hammersley's first method: obtaining information about relevant aspects of the population of cases and comparing our case to them. This is more useful because, at its simplest, this method only involves reading about other cognate studies and comparing our case to them. As we have seen, in my study of HIV counselling (Silverman, 1997b) I compared my counsellor–client interviews to Heritage and Sefi's (1992) data on interviews between health visitors and first-time mothers. Although this had little to do with establishing the representativeness of my sample, it gave a firmer basis to my generalizations about advice sequences in my data (Silverman, 1997b: 124–8).

The comparative method used here allows you to make larger claims about your analysis without leaving your library. As Peräkylä puts it:

> The comparative approach directly tackles the question of generalizability by demonstrating the similarities and differences across a number of settings. (1997: 214)

### 8.4.2   Purposive sampling

Before we can contemplate comparing our case to others, we need to have selected our case. Are there any grounds other than convenience or accessibility to guide us in this selection?

Purposive sampling allows us to choose a case because it illustrates some feature or process in which we are interested. However, this does not provide a simple approval to any case we happen to choose. Rather, purposive sampling demands that we think critically about the parameters of the population we are interested in and choose our sample case carefully on this basis. As Denzin and Lincoln put it:

> Many qualitative researchers employ . . . purposive, and not random, sampling methods. They seek out groups, settings and individuals where . . . the processes being studied are most likely to occur. (1994: 202)

Stake (1994: 243) gives the example of a study of interactive displays in children's museums. He assumes that you only have resources to study four such museums. How should you proceed?

He suggests setting up a typology which would establish a matrix of museum types as in Table 8.5. This yields six cases which could be increased further by, say, distinguishing between museums located in small and big cities – bringing up the cases to 12. Which cases should you select?

TABLE 8.5   A typology of children's museums

| | Type of museum | | |
| --- | --- | --- | --- |
| | Art | Science | History |
| Exhibitory | 1 | 2 | 3 |
| Program type Participative | 4 | 5 | 6 |

Source: adapted from Stake, 1994: 243

You will be constrained by two main factors. First, there may not be examples to fit every cell. Second, your resources will not allow you to research every existing unit. So you have to make a practical decision. For instance, if you can cover only two cases, do you choose two participatory museums in different locations or in different subjects? Or do you compare such a museum with a more conventional exhibit-based museum?

Provided you have thought through the options, it is unlikely that your selection will be criticized. Moreover, as we see below, how you set up your typology and make your choice should be grounded in the theoretical apparatus you are using. Sampling in qualitative research is neither statistical nor purely personal: it is, or should be, theoretically grounded.

**Attempt Exercise 8.6 about now**

### 8.4.3   Theoretical sampling

Theoretical and purposive sampling are often treated as synonyms. Indeed, the only difference between the two procedures applies when the 'purpose' behind 'purposive' sampling is not theoretically defined.

Bryman argues that qualitative research follows a theoretical, rather than a statistical, logic:

> the issue should be couched in terms of the generalizability of cases to *theoretical* propositions rather than to *populations* or universes. (1988: 90, my emphasis)

However, Clive Seale (personal correspondence) has pointed out that theoretical sampling may have more to do with generating theories than with empirical generalization. I take up Seale's point later in this chapter in relation to Alasuutari's argument that the idea of empirical generalization 'should be reserved for surveys only' (1995: 156).

The nature of the link between sampling and theory is set out by Jennifer Mason:

theoretical sampling means selecting groups or categories to study on the basis of their relevance to your research questions, your theoretical position . . . and most importantly the explanation or account which you are developing. Theoretical sampling is concerned with constructing a sample . . . which is meaningful theoretically, because it builds in certain characteristics or criteria which help to develop and test your theory and explanation. (1996: 93–4)

Theoretical sampling has three features which I discuss below:

- choosing cases in terms of your theory
- choosing 'deviant' cases
- changing the size of your sample during the research.

### Choosing cases in terms of your theory

Mason writes about 'the wider universe of social explanations in relation to which you have constructed your research questions' (1996: 85). This theoretically defined universe 'will make some sampling choices more sensible and meaningful than others'. Mason describes choosing a kind of sample which can represent a wider population. Here we select a sample of particular 'processes, types, categories or examples which are relevant to or appear within the wider universe' (1996: 92). Mason suggests that examples of these would include single units such as 'an organization, a location, a document . . . [or] a conversation'.

Mason gives the example of a DA study of gender relations as discourses which construct subjects of gender relations. In this approach, as she puts it:

you are . . . unlikely to perceive the social world in terms of a large set of gender relations from which you can simply draw a representative sample of people by gender. (1996: 85)

So in qualitative research the relevant or 'sampleable' units are often seen as theoretically defined. This means that it is inappropriate to sample populations by such attributes as 'gender', 'ethnicity' or even age because how such attributes are routinely defined is itself the *topic* of your research.

As an example of theoretically defined sampling, Bryman uses Glaser and Strauss's discussion of 'awareness contexts' in relation to dying in hospital:

The issue of whether the particular hospital studied is 'typical' is not the critical issue; what is important is whether the experiences of dying patients are typical of the broad class of phenomena . . . to which the theory refers. Subsequent research would then focus on the validity of the proposition in other milieux (e.g. doctors' surgeries). (1988: 91)

Further discussion of choosing a case for theoretical reasons is to be found in Silverman (2000: 106–7). Sometimes, however, we will want to choose a case because it appears to be deviant.

## Choosing 'deviant' cases

In my discussion of validity, I discussed analysing deviant cases in your data. Here we are concerned with something prior to data analysis – choosing a case to study. Mason notes that you must overcome any tendency to select a case which is likely to support your argument. Instead, it makes sense to seek out negative instances as defined by the theory with which you are working.

For instance, in a study of the forces that may make trade unions undemocratic, Lipset et al. (1962) deliberately chose to study a US printing union. Because this union had unusually strong democratic institutions it constituted a vital deviant case compared to most American unions of the period. Lipset et al.'s union was also deviant in terms of a highly respected theory which postulated an irresistible tendency towards 'oligarchy' in all formal organizations.

So Lipset et al. chose a deviant case because it offered a crucial test of a theory. As our understanding of social processes improves, we are increasingly able to choose cases on such theoretical grounds.

## Changing the size of your sample during the research

So far we have been discussing theoretical sampling as an issue at the *start* of a research study. However, we can also apply such sampling during the course of a piece of research. Indeed, one of the strengths of qualitative research design is that it often allows for far greater (theoretically informed) flexibility than in most quantitative research designs. As Mason puts it:

> Theoretical or purposive sampling is a set of procedures where the researcher manipulates their analysis, theory, and sampling activities *interactively* during the research process, to a much greater extent than in statistical sampling. (1996: 100)

Such flexibility may be appropriate in the following cases:

- As new factors emerge you may want to increase your sample in order to say more about them.
- You may want to focus on a small part of your sample in early stages, using the wider sample for later tests of emerging generalizations.
- Unexpected generalizations in the course of data analysis lead you to seek out new deviant cases.

Alasuutari has described this process through using the analogy of an hourglass:

> a narrow case-analysis is broadened . . . through the search for contrary and parallel cases, into an example of a broader entity. Thus the research process advances, in its final stages, towards a discussion of broader entities. We end up on the bottom of the hourglass. (1995: 156)

Alasuutari (1995: 155) illustrates this hourglass metaphor through his own study of the social consequences of Finnish urbanization in the 1970s. He chose local pubs as a site to observe these effects and eventually focused upon male 'regulars'. This led to a second study even more narrowly focused on a group where drinking was heavier and where many of the men were divorced. As he puts it:

> Ethnographic research of this kind is not so much generalization as extrapolation ... the results are related to broader entities. (1995: 155)

## 8.5 CONCLUSION

Unless you can convince your audience(s) that the procedures you used did ensure that your methods were reliable and that your conclusions were valid, there is little point in aiming to conclude a research study. Having good intentions, or the correct political attitude, is unfortunately never the point. Short of reliable methods and valid conclusions, research descends into a bedlam where battles are won only by those who shout the loudest.

More than 40 years ago, Becker and Geer (1960) recognized that adequate sociological description of social processes needs to look beyond purely qualitative methods. Everything depends, however, on the relation between the quantitative measures being used and the analytic issue being addressed:

> The usefulness of . . . statistics is a function of the theoretical problematic in which they are to be used and on the use to which they are to be put within it. (Hindess, 1973: 45)

However, I have also shown that quantitative measures are not the only way to test the validity of our propositions. Theoretical sampling and analytic induction, based upon deviant-case analysis and the constant comparative method, offer powerful tools through which to overcome the danger of purely 'anecdotal' quantitative research.

The time for wholesale critiques of quantitative research has passed. What we need to do now is to show the ways in which qualitative research can be every bit as credible as the best quantitative work.

## KEY POINTS

- Social science is credible to the extent that it uses appropriate methods and is rigorous, critical and objective in its handling of data.
- Qualitative research can be made credible if we make every effort to falsify our initial assumptions about our data.
- High reliability in qualitative research is associated with what Clive Seale (1999: 148) calls low-inference descriptors.
- Appropriate methods for validating studies based largely or entirely upon qualitative data include: analytic induction, the constant comparative

method, deviant-case analysis, comprehensive data treatment and the use of appropriate tabulations.

• The generalizability of a piece of qualitative research can be increased by: combining qualitative research with quantitative measures of populations; purposive sampling guided by time and resources; and theoretical sampling.

## Recommended Reading

Clive Seale (1999) offers an excellent overall treatment of the issues discussed in this chapter. A shorter but more specialized treatment is to be found in Peräkylä (1997). For a detailed discussion of analytic induction (AI) see Becker (1998: 197–212). For further discussion of AI, using Bloor's study as an exemplar, see Abrams (1984).

## Exercise 8.1

Select a qualitative research study in your own area. Now go through the following steps:

1 Review the study in terms of the ten quality criteria set out in Table 8.1.
2 If the study fails to satisfy all these criteria, consider how it could have been improved to satisfy them.
3 Consider to what extent these criteria are appropriate to your area. Are there additional or different criteria which you would choose?

## Exercise 8.2

This exercise asks you to use the fieldnote conventions set out in Table 8.2. You should gather observational data in any setting with which you are familiar and in which it is relatively easy to find a place to make notes (you may return to the setting you used for Exercise 3.3). Observe for about an hour. Ideally, you should carry out your observations with someone else who also is using the same conventions.

1 Record your notes using these fieldnote conventions. Compare your notes with your colleague's. Identify and explain any differences.
2 What conventions were difficult to use? Why was this so (e.g. because they are unclear or inappropriate to the setting)?
3 Can you think of other conventions that would improve the reliability of your fieldnotes?
4 What have you gained (or lost) compared to earlier observational exercises (e.g. Exercise 3.3)?
5 Which further fields of enquiry do your fieldnotes suggest?

---

### Exercise 8.3

This exercise gives you the opportunity to assess the reliability of your analysis of the data used in earlier exercises, using the method of inter-rater agreement.

You should find a colleague who carried out the same data analysis exercise as you did from those in Chapters 3–7. Return to your answers to that exercise and now consider:

1 What are the major differences and similarities in the way in which you used concepts and categories in that exercise?
2 Which part of either person's analysis needs to be revised or abandoned?
3 Do similarities in your analysis mean that the concepts and categories you have used are good ones (distinguish issues of reliability and usefulness)?
4 Do any differences mean that the concepts and categories you have used are badly designed and/or that you have used them inappropriately?
5 What have you learned from this comparison? How would you redo your analysis in the light of it?

---

### Exercise 8.4

This exercise is concerned with method triangulation. You should select any *two* of the methods discussed in Chapters 3–6 (i.e. observation, texts, interviews and transcripts). Then you should choose a research topic where these two methods can be applied. For example, you might want to compare your observations of a library with interviews with library users and staff. Alternatively, you could obtain official documents about the academic aims of your university and compare these to your observations, interviews or audio recordings of a teaching session (subject to everyone's agreement).

Now do the following:

1 Briefly analyse each of your two sources of data. What does each source tell you about your topic?
2 Identify different themes emerging in the two data sources. How far are these differences relevant for an overall understanding of the topic?
3 Using your data, assess the argument that evidence is only relevant in the context of the situation in which it arises.
4 In the light of the above, explain whether, if you had to pursue your topic further, you would use multiple methods.

## Exercise 8.5

This exercise is meant to accustom you to the advantages and limitations of simple tabulations. You should return to one of the settings which you have observed in a previous exercise in Chapter 3.

Now follow these steps:

1 Count whatever seems to be countable in this setting (e.g. the number of people entering and leaving or engaging in certain activities).
2 Assess what these quantitative data tell you about social life in this setting. How far can what you have counted be related to any *one* social science theory or concept with which you are familiar?
3 Beginning from the theory or concept selected in 2, indicate how you might count in terms of it rather than in terms of common-sense categories.
4 Attempt to count again on this basis. What associations can you establish?
5 Identify deviant cases (i.e. items that do not support the associations that you have established). How might you further analyse these deviant cases, using either quantitative or qualitative techniques? What light might that throw on the associations which you have identified?

## Exercise 8.6

Imagine that you have the resources to study *four* cases of the phenomenon in which you are interested. Following my discussion of Stake (Table 8.5), draw up a typology to indicate the universe of cases potentially available. This typology should include between six and 12 possible cases.

Now explain why you propose to select your four cases in terms of the logic of purposive sampling.

# 9

# Relevance and Ethics

There are several claims we might like to make about the value of qualitative research to the wider community. Here is one recent list (Hammersley, 1992a: 125):

- It is relatively flexible.
- It studies what people are doing in their natural context.
- It is well placed to study processes as well as outcomes.
- It studies meanings as well as causes.

Although I have made similar claims to both practitioners and research funding bodies, things are, unfortunately, not quite as simple as this list might suggest.

First, as we have already seen (especially in Chapter 1), the status of qualitative research as a naturalistic enterprise, concerned with meanings, is disputable. Second, as Hammersley (1992) himself points out, non-qualitative approaches can study some of these features (e.g. questionnaire panel studies can examine change over time and thus social processes). Third, as I argued in Chapter 8, the issue of the validity of qualitative research (its generalizability to larger populations, and the possible anecdotal basis of its claims) is a real one and does not exist just in the minds of policy-makers.

Finally, quantitative research tends to define its research problems in a way which makes immediate sense to practitioners and administrators. For instance, unlike many qualitative researchers, quantitative people have few qualms about taking their variables (albeit 'operationalized') from current headlines (e.g. 'crime', 'poverty' or 'effective communication') and about speaking a scientific language of cause and effect.

Faced with this competition, what can qualitative researchers offer that will be relevant to a wider audience? An example may help to set up my argument.

My example comes from the British educational system – although there are several parallel cases in many institutions and countries. In the 1960s, there was a lively debate in Britain about the pros and cons of selective education for the 11–18 age group. This debate was heavily influenced by quantitative social surveys which revealed a pool of hidden talent among children who had been unsuccessful in obtaining entry to 'academic' schools at the age of 11. Accordingly, in the late 1960s, the selective element in British secondary education was largely scrapped.

Subsequent research showed that secondary reorganization did improve the overall school performance of this age group. However, this improvement was not as great as many thought it would be. One reason seemed to be that, in non-selective or 'comprehensive' schools, many children were being put into different streams according to their perceived abilities. In some cases, streaming could reproduce the old system of selective education: although children of all abilities attend the same school, some are labelled and, perhaps, discouraged at the outset.

Now, of course, such streaming could be (and was) turned into a 'variable' to be studied by subsequent survey research. Nonetheless, I believe that the British experience of secondary reorganization suggests that policy-makers could have gained by paying more attention to non-quantitative research studies. For instance, ethnographic studies of the classroom (e.g. Mehan, 1979) and of educational decision-making (e.g. Cicourel and Kitsuse, 1963) have revealed a great deal about what actually happens inside schools. So, if such studies had been added to more familiar quantitative studies of educational 'outputs', then it is likely that policy-makers would have been much better informed.

This example fits the qualitative research strategy outlined earlier in this book (particularly in Chapters 1 and 2). This strategy involves three arguments:

- Qualitative research's greatest strength is its ability to analyse what actually happens in naturally occurring settings (unlike quantitative research which often turns this phenomenon into a 'black box', defined by the researcher at the outset).
- By refusing to allow their research topics to be defined in terms of the conceptions of 'social problems' as recognized by either professional or community groups and by beginning from a clearly defined academic perspective, qualitative researchers can later address such social problems with considerable force and persuasiveness.
- Qualitative research is not, however, competitive with quantitative work; the proper relationship is a division of labour in which qualitative researchers seek to answer 'how' and 'what' questions and then pass on their findings, so that the causes and outputs of the phenomena identified ('why' questions) can be studied by their quantitative colleagues.

These are arguments in need of further demonstration. At the end of the chapter, I will return to the possible relative contributions of qualitative and quantitative research. For the moment, however, I want to move away from the specifics of research to review the wider debate about how all forms of social science stand in relation to social problems.

## 9.1 THREE ROLES FOR THE SOCIAL SCIENTIST

The question is not whether we should take sides, since we inevitably will, but rather whose side are we on? (Becker, 1967: 239)

Not all social scientists would agree with Becker's call for moral or political partisanship. Perhaps responding to state apparatuses which are at best suspicious of the purposes of social science, many would go on the defensive. They might find it easier or more acceptable to argue that their concern is simply with the establishment of facts through the judicious testing of competing hypotheses and theories. Their only slogan, they would say, is the pursuit of knowledge. They would claim to reject political partisanship, at least in their academic work; they are only, they would say, partisans for truth.

I am not, for the moment, concerned to make a detailed assessment of either Becker's statement or the defensive response to it which I have just depicted. I believe both contain dangerous simplifications. As I shall later show, the partisans for truth are mistaken about the purity of knowledge, while Becker's rhetoric of 'sides' is often associated with a style of research which is unable to discover anything because of its prior commitment to a revealed truth (the plight of the underdog, the inevitable course of human history etc.). Curiously, both positions can be elitist, establishing themselves apart from and above the people they study.

For the moment, however, I want to stress a more positive feature of both arguments. Both recognize that no simply neutral or value-free position is possible in social science (or, indeed, elsewhere). The partisans for truth, just as much as the partisans of the 'underdog', are committed to an absolute value for which there can be no purely factual foundation. As Weber pointed out in the early years of this century, all research is contaminated to some extent by the values of the researcher. Only through those values do certain problems get identified and studied in particular ways. Even the commitment to scientific (or rigorous) method is itself, as Weber emphasizes, a value. Finally, the conclusions and implications to be drawn from a study are, Weber stresses, largely grounded in the moral and political beliefs of the researcher.

Fifty years afterwards, Gouldner (1962) pointed out how Weber had been grossly misinterpreted by positivists. Because Weber had suggested that purely scientific standards could govern the *study* of a research problem, they had used him as the standard-bearer for a value-free social science. They had conveniently forgotten that Weber had argued that the initial choice and conceptualization of a problem, as well as the subsequent attempt to seek practical implications from its study, were highly 'value-relevant' (to use Weber's term).

The 'minotaur' of a value-free social science which positivists had conjured up from misreading Weber is effectively destroyed by Gouldner. As Denzin (1970) shows, the myth of value freedom is shattered not only by the researcher's own commitments but by the social and political environment in which research is carried out. Grant-giving bodies will seek to channel research in particular directions: there is no *neutral* money, whether one is speaking about the well-meaning 'initiatives' of research councils or the more sinister funding schemes of the tobacco industry or the war machine (Horowitz, 1965). Moreover, organizations that are studied are likely to want some kind of return in terms of 'facts' (assumed to be theory-free and always quantifiable) as well as support for their current political strategy.

Finally, as Robert Dingwall (personal correspondence) has pointed out, governments may sponsor 'window-dressing' research to buy time and to legitimate inaction. So while, as Denzin points out, the researcher may desire nothing more than a publishable paper, this pressure-group activity is bound to have an impact on the work.

Given the constraints under which research takes place, how may the researcher respond? To answer this question, three different research roles have been prescribed or adopted. These are presented in summary form in Table 9.1.

TABLE 9.1   *Whose side are we on?*

| Role | Politics | Commitment | Examples |
|------|----------|------------|----------|
| Scholar | Liberal | Knowledge for knowledge's sake, protected by scholar's conscience | Weber, Denzin |
| State counsellor | Bureaucratic | Social engineering or enlightenment for policy-makers | Popper, Bulmer |
| Partisan | Left-wing Right-wing | Knowledge to support both a political theory and a political practice | Marx, Habermas, political research centres |

It will probably be helpful if I now give a summary presentation of each of these three positions.

### 9.1.1  Scholar

In his two famous lectures 'Science as a vocation' and 'Politics as a vocation' (Weber, 1946), Weber enunciated basic liberal principles to a student audience in 1917. Despite the patriotic fervour of the First World War, he insisted on the primacy of the individual's own conscience as a basis for action. Taking the classic position derived from the nineteenth-century German philosopher Immanuel Kant, Weber argued that values could not be derived from facts.

This was not because values were less important than facts (as logical positivists were soon to argue). Rather, precisely because 'ultimate evaluations' (or value choices) were so important, they were not to be reduced to purely factual judgements. The facts could tell you about the likely consequences of given actions but they could not tell you which action to choose.

For Weber, the very commitment to science was an example of an ultimate evaluation, exemplifying a personal belief in standards of logic and rationality and in the value of factual knowledge. Ironically echoing certain aspects of the 'Protestant ethic' whose historical emergence he himself had traced, Weber appealed to the scholar's conscience as the sole basis for conferring meaning and significance upon events.

Weber's appeal to Protestantism's and liberalism's 'free individual' was fully shared, 50 years on, by Norman Denzin. Denzin (1970) rejected any fixed moral standards as the basis for research. His stand was distinctively liberal and individualist: 'One mandate governs sociological activity – the absolute freedom to pursue one's activities as one sees fit' (1970: 332). What 'one sees [as] fit' will take into account that no method of sociological research is intrinsically any more unethical than any other.

Denzin does suggest that the pursuit of research in terms of one's own standards should have certain safeguards. For instance, subjects should be told of the researcher's own value judgements and biases. But he is insistent that the ultimate arbiter of proper conduct remains the conscience of the individual sociologist.

Weber's and Denzin's liberal position seems rather unrealistic. Curiously, as sociologists they fail to see the power of social organization as it shapes the practice of research. For while Denzin acknowledges the role of pressure groups, he remains silent about the privileged authority of the 'scientist' in society and about the deployment of scientific theories by agents of social control as mobilizing forms of power/knowledge.

Thirty years later, Denzin's position was very different. Now Denzin was calling for research which embodied 'a politics of hope'. This 'should criticize how things are and imagine how they could be different' (Denzin, 2000: 916). In order to achieve this, Denzin, following Mills (1959), demands a 'critical, intimate ethnography' which: 'presents the public with in-depth, intimate stories of problematic everyday life . . . These stories create moral compassion and help citizens make intelligent decisions and take public action on private troubles that have become public issues, including helping to get these action proposals carried out'. (Denzin, 2000: 901). Denzin's later position is that of the Partisan (see Table 9.1).

### 9.1.2 State counsellor

Even liberal individualists may occasionally move away from their 'hands-off' attitude towards others. Denzin, for instance, considers the value of the information that sociologists may offer to participants:

> The investigator may open new avenues of action and perception among those studied. Organizational leaders may be ignorant of the dysfunctional aspects of certain programs, and an exposure to the sociologist's findings may correct their misconceptions. (1970: 338)

Notice how Denzin uses 'organizational leaders' as his example of 'those studied'. Just as many sociologists automatically side with the underdog, so also there is a considerable weight of social science work which identifies with the problems and interests of the 'leaders' or 'top dogs'.

One such example is provided by Bulmer (1982). Despite having a general title, *The Uses of Social Research*, his book turns out to be solely a discussion of how social research may be used by 'policy-makers'. It will thus serve as an example of what I have called, in Table 9.1, *bureaucratic* politics where the researcher adopts the role of state counsellor.

It is at once clear, however, that Bulmer's bureaucrat-cum-researcher is intended to work at arm's length from the administration, offering no simple solutions and preferring to provide knowledge rather than to recommend policies. This is Bulmer's 'enlightenment model' of social research. It is based on a rejection of two other versions of the uses of research – 'empiricism' and the 'engineering model'.

I set out as follows how Bulmer depicts each of his three models.

## Empiricism

This assumes that facts somehow speak for themselves. It reflects the administrative view that research is a neutral tool for the collection of facts for the use of policy-makers. Failing to take account of the post-Weberian consensus that facts can only be recognized in terms of theoretically derived categories, its 'bucket theory of mind' (Popper) is, Bulmer suggests, wholly inadequate. This is not merely a methodological quibble, as Bulmer demonstrates. Empiricism fails because it offers no way of

> [bringing] to bear the insights of social science – rather than merely the factual products of social research. (1982: 42)

Bulmer's argument ties directly in with the second of my arguments for the relevance of qualitative research at the beginning of this chapter.

## The engineering model

This seems to be based on Popper's (1959) own version of the contribution of research to 'piecemeal social engineering'. Derived from Popper's rejection of attempts at revolutionary social changes, the engineering model takes off from the definition, presumably by the bureaucracy, of a social problem. It then proceeds, in Bulmer's version, through a sequence of four stages: (1) the identification of the knowledge that is required; (2) the acquisition of social research data; (3) the interpretation of the data in the light of the problem; and (4) a change in the policy.

Bulmer implies that the proponents of the engineering model are politically naive. Bureaucrats often know precisely what policy changes they wish to make and they commission research in such a way that the end-product is likely to legitimate their thinking. He also points out that, in large organizations, it is often action rather than research that is needed. Moreover, where problems need to be analysed, the application of common sense is often quite sufficient.

## The enlightenment model

This is Bulmer's preferred model. He sees the function of applied research as the provision of knowledge of alternative possibilities. Its role is to enlighten bureaucrats, and not to recommend policies or to choose between administrative options. This means that it *rejects* a number of research aims (1982: 153–4) including: (1) the provision of authoritative facts (because facts are only authoritative in the context of theories); (2) supplying political ammunition (because this is based, Bulmer points out, on the 'sterile' assumption that there are 'left-wing' facts as opposed to 'right-wing' facts); (3) doing tactical research, as in government think-tanks (because this reduces the social scientist to a mere technician); and (4) evaluating policies (because this is based on the rejected engineering model of applied social research).

Instead, Bulmer *proposes* two research aims which are consistent with his enlightenment model:

- interaction – offering mutual contact between researchers and policy-makers
- conceptualization – creation of new problems for policy-makers to think about through the development of new concepts.

The weaknesses of Bulmer's enlightenment model are already implied by my labelling his approach the 'state counsellor'. It offers an attractive version of how researchers who are already employed as functionaries of the state can preserve a degree of professional freedom. Pursuing 'enlightenment', they are relatively freer to define problems in terms of their own interests rather than to have them imposed on them by their political bosses (as empiricism or the engineering model implies).

However, this 'professional' freedom is to some extent a fraud, for, in Bulmer's discussion, the enlightenment model never brings into question the role of research as the supplier of concepts and information to the powers-that-be. Precisely because it represents applied research as the handmaiden of the state, 'enlightenment' offers a purely bureaucratic version of politics: as such, it totally fails to address the political and moral issues of research which is at anything other than arm's length from the state.

A case in point is the famous Project Camelot (Horowitz, 1965). This was a research project funded in 1963 by the Pentagon with a budget of 6 million dollars. Its purported aim was to gather data on the causes of revolutions in the Third World. However, when it became clear that such research was to be used as a basis for counter-insurgency techniques, it created a storm of protest and the project was withdrawn.

Horowitz points out that many social scientists had been prepared to overlook the source of the money when offered such big research funding. Presumably, they might have defended themselves as seeking merely to spread 'enlightenment' rather than to engage in political or social engineering.

However, this in no way settles the moral issue over whether social scientists should have this kind of relationship to such a government agency. Stewart Clegg (personal correspondence), for instance, suggests that we may need to call upon the organizational capacities of the state in order to produce real changes. His point reveals the dilemma that worthy ends may depend upon elitist means.

### 9.1.3 *Partisan*

If the state counsellor is co-opted by administrative interests and scholars delude themselves that they can stand apart from a socially organized world, then the partisan's role would seem to be altogether more defensible. Unlike scholars, partisans do not shy away from their accountability to the world. Unlike state counsellors, however, they hold the ruling bureaucracy at arm's length. Instead, the partisan seeks to provide the theoretical and factual resources for a political struggle aimed at transforming the assumptions through which both political and administrative games are played.

A paper called 'Medicine, superstructure and micropolitics' by the American medical sociologist Howard Waitzkin (1979) will stand here as an example of such partisanship. Waitzkin has the laudable aim of relating 'the everyday micro-level interaction of individuals' to 'macro-level structures of domination' (1979: 601).

Unfortunately, Waitzkin appeared to treat his data largely as illustrative of a preconceived theory. For instance, he asserts that doctors send ideological messages about the 'work ethic' to their patients. Yet he rests his case on a small part of a medical interview in which, hearing that his patient is tired, the doctor asks whether he is 'able . . . to work a regular day'. When the patient confirms this, the doctor says: 'Wonderful' (1979: 604–5).

At the very least, Waitzkin is making very limited data do a great deal of analytic work. Without any evidence to the contrary, the reader might prefer to read the doctor's question about the patient's employment as simply establishing the status of the latter's comment about feeling tired.

Two things never seem to strike Waitzkin:

1 that what he finds is true but not necessarily caused by the factors in his theory (for instance, Strong, 1979, suggests that doctors' use of the machine analogy in describing the body may be a feature of medical consultations in all industrialized social systems and not, as Waitzkin suggests, specific to capitalism)
2 that contrary evidence should be hunted down and followed up (for instance, Waitzkin notes – but makes nothing of – his own apparently contrary findings that women patients receive more information, while 'doctors from working-class backgrounds tend to communicate less information than doctors from upper-class backgrounds', (Waitzkin, 1979: 604).

Just as partisans do not seek to be surprised by their data, they tend to be elitist in regard to political change. Not surprisingly, Waitzkin seeks to encourage 'patient education' to invite the questioning of professional advice (1979: 608). At the same time, he makes nothing of patients' self-generated attempts to challenge professional dominance. Karl Marx's rhetorical question 'who educates the educator?' seems entirely apposite.

Waitzkin's paper illustrates some of the more unfortunate consequences of the researcher adopting the role of the partisan. In the same way as the Bible advises 'look and ye shall find', so partisans (Marxists, feminists, conservatives) look and inevitably find examples which can be used to support their theories.

Dingwall (1980) has noted how such work 'undoubtedly furnishes an element of romance, radical chic even, to liven the humdrum routine of academic inquiry'. He then goes on to note that a concern to champion the 'underdog':

> is inimical to the serious practice of ethnography, whose claims to be distinguished from polemic or investigative journalism must rest on its ability to comprehend the perspectives of top dogs, bottom dogs and, indeed, lap dogs. (1980: 874)

Dingwall concludes that social research, whatever its methods, must seek to produce valid generalizations rather than 'synthetic moral outrage' (1980: 874). This leads him into a discussion of the ethics of ethnography – a topic which I take up in Section 9.3.

**Attempt Exercise 9.1 about now**

Having taken up Becker's question 'whose side are we on?' and depicted three roles adopted by social scientists (scholar, state counsellor and partisan), I have found major problems in how these roles have been exercised. We would thus seem to be back at square one. Now, I shall try to be more positive and indicate the scope for what I believe to be a fruitful relation between qualitative social science and society. The best way to do this is to think about who are the principal audiences for research and what qualitative researchers might have to say to them.

## 9.2 THE AUDIENCES FOR QUALITATIVE RESEARCH

If you are reading this book as part of a university course, the only audiences relevant to you are your professors, who will grade your papers, and your fellow students, who will listen to your comments in classes. However, members of universities are only one of several potential audiences for qualitative researchers.

This wider audience includes policy-makers, practitioners and the general public. Each group will only want to hear about qualitative research if it relates to their needs. These four audiences and their likely expectations are set out in Table 9.2.

The expectations of academic audiences about both written work and oral presentations are discussed in Silverman (2000: 211–19). The range of other

TABLE 9.2   *Audiences and their expectations*

| Audience | Expectation |
| --- | --- |
| Academic colleagues | Theoretical, factual or methodological insights |
| Policy-makers | Practical information relevant to current policy issues |
| Practitioners | A theoretical framework for understanding clients better; factual information; practical suggestions for better procedures; reform of existing practices |
| The general public | New facts; ideas for reform of current practices or policies; guidelines for how to manage better or get better service from practitioners or institutions; assurances that others share their own experience of particular problems in life |

*Source*: adapted from Strauss and Corbin, 1990: 242–3

audiences, shown in Table 9.2, may tend to induce despair about the amount of work required to meet their separate expectations and needs. However, it contains a simple, easy to follow message: good communication requires focus and yet more focus.

The trick is to combine a recognition of the expectations and needs of such audiences with our own active shaping of our materials. In this context, Gary Marx's (1997) concept of 'leverage' is very useful. As he puts it:

> Try to leverage your work. The sociological equivalent of a bases-loaded homerun is to take material prepared for a class lecture, deliver it at a professional meeting, publish it in a refereed journal, have it reprinted in an edited collection, use it in a book you write, publish foreign versions and a more popular version and have the work inform a documentary. (1997: 115)

Marx reminds us of the range of audiences that await the qualitative researcher. Below, I consider the three non-academic audiences listed in Table 9.2: policy-makers, practitioners and lay audiences. How can qualitative researchers fashion what Marx calls 'a popular version' for such audiences?

### 9.2.1   The policy-making audience

The idea that social research might influence public policy provides an inspiration for many young social scientists. In most English-speaking countries, the sad truth is that things have never worked in this way.

Qualitative research has rarely had much appeal to civil servants and administrators geared to focus on numbers and the 'bottom line'. The one possible exception, Erving Goffman's (1961a) account of the dehumanizing consequences of 'total institutions' in his book *Asylums*, appears merely to have legitimated the cost-cutting frenzy known as 'community care'.

Moreover, it is arguable that number-crunching researchers have fared little better. As Roger Hadley (1987: 100) has pointed out, 'not being heard' is the common experience of Anglo-American social researchers who attempt to influence public policy.

Among the reasons for this, Hadley cites:

- Research is often commissioned to buy time in the face of public scandal or criticism. This means that: 'the customer's motives for commissioning a research project may not necessarily be directly related to an interest in the topic concerned' (1987: 101).
- The time lag between commissioning a study and receiving a report may mean that the customer's interests have shifted.
- Academic researchers who produce unpalatable conclusions can be written off as 'unrealistic' (1987: 102).

Of course, fashions change. At the time of writing, there is some evidence that public bodies may be starting to take qualitative research more seriously. Focus groups, in particular seem to be 'the flavour of the month', mainly, I think, because they are relatively cheap and quick and give nice 'sound-bites' for politicians and advertisers. However, such changes in fashion do little to affect the natural tendency of policy-makers to redefine the meaning of research 'findings'.

However, as Bloor (1997) has noted, the policy community is not the sole audience for social research.

### 9.2.2  The practitioner audience

> The real opportunities for sociological influence lie closer to the coalface than they do to head office . . . [they] lie in relations with practitioners, not with the managers of practice. (Bloor, 1997: 234)

Taking the example of the sociology of health and illness, Michael Bloor argues that practitioners rather than policy-makers are the most reliable and eager audience for social research:

> Sociologists who have conducted research on sociological aspects of health and medicine . . . have long been aware that there is a role for sociologists as participants in debates on public policy, but that there are also other audiences for social research, notably audiences of patients and practitioners (clinicians, nurses and other professionals). (1997: 223)

Bloor suggests that qualitative social researchers have a twofold advantage in influencing practitioners. First, they can build upon their research relationships with practitioners in order to discuss practical implications. As he puts it:

> In respect of practitioners who are research subjects, qualitative researchers can call upon their pre-existing research relationships with their research subjects as a resource for ensuring an attentive and even sympathetic response to their research findings. A close personal and working relationship, based on lengthy social contact and built up over weeks and months, is likely to ensure that, not only will practitioner research subjects have a particular interest in the findings (because of the identity of the researcher as much as a particular interest in the research topic), but also practitioner research subjects may be willing to devote an unusual amount of time and effort to discussions of the findings. (1997: 236)

Second, even if you have no research relationship with practitioners, the detail and transparency of some qualitative data have an appeal to many of them:

> the qualitative researcher has the advantage that the research methods allow rich descriptions of everyday practice which allow practitioner audiences imaginatively to juxtapose their own everyday practices with the research description. There is therefore an opportunity for practitioners to make evaluative judgments about their own practices and experiment with the adoption of new approaches described in the research findings. (1997: 236)

Bloor's argument resonates with my own recent experience with AIDS counsellors. For further discussion of how to approach such practitioner audiences, see Silverman (2000: 205–6).

### 9.2.3  The general public

There are at least four reasons why qualitative researchers may become involved in reporting back to the general public:

1  to answer questions asked by your respondents
2  to 'check' provisional findings
3  to provide 'feedback' to organizations and relevant groups
4  to provide information for the media.

Points 1 and 2 have been considered in Chapters 3 and 8. In particular, you should refer to the discussions on 'gaining access' (Section 3.3.1) for point 1 and on feedback as a validation exercise (in Section 8.3.2) for point 2.

Feedback to the general public is usually set up because of your own desire to 'give something back' from your research to ordinary people who, through their taxes, may well have funded your research. The format should vary according to whether your audience are members of an established organization or simply just a group of people with similar interests or concerns.

As an example, following my own research on hospital clinics for children, I gave a talk to the parents' association at one of the hospitals I had studied. In this talk, I discussed new facts from my research about doctor–parent communication. I also examined the implications of my findings for reform of current hospital practices. Subsequently, I was invited to write a short piece on my research for the newsletter of a British organization called the Patients' Association. In this article, I covered much the same ground as well as adding guidelines for how to manage better or get better service from hospitals that treat sick children. Finally, I spoke at a meeting of parents of children with diabetes. My aim here was to stress what my research had revealed about the painful dilemmas experienced by such parents. In this way, I sought to assure them that others share their own experience and that there is no need for them to reproach themselves.

Qualitative researchers only rarely reach a general audience through the mass media. Nearly all social science goes unreported by such media. The cautious way in which researchers are taught to write about their findings runs up against the media's need to pull in audience with sensational stories. So it is always a question of balance between the media's sense of what is 'newsworthy' and researchers' desire for an accurate, unsensationalized account of their research.

However, reporting back is only part of the issue. The people we study have also the right to expect that we behave ethically. The ethics of qualitative research is discussed in the next section.

## 9.3  ETHICS IN QUALITATIVE RESEARCH

As we saw earlier (Section 9.1), the German sociologist Max Weber (1946) pointed out in the early years of this century that all research is contaminated to some extent by the values of the researcher. Only through those values do certain problems get identified and studied in particular ways. Even the commitment to scientific (or rigorous) method is itself, as Weber emphasizes, a value. Finally, the conclusions and implications to be drawn from a study are, Weber stresses, largely grounded in the moral and political beliefs of the researcher.

From an ethical point of view, Weber was fortunate in that much of his empirical research was based on documents and texts that were already in the public sphere. In many other kinds of social science research, ethical issues are much more to the fore. For instance, both qualitative and quantitative researchers studying human subjects ponder over the dilemma of wanting to give full information to subjects but not 'contaminating' their research by informing subjects too specifically about the research question to be studied.

Moreover, when you are studying people's behaviour or asking them questions, not only the values of the researcher but the researcher's responsibilities to those studied have to be faced.

Jennifer Mason (1996: 166–7) discusses two ways in which such ethical issues impinge upon the qualitative researcher:

1  The rich and detailed character of much qualitative research can mean intimate engagement with the public and private lives of individuals.
2  The changing directions of interest and access during a qualitative study mean that new and unexpected ethical dilemmas are likely to arise during the course of your research.

Mason (1996) suggests that one way to confront these problems is to try to clarify your intentions while you are formulating your research problem. Three ways of doing this are to:

1  decide what is the purpose(s) of your research, e.g. self-advancement, political advocacy etc.
2  examine which individuals or groups might be interested or affected by your research topic

3   consider what are the implications for these parties of framing your research topic in the way you have done (1996: 29–30).

Ethical procedures can also be clarified by consulting the ethical guidelines of one's professional association. All such guidelines stress the importance of 'informed consent' where possible (see Punch, 1994: 88–94). The nature of 'informed consent' is set out in Table 9.3.

TABLE 9.3   *What is informed consent?*

- Giving information about the research which is relevant to subjects' decisions about whether to participate
- Making sure that subjects understand that information (e.g. by providing information sheets written in the subjects' language)
- Ensuring that participation is voluntary (e.g. by requiring written consent)
- Where subjects are not competent to agree (e.g. small children), obtaining consent by proxy (e.g. from their parents)

*Source*: adapted from Kent, 1996: 19–20

However, initial consent may not be enough, particularly where you are making a recording. In such cases, it often is proper to obtain further consent as to how the data may be used (see Table 9.4).

TABLE 9.4   *A sample consent form for studies of language use*

As part of this project, we have made a photographic, audio and/or video recording of you. We would like you to indicate (with ticks in the appropriate places) below what uses of these records you are willing to consent to. This is completely up to you. We will only use the records in ways that you agree to. In any use of these records, names will not be identified.

1   The records can be studied by the research team for use in the research project.
2   The records can be used for scientific publications and/or meetings.
3   The written transcript and/or records can be used by other researchers.
4   The records can be shown in public presentations to non-scientific groups.
5   The records can be used on television or radio.

*Source*: adapted from ten Have, 1998: Appendix C, based on a form developed by Susan Ervin-Tripp, Psychology Department, University of California at Berkeley

Having discussed the audiences we can reach and the ethics of research, I will pull these themes together by considering the possible contribution to society of *qualitative* social science.

## 9.4   THE CONTRIBUTION OF QUALITATIVE SOCIAL SCIENCE

As a sociologist, my own strong views on social issues are tempered by an understanding of the way in which particular practices are relative to certain cultures. Understandably, if you are looking at the ways in which things operate differently in different milieux, you tend to get to the position where it is difficult to take a stand on anything because everything is relative to its particular context. This is what is called *relativism*.

Although sociologists' and anthropologists' stress on the infinite variability of cultures is a useful critique of absolutist notions, if pushed too far it can be disabling in terms of our relationships to the wider community. For instance, in my own work (Silverman, 1987), I have been forced to question favourite liberal or progressive ideas such as 'patient-centred medicine' – doctors paying more attention to their patient's needs and language rather than looking at everything in a purely organic way. My research suggests that there are traps and power-plays present even within apparently patient-centred medicine.

So a relativist sociology needs to think about how it can present its findings in a way that will seem relevant to people who turn to social science with a naive belief in progress and an absolutist version of the role of science (see Section 1.1.2). Moreover, as the recent debate on female circumcision shows, there are some practices that even relativist academics will not usually be able to tolerate.

I want now to tackle the issue of relativism but not head-on because this would deflect us into a philosophical minefield. Instead, I want to show how qualitative social science can overcome relativism simply by making three contributions to society, namely:

1 participating in debates about public policy
2 providing new opportunities for people to make their own choices
3 offering a new perspective to practitioners and clients.

Let me consider each contribution in turn.

### 9.4.1 Debating public policy

The first task, as I see it, is to participate in debates about public policy. Let me take an example which returns us to the issue of patient-centred medicine. In a paediatric heart clinic, we became interested in how decisions (or 'disposals') were organized and announced. It seemed likely that the doctor's way of announcing decisions was systematically related not only to clinical factors (like the child's heart condition) but to social factors (such as what parents would be told at various stages of treatment).

For instance, at a first outpatients' consultation, doctors would not normally announce to parents the discovery of a major heart abnormality and the necessity for life-threatening surgery. Instead, they would suggest the need for more tests and only hint that major surgery might be needed. They would also collaborate with parents who produced examples of their child's apparent 'wellness'.

This step-by-step method of information-giving was avoided in only two cases. First, if a child was diagnosed as 'healthy' by the cardiologist, the doctor would give all the information in one go and would engage in what we called a 'search and destroy' operation, based on eliciting any remaining worries of the parent(s) and proving that they were mistaken.

Second, in the case of a group of children with Down's syndrome in addition to suspected cardiac disease, the doctor would present all the clinical information at one sitting, avoiding a step-by-step method. Moreover, atypically, the doctor would allow parents to make the choice about further treatment, while encouraging them to dwell on non-clinical matters like their child's 'enjoyment of life' or friendly personality.

We then narrowed our focus to examine how doctors talked to parents about the decision to have a small diagnostic test on their children. In most cases, the doctor would say something like:

> What we propose to do, if you agree, is a small test.

No parent disagreed with an offer which appeared to be purely formal – like the formal right (never exercised) of the Queen not to sign legislation passed by the British Parliament. For Down's syndrome children, however, the parents' right to choose was far from formal. The doctor would say things to them like the following:

> I think what we would do now depends a little bit on parents' feelings.
>
> Now it depends a little bit on what you think.
>
> It depends very much on your own personal views as to whether we should proceed.

Moreover, these consultations were longer and apparently more democratic than elsewhere. A view of the patient in a family context was encouraged and parents were given every opportunity to voice their concerns and to participate in decision-making.

In this subsample, unlike the larger sample, when given a real choice, parents refused the test – with only one exception. Yet this served to reinforce rather than to challenge the medical policy in the unit concerned. This policy was to discourage surgery, all things being equal, on such children. So the democratic form coexisted with (and was indeed sustained by) the maintenance of an autocratic policy (Silverman, 1981).

The research thus discovered the mechanics whereby a particular medical policy was enacted. The availability of tape-recordings of large numbers of consultations, together with a research method that sought to develop hypotheses inductively, meant that we were able to develop our data analysis by discovering a phenomenon for which we had not originally been looking. Such discovery is far harder to make in more structured quantitative research designs.

'Democratic' decision-making or 'whole-patient medicine' are thus revealed as discourses with no intrinsic meaning. Instead, their consequences depend upon their deployment and articulation in particular contexts. So even democracy is not something that we must appeal to in all circumstances. In contexts like this, democratic forms can be part of a power-play.

Am I still faced with the charge of relativism because I am treating what many of us would hold to be an absolute value (democracy) as having a variable meaning? Well, not necessarily, particularly if I can show that research which questions apparently 'absolute' values, like universal democracy, can have a practical relevance.

Two such practically relevant matters arose from the study of Down's syndrome consultations. First, we asked the doctor concerned to rethink his policy or at least reveal his hidden agenda to parents. We did not dispute that there are many grounds to treat such children differently from others in relation to surgery. For instance, they have a poorer post-surgical survival rate and most parents are reluctant to contemplate surgery. However, there is a danger of stereotyping the needs of such children and their parents. By 'coming clean' about his policy, the doctor would enable parents to make a more informed choice.

The second practical point, revealed by this research, has already been mentioned. Its relativistic stance about 'patient-centred' medicine rightly serves to discomfit liberal doctors wedded to this fashionable orthodoxy. For, as good practitioners realize, no style of communication is intrinsically superior to another. Everything depends upon its context.

The work I was doing in the paediatric cardiology clinic on the Down's parents already suggests one direction in which that debate could take place. Another example, already used in Section 8.3.2 (Example 8.1), arose from my research on three cancer clinics in which I looked at the practice of a doctor in the British National Health Service and compared it to his private practice (Silverman, 1984).

This study was relevant to a lively debate about the British National Health Service and whether there should be more private medicine. I was able to show that, despite these 'ceremonial' gains, patients overall got a better deal when they didn't pay than when they did pay. So this serves as a further example of how field researchers can participate in debates about public policy.

### 9.4.2  Increasing people's options

Field research can, I believe, provide new opportunities which allow people to make their own choices. Our work in the paediatric cardiology unit revealed two aspects of this. First, the study of doctors' decision-making highlighted the need for parents to make their own choices without feeling guilty. Second, the extra clinic that was offered to parents after a first outpatient consultation removed some constraints which allowed all parties to innovate in ways which we could not have predicted.

A further relevant example was the research on the mother talking to a doctor about her worries regarding her diabetic daughter (already discussed in Section 6.4.2). This naturally occurring material revealed that this mother is not *intrinsically* 'nagging' or 'irresponsible'. Instead, both are depictions which are *locally* available and *locally* resisted. Conversely, if we had interviewed mothers, the temptation would have been to search for idealized conceptions of their role.

Doctors were interested to learn about the double-binds present in their attention to the autonomy of their young patients. Likewise, parents' groups (largely mothers) of diabetic children found it very helpful to go through material of this kind. It brought out the way in which things they may feel personally guilty about in their relationships with their teenage children are not something that relates to their individual failings. Instead, such problems arise in our culture in the double-binds built into the parent–adolescent relationship.

In all these cases, we contributed to practical matters without imposing any elitist form of social engineering. By attending to the fine detail of interactions, we come to respect the practical skills of the participants. The role of the social scientist is not to be more knowledgeable than laypeople but, instead, to put an analytic method at their disposal.

### 9.4.3  Offering a new perspective

I will take one further example from my own research to illustrate the new perspectives that field research can offer.

This allows me to return to the practical implications of the study of advice sequences in HIV counselling already discussed in Section 8.3.2 (Example 8.2). As we saw, advice sequences are more effective when they either are requested by the client or derive from a specified client 'problem'.

How far can we advance from this barely newsworthy observation? In principle, the practical payoff of research grounded in the understanding of locally organized practices should be considerably more than work based simply on 'face-sheet' data (e.g. statistical tables showing correlations between predefined variables) and experimental studies based on idealized conceptions of the phenomena in question. But how can we show that our findings on advice reception go beyond the somewhat trite recommendations for 'better professional communication'?

I will attempt to show how this can be done by moving beyond *how* professionals and clients communicate to *why* they do so in the ways we have discovered. This leads us on to a more conventional address of the constraints on professional–client communication. In doing so, we return to the issue of the social contexts of interaction (already discussed in Section 6.3.4). Now, however, we will be concerned about the policy payoff of one way of settling this debate.

In my analysis of advice sequences in Chapter 8 I stayed at the level of verbal interaction. The only social context I was interested in was that locally produced by the participants. Thus I stuck closely to Schegloff's (1991) injunction about the need to identify context in observable features of the participants' activities.

I shall now argue that an understanding of the institutional contexts of talk allows us to move on from such 'how' questions to certain kinds of 'why' questions. As Maynard argues:

the structure of the interaction, while being a local production, simultaneously enacts matters whose origins are externally initiated. (1989: 139)

Maynard goes on to suggest 'combining discourse study with ethnography'. Elsewhere Maynard (1985) has demonstrated how such work can raise questions about the *functions* of communication patterns. Closely following Maynard, gathering ethnographic data on the clinics where these counsellors work allowed me to address the functions of counsellors' behaviour and, thereby, made possible a constructive input into policy debates.

In short, my argument will be that we can develop the practical payoff of qualitative research by avoiding the language of 'communication problems' (which imply that professionals are bad at their job) and instead examine the *functions* of communication sequences in a particular institutional context.

Let us look at a relevant extract from my HIV counselling data, Extract 9.1.

**Extract 9.1 (3: NH 4 42B)**

```
 1  C:  so you know it's not hh dead set on ten years hh now there
 2      are other people who could be HIV positive but not actually
 3      develop AIDS as such hh so they could be (.) carriers they
 4      could (.) stay well hh but pass the virus to people that
 5      they have sex with hh this is why we say hh if you don't
 6      know the person that you're with (0.6) and you're going to
 7      have sex with them hh it's important that you tell them to
 8      (0.3) use a condom (0.8) or to practice safe sex that's
 9      what using a condom means.
10      (1.5)
11  C:  okay?
12      (0.3)
13  P:  uhum
14      (2.4)
15  C:  has your pa:rtner ever used a condom with you?
16      (1.0)
17  P:  n:o
18      (1.5)
19  C:  do yer know what a condom looks like?
20      (0.5)
21  P:  (I don't)
22      (0.3)
23  C:  (Did you-) (0.3) have you perhaps- (1.0) a condom shown to
24      you (.) at school?= or:?
25  P:  no:
26  C:  yer didn't alright, =okay hhh
27      (2.0)
28  C:  is there anything that yer worried about in terms of yer
29      test if it's done today? (.) would you like the test first
30      of all to be done today?
31      (0.8)
32  P:  yeah
33  C:  yer would (1.0) ri::ght hh (.) if we do the test today
        (information follows on how the results of test are given)
```

Here, on lines 1–9, C offers an advice package which, as in the majority of counselling interviews we have examined, has not been based on a prior specification of P's problem (see Silverman et al., 1992). When, at line 10, she gets no acknowledgement of any kind, she pursues one (line 11) and finally gets a minimal acknowledgement at line 13.

C now moves into questions about P's knowledge of condoms (lines 15 and 19) which produce material that underlines the irrelevance to P of C's earlier advice. Now C swiftly exits from the whole topic at line 28).

Extract 9.1 thus shows the potential instability of advice-giving when patients produce material that suggests the irrelevance of the advice to them. Since professionals presumably desire clients to take up their advice, the lack of such uptake would appear to indicate bad methods of communication. So we must pose the question: why do many counsellors organize their advice in this way rather than first eliciting their patients' own concerns and knowledge?

As I have already noted, it is no part of my argument to suggest that these counsellors are short-sighted in avoiding recipient-designed advice. It does not make sense to imply that experienced professionals do not know what they are doing (even if they cannot be aware of all the consequences of their actions). Instead, we might ask, what are the *functions* of giving very generalized advice, without first eliciting clients' perceptions of their problems? We can start to look at this by examining the potential *dysfunctions* of more recipient-designed advice based on careful questioning.

Throughout our corpus of examples, counsellors exit quickly from recipient-designed advice when patients offer only minimal response tokens or when they display overt resistance. A fascinating example of such resistance is found in two of our Trinidad extracts where patients overtly resist question–answer sequences about 'safer sex' by asserting that the counsellor should not be asking about their behaviour and knowledge but, as the expert, telling them directly.

In this context, we can begin to see the function of how C constructs her advice in Extract 9.1. On the surface, it may appear strange that the advice is given (on lines 5–9) in an apparently 'depersonalized' way. C could have said something like:

> I suggest to you Sarah that you use a condom with your boyfriend.

In fact, C introduces her advice as follows:

> C:     this is why we say hh if you don't know the person that you're with

Notice the alternative readings that C thereby creates for whom is to be regarded as the sender and receiver of the advice: who is 'we'; is 'you' Sarah or just anybody; who is 'the person'? These different readings create the possibility that the client can opt to hear what is being said either as advice directed at her or as simply 'information about the kinds of things we tell people in this clinic'.

In Chapter 8 I argued that, by constructing advice sequences that can be heard as information delivery, counsellors manage to stabilize advice-giving. A function of maintaining an ambiguous communication format is that the counsellor does not have to cope with the difficult interactional problems of the failure of the patient to mark that what she is hearing is personalized advice and hence to offer more than a mere response token in reply. For, as we have shown elsewhere, information delivery can be co-operatively maintained simply by the client offering occasional response tokens, like 'mm hmm' (Peräkylä and Silverman, 1991). Indeed, C's prompt at line 11 makes remarkable the absence of such a response token from P despite the 1.5 second slot at line 10.

A second function of offering advice in this way is that it neatly handles many of the issues of delicacy that can arise in discussing sexual behaviour. First, the counsellor can be heard as making reference to what she tells 'anyone' so that this particular patient need not feel singled out for attention about her private life. Second, because there is no step-by-step method of questioning, patients are not required to expand on their sexual practices with the kinds of hesitations we saw above. Third, setting up advice sequences that can be heard as information delivery shields the counsellor from some of the interactional difficulties of appearing to tell strangers what they should be doing in the most intimate aspects of their behaviour.

### Attempt Exercise 9.2 about now

So far I seem to be arguing that counsellors are right to use communication methods quite different from those recommended in the textbooks. However, this is not my point. Rather, I am suggesting the following:

1 Researchers ought *not* to begin from normative standards of 'good' and 'bad' communication.
2 Instead the aim should be to understand the *skills* that participants deploy and the *functions* of the communication patterns that are discovered.
3 Communication patterns are only functional within a particular institutional context. Therefore, the researcher's next task is to understand the social context in which the observed patterns operate.
4 The practical import of the research can then be discussed with participants in the light of the relationship between communication and context.

This means that there is no point in suggesting reforms in how practitioners communicate when the social context pressures them in a particular direction. Such an intervention can only be irrelevant and even elitist.

Instead, by appreciating the skills of practitioners, in the context of the demands made upon them, we can open up a fruitful debate about *both* communication *and* the social and economic constraints on communication.

Counselling prior to the HIV antibody test occurs within at least two major constraints. First, it is dependent upon patient flow. This produces sudden periods of demand (usually immediately after the latest media advertising campaigns), interspersed with relatively quiet periods. The uneven flow of patients makes it difficult to design an effective use of clinic resources.

The second problem is that pre-test counselling is expected to cover a huge number of topics – from the difference between HIV and AIDS, to the meaning of positive and negative test results, to issues of insurance cover and confidentiality, and to 'safer sex'. The consequence is that, in most English testing sites, such counselling consists of largely stereotyped 'information packages' and is completed within 15 minutes (see Peräkylä and Silverman, 1991). The lack of patient uptake (Silverman et al., 1992) suggests that this is not very useful for clients. It is certainly a dull and repetitive task for the counsellors.

The analysis of the transcripts shows both that advice-giving is unstable and that, if advice is given in a personalized manner, it takes a long time. Truncated, non-personalized advice sequences are usually far shorter – an important consideration for hard-pressed counsellors.

I suggest, therefore, that the character of HIV counselling as a focused conversation on mostly delicate topics explains why ambiguous, truncated advice sequences (like that seen in Extract 9.1) predominate in our transcripts. Clearly, such sequences are functional for both local and institutional contexts.

I return to my point about the need to locate 'communication problems' in a broader structural context. Our research has much to say about how counsellors can organize their talk in order to maximize patient uptake (Silverman et al., 1992). However, without organizational change, the impact of such communication techniques alone might be minimal or even harmful. For instance, encouraging patient uptake will usually involve longer counselling sessions. Experienced counsellors will tell you that, if they take so long with one client that the waiting period for others increases, some clients will simply walk out – and hence may continue their risky behaviour without learning their HIV status.

Three simple organizational changes might allow counsellors to adopt new, more effective but time-consuming styles of communication. First, central government could keep testing centres better informed of new media AIDS campaigns so that local structures can be more responsive to sudden surges of client demand. Second, testing centres might use an appointment system rather than seeing clients on a walk-in basis. Third, certain of the topics now cursorily covered in pre-test counselling might be just as well addressed by leaflets or, still better, by videos shown to patients while they are waiting to see a counsellor. AIDS counselling might then look more like a service encounter, where the client is encouraged to ask questions of the professional, rather than a sermon.

As our own recent work shows, professionals respond to research which seeks to document the fine detail of their practice, while acknowledging the structural constraints to which they must respond. Put in another way, this means that we should aim to identify the interactional skills of the participants rather than their failings. Although the researcher cannot tell practitioners how they should behave, understanding the intended and unintended consequences of actions can provide the basis for a fruitful dialogue.

Following this extended case study, I will conclude this chapter by returning to the argument with which it began.

## 9.5 SUMMARY: THE SPECIFIC CONTRIBUTION OF QUALITATIVE RESEARCH

We are all cleverer than we can say in so many words. That is to say that the kinds of skills we are using in everyday settings, like medical consultations, are much more complicated and require much more analysis than we can actually tell the researcher in an interview study. Yet, by working with naturally occurring material we can make the skills used by all parties more available for analysis.

By analysing 'common sense' in fine detail, research can often make a direct contribution to professional practice. Moreover, the transcripts alone are an excellent resource which professionals can use to examine their own and each other's practice.

I think such research also has an implication for how phenomena can be made available for social science analysis. Researchers too readily assume that some topics, like sexuality, are private matters to which we cannot get direct access – for instance without putting a tape-recorder under everybody's bed or a video camera above it. However, this is an example of unclear thinking.

This assumes that sexuality is a unitary phenomenon that only takes place in a certain kind of setting. Instead, I would argue that most phenomena take place in a multiplicity of settings. Why can't we find sexuality present in soap-operas, cartoons or, indeed, in how clients and professionals present versions of themselves and descriptions of their partners and activities (see the discussion of Gubrium's work in Section 3.4.4)?

As I pointed out in the first few pages of Chapter 1, the problem arises from the use by researchers of essentialist conceptions of social phenomena. Once we are freed from this common-sense assumption, we can proceed to explicate common-sense practices in order to reveal their fine detail.

My favourite philosopher, Ludwig Wittgenstein, made this point for me. He writes:

> The aspects of things that are most important for us are hidden because of their simplicity and familiarity. (1968, para 129)

Now Wittgenstein, of course, is referring to what is hidden from philosophers. But the same issue often arises for social scientists – to whom things can be 'hidden because of their simplicity and familiarity'.

This means that it is often unhelpful for researchers to begin their work on a basis of a 'social problem' identified by either practitioners or managers. It is a commonplace that such definitions of 'problems' often may serve vested interests. My point, however, is that if field research has anything to offer, its theoretical imperatives drive it in a direction which can offer participants new perspectives on their problems. Paradoxically, by refusing to begin from a common conception of what is 'wrong' in a setting, we may be most able to contribute to the identification both of what is going on and, thereby, of how it may be modified in the pursuit of desired ends.

Strangely, what we are concerned with in qualitative social science is what is closest to hand. However, because it is so close to hand, both participants *and* researchers may often forget about it. Our common-sense knowledge about the way in which the world is organized is being used all the time by us in the everyday world and also to understand our research findings. But rarely do we topicalize that common-sense knowledge. Wittgenstein draws our attention to this paradox.

**Attempt Exercise 9.3 about now**

## 9.6 CONCLUSION

> There is a pressing need to show how the practices of qualitative research can help change the world in positive ways. (Denzin and Lincoln, 2000: x)

Throughout this chapter, I have been arguing that qualitative researchers can best satisfy the 'pressing need' identified by Denzin and Lincoln by resisting directly employing administrators', journalists' or even practitioners' definitions of what is a 'problem'. I have illustrated this point through my own research on outpatient clinics and HIV test counselling.

In these contexts, I have shown the gains of seeking to understand the local functions of talk rather than directly entering into normative debates about communication styles. Put in another way, this means that we should aim to identify the interactional skills of the participants rather than their failings.

I will conclude with a brief discussion of a highly relevant dialogue in David Lodge's novel *Nice Work*. This novel is about the relationship between Robyn, a lecturer (at the same university as in all Lodge's books), and Vic, a manager in an engineering firm. She has spent some time with him in order to understand the world of industry. This is, of course, very much a document of the 1980s where one version of 'free market' economics suggested that the value of academic institutions is to be judged in terms of their contribution to the needs of industry.

Just before Extract 9.2, Robyn, the cultural studies lecturer, had given a highly risqué reading of the cultural symbolism of a cigarette advertisement. Robyn's semiotic analysis of the advertisement is treated by Vic as a display of unnecessary jargon. In the extract, Vic, the manager, speaks first.

**Extract 9.2 (Lodge, 1989: 221)**
'Why can't you people take things at their face value?'
   'What people are you referring to?'

'Highbrows. Intellectuals. You're always trying to find hidden meanings in things. Why? A cigarette is a cigarette. A piece of silk is a piece of silk. Why not leave it at that?'

'When they're represented they acquire additional meanings,' said Robyn. 'Signs are never innocent. Semiotics teaches us that.'

'Semi-what?'

'Semiotics. The study of signs.'

'It teaches us to have dirty minds, if you ask me.'

It seems that Vic and Robyn talk past one another. He does not understand what on earth she is doing. And to her, the world of industry seems to be a world with no morality and little sense. However, at the end of the book they do achieve a dialogue between the world of academia and the everyday world.

I think such a dialogue, though hard to achieve, should be our aim. In practice, this probably means that both sides will have to give a little. Policy-makers will have to give up their suspicion of research which is not based on statistics and refuses to define its research topic in terms of any obvious social problem. In turn, qualitative researchers will have to demonstrate how their work can be both insightful and valid.

As part of this dialogue, quantitative researchers will have to give up their belief in the stupidity of common-sense ways of acting and be prepared to establish a division of labour with their qualitative colleagues. But, equally, qualitative researchers will have to question the siren calls of Emotionalism and its commitment to the transcendent character of 'experience'.

## KEY POINTS

- The wider audience for qualitative research includes policy-makers, practitioners and the general public. Each will have different expectations.
- Qualitative researchers can attempt to satisfy these expectations by: participating in debates about public policy; providing new opportunities for people to make their own choices; and offering a new perspective to practitioners and clients.
- Although no neutral or value-free position is possible in social science, this does not mean that 'anything goes'.
- When you are studying people's behaviour or asking them questions, not only the values of the researcher but the researcher's responsibilities to those studied have to be faced.

## Recommended Reading

Although almost a century old, Max Weber's lecture 'Science as a vocation' (1946) remains the key reading. Roger Hadley's chapter 'Publish and be ignored: proselytise and be damned', in G.C. Wenger (1987), is a vibrant account of the pitfalls of trying to reach a policy audience. Practitioner audiences are very well discussed in Michael Bloor's chapter 'Addressing social problems through qualitative research', in Silverman (1997). Gary Marx's paper (1997) is a lively and extremely helpful guide for the apprentice researcher desiring to make links with a range of audiences. Ian Shaw (1999) provides a helpful introductory account of the ways in which qualitative research can evaluate programmes and policies.

## Exercise 9.1

This exercise gives you an opportunity to think through the various ways social scientists have answered Becker's question: 'Whose side are we on?' You are asked to imagine that research funding is available for whatever topic and research design you prefer.

1 Suggest a research topic and outline a methodology using one or more of the methods set out in Chapters 3–7.
2 Justify the topic and methodology from the point of view of: (a) the scholar (b) the state counsellor and (c) the partisan.
3 Now select any one article which report research findings in a social science journal. Which of the positions referred to in 2 does it adopt?
4 Set out how this position might be criticized from the point of view of (a) the other positions and (b) your own views of the relevance of social science research.

**Exercise 9.2**

This exercise offers you an opportunity to address the practical relevance of field research in the context of the conversation analysis skills you learned in Chapter 6. It is based on Extract 9.1.

1 Using any of the concepts mentioned in Chapter 6, attempt a further analysis of Extract 9.1.
2 What does your analysis show that is different from or adds to the analysis given in this chapter?
3 Imagine you are talking to counsellors about their work. What kinds of practical implications could you suggest in relation to how they communicate with their clients?
4 Imagine you are talking to people coming for HIV counselling. What kinds of practical implications could your analysis have for them?

**Exercise 9.3**

Select any published account of qualitative research. Reread it in order to answer the following questions:

1 In what way(s), if at all, did the author(s) address ethical matters arising in this research?
2 Were there any unacknowledged ethical issues? If so, how might they have been addressed?
3 In what way(s), if at all, did the author(s) discuss the contribution of this research for non-academic audiences?
4 What unacknowledged relevance for the wider community might this research have? Explain this (in no more than 200 words) without using any specialist jargon.

# 10
## The Potential of Qualitative Research: Eight Reminders

The author of a textbook is always torn between two different impulses. Naturally, one wants to provide a comprehensive and fair coverage of the field. On the other hand, it is impossible to escape one's own assumptions, preferences and (dare one say it?) prejudices.

However, providing the reader is given the opportunity to register the intellectual baggage that authors bring to their writing, we should not see such baggage as a drawback. Even if we could imagine a textbook freed from authorial prejudice, it would be a pretty dull affair – rather like those awful book reviews which do little more than list the titles of each chapter.

In this book, I hope that my own intellectual baggage has given flavour and spice to my depiction of the field. Throughout I have tried to be open about the way that this has shaped the route we have followed.

This final chapter gives me the opportunity to pull together these authorial threads. However, it is not meant as an indulgence to myself, still less as a kind of *mea culpa*, where I apologize for my inability to be sufficiently objective. It is one voice in a debate that I believe matters both to social scientists and to our audiences. I hope, therefore, that you will find this chapter worth reading as a way of further stimulating your interest in the potential of qualitative research.

In formulating my ideas as 'reminders', I have followed my favourite philosopher, Ludwig Wittgenstein. Wittgenstein came to reject philosophies based on principles or rules. Instead, he favoured assembling fragments of everyday understandings to serve as reminders of what we know already. For Wittgenstein, these reminders would have a 'hygienic' purpose. They would aim to clear our heads of the babble that sometimes passes as intellectual argument in order to look at the world afresh.

In this chapter, my aims are less grand. I would not, for a moment, claim to have transcended that babble. While much has had to be crammed into a small space, a common thread will emerge which, I hope, will tie together the preceding chapters. For my own position rests firmly on the models that have been described in this book as constructionism and ethnomethodology. So, in this chapter, I return to the theme of the situated character of accounts and other practices and to the dangers of seeking to identify phenomena apart from these practices and the forms of representation which they embody.

Yet, because I have no time for self-contained 'schools' of social science, I hope that what I have to say will be debated by those researchers with other kinds of preferences and allegiances. Conceived as 'reminders', rather than as rules or dictums, what follows is meant to encourage, rather than stifle, debate.

## 10.1 TAKE ADVANTAGE OF NATURALLY OCCURRING DATA

In the preface to this book, I referred to my preference for working with 'naturally occurring' data. This seems logical if your interest is in the practices through which phenomena like 'families', 'tribes' or 'laboratory science' are constructed or assembled. Despite this, however, many ethnographers move relatively easily between observational data and data that are an artifact of a research setting, usually an interview. In Chapters 3 and 4, I pointed out the difficulties this can create, especially where triangulation is used to compare findings from different settings and to assemble the context-free 'truth' (see Section 8.3.2).

We often falsely assume that there is inherent difficulty in obtaining naturally occurring data because of the supposedly 'private' character of many settings, e.g. 'family life' or 'sexuality'. However, this assumption trades off a common-sense perception that these are *unitary* phenomena whose meaning is constructed in a single site (e.g. households, bedrooms).

Yet 'family life' is going on all around us – in courtrooms and social security offices as well as households (see Gubrium, 1992). Equally, 'sexuality' is hardly confined to the bedroom; discourses of sexuality are all around us too (see Foucault, 1979).

Given the availability of such naturally occurring data, I share naturalism's enthusiasm to get out 'into the field' to study what participants are doing. Being 'in the field' gives us exposure to the categories that members actually use in their day-to-day activities. Categories abstracted from the business of daily life usually impose a set of polarities (or continuums) with an unknown relationship to that business.

One obvious example of such *a priori* polarized theorizing is in abstract models of organizational behaviour in terms of rational/non-rational action (e.g. Cyert and March, 1963). As Anderson et al. point out, such models fail to address:

> the essentially socially organized character of the discovery, recognition, determination and solution of problems. (1987: 144)

This 'socially organized character' cannot be inferred by armchair thinking or read off interviewees' accounts. Instead, we need to get out 'into the field' to study how the participants themselves constitute 'organizational behaviour'.

Using materials from audiotapes of business negotiations, Anderson et al. show that the parties focus on problems and their provision of candidate solutions is embedded in how they play with the sequencing rules of natural language (see my discussion of 'institutional talk' in Section 6.3.4). For instance, an available turn transition point may not be taken up and so a party can avoid a commitment until more is known of the other party's game. Equally, requests for clarification both buy time and give the ball back to the first speaker in a three-part sequence (clarification request, clarification response).

In turn, these sequencing rules are enacted in the context of a set of 'business' relevances which, as Anderson et al. show, depend on the display of 'competitiveness' coupled with a form of 'urbane affability' which takes for granted the reciprocity of personal and commercial relevances.

Anderson et al.'s analysis reveals 'what adopting a businesslike attitude to the solution of routine problems means as an observable, interactional feature of daily life' (1987: 155). In doing so, it shows how 'business' disappears as a unitary phenomenon (see Section 10.5). As Anderson et al. note, 'business life' is interwoven with social life: the purely 'rational' cannot be filtered out from the social.

However, there are two dangers in pushing this argument very far. First, we can become smug about the status of 'naturally occurring' data. I have already referred to Hammersley and Atkinson's (1983) observation that there are no 'pure' data; all data are mediated by our own reasoning as well as that of participants. So to assume that 'naturally occurring' data are unmediated data is, self-evidently, a fiction of the same kind as put about by survey researchers who argue that techniques and controls suffice to produce data which are not an artefact of the research setting.

The second danger implicit in the purist response is that it can blind us to the really powerful, compelling nature of interview accounts. Consider, for instance, the striking 'atrocity stories' told by mothers of handicapped children and their appeal to listeners to hear them as 'coping splendidly' (see my discussion in Section 4.8, of 'moral tales').

This leads me to the problem of how to make the best use of interview data and to the dead-ends identified in Chapter 4.

## 10.2 AVOID TREATING THE ACTOR'S POINT OF VIEW AS AN EXPLANATION

How could anybody have thought this was the case in social science? How could anybody think that what we ought to do is to go out into the field to report people's exciting, gruesome or intimate experiences (see Section 10.5 for one answer)?

Yet, judging by the prevalence of what I will call 'naive' interview studies in qualitative research, this indeed seems to be the case. Naive interviewers believe that the supposed limits of quantitative research are overcome by an open-ended interview schedule and a desire to catch 'authentic' experience.

They fail to recognize what they have in common with media interviewers (whose perennial question is 'How do you/does it feel?') and with tourists (who, in their search for the 'authentic' or 'different', invariably end up with more of the same). They also totally fail to recognize the problematic analytic status of interview data which are never simply raw but are both situated and textual (Mishler, 1986). Such analytic issues, moreover, are not even touched upon in the elegant methodological 'remedies' of survey research.

Of course, the crasser forms of emotionalism are restricted to student essays and to some of the speeches of the British ex-Prime Minister Margaret Thatcher ('there is no such thing as society' she once commented). Nevertheless, professional social science often still responds to the emotionalist impulse, particularly in fieldworkers' commitment to the sanctity of what respondents say in open-ended interviews. As we saw in Chapter 4, we are thus sometimes left with the unappetizing choice between treating accounts as privileged data or as 'perspectival' and subject to check via the method of triangulation with other observations.

If we reduce qualitative research to the emotionalist interview, we lose much of the thrust of the tradition from which it emerged. As I noted in Chapter 3, you only have to look at interactionist work from the Chicago School in the 1930s and 1940s to see the presence of a much more vital approach.

Using their eyes as well as listening to what people were saying, these sociologists invariably located 'consciousness' in specific patterns of social organization. As we saw, Whyte (1949) showed how the behaviour of barmen and waitresses was a response to the imperatives of status and the organization of work routines. The experiences of such staff needed to be contexted by knowledge of such features and by precise observation of the territorial organization of restaurants (see the beginning of Chapter 3).

This issue of the situated nature of people's accounts directly arose in my study of a paediatric cardiology unit (Silverman, 1987). As noted in Section 9.4.2, when we interviewed parents after their child's first clinic visit, most said that they had a problem taking anything in. They reported that one of their major problems in concentrating properly was caused by the crowded room in which the consultation took place – for this was a teaching hospital, where several student doctors as well as nurses and researchers were usually present.

Although we could empathize with the parents' response, we thought it worthwhile to go back to our tapes of the encounters they were discussing. It turned out that the number of questions parents asked was directly related to the number of staff present (not inversely related as their interview answers would have suggested).

As is often the case after such a counter-intuitive finding, we found quite a simple explanation. Perhaps when the senior doctor broke off the consultation to ask questions of the junior doctors present, quite unintentionally this created a space for parents to think about what they had been told so far and to formulate their questions without being 'on stage', in direct eye contact with the doctor. This explanation was supported in another unit where parents also asked many questions after they had had some time on their own while the doctor studied clinical data (Silverman, 1987: 91–4).

This took us back to our interview material with the parents. We were not prepared to treat what they had told us ironically, i.e. as self-evidently mistaken in the light of the 'objective' data.

As already noted, such simple-minded triangulation of data fails to do justice to the embedded, situated nature of accounts (see Section 8.3.2). Instead, we came to see parents' accounts as 'moral tales' (Baruch, 1982; Voysey, 1975). Our respondents struggled to present their actions in the context of moral versions of responsible parenthood in a situation where the dice were loaded against them (because of the risks to life and the high-technology means of diagnosis and treatment).

Parents' reference to the problems of the crowded consultation room were now treated not as an explanation of their behaviour at the time but as a situated appeal to the rationality and moral appropriateness of that behaviour. Similarly, in a study of 50 British general practice consultations, Webb and Stimson (1976) noted how the subsequent accounts of patients took on a dramatic quality in which the researcher was encouraged to empathize with the patient's difficulties in the consultation.

A story was told in which a highly rational patient had behaved actively and sensibly. By contrast, doctors were routinely portrayed as acting insensitively or with poor judgement. By telling 'atrocity stories', Webb and Stimson suggest that patients were able to give vent to thoughts which had gone unvoiced at the time of the consultation, to redress a real or perceived inequality between doctor and patient and to highlight the teller's own rationality. Equally, atrocity stories have a dramatic form which captures the hearer's attention – a point which qualitative researchers become aware of when asked to give brief accounts of their findings.

There are powerful cultural forms at work in such 'moral tales'. Consequently, the last thing you want to do is to treat them as simple statements of events to be triangulated with other people's accounts or observations. For the fact is that, as societal members, we can see the 'good sense' of such tales.

In many respects, an 'atrocity story' is no less powerful because there is no corroborating evidence. It reveals the 'moral work' involved in displays of 'responsible' parenthood, particularly, as in Baruch's study, where that responsibility had to be demonstrated in the context of potentially unintelligible, high-technology cardiac medicine.

In a certain sense, once again we see how qualitative researchers have come back, in a full circle, to a position held by their quantitative colleagues. Neither wants to take the actor's point of view as an explanation because this would be to equate common sense with social science – a recipe for the lazy qualitative researcher who settles for simply reporting people's 'experiences'. Only when such a researcher moves beyond the gaze of the tourist, bemused with a sense of bizarre cultural practices ('Goodness, you do things differently here'), do the interesting analytic questions begin.

Such questions can be derived from two very different but equally neglected sources. In his later philosophical writing, Wittgenstein (1968) implies that we should not treat people's utterances as standing for their unmediated inner experiences. This is particularly striking in his discussion of statements about pain (1968, paras 244–6, 448–9). Wittgenstein asks: what does it mean when I say 'I'm in pain'? And why is it that we feel unable to deny this assertion when someone makes it?

In our community, it seems, we talk about pain as if it belongs to individuals. So, in understanding the meaning of someone saying 'I'm in pain' we reveal what our community takes for granted about private experience (but not private experience itself – see Peräkylä and Silverman, 1991). So Wittgenstein makes the point that, in analysing another's activities, we are always describing what is appropriate to a communal 'language game'.

A second source for understanding the public sense of interview accounts is to be found in Mills's (1940) discussion of 'vocabularies of motive'. Mills reminds us that, for sociological purposes, nothing lies 'behind' people's accounts. So when people describe their own or other's motives, the appropriate questions to ask are: when does such talk get done, what motives are available and what work does 'motive talk' do in the context in which it arises? As Gilbert and Mulkay were to argue, many years later:

> the goal of the analyst no longer parallels that of the participants, who are concerned to find out what they and others did or thought, but becomes that of reflecting upon the patterned character of participants' portrayals of action. (1983: 24)

Conceived in this sort of way, interview data become a fascinating topic for analytically sensitive case study work. As I have already suggested, with a little lateral thinking, it is also possible to derive from this approach practical as well as analytic insights.

## 10.3 STUDY THE INTERRELATIONSHIPS BETWEEN ELEMENTS

The distinctive contribution qualitative research can make is by utilizing its theoretical resources in the deep analysis of small bodies of publicly shareable data. This means that, unlike much quantitative research, we are not satisfied with a simple coding of data in order to produce explanations of statistical variance. Instead, through comprehensive data treatment, we have to show how the (theoretically defined) elements we have identified are assembled or mutually laminated (see Section 8.3.2).

Yet there are also similarities between good qualitative and quantitative research. In both, multi-factorial explanation is likely to be more satisfactory than explanations which appeal to what I have called a 'single element'. Just because one is doing a case study, limited to a particular set of interactions, does not mean that one cannot examine how particular sayings and doings are embedded in particular patterns of social organization.

Despite their very different theoretical frameworks, this is the distinctive quality shared by, say, Whyte (1949) and Moerman's (1974) discussion of a Thai tribe. A further classic case is found in Mary Douglas's (1975) work on a central African tribe, the Lele (discussed in Section 3.1.1).

Douglas's study of the Lele exemplifies the need to locate how individual elements are embedded in forms of social organization. In her case, this is done in the manner of structural anthropology where behaviour is seen as the expression of a 'society' which works as a 'hidden hand' constraining and forming human action.

By contrast, Moerman's and Anderson et al.'s work indicates how one can avoid single-element explanations without treating social organization as a purely external force. In the latter case, people cease to be 'cultural dopes' (Garfinkel, 1967) and skilfully reproduce a moral order.

Saussure provides a message appropriate to both these traditions when he reminds us that no meaning ever resides in a single term (see the discussion of Saussure in Section 7.2). This is an instruction equally relevant to Douglas's structural anthropology and to Garfinkel and Anderson et al.'s ethnomethodology.

So we can take Saussure's message out of context from the kind of linguistics that Saussure himself was doing and use it as a very general methodological principle in qualitative research.

What we are concerned with, as Saussure (1974) showed us, is not individual elements but their relations. As Saussure points out, these relations may be organized in terms of paradigmatic oppositions (Ancient Israelites, British sociologists etc.) or in terms of systems of relations which are organized through what precedes and what follows each item.

An example that Saussure himself gives shows the importance of organization and sequence in social phenomena. The 8.15 train from Zurich to Geneva remains the 8.15 train even if it does not depart till 8.45. The meaning of the train – its identity – only arises within the oppositions and relationships set out in the railway timetable.

Let me illustrate the significance of this with an example drawn from an ethnographic case in a study influenced by constructionism. Dingwall and Murray (1983) were concerned with how medical staff responded to patients presenting themselves at a British 'casualty' or emergency hospital unit. They note that Jeffery (1979) suggests that patients are typified by staff as either 'good' and 'interesting' or 'bad' and 'rubbish'. The former might be patients who tested the specialized competences of staff; the latter might be patients with trivial complaints and/or responsible for their own illnesses.

Dingwall and Murray argue that Jeffery's polarity inadequately spells out the system of relations in which these labels are embedded. They note, for instance, that children often have trivial complaints for which they themselves are responsible and yet are not usually defined by staff as 'bad' or 'rubbish' patients.

Drawing upon McHugh's (1970) treatment of deviance, Dingwall and Murray suggest that casualty staff assign such labels only after assessing whether the patient is 'theoretic' (i.e. perceived to be able to make choices) and the situation is 'conventional' (i.e. that it offers a choice for the patient to make). On this basis, Dingwall and Murray offer a 2 × 2 table which reveals the staff's decision-making rules. This is set out in Table 10.1.

TABLE 10.1  *Casualty department rules*

|  |  | Situation | |
|  |  | *Conventional* | *Non-conventional* |
| --- | --- | --- | --- |
|  | *Theoretic* | Bad patients | Inappropriate patients |
| Actor |  |  |  |
|  | *Non-theoretic* | Children | Naive patients |

*Source*: adapted from Dingwall and Murray, 1983

So, in a conventional situation, a patient who does not co-operate with staff is normally defined as 'bad'. Children, however, because they may be perceived as non-theoretic, will not find that such behaviour leads to this label. Similarly, in a situation offering no choice (i.e. 'non-conventional'), patients will be labelled as 'inappropriate' ('theoretic') or 'naive' ('non-theoretic').

Indeed, as Dingwall and Murray show, the attribution of deviance to a patient arises only within one of three 'frames' (see Section 3.3.2) which shape the perceived clinical priority of a presenting patient as follows:

1 A *special* frame sorts out patients according to their perceived moral worth (e.g. as 'bad', 'inappropriate', 'naive' or simply a child).
2 A *clinical* frame judges patients simply by whether they constitute what staff perceive to be an 'interesting' case.
3 A *bureaucratic* frame categorizes patients as 'routine', i.e. without perceived deviant features or special clinical interest. 'Routine' patients get routine treatment.

Just as Douglas discovered that the pangolin's anomalous characteristics were the key to unravelling the social organization of the Lele, so the anomaly created by children who break rules and yet are not treated as 'bad' patients shows the complexity of decision-making in a hospital setting. In both cases, the importance is revealed of avoiding single-element explanations and of focusing upon the processes through which the relations between elements are articulated.

## 10.4  ATTEMPT THEORETICALLY FERTILE RESEARCH

In any text on social research methodology, there is a danger of reducing analytical questions to technical issues to be resolved by cookbook means, e.g. good interviewing techniques, grounded theory or the appropriate computer-aided qualitative data analysis system. I do not wish to criticize these methods but to underline that, as most of their proponents recognize, they are no substitute for theoretically inspired reasoning.

As we have already seen, such theoretical issues lurk behind some apparently technical questions like observing 'private' encounters or interpreting interview data. Following Wittgenstein once more, a touch of 'hygiene' may be useful in clearing our minds about the nature of the phenomena that qualitative researchers attempt to study.

One way of achieving such hygiene is by mobilizing the social science discipline in which you have been trained and the models it offers. In Chapter 1, I referred to Martin O'Brien's (1993) use of the example of a kaleidoscope as a way to think of how models and theories can inspire the way we think about our data. Let me repeat what O'Brien says about this:

> a kaleidoscope . . . [is] the child's toy consisting of a tube, a number of lenses and fragments of translucent, coloured glass or plastic. When you turn the tube and look down the lens of the kaleidoscope the shapes and colours, visible at the bottom, change. As the tube is turned, different lenses come into play and the combinations of colour and shape shift from one pattern to another. In a similar way, we can see social theory as a sort of kaleidoscope – by shifting theoretical perspective the world under investigation also changes shape. (1993: 10–11)

I have space for only one example. How we code or transcribe our data is a crucial matter for qualitative researchers (see Sections 3.3.5 and 6.2). Often, however, such researchers simply replicate the positivist model routinely used in quantitative research. According to this model, coders of data are usually trained in procedures with the aim of ensuring a uniform approach. This is a tried and trusted method designed to improve the reliability of a research method.

However, ethnomethodology reminds us that 'coding' is not the preserve of research scientists. In some sense, researchers, like all of us, 'code' what they hear and see in the world around them. Moreover, this 'coding' has been shown to be mutual and interactive (Sacks, 1992; Silverman, 1998).

The ethnomethodological response is to make this everyday 'coding' (or 'interpretive practice') the object of inquiry. Alternatively, we can proceed in a more conventional manner but mention and respond to this well-established critique (for an example, see Clavarino et al., 1995, discussed in Section 8.2.5).

Of course, as I have emphasized throughout, the research 'cake' can be legitimately sliced in many ways: there is no 'correct' kaleidoscope through which to view all data. So I am *not* suggesting that the vast mass of researchers who treat 'coding' as purely an analyst's problem abandon their work. Instead, my minimalist suggestion is that they examine how far the categories they are using can be shown to be used by the participants in their ordinary behaviours.

The example of coding our data shows, I hope, how theory can make our data analysis more fertile. It is also useful because it emphasizes my own view of theory building as being done with data and not from the armchair.

Unfortunately, however, the armchair is a favoured position in much contemporary social science, notably in my own discipline of sociology. One reason for this concentration on armchair thinking is that, unlike many natural sciences, we lack one agreed model of our part of reality.

As the philosopher of science Thomas Kuhn (1970) has argued, many social sciences lack a single, agreed set of concepts deriving from a common model of 'reality'. In Kuhn's terms, this makes social research 'pre-paradigmatic' or at least in a state of competing paradigms. Unfortunately, this has generated a whole series of social science courses which pose different social science approaches in terms of either/or questions.

Such courses are much appreciated by some students. They learn about the paradigmatic oppositions in question, choose A rather than B, and report back, parrot fashion, all the advantages of A and the drawbacks of B. It is hardly surprising that such courses produce very little evidence that such students have ever thought about anything: even their choice of A is likely to be based on their teacher's implicit or explicit preferences. This may, in part, explain why so many undergraduate sociology courses actually provide a learned incapacity to go out and do research.

Learning about rival 'armed camps' in no way allows you to confront research data. In the field, material is much more messy than the different camps would suggest. Perhaps there is something to be learned from both sides, or, more constructively, perhaps we start to ask interesting questions when we reject the polarities that such a course markets?

So when I call for theoretically fertile research it is because I believe that theory only becomes worthwhile when it is used to explain something. Howard Becker (1998: 1) reports that the great founder of the Chicago School, Everett Hughes, responded grumpily when students asked what he thought about theory. 'Theory of what?,' he would reply. For Hughes, as for me, theory without some observation to work upon is like a tractor without a field.

Theory, then, should be neither a status symbol nor an optional extra in a research study. Without theory, research is impossibly narrow. Without research, theory is mere armchair contemplation.

## 10.5  ADDRESS WIDER AUDIENCES

To call for more theory in research might seem to drive off our non-academic audiences: policy-makers, practitioners, the general public and others (see Section 9.2). However, by a somewhat roundabout route, our internal debate between theory and data can lead to data sources and findings of great interest to wider audiences. To simplify, I discuss here the policy-making audience (see Silverman, 1997b: 23–5).

There are two potentially dangerous orthodoxies shared by many social scientists and by policy-makers who commission social research. The first orthodoxy is that people are puppets of social structures. According to this model, what people do is defined by 'society'. In practice, this reduces to explaining people's behaviour as the outcome of certain 'face-sheet' variables (like social class, gender or ethnicity).

We will call this the *explanatory orthodoxy*. According to it, social scientists do research to provide explanations of given problems, e.g. why do individuals engage in unsafe sex? Inevitably, such research will find explanations based on one or more 'face-sheet' variables.

The second orthodoxy is that people are 'dopes'. Interview respondents' knowledge is assumed to be imperfect, indeed they may even lie to us. In the same way, practitioners (like doctors or counsellors) are assumed always to depart from normative standards of good practice. This is the *divine orthodoxy*. It makes the social scientist into the philosopher-king (or queen) who can always see through people's claims and know better than they do.

What is wrong with these two orthodoxies? The explanatory orthodoxy is so concerned to rush to an explanation that it fails to ask serious questions about what it is explaining. There is a parallel here with what we must now call a 'postmodern' phenomenon. It seems that visitors to the Grand Canyon in Arizona are now freed from the messy business of exploring the Canyon itself. Instead, they can now spend an enlightening hour or so in a multi-media 'experience' which gives them all the thrills in a predigested way. Then they can be on their way, secure in the knowledge that they have 'done' the Grand Canyon.

This example is part of something far larger. In contemporary culture, the environment around phenomena has become more important than the phenomenon itself. So people are more interested in the lives of movie stars than in the movies themselves. Equally, on sporting occasions, pre- and post-match interviews become as exciting (or even more exciting) than the game itself. Using a phrase to which we shall shortly return, in both cases, *the phenomenon escapes*.

This is precisely what the explanatory orthodoxy encourages. Because we rush to offer explanations of all kinds of social phenomena, we rarely spend enough time trying to understand how the phenomenon works. So, for instance, we may simply impose 'operational definitions' of phenomena, failing totally to examine how such activities come to have meaning in what people are actually doing in everyday (naturally occurring) situations.

This directly leads to the folly of the divine orthodoxy. Its methods preclude seeing the good sense of what people are doing or understanding their skills in local contexts. It prefers interviews where people are forced to answer questions that never arise in their day-to-day life. Because it rarely looks at this life, it condemns people to fail without understanding that we are all cleverer than we can say in so many words. Even when it examines what people are actually doing, the divine orthodoxy measures their activities by some idealized normative standards, like 'good communication'. So, once again, like ordinary people, practitioners are condemned to fail.

Both kinds of research are fundamentally concerned with the environment around the phenomenon rather than the phenomenon itself. In quantitative studies of 'objective' social structures and qualitative studies of people's 'subjective' orientations, we may be deflected away from the phenomenon towards what follows and precedes it (causes and consequences in the 'objective' approach) or to how people respond to it (the 'subjective' approach). This can be illustrated in two simple diagrams:

*Objectivism*
causes > the phenomenon > consequences

*Subjectivism*
perceptions > the phenomenon > responses

In both approaches, the phenomenon with which ostensibly we are concerned disappears. In 'objectivism', it is defined out of existence (by fiat, as Cicourel, 1964, puts it). Equally, what I have called 'subjectivism' is so romantically attached to the authentic rush of human experience that it merely reproduces tales of a subjective world without bringing us any closer to the local organization of the phenomena concerned.

How can these theoretically informed reflections aid policy-makers? In the first place, abandoning the divine orthodoxy means that we may be able to offer more original suggestions than simply to improve practitioner communication so that it better approximates some idealized model.

Take the example of my research in cardiac and diabetic clinics (Silverman, 1987). Among other things, this revealed that parents, particularly mothers, sought ways to display their 'responsible parenthood'. How could this massively recurrent cultural compunction to treat parenthood as a moral activity be incorporated into medical consultations?

In the study of the paediatric cardiology unit (PCU) discussed earlier, it would have been tempting to follow other researchers (e.g. Byrne and Long, 1976) and to suggest that parents' reported problems derive from doctors' inadequate communication skills. Our analysis suggested, however, that the constraints of the setting and of the task at hand (speedy diagnosis and treatment) meant that the first outpatients' clinic had no space for some parental concerns and that, in any event, many parents needed time to come to terms with what they were being told. If time was allowed to pass (when, for instance, parents had faced the questions of other anxious relatives and had consulted popular medical manuals or the family physician) and the family was invited to revisit the hospital, things might turn out differently.

Such a clinic was indeed established at the PCU and the constraints were further altered by informing parents in advance that their child would not be examined this time. An evaluation study indicated that, in the eyes of the participants, this was a successful innovation (1987: 86–103).

Yet at no point had we set out to teach doctors communication skills. So a sociological truism (change the constraints of the setting and people will behave differently) had paid off in ways that we had not foreseen. People responded to the new setting in innovatory ways: parents bringing their children along to see the playroom and to discover that the ward was not such a frightening place after all.

This study of a medical clinic indicates the gains of avoiding the divine orthodoxy. But what of the explanatory orthodoxy? In particular, how are we to satisfy our fellow social scientists, let alone our wider audiences, if we fail to base our research on the study of *causes*? As I argue below, it is all a matter of timing.

## 10.6 BEGIN WITH 'HOW?' QUESTIONS, THEN ASK 'WHY?'

The kind of detailed ethnographic research discussed above, as well as my conversation analytic study of counselling (Silverman, 1997b), lay themselves open to the charge that they deal 'only' with talk. The implication is that, because such research supposedly refuses to look beyond the talk, it is unable to offer adequate explanations of its findings. As critics continually reiterate: what about the *context* of your data?

Of course, I have already offered a critical review of this approach in my comments on the explanatory orthodoxy. Such contexts do not speak for themselves but must be carefully identified in the practices and orientations of the participants.

Nonetheless, I do *not* want to suggest that it is always improper to look beyond talk-in-interaction. Instead, my position is that we are faced not with either/or choices but with issues largely of *timing*.

My assumption is that it is usually necessary to refuse to allow our research topics to be defined in terms of, say, the 'causes' of 'bad' counselling or the 'consequences of 'good' counselling. Such topics merely reflect the conceptions of 'social problems' as recognized by either professional or community groups. Ironically, by beginning from a clearly defined analytical perspective, we show how we can later address such social problems with, we believe, considerable force and persuasiveness.

My argument suggests that one's initial move should be to give close attention to how participants locally produce contexts for their interaction. By beginning with this question of 'how', we can then fruitfully move on to 'why' questions about institutional and cultural constraints. Such constraints reveal the functions of apparently irrational practices and help us to understand the possibilities and limits of attempts at social reform.

Using CA, Schegloff has shown that a great deal depends on the pace at which we proceed:

> the study of talk should be allowed to proceed under its own imperatives, with the hope that its results will provide more effective tools for the analysis of distributional, institutional and social structural problems *later on* than would be the case if the analysis of talk had, from the outset, to be made answerable to problems extrinsic to it. (1991: 64, my emphasis)

Quite properly, this will mean delaying what I have called 'why' questions until we have asked the appropriate 'how' questions. But how, eventually, are we to make the link between the two?

A solution is suggested in Douglas Maynard's (1991) account of how paediatricians give diagnostic information to parents. Maynard identifies a 'perspective-display sequence' where doctors invite the parents' views first and then tailor their diagnostic statements to what they have elicited from parents.

So far, this addresses the 'how?' question. However, Maynard then moves on to the 'why?' question, relating the 'perspective-display sequence' to the functions of avoiding open conflict over unfavourable diagnoses. In this way, the device serves to preserve social solidarity.

So Maynard's close focus on *how* the parties locally produce patterns of communication ends up by considering the 'functions' of the forms so discovered. The lesson is clear. We cannot do everything at the same time without muddying the water. For policy reasons, as well as from conventional social science concerns, we may well want to ask what I have called 'why' questions. There is no reason not to, providing that we have first closely described how the phenomenon at hand is locally produced. If not, we are limited to an explanation of something that we have simply defined by fiat.

This means that there is nothing wrong with the search for explanations, providing that this search is grounded in a close understanding of how the phenomena being explained are 'put together' at an interactional level. This means that, wherever possible, one should seek to obtain 'naturally occurring' data in order to obtain adequate understanding, leading to soundly based policy interventions.

## 10.7 STUDY 'HYPHENATED' PHENOMENA

When we attempt to unravel the 'black box' of social phenomena, we invariably start to see the multiple ways in which apparently uniform phenomena are locally constructed. This emphasizes that a botanist classifying a plant is engaged in a less problematic activity than an anthropologist classifying a tribe (see my discussion of Moerman's research on the Lue in Section 4.1).

Let me take some examples of research which disabuses us of our common-sense assumptions about the stable realities of particular collectivities. As we saw in Section 6.4.2, Gilbert and Mulkay's (1983) study of scientists' accounts of their work showed that there are better research questions than 'What is science?' Instead, it is more fruitful to ask: 'How is a particular scientific discourse invoked? When is it invoked? How does it stand in relation to other discourses?' In this way, Gilbert and Mulkay lead us to see that 'science', like other social institutions, is a **hyphenated phenomenon** which takes on different meanings in different contexts.

So scientists, treated as a collectivity having stable goals and practices, also escaped in Gilbert and Mulkay's work. As I noted in Section 10.2, patients, conceived as a stable phenomenon, escaped in the Webb and Stimson study.

A second example of hyphenated phenomena can be drawn from Steve Woolgar's account of 'artificial intelligence'. Woolgar (1985) notes how participants themselves may be reluctant to treat their own activities as instances of particular idealized phenomena. Like Gilbert and Mulkay, Woolgar was interested in the sociology of science. Yet he reports, that, when he tried to get access to laboratories to study scientists at work, each laboratory team would uniformly respond that, if he was interested in science, this really was not the best place to investigate it. For whatever reason, what was going on in this laboratory did not really fit what scientific work really should be. On the other hand, the work being done at some other place was much more truly scientific.

Curiously, Woolgar tells us that he has yet to find a laboratory where people are prepared to accept that whatever they do is 'real' science. He was perpetually being referred to some other site as the home of 'hard' science.

Like 'science', Woolgar also found that 'artificial intelligence' (AI), conceived as an indisputably 'real' phenomenon, was also perceived to be 'elsewhere'. As each new test of what might constitute 'real' AI appeared, grounds were cited to find it inadequate. The famous Turing test, based upon asking subjects whether they can tell if the communication they are hearing is from a person or a machine, is now largely rejected.

Even if a hearer cannot tell the difference between human reasoning and AI, a machine may be held to be only 'simulating intelligence' without being 'intelligent'. Even machines which successfully switch off televisions during commercials will not be recognized as an example of AI since, it is held, this is a response to changes in the broadcast signal rather than in programme content. Hence the search for 'genuine' AI, Woolgar argues, has generated a seemingly endless research programme in which the phenomenon always escapes.

These kinds of studies point to the way in which idealized conceptions of phenomena become like a will-o'-the-wisp on the basis of systematic field research, dissolving into sets of practices embedded in particular milieux. Nowhere is this clearer than in the field of studies of the 'family' (see Section 3.5). As Gubrium and Holstein (1987) note, researchers have unnecessarily worried about getting 'authentic' reports of family life, given the privacy of the household. But this implies an idealized reality – as if there were some authentic site of family life which could be isolated and put under the researcher's microscope. Instead, discourses of family life are applied in varying ways in a range of contexts, many of which, like courts of law, clinics and radio call-in programmes, are public and readily available for research investigation.

If 'the family' is present wherever it is invoked, then the worry of some qualitative researchers about observing 'real' family life looks to be misplaced. Their assumption that the family has a unitary reality looks more like a common-sense way of approaching the phenomenon with little analytic basis.

Finding the family is no problem at all for laypeople. In our everyday life, we can always locate and understand 'real' families by using the documentary method of interpretation (Garfinkel, 1967) to search beneath appearances to locate the 'true' reality. In this regard, think of how social workers or lawyers in juvenile or divorce courts 'discover' the essential features of a particular family.

Yet, for social scientists, *how* we invoke the family, *when* we invoke the family and *where* we invoke the family become central analytic concerns. Because we cannot assume, as laypeople must, that families are 'available' for analysis in some kind of unexplicated way, the 'family', conceived as a self-evident phenomenon, always escapes.

Note that this wholly fits with my earlier argument (Section 10.5) about the disappearing phenomenon in 'objectivist' and 'subjectivist' social science. The phenomenon that *always* escapes is the 'essential' reality pursued in such work. The phenomenon that can be made to *reappear* is the practical activity of participants in establishing a phenomenon in context – the hyphenated phenomenon.

## 10.8 TREAT QUALITATIVE RESEARCH AS DIFFERENT FROM JOURNALISM

My final reminder will be brief. Presupposed in all I have written is an appeal to treat qualitative research as different from journalism. This is *not* because I have no regard for the skills (as well as the sins) of journalists. It is simply because, contrary to how much qualitative research is written, I believe that if qualitative research has anything to offer it is because we possess different (not better) skills to those of journalists.

The skills of journalists are related to the ephemeral nature of their products. They pursue stories which are 'newsworthy'. Their interests (and that of their readers) is in what can be treated as 'new'. However, many things can be 'new' without being 'newsworthy' (for instance, I would not expect my purchase of a new pullover to be reported in a newspaper!).

Because of this, journalists seek the 'new' in what can be seen as previously 'hidden' or 'concealed'. In this regard, particularly powerful journalistic motifs are ironic contrasts (say between the public statements and private lives of celebrities) or 'in-depth' accounts of the experiences and feelings of ordinary people who have found themselves in extraordinary situations (falling off a cliff, winning a lottery).

Of course, this is a very crude account of journalism which fails to do justice to the range of media outlets or to the audience sought. Nonetheless, even at this level, the similarities with much qualitative research, I believe, speak for themselves. For instance, ironic contrasts and 'in-depth' accounts are the meat and drink of many of our research findings.

By contrast, I suggest that qualitative researchers make use of quite *different* skills. These skills should allow us to:

- avoid the assumption that research is only newsworthy if it reveals what is hidden or secret
- recognize that what is usually of most interest is what is *unremarkable* to participants

- avoid ironic comparisons between what people say and what we (think we) know about what they do
- recognize that 'experience' is not more or less 'authentic' but is narrated in ways that are open to lively investigation.

**Attempt Exercise 10.1 about now**

## 10.9   CONCLUDING REMARKS

Despite the *negative* form of some of my comments, I have intended throughout this chapter to convey a sense of the good things that research can do. I tried to show this in the examples of successful case studies and, above all, in my implicit appeal to lateral thinking. If, as I heard somebody say the other day, the world is divided into two sorts of people – those who make such a statement and those who don't – then I am firmly with the latter group.

Perhaps, as Douglas implies, we have something to learn from the Lele. Part of what we might learn is living with uncertainty. Curiously, the critics of such apparently disparate theorists as Garfinkel and Saussure and his heirs have one argument in common. If everything derives from forms of representation, how can we find any secure ground from which to speak? Are we not inevitably led to an infinite regress where ultimate truths are unavailable (see Bury, 1986)?

Three responses suggest themselves. First, isn't it a little surprising that such possibilities should be found threatening when the natural sciences, particularly quantum physics, seem to live with them all the time and adapt accordingly, even ingeniously? Second, instead of throwing up our hands in horror at the context-boundedness of accounts, why not marvel at the elegant solutions that societal members use to remedy this? For practical actors, the regress becomes no problem at all. Finally, like members, why not use practical solutions to practical problems? For instance, as I argued in Chapter 8, even sophisticated qualitative analysis can find practical solutions to the problem of validity (counting where it makes sense to count, using the constant comparative method, and so on).

The worse thing that contemporary qualitative research can imply is that in this postmodern age, anything goes. The trick is to produce intelligent, disciplined work on the very edge of the abyss.

## KEY POINTS

This chapter draws together the arguments present in the rest of my book. These arguments are offered not as self-evident truths but as one voice in a debate that I believe matters both to social scientists and to our audiences. To this end, I provided eight reminders:

1 Take advantage of naturally occurring data.
2 Avoid treating the actor's point of view as an explanation.
3 Study the interrelationships between elements.
4 Attempt theoretically fertile research.
5 Address wider audiences.
6 Begin with 'how?' questions, then ask 'why?'.
7 Study 'hyphenated' phenomena.
8 Treat qualitative research as different from journalism.

## Recommended Reading

State of the art accounts of qualitative research which fit the reminders presented in this chapter are to be found in David Silverman (1997a) (ed.). That book can be contrasted with the wider range of positions in Norman Denzin and Yvonna Lincoln (2000, 2nd edition).

Good discussions of theoretically inspired but rigorous qualitative research are to be found in: Pertti Alasuutari (1995), Jennifer Mason (1996), Amanda Coffey and Paul Atkinson (1996) and Anselm Strauss and Juliet Corbin (1990).

The various theoretical traditions that comprise qualitative research are skilfully dissected in Jaber Gubrium and James Holstein (1997).

Gary Marx's paper (1997), is a lively and extremely helpful short guide for the apprentice researcher.

## Exercise 10.1

Select any qualitative research report with which you are familiar. Now proceed as follows:

1 Apply to it the eight 'reminders' discussed in this chapter.
2 Consider how well it stands in relation to each.
3 In the light of your reading, assess how the research could be improved to satisfy any *one* of these reminders.
4 Assess whether, in the light of your analysis, any of these reminders needs to be modified or rejected.

# Appendix

*Simplified transcription symbols*

| | | | |
|---|---|---|---|
| [ | C2: quite a  [ while<br>Mo:          [ yea | | Left brackets indicate the point at which a current speaker's talk is overlapped by another's talk |
| = | W:<br>C: | that I'm aware of =<br>= Yes. Would you confirm that? | Equal signs, one at the end of a line and one at the beginning, indicate no gap between the two lines |
| (0.4) | Yes (0.2) yeah | | Numbers in parentheses indicate elapsed time in silence in tenths of a second |
| (.) | to get (.) treatment | | A dot in parentheses indicates a tiny gap, probably no more than one-tenth of a second |
| _ | What's up? | | Underscoring indicates some form of stress, via pitch and/or amplitude |
| :: | O:kay? | | Colons indicate prolongation of the immediately prior sound. The length of the row of colons indicates the length of the prolongation |
| WORD | I've got ENOUGH TO WORRY ABOUT | | Capitals except at the beginnings of lines, indicate especially loud sounds relative to the surrounding talk |
| .hhhh | I fell that (0.2) .hhh | | A row of h's prefixed by a dot indicates an inbreath; without a dot, an outbreath. The length of the row of h's indicates the length of the inbreath or outbreath |
| ( ) | future risks and ( ) and life ( ) | | Empty parentheses indicate the transcriber's inability to hear what was said |
| (word) | Would you see (there) anything positive | | Parenthesized words are possible hearings |
| (( )) | confirm that ((continues)) | | Double parentheses contain author's descriptions rather than transcriptions |
| . | That's that. | | Indicates a stopping fall in tone |
| , | one, two, | | Indicates a continuing intonation |
| >< | >so that's it< | | Shows talk that is noticeably faster than surrounding talk |
| ? | What do you think? | | Indicates a rising intonation |

# Glossary

**Analytic induction**  The equivalent to the statistical testing of quantitative associations to see if they are greater than might be expected at random (random error). Using AI, the researcher examines a case, and, where appropriate, redefines the phenomenon and reformulates a hypothesis until a universal relationship is shown (Fielding, 1988: 7–8).

**Anecdotalism**  Found where research reports appear to tell entertaining stories or anecdotes but fail to provide an analytic or methodological framework within which to convince the reader of their scientific credibility.

**Chicago School**  This form of sociological ethnography is usually assumed to originate in the 1920s when students at the University of Chicago were instructed to put down their theory textbooks and get out on to the streets of their city and use their eyes and ears. It led to a series of studies of the social organization of the city and of the daily life of various occupational groups.

**Cognitive anthropology**  Seeks to understand the structures that organize how people perceive the world. This leads to the production of ethnographies, or conceptually derived descriptions, of whole cultures, focused on how people communicate.

**Concepts**  Clearly specified ideas deriving from a particular model.

**Constructionism**  A model which encourages researchers to focus upon how particular phenomena are put together through the close study of particular behaviours.

**Content analysis**  Involves establishing categories, and systematic linkages between them, and then counting the number of instances when those categories are used in a particular item of text.

**Conversation analysis** (CA)  Based on an attempt to describe people's methods for producing orderly talk-in-interaction. It derives from the work of Harvey Sacks (1992).

**Critical rationalism**  A concept deriving from the work of the philosopher of science Karl Popper. It demands that we must seek to falsify assumed relations between phenomena. Then, only if we cannot falsify the existence of a certain relationship are we in a position to speak about 'objective' knowledge. Even then, however, our knowledge is always provisional, subject to a subsequent study which may come up with disconfirming evidence.

**Deviant-case analysis**  In qualitative research, involves testing provisional hypotheses by 'negative' or 'discrepant' cases until all the data can be incorporated in your explanation.

**Diachronic analysis**   A linguistic method concerned with historical changes in language (see *etymology*). It is opposed to *synchronic analysis.*

**Discourse analysis** (DA)   The study of the rhetorical and argumentative organization of talk and texts.

**Emic analysis**   A term mainly used by anthropologists to describe culture based on subjects' concepts and descriptions (see *etic analysis*).

**Emotionalism**   A model of social research in which the primary aim is to generate deeply authentic insights into people's experiences. Emotionalists draw from *romantic* perspectives and favour open-ended interviews (see Gubrium and Holstein, 1997).

**Ethnography**   Puts together two different words: 'ethno' means 'folk' or 'people', while 'graph' derives from 'writing'. Ethnography refers, then, to highly descriptive writing about particular groups of people.

**Ethnomethodology**   The study of folk – or members' – methods. It seeks to describe methods persons use in doing social life. Ethnomethodology is not a methodology but a theoretical model.

**Etymology**   The study of historical changes in the meanings of words.

**Etic analysis**   A term used mainly by anthropologists to describe concepts and descriptions based on the researcher's own concepts (as opposed to those of research subjects).

**Frame**   Drawing on the metaphor of a picture frame, Goffman (1974) uses this term to reference how people treat what is currently relevant and irrelevant. Such treatment defines the frame through which a setting is constituted.

**Grounded theory**   Involves three stages: an initial attempt to develop categories which illuminate the data; an attempt to 'saturate' these categories with many appropriate cases in order to demonstrate their relevance; and trying to develop these categories into more general analytic frameworks with relevance outside the setting.

**Hyphenated phenomena**   A concept which refers to the way in which apparently stable social phenomena (a 'tribe' or a 'family') take on different meanings in different contexts. Thus 'a family as seen by the oldest child' takes on a different meaning than 'a family as seen by the youngest' (see *constructionism*).

**Hypotheses**   Testable propositions.

**Interpretive repertoires**   'Systematically related sets of terms that are often used with stylistic and grammatical coherence and often organized around one or more central metaphors' (Potter, 1996a:131) (see *discourse analysis*).

**Low-inference descriptors**   Seek to record observations 'in terms that are as concrete as possible, including verbatim accounts of what people say, for example, rather than researchers' reconstructions of the general sense of what a person said, which would allow researchers' personal perspectives to influence the reporting' (Seale, 1999:148) (see *reliability*).

**Member** A term used by Garfinkel (1967) to refer to participants in society or particular social groups. It is a shorthand term for 'collectivity member' (see *ethnomethodology*).

**Membership categorization device** (MCD) A collection of categories (e.g. baby, mommy, father = family; male, female = gender) and some rules about how to apply these categories.

**Methodology** Refers to the choices we make about cases to study, methods of data gathering, forms of data analysis etc., in planning and executing a research study.

**Methods** Specific research techniques. These include quantitative techniques, like statistical correlations, as well as techniques like observation, interviewing and audio recording.

**Models** Provide an overall framework for how we look at reality. They tell us what reality is like and the basic elements it contains ('ontology') and what is the nature and status of knowledge ('epistemology').

**Naturalism** A model of research which seeks to minimize presuppositions in order to witness subjects' worlds in their own terms.

**Naturally-occurring data** Derive from situations which exist independently of the researcher's intervention.

**Participant observation** A method that assumes that, in order to understand the world 'firsthand', you must participate yourself rather than just observe it at a distance. This method was championed by the early anthropologists but is shared by some ethnographers (e.g. the Chicago School).

**Positivism** A model of the research process which treats 'social facts' as existing independently of the activities of both participants and researchers. For positivists, the aim is to generate data which are valid and reliable, independently of the research setting.

**Post-modernism** A contemporary approach which questions or seeks to deconstruct both accepted concepts (e.g. the 'subject' and the 'field') and scientific method (see *critical rationalism*). Postmodernism is both an analytical model and a way of describing contemporary society as a pastiche of insecure and changing elements.

**Relational views of language** Analyse the system of relations between words; they do not assume a simple correspondence between individual words and their meanings (cf. Saussure).

**Relativism** A value position where we resist taking a position because we believe that, since everything is relative to its particular context, it should not be criticized.

**Reliability** Refers to 'the degree of consistency with which instances are assigned to the same category by different observers or by the same observer on different occasions' (Hammersley, 1992a: 67) (see *validity*).

**Respondent validation** Sometimes known as 'member validation', this involves taking one's findings back to the subjects being studied. Where these people verify one's findings, it is argued, one can be more confident of their validity.

**Researcher-provoked data**   Data which are actively created and, therefore, would not exist apart from the researcher's intervention (e.g. interviews, focus groups).

**Romantic(ism)**   An approach taken from nineteenth-century thought in which authenticity is attached to personal experiences (see *emotionalism*).

**Scripts**   Members' devices used to invoke the routine character of described events in order to imply that they are features of some (approved or disapproved) general pattern (see *discourse analysis*).

**Semiotics**   The study of signs (from speech to fashion to Morse code).

**Structural anthropology**   While cognitive anthropology is usually content with single case studies of particular peoples, structural anthropology is only interested in single cases in so far as they relate to general social forms. Structural anthropologists draw upon French social and linguistic theory of the early twentieth century, notably Ferdinand de Saussure and Emile Durkheim. They view behaviour as the expression of a 'society' which works as a 'hidden hand' constraining and forming human action (see Lévi-Strauss, 1967).

**Synchronic analysis**   This is ahistorical: it is concerned with any language's present functioning. It treats language as a complete system whose meaning derives not from history but from the relation of each of its parts to the others.

**Text(ual) data**   Consist of words and/or images which have become recorded without the intervention of a researcher (e.g. through an interview).

**Theories**   Arrange sets of concepts to define and explain some phenomenon.

**Triangulation**   Involves comparing different kinds of data (e.g. quantitative and qualitative) and different methods (e.g. observation and interviews) to see whether they corroborate one another.

**Validity**   'The extent to which an account accurately represents the social phenomena to which it refers' (Hammersley, 1990: 57). Researchers respond to validity concerns by describing 'the warrant for their inferences' (Fielding and Fielding, 1986:12) (see *reliability*).

# References

Abrams, P. (1984) 'Evaluating soft findings: some problems of measuring informal care', *Research Policy and Planning*, 2 (2): 1–8.

Adler, P.A. and Adler, P. (1994) 'Observational techniques', in N. Denzin and Y. Lincoln (eds), *Handbook of Qualitative Research*. Thousand Oaks, CA: Sage. pp. 377–92.

Agar, M. (1986) *Speaking of Ethnography*. London: Sage.

Alasuutari, P. (1990) *Desire and Craving: Studies in a Cultural Theory of Alcoholism*. Finland: University of Tampere.

Alasuutari, P. (1995) *Researching Culture*. London: Sage.

Anderson, R., Hughes, J. and Sharrock, W.L. (1987) 'Executive problem finding: some material and initial observations', *Social Psychology Quarterly*, 50 (2): 143–59.

Angosino, M. and Mays de Perez, K. (2000) 'Rethinking observation: from method to context', in N. Denzin and Y. Lincoln (eds), *Handbook of Qualitative Research*, 2nd edn. Thousand Oaks, CA: Sage. pp. 673–702.

Antaki, C. and Rapley, M. (1996) '"Quality of life" talk: the liberal paradox of psychological testing', *Discourse & Society*, 7 (3): 293–316.

Arber, S. (1993) 'The research process', in N. Gilbert (ed.), *Researching Social Life*. London: Sage. pp. 32–50.

Ashmore, M. (1989) *The Reflexive Thesis: Wrighting Sociology of Scientific Knowledge*. Chicago: University of Chicago Press.

Atkinson, P. (1990) *The Ethnographic Imagination*. London: Routledge.

Atkinson, P. (1992) 'The ethnography of a medical setting: reading, writing and rhetoric', *Qualitative Health Research*, 2 (4): 451–74.

Atkinson, P. and Coffey, A. (1997) 'Analysing documentary realities', in D. Silverman (ed.), *Qualitative Research: Theory, Method and Practice*. London: Sage. pp. 45–62.

Atkinson, P. and Hammersley, M. (1994) 'Ethnography and participant observation', in N. Denzin and Y. Lincoln (eds), *Handbook of Qualitative Research*. Thousand Oaks, CA: Sage. pp. 248–61.

Atkinson, P. and Silverman, D. (1997) 'Kundera's *Immortality*: the interview society and the invention of self', *Qualitative Inquiry*, 3 (3): 324–45.

Austin, J.L. (1962) *How To Do Things with Words*. Oxford: Clarendon.

Baker, C.D. (1982) 'Adolescent–adult talk as a practical interpretive problem', in G. Payne and E. Cuff (eds), *Doing Teaching: the Practical Management of Classrooms*. London: Batsford. pp. 104–25.

Baker, C.D. (1984) 'The search for adultness: membership work in adolescent–adult talk', *Human Studies*, 7: 301–23.

Bales, R.F. (1950) *Interaction Process Analysis*. Cambridge, MA: Addison-Wesley.

Barthes, R. (1967) *Elements of Semiology*. London: Cape.

Barthes, R. (1973) *Mythologies*. London: Cape.

Barthes, R. (1977) *Image, Music, Text*. London: Fontana.

Barthes, R. (1981) *Camera Lucida: Reflections on Photography*, New York: Hill and Wang.

Baruch, G. (1981) 'Moral tales: parents' stories of encounters with the health profession', *Social Health and Illness*, 3 (3): 275–96.

Baruch, G. (1982) 'Moral tales: interviewing parents of congenitally ill children'. Unpublished PhD thesis, University of London.

Basso, C. (1972) '"To give up on words": silence in western Apache culture', in P.-P. Giglioli (ed.), *Language and Social Context*. Harmondsworth: Penguin.

Becker, H.S. (1953) 'Becoming a marihuana user', *American Journal of Sociology*, 59: 235–42.

Becker, H.S. (1967a) 'Whose side are we on?', *Social Problems*, 14: 239–48.

Becker, H.S. (1998) *Tricks of the Trade: How to Think about your Research while Doing It.* Chicago and London: University of Chicago Press.

Becker, H.S. and Geer, B. (1960) 'Participant observation: the analysis of qualitative field data', in R. Adams and J. Preiss (eds), *Human Organization Research: Field Relations and Techniques*. Homewood, IL: Dorsey.

Berelson, B. (1952) *Content Analysis in Communicative Research*. New York: Free Press.

Billig, M. (1992) *Talking of the Royal Family*. London: Routledge.

Billig, M. (1995) *Banal Nationalism*. London: Sage.

Blau, P. and Schoenherr, R. (1971) *The Structure of Organizations*. New York: Basic.

Bloor, M. (1978) 'On the analysis of observational data: a discussion of the worth and uses of inductive techniques and respondent validation', *Sociology*, 12 (3): 545–57.

Bloor, M. (1983) 'Notes on member validation', in R. Emerson (ed.), *Contemporary Field Research: a Collection of Readings*. Boston: Little Brown.

Bloor, M. (1997) 'Addressing social problems through qualitative research', in D. Silverman (ed.), *Qualitative Research: Theory, Method and Practice*. London: Sage. pp. 221–38.

Bloor, M., Frankland, J., Thomas, M. and Robson, K. (2001) *Focus Groups in Social Research*. Introducing Qualitative Methods Series. London: Sage.

Blumer, H. (1956) 'Sociological analysis and the "variable"', *American Sociological Review*, 21: 633–60.

Boden, D. (1994) *The Business of Talk*. Cambridge: Polity.

Brenner, M. (ed.) (1981) *Social Method and Social Life*. London: Academic.

Brown, J. and Sime, J. (1981) 'A methodology for accounts', in M. Brenner (ed.), *Social Method and Social Life*. London: Academic.

Bryman, A. (1988) *Quantity and Quality in Social Research*. London: Unwin Hyman.

Bulmer, M. (1982) *The Uses of Social Research*. London: Allen and Unwin.

Burgess, R. (ed.) (1980) *Field Research: a Sourcebook and Field Manual*. London: Allen and Unwin.

Burton, L. (1975) *The Family Life of Sick Children*. London: Routledge.

Bury, M. (1986) 'Social constructionism and the development of medical sociology', *Sociology of Health and Illness*, 8: 137–69.

Byrne, P. and Long, B. (1976) *Doctors Talking to Patients*. London: Her Majesty's Stationery Office.

Cain, M. (1986) 'Realism, feminism, methodology and law', *International Journal of the Sociology of Law*, 14: 255–67.

Charmaz, K. (2000) 'Grounded theory: objectivist and constructivist methods', in N. Denzin and Y. Lincoln (eds), *Handbook of Qualitative Research*, 2nd edn. Thousand Oaks, CA: Sage. pp. 509–36.

Cicourel, A. (1964) *Method and Measurement in Sociology*. New York: Free Press.

Cicourel, A. (1968) *The Social Organization of Juvenile Justice*. New York: Wiley.

# REFERENCES

Cicourel, A. and Kitsuse, J. (1963) *The Educational Decision-Makers*. New York: Bobbs-Merrill.

Clavarino, A., Najman, J. and Silverman, D. (1995) 'Assessing the quality of qualitative data', *Qualitative Inquiry*, 1 (2): 223–42.

Clayman, S.C. (1992) 'Footing in the achievement of neutrality: the case of news-interview discourse', in P. Drew and J.C. Heritage (eds), *Talk at Work*. Cambridge: Cambridge University Press. pp. 163–98.

Coffey, A. and Atkinson, P. (1996) *Making Sense of Qualitative Data*. London: Sage.

Cuff, E.C. and Payne, G.C. (eds) (1979) *Perspectives in Sociology*. London: Allen and Unwin.

Culler, J. (1976) *Saussure*. London: Fontana.

Cyert, R.M. and March, J.G. (1963) *A Behavioural Theory of the Firm*. New York: Wiley.

Czarniawska, B. (1998) *A Narrative Approach to Organization Studies*. London: Sage.

Dalton, M. (1959) *Men Who Manage*. New York: Wiley.

Denzin, N. (1970) *The Research Act in Sociology*. London: Butterworth.

Densin, N. (2000) 'The practice and politics of interpretation', in *Handbook of Qualitative Research*, 2nd edn. Thousand Oaks, CA: Sage.

Denzin, N. and Lincoln, Y. (eds) (1994) *Handbook of Qualitative Research*. Thousand Oaks, CA: Sage.

Denzin, N. and Lincoln, Y. (eds) (2000) *Handbook of Qualitative Research*, 2nd edn. Thousand Oaks, CA: Sage.

Dingwall, R. (1980) 'Ethics and ethnography', *Social Science and Medicine*.

Dingwall, R. (1992) 'Don't mind him – he's from Barcelona: qualitative methods in health studies', in J. Daly, I. MacDonald and E. Willis (eds), *Researching Health Care: Designs, Dilemmas, Disciplines*. London: Routledge.

Dingwall, R. and Murray, T. (1983) 'Categorization in accident departments: "good" patients, "bad" patients and children', *Sociology of Health and Illness*, 5 (12): 121–48.

Douglas, M. (1975) 'Self-evidence', in M. Douglas, *Implicit Meanings*. London: Routledge.

Drew, P. (1978) 'Accusations: the occasioned use of members' knowledge of "religious geography" in describing events', *Sociology*, 12: 1–22.

Drew, P. and Heritage, J.C. (eds) (1992) *Talk at Work*. Cambridge: Cambridge University Press.

Edwards, D. (1995) 'Two to tango: script formulations, dispositions, and rhetorical symmetry in relationship troubles talk', *Research on Language and Social Interaction*, 28: 319–50.

Edwards, D. (1997) *Discourse and Cognition*. London: Sage.

Eglin, P. and Hester, S. (1992) 'Category, predicate and task: the pragmatics of practical action', *Semiotica*, 88 (3/4): 243–68.

Emmison, M. (1988) 'On the interactional management of defeat', *Sociology*, 22: 233–51.

Emmison, M. and McHoul, A. (1987) 'Drawing on the economy: cartoon discourse and the production of a category', *Cultural Studies*, 1 (10): 93–112.

Emmison, M. and Smith, P. (2000) *Researching the Visual*. London: Sage.

Engebretson, J. (1996) 'Urban healers: an experiential description of American healing touch groups', *Qualitative Health Research*, 6 (4): 526–41.

Fielding, N.G. (1982) 'Observational research on the National Front', in M. Bulmer (ed.), *Social Research Ethics: an Examination of the Merits of Covert Participant Observation*. London: Macmillan.

Fielding, N.G. (ed.) (1988) *Actions and Structure*. London: Sage.

Fielding, N.G. and Fielding, J.L. (1986) *Linking Data*. London: Sage.

Filmer, P., Phillipson, M., Silverman, D. and Walsh, D. (1972) *New Directions in Sociological Theory*. London: Collier Macmillan.

Finch, J. (1984) '"It's great to have someone to talk to": the ethics and politics of interviewing women', in C. Bell and H. Roberts (eds) *Social Researching*. London: Routledge.

Fontana, A. and Frey, J. (2000) 'The interview: from structured questions to negotiated text', in N. Denzin and Y. Lincoln (eds), *Handbook of Qualitative Research*, 2nd edn. Thousand Oaks, CA: Sage. pp. 645–72.

Foucault, M. (1977) *Discipline and Punish*. Harmondsworth: Penguin.

Foucault, M. (1979) *The History of Sexuality: Volume 1*. Harmondsworth: Penguin.

Frake, C. (1964) 'Notes on queries in ethnography', *American Anthropologist*, 66: 132–45.

Frake, C. (1972) 'How to ask for a drink in Subanun', in P.-P. Giglioli (ed.), *Language and Social Context*. Harmondsworth: Penguin.

Frith, H. and Kitzinger, C. (1998) 'Emotion work as a participant resource: a feminist analysis of young women's talk-in-interaction', *Sociology*, 32 (2): 299–320.

Garfinkel, E. (1967) *Studies in Ethnomethodology*, Englewood Cliffs, NJ: Prentice-Hall.

Gilbert, N. (ed.) (1993) *Researching Social Life*. London: Sage.

Gilbert, N. and Mulkay, M. (1983) 'In search of the action', in N. Gilbert and P. Abell (eds), *Accounts and Action*. Aldershot: Gower.

Gladwin, T. (1964) 'Culture and logical process', in W. Goodenough (ed.), *Explorations in Cultural Anthropology*. New York: McGraw-Hill.

Glaser, B. and Strauss, A. (1967) *The Discovery of Grounded Theory*. Chicago: Aldine.

Glassner, B. and Loughlin, J. (1987) *Drugs in Adolescent Worlds: Burnouts to Straights*. New York: St Martin's Press.

Goffman, E. (1959) *The Presentation of Self in Everyday Life*. New York: Doubleday Anchor.

Goffman, E. (1961a) *Asylums*. New York: Doubleday Anchor.

Goffman, E. (1961b) *Encounters: Two Studies in the Sociology of Interaction*. Indianapolis: Bobbs-Merrill.

Goffman, E. (1974) *Frame Analysis*. New York: Harper & Row.

Goffman, E. (1981) *Forms of Talk*. Oxford: Basil Blackwell.

Goodwin, C. (1981) *Conversational Organization: Interaction between Speakers and Hearers*. New York: Academic.

Goodwin, M.H. and Goodwin, C. (1986) 'Gesture and co-participation in the activity of searching for a word', *Semiotica*, 62 (1/2): 51–75.

Gouldner, A. (1962) '"Anti-minotaur": the myth of a value-free sociology', *Social Problems*, 9: 199–213.

Grahame, P. (1999) 'Doing qualitative research: three problematics', *Graduate Program in Applied Sociology*, 2 (1): 4–10. Boston: University of Massachusetts.

Greatbatch, D. (1992) 'On the management of disagreement among news interviewers', in P. Drew and J.C. Heritage (eds), *Talk at Work*. Cambridge: Cambridge University Press. pp. 268–301.

Greimas, A.J. (1966) *Semantique Structurale*. Paris: Larousse.

Guba, E. and Lincoln, Y. (1994) 'Competing paradigms in qualitative research', in N. Denzin and Y. Lincoln (eds), *Handbook of Qualitative Research*. Thousand Oaks, CA: Sage. pp. 105–17.

Gubrium, J. (1988) *Analyzing Field Reality*. Newbury Park, CA: Sage.

## REFERENCES

Gubrium, J. (1992) *Out of Control: Family Therapy and Domestic Disorder*. London: Sage.

Gubrium, J. (1997) *Living and Dying in Murray Manor*. Charlottesville, VA: University Press of Virginia.

Gubrium, J. and Buckholdt, D. (1982) *Describing Care: Image and Practice in Rehabilitation*. Cambridge, MA: Oelschlager, Gunn & Hain.

Gubrium, J. and Holstein, J. (1987) 'The private image: experiential location and method in family studies', *Journal of Marriage and the Family*, 49: 773–86.

Gubrium, J. and Holstein, J. (1990) *What is Family?* Mountain View, CA: Mayfield.

Gubrium, J. and Holstein, J. (1997) *The New Language of Qualitative Method*. New York: Oxford University Press.

Hadley, R. (1987) 'Publish and be ignored: proselytise and be damned', in G.C. Wenger (ed.), *The Research Relationship: Practice and Politics in Social Policy Research*. London: Allen and Unwin. pp. 98–110.

Halfpenny, P. (1979) 'The analysis of qualitative data', *Sociological Review*, 27 (4): 799–825.

Hall, E. (1969) *The Hidden Dimension*. London: Bodley Head.

Hammersley, M. (1990) *Reading Ethnographic Research: A Critical Guide*. Longmans: London.

Hammersley, M. (1992) *What's Wrong with Ethnography: Methodological Explorations*. Routledge: London.

Hammersley, M. and Atkinson, P. (1983) *Ethnography: Principles in Practice*. Tavistock: London.

Hawkes, T. (1977) *Structuralism and Semiotics*. London: Methuen.

Heath, C. (1981) 'The opening sequence in doctor–patient interaction', in P. Atkinson and C. Heath (eds), *Medical Work: Realities and Routines*. Farnborough: Gower.

Heath, C. (1986) *Body Movement and Speech in Medical Interaction*. Cambridge: Cambridge University Press.

Heath, C. (1997) 'Using video: analysing activities in face to face interaction', in D. Silverman (ed.), *Qualitative Research: Theory, Method and Practice*. London: Sage. pp. 183–200.

Heath, C. and Luff, P. (1992) 'Collaboration and control: crisis management and multimedia technology in London Underground line control rooms', *Journal of Computer Supported Cooperative Work*, 1 (1–2): 69–94.

Heath, S. (1981) *Questions of Cinema*. London: Macmillan.

Heritage, J. (1984) *Garfinkel and Ethnomethodology*. Cambridge: Polity.

Heritage, J. and Sefi, S. (1992) 'Dilemmas of advice: aspects of the delivery and reception of advice in interactions between health visitors and first time mothers', in P. Drew and J.C. Heritage (eds), *Talk at Work*. Cambridge: Cambridge University Press. pp. 359–417.

Hindess, B. (1973) *The Use of Official Statistics in Sociology*. London: Macmillan.

Holstein, J. and Gubrium, J. (1995) *The Active Interview*. Thousand Oaks, CA: Sage.

Holstein, J. and Gubrium, J. (1997) 'Active interviewing', in D. Silverman (ed.), *Qualitative Research: Theory, Method and Practice*. London: Sage. pp. 113–29.

Hornsby-Smith, M. (1993) 'Gaining access', in N. Gilbert (ed.), *Researching Social Life*. London: Sage. pp. 52–67.

Horowitz, I.L. (1965) 'The life and death of Project Camelot', *Transaction*, 3: 44–7.

Humphrey, J. (1970) *Tea Room Trade*. London: Duckworth.

Hyman, H. (1954) *Interviewing in Social Research*. Chicago: Chicago University Press.

Jacques, M. and Mulhern, F. (eds) (1981) *The Forward March of Labour Halted*. London: Verso.

Jeffery, R. (1979) 'Normal rubbish: deviant patients in casualty departments', *Sociology of Health & Illness*, 1 (1): 90–107.

Kendall, G. and Wickham, G. (1999) *Using Foucault's Methods*. London: Sage.

Kent, G. (1996) 'Informed consent', in 'The Principled Researcher'. Unpublished manuscript, Social Science Division, The Graduate School, University of Sheffield. pp. 18–24.

Kirk, J. and Miller, M. (1986) *Reliability and Validity in Qualitative Research*. London: Sage.

Kitzinger, J. and Miller, D. (1992) '"African AIDS": the media and audience beliefs', in P. Aggleton, P. Davies and G. Hart (eds), *AIDS: Rights, Risk and Reason*. London: Falmer.

Kuhn, T.S. (1970) *The Structure of Scientific Revolutions*, 2nd edn. Chicago: University of Chicago Press.

Laclau, E. (1981) 'Politics as the construction of the unthinkable', unpublished paper, translated from the French by D. Silverman, mimeo, Department of Sociology, Goldsmiths' College.

Landsberger, H. (1958) *Hawthorne Revisited*. New York: Cornell University Press.

Lepper, G. (1995) 'Making trouble: the uses of "formal organization" as an institutional resource', *Studies in Cultures, Organizations and Societies*, 1: 189–207.

Levinson, S.C. (1983) *Pragmatics*. Cambridge: Cambridge University Press.

Lévi-Strauss, C. (1967) *Structural Anthropology*. New York: Basic.

Lipset, S.M., Trow, M. and Coleman, J. (1962) *Union Democracy*. Garden City, NY: Anchor Doubleday.

Livingston, E. (1987) *Making Sense of Ethnomethodology*. London: Routledge.

Lodge, D. (1989) *Nice Work*. London: Penguin.

Lynch, M. (1984) *Art and Artifact in Laboratory Science*. London: Routledge.

Malinowski, B. (1922) *Argonauts of the Western Pacific*. London: Routledge.

Mann, C. and Stewart, F. (eds) (2000) *Internet Communication and Qualitative Research: A Handbook for Researching Online*. London: Sage.

Marsh, C. (1982) *The Survey Method*. London: Allen & Unwin.

Marshall, C. and Rossman, G. (1989) *Designing Qualitative Research*. London: Sage.

Marx, G. (1997) 'Of methods and manners for aspiring sociologists: 37 moral imperatives', *The American Sociologist*, Spring: 102–25.

Maseide, P. (1990) 'The social construction of research information', *Acta Sociologica*, 33 (1): 3–13.

Mason, J. (1996) *Qualitative Researching*. London: Sage.

Maynard, D. (1985) 'On the functions of social conflict among children', *American Sociological Review*, 50: 207–23.

Maynard, D. (1989) 'On the ethnography and analysis of discourse in institutional settings', *Perspectives on Social Problems*, 1: 127–46.

Maynard, D. (1991) 'Interaction and asymmetry in clinical discourse', *American Journal of Sociology*, 97 (2): 448–95.

Maynard, D. and Clayman, S. (1991) 'The diversity of ethnomethodology', *Annual Review of Sociology*, 17: 385–418.

McHoul, A. and Watson, D.R. (1984) 'Two axes for the analysis of "commonsense" and "formal" geographical knowledge in classroom talk', *British Journal of the Sociology of Education*, 5 (3): 281–302.

McHugh, P. (1970) 'A commonsense conception of deviance', in H.P. Dreitzel (ed.), *Recent Sociology, No. 2*. New York: Macmillan.

McKeganey, N. and Bloor, M. (1991) 'Spotting the invisible man: the influence of male gender on fieldwork relations', *British Journal of Sociology*, 42 (2): 195–210.

# REFERENCES

Mead, G.H. (1934) *Mind, Self and Society*. Chicago: University of Chicago Press.

Mehan, H. (1979) *Learning Lessons: Social Organization in the Classroom*. Cambridge, MA: Harvard University Press.

Mercer, K. (1990) 'Powellism as a political discourse'. Unpublished PhD thesis, Goldsmiths College, University of London.

Miles, M. and Huberman, A. (1984) *Qualitative Data Analysis*. London: Sage.

Miller, J. (1996) 'Female Gang Involvement in the Midwest: A Two-City Comparison'. Doctoral dissertation, Department of Sociology, University of Southern California.

Miller, G. and Silverman, D. (1995) 'Troubles talk and counseling discourse: a comparative study', *The Sociological Quarterly*, 36 (4): 725–47.

Miller, J. and Glassner, B. (1997) 'The "inside" and the "outside": finding realities in interviews', in D. Silverman (ed.), *Qualitative Research: Theory, Method and Practice*. London: Sage. pp. 99–112.

Miller, R.L. (2000) *Researching Life Stories and Family Histories*. London: Sage.

Mills, C.W. (1940) 'Situated actions and vocabularies of motive', *American Sociological Review*, 5: 904–13.

Mills, C.W. (1959) *The Sociological Imagination*. New York: Oxford University Press.

Mishler, E.G. (1986) *Research Interviewing: Context and Narrative*. London: Harvard University Press.

Moerman, M. (1974) 'Accomplishing ethnicity', in R. Turner (ed.), *Ethnomethodology*. Harmondsworth: Penguin.

Molotch, H. and Boden, D. (1985) 'Talking social structure: discourse, domination and the Watergate Hearings', *American Sociological Review*, 50 (3): 273–88.

Mulkay, M. (1984) 'The ultimate compliment: a sociological analysis of ceremonial discourse', *Sociology*, 18: 531–49.

Nash, J. (1975) 'Bus riding: community on wheels', *Urban Life*, 4: 99–124.

Nash, J. (1981) 'Relations in frozen places: observations on winter public order', *Qualitative Sociology*, 4: 229–43.

Nelson, B. (1984) *Making an Issue of Child Abuse: Political Agenda Setting for Social Problems*. Chicago: University of Chicago Press.

Oakley, A. (1981) 'Interviewing women: a contradiction in terms', in H. Roberts (ed.), *Doing Feminist Research*. London: Routledge & Kegan Paul.

Oboler, R. (1986) 'For better or for worse: anthropologists and husbands in the field', in T. Whitehead and M. Conway (eds), *Self, Sex and Gender in Cross-Cultural Fieldwork*. Urbana: University of Illinois Press. pp. 28–51.

O'Brien, M. (1993) 'Social research and sociology', in N. Gilbert (ed.), *Researching Social Life*. London: Sage. pp. 1–17.

Peräkylä, A. (1989) 'Appealing to the experience of the patient in the care of the dying', *Sociology of Health & Illness*, 11(2): 117–34.

Peräkylä, A. (1995) *AIDS Counselling*. Cambridge: Cambridge University Press.

Peräkylä, A. (1997) 'Reliability and validity in research based upon transcripts', in D. Silverman (ed.), *Qualitative Research*. London: Sage. pp. 201–19.

Peräkylä, A. and Silverman, D. (1991) 'Owning experience: describing the experience of others', *Text*, 11 (3): 441–80.

Pollner, M. (1987) *Mundane Reason: Reality in Everyday and Sociological Discourse*. Cambridge: Cambridge University Press.

Popper, K. (1959) *The Logic of Scientific Discovery*. New York: Basic.

Potter, J. (1996a) 'Discourse analysis and constructionist approaches: theoretical background', in J. Richardson (ed.), *Handbook of Qualitative Research Methods for Psychology and the Social Sciences*. Leicester: BPS. pp. 125–40.

Potter, J. (1996b) *Representing Reality: Discourse, Rhetoric and Social Construction.* London: Sage.

Potter, J. (1997) 'Discourse analysis as a way of analysing naturally-occurring talk', in D. Silverman (ed.), *Qualitative Research: Theory, Method and Practice.* London: Sage. pp. 144–60.

Potter, J. and Wetherell, M. (1987) *Discourse and Social Psychology: Beyond Attitudes and Behaviour.* London: Sage.

Prior, L. (1987) 'Policing the dead: a sociology of the mortuary', *Sociology*, 21 (3): 355–76.

Prior, L. (1997) 'Following in Foucault's footprints: text and context in qualitative research', in D. Silverman (ed.), *Qualitative Research.* London: Sage. pp. 63–79.

Procter, M. (1993) 'Analysing survey data', in N. Gilbert (ed.), *Researching Social Life.* London: Sage. pp. 239–54.

Propp, V.I. (1968) *Morphology of the Folktale*, 2nd rev. edn, L.A. Wagner (ed.). Austin, TX and London: University of Texas Press.

Psathas, G. (1979) 'Organizational features of direction maps', in G. Psathas (ed.), *Everyday Language: Studies in Ethnomethodology.* New York: Irvington. pp. 203–25.

Punch, M. (1994) 'Politics and ethics in fieldwork', in N. Denzin and Y. Lincoln (eds), *Handbook of Qualitative Research.* Thousand Oaks, CA: Sage. pp. 83–97.

Radcliffe-Brown, A.R. (1948) *The Andaman Islanders.* Glencoe, IL: Free Press.

Rayner, G. and Stimson, G. (1979) 'Medicine, superstructure and micropolitics: a response', *Social Science and Medicine*, 13A: 611–12.

Reason, P. and Rowan, J. (1981) *Human Inquiry: a Sourcebook of New Paradigm Research.* Chichester: Wiley.

Richards, L. and Richards, T. (1987) 'Qualitative data analysis: can computers do it?', *Australia and New Zealand Journal of Sociology*, 23: 23–35.

Richardson, L. (1990) *Writing Strategies: Reaching Diverse Audiences.* Newbury Park, CA: Sage.

Ryen, A. and Silverman, D. (2000) 'Marking boundaries: culture as category-work', *Qualitative Inquiry*, 6 (1): 107–28.

Sacks, H. (1972a) 'On the analysability of stories by children', in J. Gumperz and D. Hymes (eds), *Directions in Sociolinguistics.* New York: Holt, Rinehart & Winston.

Sacks, H. (1972b) 'Notes on police assessment of moral character', in D. Sudnow (ed.), *Studies in Social Interaction.* New York: Free Press. pp. 280–93.

Sacks, H. (1974) 'On the analyzability of stories by children', in R. Turner (ed.), *Ethnomethodology.* Harmondsworth: Penguin. pp. 216–32.

Sacks, H. (1984) 'On doing "being ordinary"', in J.M. Atkinson and J. Heritage (eds), *Structures of Social Action: Studies in Conversation Analysis.* Cambridge: Cambridge University Press. pp. 513–29.

Sacks, H. (1992) *Lectures on Conversation*, vols I and II, edited by Gail Jefferson with an introduction by Emmanuel Schegloff. Oxford: Blackwell. Page references in the text refer to each volume in the following format: 1992, I: 467–8; 1992, II: 54–5.

Sacks, H., Schegloff, E.A. and Jefferson, G. (1974) 'A simplest systematics for the organization of turn-taking in conversation', *Language*, 50 (4): 696–735.

Saussure, F. de (1974) *Course in General Linguistics.* London: Fontana.

Schegloff, E.A. (1968) 'Sequencings in conversational openings', *American Anthropologist*, 70: 1075–95.

Schegloff, E.A. (1972) 'Notes on a conversational practice: formulating place', in D. Sudnow (ed.), *Studies in Social Interaction.* New York: Free Press. pp. 75–119.

Schegloff, E.A. (1982) 'Discourse as an interactional accomplishment: some uses of "uh huh" and other things that come between sentences', in D. Tannen (ed.), *Georgetown University Round Table on Language and Linguistics: Analyzing Discourse: Text and Talk*. Washington, DC: Georgetown University Press. pp. 71–93.

Schegloff, E.A. (1991) 'Reflections on talk and social structure', in D. Boden and D. Zimmerman (eds), *Talk and Social Structure: Studies in Ethnomethodology and Conversation Analysis*. Cambridge: Polity. pp. 44–70.

Schegloff, E.A. (1992) 'On talk and its institutional occasions', in P. Drew and J.C. Heritage (eds), *Talk at Work*. Cambridge: Cambridge University Press. pp. 101–36.

Schegloff, E.A. (1997) 'Whose text? Whose context?', *Discourse and Society*, 8: 165–87.

Schreiber, R. (1996) '(Re)defining my self: women's process of recovery from depression', *Qualitative Health Research*, 6 (4): 469–91.

Schwartz, H. and Jacobs, J. (1979) *Qualitative Sociology: a Method to the Madness*. New York: Free Press.

Seale, C. (ed.) (1998) *Researching Society and Culture*. London: Sage.

Seale, C. (1999) *The Quality of Qualitative Research*. London: Sage.

Seale, C. (2000) 'Using computers to analyse qualitative data', in D. Silverman, *Doing Qualitative Research: a Practical Handbook*. London: Sage. pp. 154–74.

Searle, J. (1969) *Speech Acts*. Cambridge: Cambridge University Press.

Selltiz, C., Jahoda, M., Deutsch, M. and Cook, S. (1964) *Research Methods in Social Relations*. New York: Holt, Rinehart & Winston.

Shaw, I. (1999) *Qualitative Evaluation*. London: Sage.

Silverman, D. (1968) 'Clerical ideologies: a research note', *British Journal of Sociology*, XIX (3): 326–33.

Silverman, D. (1970) *The Theory of Organizations*. London: Heinemann. New York: Basic, 1971.

Silverman, D. (1973) 'Interview talk: bringing off a research instrument', *Sociology*, 7 (1): 31–48.

Silverman, D. (1975) 'Accounts of organizations: organizational structures and the accounting process', in J. McKinlay (ed.), *Processing People: Cases in Organizational Behaviour*. London: Holt, Rinehart & Winston.

Silverman, D. (1981) 'The child as a social object: Down's syndrome children in a paediatric cardiology clinic', *Sociology of Health and Illness*, 3 (3): 254–74.

Silverman, D. (1982) 'Labour's marches: the discursive politics of a current debate', mimeo, Department of Sociology, Goldsmiths' College.

Silverman, D. (1984) 'Going private: ceremonial forms in a private oncology clinic', *Sociology*, 18: 191–202.

Silverman, D. (1985) *Qualitative Methodology and Sociology*. Aldershot: Gower.

Silverman, D. (1987) *Communication and Medical Practice*. London: Sage.

Silverman, D. (1989a) 'Telling convincing stories: a plea for cautious positivism in case-studies', in B. Glassner and J. Moreno (eds), *The Qualitative–Quantitative Distinction in the Social Sciences*. Dordrecht: Kluwer.

Silverman, D. (1989b) 'The impossible dreams of reformism and romanticism', in J. Gubrium and D. Silverman (eds), *The Politics of Field Research: Sociology beyond Enlightenment*. London: Sage.

Silverman, D. (1989c) 'Making sense of a precipice: constituting identity in an HIV clinic', in P. Aggleton, G. Hart and P. Davies (eds), *AIDS: Social Representations, Social Practices*. Lewes: Falmer.

Silverman, D. (1991) 'Unfixing the subject: viewing "Bad Timing"', *Continuum: An Australian Journal of the Arts*, 5 (1): 9–31. Reprinted in C. Jenks (ed.), *Cultural Reproduction* (1993). Routledge: London.

Silverman, D. (1993) *Interpreting Qualitative Data: Methods for Analysing Talk, Text and Interaction*. London: Sage.

Silverman, D. (ed.) (1997a) *Qualitative Research: Theory, Method and Practice*. London: Sage.

Silverman, D. (1997b) *Discourses of Counselling: HIV Counselling as Social Interaction*. London: Sage.

Silverman, D. (1998) *Harvey Sacks: Social Science and Conversation Analysis*. Cambridge: Polity. New York: Oxford University Press.

Silverman, D. (2000) *Doing Qualitative Research: a Practical Handbook*, London: Sage.

Silverman, D. and Jones, J. (1976) *Organizational Work: the Language of Grading/the Grading of Language*. London: Collier Macmillan.

Silverman, D. and Torode, B. (1980) *The Material Word: Some Theories of Language and its Limits*. London: Routledge.

Silverman, D., Bor, R., Miller, R. and Goldman, E. (1992) 'Advice-giving and advice-reception in AIDS counselling', in P. Aggleton, P. Davies and G. Hart (eds), *AIDS: Rights, Risk and Reason*, London: Falmer Press.

Simmel, G. (1950) *Sociology*. Glencoe, IL: Free Press.

Singleton, R., Straits, B., Straits, M. and McAllister, R. (1988) *Approaches to Social Research*. Oxford: Oxford University Press.

Slater, D. (1989) 'Corridors of power', in J. Gubrium and D. Silverman (eds), *The Politics of Field Research: Sociology beyond Enlightenment*. London: Sage.

Sontag, S. (1979) *Illness as Metaphor*. Harmondsworth: Penguin.

Spradley, J.P. (1979) *The Ethnographic Interview*. New York: Holt, Rinehart & Winston.

Stake, R. (1994) 'Case studies', in N. Denzin and Y. Lincoln (eds), *Handbook of Qualitative Research*. Thousand Oaks, CA: Sage. pp. 236–47.

Stanley, L. and Wise, S. (1983) *Breaking Out: Feminist Consciousness and Feminist Research*. London: Routledge.

Stimson, G. (1986) 'Place and space in sociological fieldwork', *Sociological Review*, 34 (3): 641–56.

Strauss, A. and Corbin, J. (1990) *Basics of Qualitative Research*. Thousand Oaks, CA: Sage.

Strauss, A. and Corbin, J. (1994) 'Grounded theory methodology: an overview', in N. Denzin and Y. Lincoln (eds), *Handbook of Qualitative Research*. Thousand Oaks, CA: Sage. pp. 273–85.

Strong, P. (1979a) *The Ceremonial Order of the Clinic*. London: Routledge.

Stubbs, M. (1981) 'Scratching the surface', in C. Adelman (ed.), *Uttering, Muttering: Collecting, Using and Reporting Talk for Educational Research*. London: Grant McIntyre.

Suchman, L. (1987) *Plans and Situated Actions: the Problem of Human–Machine Communication*. Cambridge: Cambridge University Press.

Sudnow, D. (1968a) *Passing On: the Social Organization of Dying*. Englewood Cliffs, NJ: Prentice-Hall.

Sudnow, D. (1968b) 'Normal crimes', in E. Rubington and M. Weinberg (eds), *Deviance: the Interactionist Perspective*. New York: Macmillan.

Tedlock, B. (2000) 'Ethnography and ethnographic representation', in N. Denzin and Y. Lincoln (eds), *Handbook of Qualitative Research*, 2nd edn. Thousand Oaks, CA: Sage. pp. 455–86.

ten Have, P. (1998) *Doing Conversation Analysis: a Practical Guide*. London: Sage.

Tesch, R. (1991) *Qualitative Research: Analysis Types and Software Tools*. Basingstoke: Falmer.

# REFERENCES

Thomas, W. and Znaniecki, F. (1927) *The Polish Peasant in Europe and America*. New York: Alfred Knopf.

Waitzkin, H. (1979) 'Medicine, superstructure and micropolitics', *Social Science and Medicine*, 13A: 601–9.

Walsh, D. (1998) 'Doing ethnography', in C. Seale (ed.), *Researching Society and Culture*. London: Sage. pp. 217–32.

Warren, A. (1988) *Gender Issues in Field Research*. Newbury Park, CA: Sage.

Warren, A. and Rasmussen, P. (1977) 'Sex and gender in fieldwork research', *Urban Life*, 6: 359–69.

Watson, R. (1997) 'Ethnomethodology and textual analysis', in D. Silverman (ed.), *Qualitative Research: Theory, Method and Practice*. London: Sage. pp. 80–98.

Weatherburn, P. and Project SIGMA (1992) 'Alcohol use and unsafe sexual behaviour: any connection?', in P. Aggleton, P. Davies and G. Hart (eds), *AIDS: Rights, Risk and Reason*. London: Falmer.

Webb, B. and Stimson, G. (1976) 'People's accounts of medical encounters', in M. Wadsworth (ed.) *Everyday Medical Life*. London: Martin Robertson.

Weber, M. (1946) 'Science as a vocation', in H. Gerth and C.W. Mills (eds), *From Max Weber*. New York: Oxford University Press.

Weber, M. (1949) *Methodology of the Social Sciences*. New York: Free Press.

Wetherell, M. (1998) 'Positioning and interpretative repertoires: conversation analysis and post-structuralism in dialogue', *Discourse and Society*, 9: 387–412.

Wetherell, M. and Potter, J. (1992) *Mapping the Language of Racism: Discourse and the Legitimation of Exploitation*. London: Harvester. New York: Columbia University Press.

Whyte, W.F. (1949) 'The social structure of the restaurant', *American Journal of Sociology*, 54: 302–10.

Whyte, W.F. (1980) 'Interviewing in field research', in R. Burgess (ed.) *Field Research: a Sourcebook and Field Manual*. London: Allen and Unwin.

Wittgenstein, L. (1968) *Philosophical Investigations*. Oxford: Basil Blackwell.

Wittgenstein, L. (1971) *Tractatus Logico-Philosophicus*. London: Routledge.

Wolcott, H. (1990) *Writing Up Qualitative Research*. Newbury Park, CA: Sage.

Woolgar, S. (1985) 'Why not a sociology of machines: the case of sociology and artificial intelligence', *Sociology*, 19 (4): 557–72.

Zimmerman, D. (1992) 'The interactional organization of calls for emergency assistance', in P. Drew and J.C. Heritage (eds), *Talk at Work*. Cambridge: Cambridge University Press. pp. 418–69.

Zimmerman, D. and West, C. (1975) 'Sex roles, interruptions and silences in conversations', in B. Thorne and N. Henley (eds), *Language and Sex*. Rowley, MA: Newbury House. pp. 105–29.

# Name Index

# NAME INDEX

# Subject Index